The Pragmatic Enlightenment

This is a study of the political theory of the Enlightenment, focusing on four leading eighteenth-century thinkers: David Hume, Adam Smith, Montesquieu, and Voltaire. Dennis C. Rasmussen calls attention to the particular strand of the Enlightenment these thinkers represent, which he terms the "pragmatic Enlightenment." He defends this strand of Enlightenment thought against both the Enlightenment's critics and some of the more idealistic Enlightenment figures who tend to have more followers today, such as John Locke, Immanuel Kant, and Jeremy Bentham. Professor Rasmussen argues that Hume, Smith, Montesquieu, and Voltaire exemplify an especially attractive type of liberalism, one that is more realistic, moderate, flexible, and contextually sensitive than most other branches of this tradition.

Dennis C. Rasmussen is Assistant Professor of Political Science at Tufts University. He is the author of *The Problems and Promise of Commercial Society: Adam Smith's Response to Rousseau* (2008), which received an honorable mention for the Delba Winthrop Award for Excellence in Political Science.

The Pragmatic Enlightenment

Recovering the Liberalism of Hume, Smith, Montesquieu, and Voltaire

DENNIS C. RASMUSSEN
Tufts University

CAMBRIDGE
UNIVERSITY PRESS

University Printing House, Cambridge CB2 8BS, United Kingdom

One Liberty Plaza, 20th Floor, New York, NY 10006, USA

477 Williamstown Road, Port Melbourne, VIC 3207, Australia

4843/24, 2nd Floor, Ansari Road, Daryaganj, Delhi - 110002, India

79 Anson Road, #06-04/06, Singapore 079906

Cambridge University Press is part of the University of Cambridge.

It furthers the University's mission by disseminating knowledge in the pursuit of education, learning and research at the highest international levels of excellence.

www.cambridge.org
Information on this title: www.cambridge.org/ 9781107622999

© Dennis C. Rasmussen 2014

This publication is in copyright. Subject to statutory exception and to the provisions of relevant collective licensing agreements, no reproduction of any part may take place without the written permission of Cambridge University Press.

First published 2014
First paperback edition 2017

A catalogue record for this publication is available from the British Library

Library of Congress Cataloging in Publication data
Rasmussen, Dennis Carl, 1978–
The pragmatic enlightenment : recovering the liberalism of Hume, Smith, Montesquieu, and Voltaire / Dennis C. Rasmussen, Tufts University.
    pages   cm
Includes bibliographical references and index.
ISBN 978-1-107-04500-2 (hardback)
1. Enlightenment.   2. Liberalism.   3. Hume, David, 1711–1776.   4. Smith, Adam, 1723–1790.   5. Montesquieu, Charles de Secondat, baron de, 1689–1755.   6. Voltaire, 1694–1778.   I. Title.
B802.R375   2013
148–dc23   2013022249

ISBN   978-1-107-04500-2   Hardback
ISBN   978-1-107-62299-9   Paperback

Cambridge University Press has no responsibility for the persistence or accuracy of URLs for external or third-party internet websites referred to in this publication, and does not guarantee that any content on such websites is, or will remain, accurate or appropriate.

Contents

A Note on the Citations	*page* vii
Acknowledgments	ix
Introduction	1
HEGEMONIC UNIVERSALISM?	25
1. Morality in Context	27
2. Pragmatic Liberalism	80
BLIND FAITH IN REASON?	133
3. The Age of the Limits of Reason	135
4. The Perils of Political Rationalism	191
ATOMISTIC INDIVIDUALISM?	231
5. The Social and Encumbered Self	233
6. Negative Liberty for a Positive Community	260
Conclusion	294
Bibliography	303
Index	329

v

A Note on the Citations

Because I hope this book will find an audience beyond specialists in Enlightenment thought, I have wherever possible cited widely available English translations of the works of Montesquieu and Voltaire, rather than the critical French editions. Where reliable translations are not available, I cite standard French versions; in these cases, the translations are my own. In some instances I have also made small alterations to the existing translations for the sake of a more literal rendering.

For some of the more frequently cited texts, I use the following in-text abbreviations. Where appropriate, I include references to volume, book, part, chapter, and/or paragraph numbers in addition to the page number.

Works of David Hume

EHU   *An Enquiry Concerning Human Understanding*, ed. Tom L. Beauchamp (Oxford: Clarendon Press, [1748] 2000).

EMPL   *Essays, Moral, Political, and Literary*, ed. Eugene F. Miller (Indianapolis: Liberty Fund, [1741–77] 1987).

EPM   *An Enquiry Concerning the Principles of Morals*, ed. Tom L. Beauchamp (Oxford: Clarendon Press, [1751] 1998).

HE   *The History of England, from the Invasion of Julius Caesar to the Revolution in 1688*, six volumes (Indianapolis: Liberty Fund, [1754–62] 1983).

THN   *A Treatise of Human Nature*, ed. David Fate Norton and Mary J. Norton (Oxford: Clarendon Press, [1739–40] 2007).

viii   *A Note on the Citations*

Works of Adam Smith

LJ   *Lectures on Jurisprudence*, ed. R. L. Meek, D. D. Raphael, and
          P. G. Stein (Indianapolis: Liberty Fund, [1762–66] 1982).
TMS   *The Theory of Moral Sentiments*, ed. D. D. Raphael and A. L.
          Macfie (Indianapolis: Liberty Fund, [1759–90] 1982).
WN   *An Inquiry into the Nature and Causes of the Wealth of
          Nations*, ed. R. H. Campbell, A. S. Skinner, and W. B. Todd,
          two volumes (Indianapolis: Liberty Fund [1776], 1981).

Works of Montesquieu

Pensées   *My Thoughts*, trans. Henry C. Clark (Indianapolis: Liberty
          Fund, [c. 1720–55] 2012).
PL   *The Persian Letters*, trans. George R. Healy (Indianapolis:
          Hackett, [1721] 1999).
SL   *The Spirit of the Laws*, trans. Anne M. Cohler, Basia C. Miller,
          and Harold S. Stone (Cambridge: Cambridge University
          Press, [1748] 1989).

Works of Voltaire

EM   *Essai sur les moeurs et l'esprit des nations*, ed. René Pomeau,
          two volumes (Paris: Garnier, [1756–69] 1963).
LCE   *Letters Concerning the English Nation*, ed. Nicholas Cronk
          (Oxford: Oxford University Press, [1733] 1994).
PD   *Philosophical Dictionary*, trans. Theodore Besterman
          (London: Penguin, [1764–69] 2004).
TM   *A Treatise on Metaphysics*, in *Voltaire: Selections*, trans. Paul
          Edwards (New York: Macmillan, [1736] 1989).

Acknowledgments

Given the somewhat peripatetic nature of my early academic career, I have accumulated numerous debts, both individual and institutional, in the course of writing this book. The project was first conceived during my time as a visiting faculty member at Bowdoin College. Paul Franco imparted sound advice at the outset, has remained a good friend, and provided thoughtful feedback on the entire manuscript at a late stage. I began research on the book in earnest while at Brown University's Political Theory Project, where I enjoyed engaging discussion with Corey Brettschneider, Sharon Krause, John Tomasi, and my fellow postdocs on all things political theory. More recently, Emily Nacol provided valuable comments on each chapter as it was written (some of them more than once). My next stop was the University of Houston, where Jeremy Bailey and Sue Collins were both excellent colleagues. My greatest institutional debt is to my academic home since 2009, Tufts University, whose Faculty Research Awards Committee and generous junior leave policy afforded me the time to write the book with limited interruptions. My fellow political theorists at Tufts, Rob Devigne, Yannis Evrigenis, and Vickie Sullivan, have all provided crucial advice and feedback.

My debts are by no means limited to these institutions. I also received helpful comments on the manuscript from my friends and former graduate school colleagues Bill Curtis and Ari Kohen, and my fellow Boston-area student of the Enlightenment, Michael Frazer. For reading parts of the manuscript and/or for conversations that influenced my thinking on these matters, I am grateful to Josh Bandoch, Richard Boyd, Keegan Callanan, Patrick Deneen, Graeme Garrard, Michael Gillespie, Ruth Grant, Charles Griswold, Ryan Hanley, Louis Hunt, Jonathan Israel,

Steve Kautz, Ben Kleinerman, Alan Levine, Jacob Levy, Folke Lindahl, Arthur Melzer, Michael Mosher, Eric Petrie, Andy Sabl, Diana Schaub, David Lay Williams, and Richard Zinman. I would also like to thank Henry Clark for kindly sharing his excellent translation of Montesquieu's *Pensées* prior to publication. Finally, I am indebted to Aurelian Craiutu and an anonymous reviewer for Cambridge University Press for their insightful comments and queries, and to my editor, Robert Dreesen, for the confidence that he showed in the project. While all of these individuals have helped to improve the book in ways large or small, any errors or oversights that remain are, of course, my responsibility alone.

As is often the case, my greatest debts are of the nonacademic variety. I owe more than I can say to my family and friends, above all to my wife Emily, for her love, support, encouragement, and willingness to endure my ramblings about the eighteenth century. The book is dedicated to her.

Introduction

The Enlightenment has fallen on hard times in recent years. It is true, of course, that the modern West is to a large extent a product of the Enlightenment. Our liberal democratic politics, our market capitalist economies, our embrace of technological progress and scientific inquiry, our toleration of religious pluralism – all were inspired or encouraged by the Enlightenment. As Paul Hazard declared many decades ago, "Rich and weighty as were the legacies bequeathed to us by old Greece and Rome, by the Middle Ages and by the Renaissance, the fact remains that it is the eighteenth century of which we are the direct and lineal descendants."[1] Yet there is widespread agreement across much of today's academy that Enlightenment thought falls somewhere on the spectrum from hopelessly naive and archaic to fundamentally and dangerously misguided. On both the Left and Right, the Enlightenment is routinely associated with a hegemonic form of moral and political universalism, a blind faith in abstract reason, and a reductive and isolating focus on the individual, among other sins. My aim in this book is to contest these charges through a recovery and defense of a central strand of Enlightenment thought that I call the "pragmatic Enlightenment."

While numerous thinkers throughout eighteenth-century Europe could be included in this category, I focus on four of the leading figures of the period: David Hume, Adam Smith, Montesquieu, and Voltaire. These thinkers, I argue, exemplify an especially attractive type of liberalism, one that is more realistic, moderate, flexible, and contextually sensitive than

---

[1] Paul Hazard, *European Thought in the Eighteenth Century: From Montesquieu to Lessing*, trans. J. Lewis May (Cleveland: Meridian Books, [1946] 1965), xvii.

many other branches of this tradition.[2] Some forms of liberalism that emerged during the Enlightenment, such as Lockean contractarianism, Kantian deontology, and Benthamite utilitarianism, were highly idealistic in character, grounded in first principles such as the immutable dictates of natural law, the rational (and therefore categorical) requirements of human dignity, or the universal imperative to maximize the greatest good for the greatest number. In contrast, the liberalism of Hume, Smith, Montesquieu, and Voltaire was far more pragmatic, in many senses of that term: it was grounded in experience and empirical observation instead of transcendent or a priori first principles; it addressed practical human concerns rather than aiming to satisfy abstract standards of right derived from God, Nature, or Reason; it was flexible in its application and attentive to the importance of historical and cultural context; and it favored gradual, piecemeal reform over the pursuit of perfection or the imposition of strict requirements for legitimacy. Thus, the outlooks of these four thinkers demonstrate that "pragmatic Enlightenment" is far from a contradiction in terms.[3]

This defense of the pragmatic strand of Enlightenment thought is meant in part, but only in small part, as a response to Jonathan Israel's recent vindication of what he calls the "Radical Enlightenment."[4] Throughout his weighty tomes, Israel argues that "from beginning to end" the Enlightenment was "always fundamentally divided ... into irreconcilably opposed intellectual blocs," the Radical Enlightenment and the "moderate mainstream," and he consistently champions the former.[5] In fact, much of his intellectual energy is devoted to unmasking and

[2] This use of the term "liberalism" is, of course, anachronistic when applied to the eighteenth century, but the outlooks of these thinkers fit readily into the tradition that we now call by that name.

[3] While there are certain similarities between my reading of these Enlightenment thinkers and the later school of American pragmatism, I use "pragmatic" as a generic term rather than a reference to Charles Sanders Peirce, William James, John Dewey, et al.

[4] See Jonathan I. Israel, *Radical Enlightenment: Philosophy and the Making of Modernity, 1650–1750* (Oxford: Oxford University Press, 2001); Jonathan I. Israel, *Enlightenment Contested: Philosophy, Modernity, and the Emancipation of Man, 1670–1752* (Oxford: Oxford University Press, 2006); and Jonathan I. Israel, *Democratic Enlightenment: Philosophy, Revolution, and Human Rights, 1750–1790* (Oxford: Oxford University Press, 2011). For a more concise statement of some of the themes that run through Israel's lengthy trilogy, see Jonathan I. Israel, *A Revolution of the Mind: Radical Enlightenment and the Intellectual Origins of Modern Democracy* (Princeton, NJ: Princeton University Press, 2010). Obviously, the present book contains neither the immense historical and geographic breadth nor the sweeping narrative that Israel's volumes do. On the other hand, my focus on just four thinkers allows for much more sustained analysis of their texts and arguments than is possible in works like Israel's.

[5] Israel, *Enlightenment Contested*, x.

Introduction 3

criticizing the moderate Enlightenment, including the four thinkers who are the focus of this book, for its intellectual modesty and social conservatism. Taken together, Israel's books constitute the most ambitious and comprehensive attempt to come to terms with the Enlightenment since the work of Peter Gay – perhaps since the Enlightenment itself – and his breadth of knowledge is extraordinary. However, I disagree profoundly with his basic claim that the neat "package" of Radical Enlightenment ideals that he derives from Spinoza, Bayle, Diderot, and others (but that none of these thinkers embraced in its entirety) is the only truly coherent and emancipatory philosophical outlook, and conversely that the moderate Enlightenment, with its doubts about the power and scope of human reason and its compromises with the existing order, was ultimately a blind alley and a source of oppression.[6]

The main target of this book, however, is neither Israel nor his Radical Enlightenment but rather the Enlightenment's (many) critics. The Enlightenment was condemned in some circles almost from the moment of its inception, and since World War II the opposition has emerged with renewed vigor and from nearly every direction, uniting liberals and conservatives, pluralists and communitarians, postmodernists and religious fundamentalists.[7] Indeed, Darrin McMahon summarizes the current climate well when he remarks that "Enlightenment bashing has developed into something of an intellectual blood-sport, uniting elements of both the Left and the Right in a common cause."[8] While the Enlightenment is criticized from a wide variety of perspectives and for a wide variety of reasons, the main lines of criticism can be grouped into three broad categories:

- *Hegemonic Universalism.* One of the most pervasive criticisms of the Enlightenment in recent years relates to its supposed belief in the

---

[6] Israel's clearest summary of the Radical Enlightenment "package" – which includes atheism, materialism, political radicalism, democracy, egalitarianism, and comprehensive religious toleration – can be found at ibid., 866.

[7] Given that one of the chief aims of this book is to combat the misperceptions about the Enlightenment that still pervade contemporary political theory, I will be concerned especially with the more recent critics of the Enlightenment, but it should be kept in mind that almost all of their critiques can be traced back to the nineteenth and even eighteenth centuries. For a helpful survey of the opponents of the Enlightenment since the eighteenth century, see Graeme Garrard, *Counter-Enlightenments: From the Eighteenth Century to the Present* (New York: Routledge, 2006). For a more polemical account that links Counter-Enlightenment discourse to moral relativism and fascist ideology, see Zeev Sternhell, *The Anti-Enlightenment Tradition*, trans. David Maisel (New Haven, CT: Yale University Press, 2010).

[8] Darrin McMahon, *Enemies of the Enlightenment: The French Counter-Enlightenment and the Making of Modernity* (Oxford University Press, 2001), 12.

4 *The Pragmatic Enlightenment*

existence of universal, ahistorical, transcultural truths in morality and politics. It is widely assumed that Enlightenment thinkers were either unaware of or dismissive of the historical and cultural differences among peoples and beliefs, and that this renders their outlook utterly implausible and dangerously exclusive.

- *Blind Faith in Reason.* Another prevalent charge leveled against the thinkers of this period is that they believed reason could do anything and everything. Critics have long contended that the key to the Enlightenment outlook was an overconfidence – many have said "faith" – in reason's power and compass. This charge is often accompanied by the claim that the Enlightenment outlook entails a naive belief in progress, a conviction that the spread of reason will inevitably produce a corresponding advance in human well-being.
- *Atomistic Individualism.* A final major criticism is that the Enlightenment focused on individuals and rights rather than communal ties and duties, thereby undermining the moral fabric of the community. By ignoring the shared values and attachments that give meaning to people's lives, the critics claim, the Enlightenment outlook reduces people to self-interested, rights-bearing atoms and thereby makes a healthy community impossible.

A closer look at these critiques will have to wait until the following chapters, where we will see that for each of these vices that are attributed to the Enlightenment, Hume, Smith, Montesquieu, and Voltaire – all of whom are central to the Enlightenment on any plausible understanding of its meaning – actually exhibited the contrary virtue. Far from adopting a hegemonic form of moral and political universalism, they emphasized the importance of context in the formulation of moral standards and adopted a flexible, nonfoundationalist form of liberalism. Far from having a blind faith in reason, they continually stressed the limits and fallibility of human understanding and advocated a cautious reformism in politics. And far from promoting atomistic individualism, they saw people as inherently social and sought a healthier and more reliable way to unite them than the traditional bonds of blood, religion, and nationalism, which they found above all in commerce.

Before turning to a more detailed examination and defense of these four thinkers, however, it may be helpful to situate my broader argument within the present state of Enlightenment studies. Most contemporary scholars of eighteenth-century thought concur that the "Enlightenment" that is so reviled by its critics is often a gross caricature of the actual ideas of the period. The recent boom in scholarship on this period has

Introduction 5

produced a number of valuable works that aim to defend certain aspects of Enlightenment thought or to reclaim individual Enlightenment thinkers, which I will have the advantage of drawing upon in making my own case. Nevertheless, my approach runs against the grain of contemporary Enlightenment studies in several respects.

To begin with, many historians of the Enlightenment now regard the study of the leading figures of the period – a small canon of almost exclusively male thinkers – as unacceptably elitist. Beginning with the work of Daniel Mornet in the early twentieth century, and continuing with such leading scholars of the period as Robert Darnton, Daniel Roche, and Roger Chartier and the Annales school, historians have tended to focus on the social milieus in which Enlightenment thinkers lived and wrote and on the diffusion of their ideas, to the almost total exclusion of the ideas themselves.[9] Much attention has been paid to the rise of sociability and the public sphere – academies and salons, coffeehouses and cafés, debating societies and Masonic lodges, the book industry and Grub Street – while far less has been paid to the arguments of the leading thinkers of the period. Indeed, alongside the move toward what the historians proudly call the "low" Enlightenment has come a kind of scorn for the "high" Enlightenment of the leading thinkers; Roy Porter derisively calls these latter thinkers the "superstars" of the period and suggests that we move beyond conceiving of the Enlightenment in terms of "periwigged poseurs prattling on in Parisian salons."[10]

As a work of political theory, however, this book will necessarily focus on the so-called high Enlightenment – indeed, the very highest of the high Enlightenment. This is not to deny the historical importance or intrinsic interest of the "low" Enlightenment, of course, but in terms of significance for the present, it is the *ideas* of the period – and the leading exponents of those ideas – that matter most. The Parisian salons, Grub Street pamphleteers, and international book industry may have helped to *propagate* the liberal values that we in the modern West have inherited from the eighteenth century, but it is the values themselves that concern us today. As Robert Wokler has argued, when historians of the Enlightenment disdain the study of the ideas and leading thinkers of the period, they thereby

[9] Useful overviews of the scholarship on the social and cultural history of the Enlightenment can be found in Dorinda Outram, *The Enlightenment*, second edition (Cambridge: Cambridge University Press, 2005), chapter 2; and John Robertson, *The Case for the Enlightenment: Scotland and Naples, 1680–1760* (Cambridge: Cambridge University Press, 2005), 16–21.

[10] Roy Porter, *The Creation of the Modern World: The Untold Story of the British Enlightenment* (New York: W. W. Norton, 2000), 11, 4.

6   *The Pragmatic Enlightenment*

abandon the legacy of these ideas and thinkers to the Enlightenment's critics.[11] It is for its ideas that the Enlightenment is attacked, and so it is by its ideas that it must be defended.

Those scholars who *do* focus on the ideas and leading thinkers of the eighteenth century, for their part, commonly deny the very existence of the Enlightenment as a coherent movement. As James Schmidt and others have emphasized, the term "the Enlightenment," used to designate a specific period and movement of thought, did not arise until the late nineteenth century, and the growing consensus among scholars of eighteenth-century thought seems to be that this term – particularly in the singular, with the definite article and a capital "E" – has become analytically useless and even harmful, insofar as it serves to paper over the great diversity of thought in this period.[12] As Schmidt writes, "the explosion of eighteenth-century studies over the last several decades has had one notable consequence: an incredulity towards generalizations about 'the Enlightenment.'"[13] Thus, many scholars now insist that it is only in the plural that the many different "Enlightenments" of the eighteenth century can be understood properly. The leading advocate of this perspective is probably J. G. A. Pocock, who contends that the process of Enlightenment "occurred in too many forms to be comprised within a single definition and history," and so "we do better to think of a family of Enlightenments, displaying both family resemblances and family quarrels (some of them bitter and even bloody)."[14] Pocock is far from alone in holding this view, however: most political theorists and philosophers who specialize in eighteenth-century thought now concur with Sankar

---

[11] See Robert Wokler, "Ernst Cassirer's Enlightenment: An Exchange with Bruce Mazlish" *Studies in Eighteenth Century Culture* 29 (2000), 336–7. See also Robertson, *The Case for the Enlightenment*, 21.

[12] On the rise of the term "the Enlightenment" and its foreign cognates, see John Lough, "Reflections on Enlightenment and Lumières" *Journal for Eighteenth-Century Studies* 8.1 (March 1985): 1–15; James Schmidt, "Inventing the Enlightenment: Anti-Jacobins, British Hegelians, and the *Oxford English Dictionary*" *Journal of the History of Ideas* 64.3 (July 2003): 421–43; and James Schmidt, "What the Enlightenment Was, What It Still Might Be, and Why Kant May Have Been Right After All" *American Behavioral Scientist* 49.5 (January 2006): 647–63.

[13] James Schmidt, "The Legacy of the Enlightenment" *Philosophy and Literature* 26.2 (October 2002), 440. See also James Schmidt, "What Enlightenment Project?" *Political Theory* 28.6 (December 2000): 734–57.

[14] J. G. A. Pocock, *Barbarism and Religion*, vol. 1: *The Enlightenments of Edward Gibbon, 1737–1764* (Cambridge: Cambridge University Press, 1999), 9; see also 7, 13; J. G. A. Pocock, "The Re-description of Enlightenment" *Proceedings of the British Academy* 125 (2004), 105–8, 114, 117; and J. G. A. Pocock, "Historiography and Enlightenment: A View of Their History" *Modern Intellectual History* 5.1 (April 2008), 83–4, 91, 94–5.

Introduction 7

Muthu's conclusion "that 'the Enlightenment' *as such* and the notion of an overarching 'Enlightenment project' simply do not exist" and thus that "it is high time ... that we pluralize our understanding of 'the Enlightenment' both for reasons of historical accuracy and because, in doing so, otherwise hidden or understudied moments of Enlightenment-era thinking will come to light."[15]

Here I agree in part, but also disagree in part. There is no question that the Enlightenment was a multifaceted, diverse movement; I myself am focusing primarily on one strand of Enlightenment thought – the pragmatic Enlightenment of Hume, Smith, Montesquieu, and Voltaire – which I distinguish throughout from other strands, above all those exemplified by Locke, Kant, Bentham, and some of the more radical philosophes. On the other hand, the larger claim that the Enlightenment simply *did not exist* seems to me to go much too far. It is important not to miss the forest for the trees here: the presence of diversity within a movement does not render it any less of a movement, and the existence of national, ideological, or other subgroups does not mean that the broader category "the Enlightenment" does not exist. (Do the differences between Luther and Calvin render the very notion of a Protestant Reformation unintelligible?) Nor must such a category encompass every thinker and idea in the eighteenth century. Critics of the idea of *the* Enlightenment often argue that, since there are no principled grounds on which to choose one set of thinkers or ideas over another, the term "Enlightenment" should be used strictly as a temporal adjective to designate the entirety of the period.[16] Yet this would render the term superfluous, since the period designation alone would suffice for this purpose. It seems to me more sensible to narrow the scope and to ask instead whether a certain kind of thinker or a certain set of widely shared principles and values can plausibly be said to make up the Enlightenment.[17]

One powerful reason to suppose that it *is* possible to identify the Enlightenment in this manner is that many of the leading thinkers of

---

[15] Sankar Muthu, *Enlightenment against Empire* (Princeton, NJ: Princeton University Press, 2003), 264.

[16] See, for example, ibid., 1–2.

[17] As Robert Darnton suggests, the recent tendency to expand the Enlightenment to encompass the entirety of the eighteenth century, and often a large part of the seventeenth, has meant that "the Enlightenment is beginning to be everything and therefore nothing." To counteract this tendency Darnton sensibly proposes a "deflation," although the physical and chronological boundaries that he sets – which confine the Enlightenment exclusively to Paris in the early eighteenth century – seem to me a bit *too* restrictive. See Robert Darnton, *George Washington's False Teeth: An Unconventional Guide to the Eighteenth Century* (New York: W. W. Norton, 2003), 4.

8 — The Pragmatic Enlightenment

eighteenth-century Europe saw *themselves* as part of a collective enterprise. As Wokler observes, there was a widespread sense in the eighteenth century of "shared principles, a campaign, an international society of the republic of letters, a party of humanity."[18] Indeed, one of the most striking features of the Enlightenment was the deliberate, self-conscious nature of the movement – the awareness, on the part of its proponents, of a broad set of shared goals and of their distinctive place in history. Even Pocock concedes that many eighteenth-century thinkers "were aware ... of what they and their colleagues and competitors were doing – aware even of their historical significance, to a degree itself new in European culture – and the metaphor of light (*lumière, lume, Aufklärung*) is strongly present in their writings."[19] As the prevalence of this metaphor suggests, even if the term "the Enlightenment" did not yet exist in English in the eighteenth century, it *did* exist in some form in French, Italian, and German, and the idea was certainly present in Britain and America as well.[20] Nor were the proponents of the Enlightenment alone in ascribing to themselves a common identity: their enemies too saw them as a single group.[21]

What, then, did the Enlightenment outlook consist of? A conclusive or comprehensive answer to this question is probably impossible, but the definition offered by John Robertson – one of the relatively few contemporary scholars to embrace the idea of a unitary Enlightenment – constitutes a reasonable starting point: "the commitment to understanding,

---

[18] For this reason, Wokler allows, "I am not so unhappy as are some other historians of eighteenth-century thought with the idea of an Enlightenment Project." Robert Wokler, "The Enlightenment Project and Its Critics," in *The Postmodernist Critique of the Project of Enlightenment*, ed. Sven-Eric Liedman (Amsterdam: Rodopi, 1997), 18–19. See also Robert Wokler, "The Enlightenment Project as Betrayed by Modernity" *History of European Ideas* 24.4–5 (1998), 302–3.

[19] Pocock, *Barbarism and Religion*, vol. 1, 5. Dan Edelstein has recently claimed that even if "the narrative of Enlightenment was open to different and evolving interpretations ... it still makes sense for historians to speak of 'the Enlightenment,' as the plural-only rule contradicts the lived experience that *Aufklärer* and *philosophes* were made of the same wood – a slightly less crooked timber." Dan Edelstein, *The Enlightenment: A Genealogy* (Chicago: University of Chicago Press, 2010), 14.

[20] Moreover, as Schmidt acknowledges, it is clearly possible for there to have been a movement – even a self-conscious one – without a word for it. See Schmidt, "What the Enlightenment Was, What It Still Might Be, and Why Kant May Have Been Right After All," 649.

[21] See McMahon, *Enemies of the Enlightenment*, especially 11–12, 28–32, 192–5, 200–1. The same could be said of the Enlightenment's greatest eighteenth-century opponent: Wokler writes that "Rousseau himself, I have no doubt, believed that there was an Enlightenment Project, by which I do not just mean the international conspiracy to defame him." Wokler, "The Enlightenment Project as Betrayed by Modernity," 302.

Introduction 9

and hence to advancing, the causes and conditions of human betterment in this world."[22] A number of broadly liberal principles and values generally followed from this desire to improve the human condition in the here and now, including support for limited government, religious toleration, freedom of expression, commerce, and humane criminal laws.[23] Indeed, I would submit that those eighteenth-century thinkers and groups who diverged from these broad liberal ideals, to the extent of the divergence, also diverged from the Enlightenment.[24] Of course, there were important differences even among those who supported these ideals. To borrow the concept made famous by John Rawls, the Enlightenment can be conceived as an overlapping consensus in which the members of the movement all supported a number of basic liberal ideals but did so in different ways, and for different reasons. For example, some Enlightenment thinkers, such as Locke, promoted these liberal ideals on natural law or natural rights grounds; others, such as Kant, grounded them in the requirements of human dignity; still others, like Bentham, based them on the imperative to maximize utility; while yet others, including Hume, Smith, Montesquieu, and Voltaire, advocated these ideals on nonfoundationalist grounds. Moreover, the various ways of grounding these ideals frequently led to differences in the *character* of the liberalism espoused by different Enlightenment thinkers. For some, liberalism was a radical or even revolutionary outlook, while for others – including, again, the four thinkers who are the focus of this book – it was a more moderate and reformist one. Similarly, the liberalism of some Enlightenment thinkers was highly individualistic in conception, rooted in individual

---

[22] Robertson, *The Case for the Enlightenment*, 28.

[23] These liberal ideals may seem unexceptionable to many today, but we should recall that throughout much of Europe the eighteenth century was still an age of royal absolutism, hereditary hierarchy, religious persecution as a formal policy, political and ecclesiastical censorship, slavery, colonialism, and routine judicial torture, and that France did not burn its last witch until 1745. When viewed in historical context, both the intellectual coherence and the importance of the Enlightenment become more apparent.

[24] I have made this case at some length regarding the eighteenth-century thinker who most resists all categorization, Jean-Jacques Rousseau. The case is even more obvious for, say, the conservative Catholic "anti-*philosophes*" who have been called to our attention by Darrin McMahon. Simply having lived in the eighteenth century does not make one an Enlightenment thinker. See Dennis C. Rasmussen, *The Problems and Promise of Commercial Society: Adam Smith's Response to Rousseau* (University Park: Pennsylvania State University Press, 2008), chapter 1; Dennis C. Rasmussen, "Adam Smith and Rousseau: Enlightenment and Counter-Enlightenment," in *The Oxford Handbook of Adam Smith*, ed. Christopher J. Berry, Maria Pia Paganelli, and Craig Smith (Oxford: Oxford University Press, 2013); and McMahon, *Enemies of the Enlightenment*.

rights, choices, and interests, while that of the pragmatic strand of the Enlightenment was much more insistent on the social nature of human beings and concerned with the character of the community.

Thus, while the Enlightenment's critics commonly assume that Enlightenment thought necessarily appeals to universal moral and political foundations, that it necessarily places a great deal of confidence in the power and scope of abstract reason, and that it necessarily rests on individualistic premises, I show that the pragmatic Enlightenment does not fall prey to *any* of these charges. This is an absolutely crucial strand of the Enlightenment, at that: Hume, Smith, Montesquieu, and Voltaire are each every bit as central to the movement as are thinkers such as Locke and Kant. Hume and Smith are almost universally seen as the two towering thinkers of the Scottish Enlightenment, and the importance of the Scottish Enlightenment for the Enlightenment as a whole is now well established. Hume was, in the judgment of many, the greatest philosopher of the eighteenth century – or at least the greatest rival to the "sage of Königsberg" – and even the greatest philosopher ever to write in the English language. Partly for this reason, Alfred Cobban dubs him "the philosopher, par excellence, of the Enlightenment," and Peter Gay casts him as the signature "modern pagan" in his study of the period.[25] Smith, for his part, has long been recognized as the leading theorist of commercial society in the eighteenth century; indeed, Wokler claims that *The Wealth of Nations* is "perhaps the most influential of all Enlightenment contributions to human science."[26] Moreover, Smith's philosophy as a whole is now starting to be appreciated for the achievement that it was, and we will see that his writings exemplify many of the key ideals of this pragmatic strand of the Enlightenment.

Similarly, Montesquieu and Voltaire were plainly two of the leading figures among the French philosophes. Given Montesquieu's enormous influence not only in France but also in Scotland, North America, and beyond, Gay concludes "after due deliberation and with due consideration for the claims of potential rivals" that "Montesquieu was the most

---

[25] Alfred Cobban, *In Search of Humanity: The Role of the Enlightenment in Modern History* (New York: George Braziller, 1960), 133; Peter Gay, *The Enlightenment: An Interpretation*, vol. 1: *The Rise of Modern Paganism* (New York: W. W. Norton, 1966), 401–19.

[26] Robert Wokler, "The Enlightenment Science of Politics," in *Inventing Human Science*, ed. Christopher Fox, Roy Porter, and Robert Wokler (Berkeley: University of California Press, 1995), 336. See also Charles L. Griswold, *Adam Smith and the Virtues of Enlightenment* (Cambridge: Cambridge University Press, 1999), especially 9–26.

Introduction 11

influential writer of the eighteenth century."[27] More recently, Thomas Pangle has proclaimed that *The Spirit of the Laws* "towers as the most ambitious expression of the Enlightenment political philosophizing that lays the principled basis for our liberal republican civilization."[28] Yet even Montesquieu cannot rival Voltaire for the sheer extent to which he was and is associated with this period; indeed, the Enlightenment is sometimes referred to as "the Age of Voltaire."[29] While Voltaire's thought has garnered strikingly little attention from political theorists and philosophers in recent years, Friedrich Nietzsche calls him "the man of his century," and Isaiah Berlin dubs him "the central figure of the Enlightenment."[30] So great was Voltaire's influence during the eighteenth century that John Adams, in Paris as the American ambassador to France, gave voice to the widespread worry that the "republic of letters" was in danger of becoming a monarchy.[31] To repeat, these four thinkers by no means make up the whole of the Enlightenment; I make no claims to comprehensiveness in these pages. Still, these thinkers are all sufficiently central to the movement that any critique of the Enlightenment that does not apply to any of them stands in need of immense revision, if not of being discarded altogether.[32]

Nor were Hume, Smith, Montesquieu, and Voltaire alone, among Enlightenment thinkers, in adopting a generally pragmatic outlook;

[27] Peter Gay, *The Enlightenment: An Interpretation*, vol. 2: *The Science of Freedom* (New York: W.W. Norton, 1969), 325. For an account of the enormous praised heaped upon *The Spirit of the Laws* by Montesquieu's contemporaries and successors throughout Europe and North America, see David W. Carrithers, "Introduction: An Appreciation of *The Spirit of Laws*," in *Montesquieu's Science of Politics: Essays on The Spirit of Laws*, ed. David W. Carrithers, Michael A. Mosher, and Paul A. Rahe (Lanham, MD: Rowman & Littlefield, 2001), 1–5.

[28] Thomas L. Pangle, *The Theological Basis of Liberal Modernity in Montesquieu's Spirit of the Laws* (Chicago: University of Chicago Press, 2010), 1.

[29] See, for instance, Will and Ariel Durant, *The Age of Voltaire: A History of Civilization in Western Europe from 1715 to 1756* (New York: Simon & Schuster, 1965).

[30] Friedrich Nietzsche, *The Will to Power*, trans. Walter Kaufmann (New York: Vintage, 1968), 63; Isaiah Berlin, "The Divorce between the Sciences and the Humanities," in *The Proper Study of Mankind: An Anthology of Essays*, ed. Henry Hardy and Roger Hausheer (New York: Farrar, Straus & Giroux [1979] 1998), 334.

[31] See John Adams, *Diary and Autobiography of John Adams*, ed. L. H. Butterfield, vol. 4 (Cambridge: Harvard University Press, [1778] 1961), 61–2.

[32] What Daniel Gordon writes of Voltaire is equally true of the other three: "Voltaire was a figure of such symbolic importance to his contemporaries that any characterization of the Enlightenment that does violence to his thought is open to question." Daniel Gordon, "On the Supposed Obsolescence of the French Enlightenment," in *Postmodernism and the Enlightenment: New Perspectives in Eighteenth-Century French Intellectual History*, ed. Daniel Gordon (New York: Routledge, 2001), 201.

The Pragmatic Enlightenment

many others did so as well. Any list is bound to remain incomplete, but other candidates for membership in this strand of the Enlightenment would include, for example, d'Alembert, Condillac, Condorcet, and Diderot in France; Adam Ferguson, John Millar, and William Robertson in Scotland; Edward Gibbon, Samuel Johnson,[33] and Josiah Tucker in England; Gotthold Lessing, Moses Mendelssohn, and Christoph Wieland in Germany; and Cesare Beccaria, Ferdinando Galiani, Antonio Genovesi, and Pietro Verri in Italy.[34] Of course, it is neither possible nor desirable to divide the thinkers of the period into a number of discrete and rigidly defined groups that are set in opposition to one another; the

[33] Johnson is sometimes seen as an anti-Enlightenment thinker because of his self-professed aversion to some of the philosophes and because of his reputation as a staunch Tory and bigoted Anglican, a reputation that James Boswell's *Life of Samuel Johnson* did much to promote. However, as Donald Greene has stressed, an examination of Johnson's political writings themselves shows him to be a skeptical conservative who fits well within the tradition of Gibbon and Hume. See Donald Greene, *The Politics of Samuel Johnson*, second edition (Athens: University of Georgia Press, [1960] 1990); and Samuel Johnson, *Political Writings*, ed. Donald Greene (Indianapolis: Liberty Fund, 1977).

[34] Readers of Jonathan Israel's volumes will notice that several of his Radical Enlightenment figures appear in this list, including Condorcet, Millar, Lessing, and above all Diderot, who plays a central role in Israel's Radical Enlightenment pantheon. I read each of these thinkers as more moderate and flexible in outlook than he does. Condorcet is often seen as a veritable poster child for the alleged rigid universalism and cold rationalism of the Enlightenment, but recent scholarship has shown that he was actually by and large a pragmatist and sentimentalist. See especially Emma Rothschild, *Economic Sentiments: Adam Smith, Condorcet, and the Enlightenment* (Cambridge: Harvard University Press, 2001), chapter 7; and David Williams, *Condorcet and Modernity* (Cambridge: Cambridge University Press, 2004). While Millar was a more strident Whig than most other members of the Scottish Enlightenment, he followed his teacher Smith in counseling prudence when making political change and in being largely satisfied with the settlement of the revolution of 1688. See Duncan Forbes, "'Scientific' Whiggism: Adam Smith and John Millar" *Cambridge Journal* 7.2 (August 1954): 643–70. Lessing may have found some aspects of Spinoza's thought congenial late in life, but the general contours of his outlook more closely resemble the skepticism of Montaigne and Bayle than Spinoza's thoroughgoing rationalism. See H. B. Nisbet, "Lessing and Philosophy," in *A Companion to the Works of Gotthold Ephraim Lessing*, ed. Barbara Fischer and Thomas C. Fox (Rochester, NY: Camden House, 2005). Finally, I have argued elsewhere that Diderot adopted a reformist, rather than radical or revolutionary, stance toward political change: see Dennis C. Rasmussen, "Burning Laws and Strangling Kings? Voltaire and Diderot on the Perils of Rationalism in Politics" *Review of Politics* 73.1 (winter 2011): 77–104. I will only add here that, contrary to Israel's suggestion, Diderot was every bit as aware of the limits of human reason as Hume or Voltaire, and that he thus took a similarly skeptical view of the rationalist *esprit de système* of thinkers like Spinoza. On the self-consciously antisystematic character of Diderot's thought, see John Hope Mason, *The Irresistible Diderot* (London: Quartet Books, 1982), 13–14; and the translators' introduction in Denis Diderot, *Political Writings*, trans. John Hope Mason and Robert Wokler (Cambridge: Cambridge University Press, 1992), xxxi–xxxii.

Introduction   13

various strands of the Enlightenment are, like the Enlightenment itself, bound to have blurry edges. I only mean to stress here that Hume, Smith, Montesquieu, and Voltaire were far from outliers, and that the pragmatic strand of the Enlightenment includes not only these four leading figures but also a host of others.

The obvious question arises: Why has the Enlightenment been so widely and so persistently seen as rigidly universalist, dogmatically rationalist, and narrowly individualist, given that such key figures of the period as Hume, Smith, Montesquieu, and Voltaire – among many others – controvert each aspect of this caricature? Answering this complex historical question fully would likely require at least a book of its own, but a few preliminary suggestions are possible here. One source of this caricature, surely, is the Enlightenment's perceived relationship to the French Revolution. During the revolutionary period and the succeeding years, both the proponents and the critics of the revolution had a vested interest in depicting philosophes such as Voltaire (and, to a lesser extent, Montesquieu) as adherents of the revolutionary ideology – the proponents in order to claim the authority of the philosophes for their cause, and the critics in order to demonstrate that the crisis was brought on by a relatively small cabal of instigators, rather than by fundamental and deep-seated problems in the ancien régime.[35] The reputations of Hume and Smith, on the other hand, were distorted in the opposite direction: they were read as narrow conservatives, even reactionaries, by those who wished to save them from association with the revolution.[36] In other words, the supporters of Hume and Smith sought to *distance* them from the Enlightenment (which they associated above all with France) and its presumed radicalism and rationalism. As a result, the narrative that the revolutionary generation handed down to posterity tended to exaggerate the divergences between the leading philosophes, on the one hand, and the preeminent Scottish thinkers, on the other, making what were

[35] On Voltaire's reputation in the revolutionary and postrevolutionary periods, see Stephen Bird, *Reinventing Voltaire: The Politics of Commemoration in Nineteenth-Century France* (Oxford: Voltaire Foundation, 2000), chapter 1; and Renée Waldinger, *Voltaire and Reform in the Light of the French Revolution* (Geneva: Droz, 1959), chapter 4. On Montesquieu, see Norman Hampson, *Will and Circumstance: Montesquieu, Rousseau and the French Revolution* (Norman: University of Oklahoma Press, 1983); and C. P. Courtney, "Montesquieu and Revolution," in *Lectures de Montesquieu*, ed. Edgar Mass and Alberto Postigliola (Naples: Liguori Editore, 1993), 43–50.

[36] On Hume, see Laurence L. Bongie, *David Hume: Prophet of the Counter-Revolution*, second edition (Indianapolis: Liberty Fund, 2000). On Smith, see Rothschild, *Economic Sentiments*, chapter 2.

14 *The Pragmatic Enlightenment*

mostly differences in tone and temperament seem like crucial differences in substantive ideals. More broadly, the Enlightenment itself came to be associated with revolutionary notions of universal natural rights and the triumph of reason, rather than with the kind of moderate, flexible liberalism that was characteristic of so many of the leading figures of the period.

A more recent, but equally conspicuous source of the Enlightenment's reputation for universalism, rationalism, and individualism has been the staggeringly disproportionate scholarly focus on Kant as the chief representative of the period. Kant is regularly taken to be *the* prototypical Enlightenment thinker, for several reasons. First, he wrote a famous essay answering the question "What Is Enlightenment?" that is conveniently (although inappropriately) taken as the definitive account of what the Enlightenment stood for.[37] Second, Kant has arguably exerted greater influence over contemporary moral and political philosophy than any other canonical thinker; the many followers of Rawls and Habermas, for example, are far more likely to appeal to Kant as their intellectual forebear than to thinkers such as Hume, Smith, Montesquieu, and Voltaire. Finally, the Enlightenment's critics tend to find this focus on Kant congenial, for, as James Schmidt notes, his "emphasis on the themes of universalism, autonomy, and self-legislation, is tailor-made for critics seeking to arraign the Enlightenment on the familiar charges of arid intellectualism and abstract individualism."[38] Yet Kant represents only one strand of Enlightenment thought, and far from the dominant one, at that; to equate the Enlightenment with his outlook is to miss much of what it stood for.[39]

---

[37] See Immanuel Kant, "An Answer to the Question: What Is Enlightenment?" in *Practical Philosophy*, trans. Mary J. Gregor (Cambridge: Cambridge University Press, [1784] 1996). As James Schmidt has stressed, those who see this essay as the manifesto of the Enlightenment ignore the fact that there were "many *other* answers to the question 'What is Enlightenment?' that appeared in Prussia during the 1780s and ... thus remain blissfully unaware of the degree to which Kant's definition of Enlightenment represented a significant departure from those of his contemporaries." Schmidt, "What Enlightenment Project?" 740. See also James Schmidt, ed., *What Is Enlightenment?: Eighteenth-Century Answers and Twentieth-Century Questions* (Berkeley: University of California Press, 1996).

[38] Schmidt, "What Enlightenment Project?" 739–40.

[39] Indeed, many aspects of Kant's outlook mark a self-conscious *departure* from the other leading strands of eighteenth-century thought. Perhaps most obviously, Kant criticizes most of his Enlightenment predecessors for basing morality on empirical or "heteronomous" (and hence contingent) factors such as human desires or sentiments, the consequences of one's actions, and the norms of one's society. Other notable departures include

Introduction   15

Connected with both of these points is perhaps the most fundamental reason for the prevalence and persistence of the caricatured view of the Enlightenment: because the Enlightenment did so much to inspire and encourage liberal values, practices, and institutions, critics of liberalism from across the political spectrum and from the eighteenth century to the present have sought to portray the thinkers of this period as rigid universalists, dogmatic rationalists, and narrow individualists in an attempt to color the way liberalism itself is viewed. From Rousseau to Foucault and from Maistre to MacIntyre, those who have found liberal principles or societies wanting have almost invariably laid much of the blame at the Enlightenment's doorstep. The critics seek to render their attacks on liberalism all the more comprehensive and conclusive by showing that the alleged shortcomings – the undermining of community and religion, the injustices of capitalism, the ills wrought by modern science, and the rest – are not incidental or avoidable aspects of liberalism but rather inherent in its very origins. As we will see in the following chapters, liberals from Tocqueville to Rawls have, for whatever reason, proven all too willing to distance themselves from the Enlightenment and thereby, in effect, to abandon its legacy to the critics. When these liberals accept or even embrace the damning depiction of the Enlightenment advanced by the critics, they not only make an interpretive mistake but also thereby cede the argumentative high ground. Indeed, it is precisely because our conception of the Enlightenment so deeply colors our views of liberalism and the modern West that it is crucial for us to understand it for ourselves rather than allow our views to be shaped by phenomena such as the politics of the French Revolution, the scholarly fascination with Kant, and the biases of liberalism's critics.

While critics tend to denounce the Enlightenment in fairly broad strokes, among those who do single out specific thinkers or groups, many focus on those who fall outside the pragmatic strand of the movement,

---

his radical separation of the phenomenal world (perceived by the senses) and the noumenal world (accessible by pure reason); his understanding of freedom in terms obeying a self-prescribed law out of pure respect for the universality of the law itself, regardless of the consequences; his hypothetical contractarianism and insistence on unconditional obedience to the established authorities; and his belief in the inevitability of perpetual peace. Nor, for all of his influence on recent moral and political *philosophy*, was Kant the Enlightenment thinker with the greatest *practical* impact. On the contrary, thinkers such as Locke, Hume, Smith, Montesquieu, Voltaire, Diderot, and Bentham *all* probably had a greater influence on the rise and spread of liberal democracy, market capitalism, religious toleration, science and technology, and/or the reform of inhumane criminal laws in the modern West.

such as Locke, Kant, Bentham, or the more radical philosophes, or even on pre-Enlightenment thinkers such as Bacon, Descartes, or Hobbes.[40] Thus, my responding to their criticisms through an examination of Hume, Smith, Montesquieu, and Voltaire may seem to miss the mark. Yet we will see that many of the critics do include these four thinkers, explicitly or implicitly, in their charges. Moreover, even for those who do not, the main purpose and effect of their criticisms are to color our view of the Enlightenment as a whole – an issue that is not, I would suggest, merely academic. Given all that we have inherited from the Enlightenment, its legacy is necessarily of great importance for us. Just as our understanding of the American founding (Lockean liberal or classical republican? Christian or secular? "We the people" or a conspiracy of the propertied elite?) influences the way we view the contemporary United States, our understanding of the Enlightenment forms an important part of how we view liberalism and the modern West. If all strands of Enlightenment thought did in fact have the rigidly universalist, dogmatically rationalist, and narrowly individualist character that the critics ascribe to it, then it might very well make sense for us to disown it, as they urge. If, however, at least one central and influential strand of the movement does not fall prey to these charges, then perhaps today's liberals should turn to their Enlightenment origins with a more open and sympathetic mind than they have often done in recent years. Perhaps, indeed, the Enlightenment still has something to teach us.

In the remaining chapters of the book I examine the political theory of Hume, Smith, Montesquieu, and Voltaire, broadly construed to include their views on human nature, morality, and commerce, as well as some features of their attitudes toward epistemology, science, and religion. This is not, however, a comprehensive study of their political thought. I say

---

[40] As Schmidt rightly notes, when critics subsume these latter thinkers into the Enlightenment, "utility trumps chronology: certain thinkers prove irresistible to critics of the Enlightenment project because they offer more forceful formulations of what are assumed to be central components of the project than can typically be found among thinkers whose work falls more squarely within the historical Enlightenment. Bacon is irreplaceable as an advocate for the scientific domination of nature, Hobbes is priceless as a representative of that individualist, rights- and contract-centered theory that critics assume lies at the heart of Enlightenment political thought, and Descartes serves as the epitome of that foundationalist and subject-centered conception of reason that philosophers have spent most of [the twentieth] century dismantling. It seems to have escaped critics of the Enlightenment that Hobbes's account of the social contract was one of the more popular whipping boys of Enlightenment moralists and natural law theorists, that the appropriation of Descartes within the Enlightenment was complex and often quite critical, and that Bacon died in 1626." Schmidt, "What Enlightenment Project?" 739.

Introduction

little in these pages about their views on international relations, including their (almost uniformly hostile) attitude toward empire and colonialism, in part because this topic has been well canvassed by others.[41] I also largely omit discussion of their views on race, ethnicity, and gender. There is no question that these thinkers occasionally expressed views on these scores that are deplorable by today's standards – Voltaire's anti-Semitism, Montesquieu's "Orientalism," Hume's infamous racist footnote – but, contrary to the claims of some of the Enlightenment's critics, these views were not integral to their thought. After all, it is easy to find passages in their works that are nearly the opposite of racist or Eurocentric,[42] and many of the retrograde statements that they did make were put forward in the service of other aims[43] or represented a *deviation* from their

---

[41] Sankar Muthu and Jennifer Pitts have shown that the widespread opposition to the idea of empire during the Enlightenment made it "an era unique in the history of modern political thought: strikingly, virtually every prominent and influential European thinker in the three hundred years before the eighteenth century and nearly the full century after it were either agnostic toward or enthusiastically in favour of imperialism." Muthu, *Enlightenment against Empire*, 1, see also 3–6, 259; and Jennifer Pitts, *A Turn to Empire: The Rise of Imperial Liberalism in Britain and France* (Princeton, NJ: Princeton University Press, 2005), 1. On Hume and empire, see Emma Rothschild, "The Atlantic Worlds of David Hume," in *Soundings in Atlantic History: Latent Structures and Intellectual Currents, 1500–1830*, ed. Bernard Bailyn and Patricia L. Denault (Cambridge, MA: Harvard University Press, 2009). On Smith, see Pitts, *A Turn to Empire*, chapter 2; and Emma Rothschild, "Adam Smith in the British Empire," in *Empire and Modern Political Thought*, ed. Sankar Muthu (Cambridge: Cambridge University Press, 2012). On Montesquieu, see Jean Ehrard, "Idée et figures de l'empire dans *l'Esprit des lois*," in *L'Empire avant l'Empire: État d'une notion au XVIIIe siècle*, ed. Gérard Loubinoux (Clermont-Farrand, France: Presses universitaires Blaise-Pascal, 2004); and Michael Mosher, "Montesquieu on Empire and Enlightenment," in *Empire and Modern Political Thought*, ed. Sankar Muthu (Cambridge: Cambridge University Press, 2012). On Voltaire, see Simon Davies, "Reflections on Voltaire and His Idea of Colonies" *Studies on Voltaire and the Eighteenth Century* 332 (1995): 61–9.

[42] For instance, Smith writes that "there is not a negro from the coast of Africa who does not ... possess a degree of magnanimity which the soul of his sordid master is too often scarce capable of conceiving. Fortune never exerted more cruelly her empire over mankind, than when she subjected those nations of heroes to the refuse of the jails of Europe" (TMS V.2.9, 206). Similarly, in contrast to Montesquieu's negative depiction of the East, Voltaire was a consistent and unabashed Sinophile. See Basil Guy, *The French Image of China before and after Voltaire* (Geneva: Institut et Musée Voltaire, 1963), chapter 5.

[43] Voltaire's criticisms of Judaism, for example, were largely (even if not wholly) a foil or cloak for his criticisms of Christianity. See Pierre Aubery, "Voltaire et les Juifs: Ironie et démystification" *Studies on Voltaire and the Eighteenth Century* 24 (1963): 67–79; Peter Gay, *The Party of Humanity: Essays in the French Enlightenment* (New York: W. W. Norton, 1964), chapter 3; and Bertram Eugene Schwarzbach, "Voltaire et les juifs: Bilan et plaidoyer" *Studies on Voltaire and the Eighteenth Century* 358 (1997): 27–91. Similarly, Montesquieu's criticisms of "Oriental despotism" were meant above all as a warning about the possible emergence of despotism closer to home, in the France of

broader outlook.[44] Moreover, all four of these thinkers were vigorous opponents of religious intolerance, colonialism, slavery, and the oppression of women.[45]

While this book seeks to defend the pragmatic strand of the Enlightenment, it does not adopt an entirely uncritical view of Hume, Smith, Montesquieu, and Voltaire. However sympathetic to them one might be, there is no need to suppose or pretend that these thinkers were without faults. In addition to holding some views that no reasonable person of the twenty-first century would accept, such as Voltaire's casual disdain of the ignorant masses, we will see that these thinkers sometimes contradicted themselves, they sometimes failed to live up to their own ideals, and they sometimes fell short of resolving the problems they

Louis XV and in the Catholic Church. See Sharon R. Krause, "Despotism in *The Spirit of Laws*," in *Montesquieu's Science of Politics: Essays on The Spirit of Laws*, ed. David W. Carrithers, Michael A. Mosher, and Paul A. Rahe (Lanham, MD: Rowman & Littlefield, 2001), especially 251–5.

[44] As several scholars have noted, Hume's racist footnote in his essay "Of National Characters" is a clear instance of a failure to follow faithfully his own empirical method. See, for instance, Richard H. Popkin, "Hume's Racism," in *The High Road to Pyrrhonism*, ed. Richard A. Watson and James E. Force (San Diego: Austin Hill Press, 1980), 258–9; Richard H. Popkin, "Hume's Racism Reconsidered," in *The Third Force in Seventeenth-Century Thought* (Leiden: Brill, 1992), 71–2, 75; John Immerwahr, "Hume's Revised Racism" *Journal of the History of Ideas* 53.3 (July–September 1992), 485; Claudia M. Schmidt, *David Hume: Reason in History* (University Park: Pennsylvania State University Press, 2003), 409–12; Aaron Garrett, "Hume's 'Original Difference': Race, National Character and the Human Sciences" *Eighteenth-Century Thought* 2 (2004), 151; and Andrew Valls, "'A Lousy Empirical Scientist': Reconsidering Hume's Racism," in *Race and Racism in Modern Philosophy*, ed. Andrew Valls (Ithaca: Cornell University Press, 2005), 127, 135–6, 139.

[45] On Hume's attitude toward women and gender, see Annette C. Baier, *Moral Prejudices: Essay on Ethics* (Cambridge: MA: Harvard University Press, 1994), chapters 4–5; and Anne Jaap Jacobson, ed., *Feminist Interpretations of David Hume* (University Park: Pennsylvania State University Press, 2000), especially chapters 9–10. On Smith, see Henry C. Clark, "Women and Humanity in Scottish Enlightenment Social Thought: The Case of Adam Smith" *Historical Reflections/Réflexions Historiques* 19.3 (summer 1993): 335–61; and Chris Nyland, "Adam Smith, Stage Theory, and the Status of Women" *History of Political Economy* 25.4 (winter 1993): 617–36. On Montesquieu, see Pauline Kra, "Montesquieu and Women," in *French Women and the Age of Enlightenment*, ed. Samia I. Spencer (Bloomington: Indiana University Press, 1984); Michael A. Mosher, "The Judgmental Gaze of European Women: Gender, Sexuality, and the Critique of Republican Rule" *Political Theory* 22.1 (February 1994): 25–44; and Diana J. Schaub, "Montesquieu on 'The Woman Problem'," in *Finding a New Feminism: Rethinking the Woman Question for Liberal Democracy*, ed. Pamela Jensen (Lanham, MD: Rowman & Littlefield, 1996). On Voltaire, see Katherine B. Clinton, "Femme et Philosophe: Enlightenment Origins of Feminism" *Eighteenth-Century Studies* 8.3 (spring 1975): 283–99; and Arthur Scherr, "Candide's Garden Revisited: Gender Equality in a Commoner's Paradise" *Eighteenth-Century Life* 17 (November 1993): 40–59.

Introduction

addressed. My aim is not to show that there is a flawless and comprehensive worldview to be found in the writings of these thinkers, or that the pragmatic Enlightenment somehow contains the hidden keys to solving all of today's problems. Rather, I seek to demonstrate that the outlooks of these leading Enlightenment thinkers were far more compelling than the caricature presented by the critics of this movement, and that they still have a number of important lessons to teach us.

The six substantive chapters of the book focus on the three broad criticisms of the Enlightenment mentioned earlier, with two chapters devoted to each one: Chapters 1 and 2 address the Enlightenment's supposed hegemonic universalism, Chapters 3 and 4 address its alleged blind faith in reason, and Chapters 5 and 6 address its perceived atomistic individualism. Chapter 1, "Morality in Context," shows that, far from positing a universally applicable set of moral standards, Hume, Smith, Montesquieu, and Voltaire all held that moral standards can, do, and should vary according to context. While the moral theories of Hume and Smith were far more developed and sophisticated than those of their French counterparts, all four of these thinkers sought to ground morality in the sentiments and evolving communal standards rather than in the dictates of God, transcendent natural law, or Kantian universal reason. For these thinkers, morality *begins* with the sentiments, but it is developed through sympathy and other forms of social interaction. Thus, the way in which moral standards are *formulated* may be the same everywhere and always, but the *content* of morality – what actually counts as moral – is in large part socially determined, and so differs in different contexts. Needless to say, this view does not entail complete moral relativism: these thinkers saw the morality that originates in people's sentiments as "real" and binding, which means that individuals are subject to moral standards that they do not choose in any direct or immediate sense. Thus, there is an element of indeterminacy or cultural relativism inherent in their view, but also a basis for moral standards that place limits on what individuals can morally do.

In Chapter 2, "Pragmatic Liberalism," I argue that while these four thinkers were all liberals, broadly speaking, their liberalism was quite pragmatic and flexible in terms of both its basis and its implications. They adopted a nonfoundationalist approach to politics, concluding that liberal practices and institutions are preferable not because they are in accord with Reason or Nature – as Locke, for instance, had done – but because historical and comparative analysis revealed them to be relative improvements on the alternatives. Nor did they rely on a single standard or benchmark in making these comparisons: sometimes they lauded liberal regimes and practices for the personal freedom they afforded, while at other times they lauded the security they provided, the happiness they produced, the prosperity they made possible, and/or the character traits they encouraged. Moreover, none of these thinkers believed in a perfect, single best, or uniquely legitimate form of government. On the contrary, they stressed that different laws and practices are appropriate for societies with different circumstances, histories, customs, and so on, and they essentially set aside the notion that there is a specific set of criteria that all regimes must meet in order to attain legitimacy. To repeat, this does not mean that these thinkers had no political principles or preferences, but rather that their liberal principles and preferences were sufficiently flexible that they did not insist on (or even allow for) a single set of institutions or a comprehensive view of the good life that would be applicable in all times and places.

Chapter 3, "The Age of the Limits of Reason," demonstrates that, despite the moniker "the Age of Reason" that has been affixed irrevocably to this period, the leading Enlightenment thinkers I examine all stressed the *limits* of human reason. Hume, Smith, Montesquieu, and Voltaire all advocated relying on observation and experience rather than a priori first principles, mocked rational "systems" and system builders, and stressed the fallibility of human understanding. Thus, their conceptions of reason were far humbler than those of the great rationalist thinkers of the seventeenth century such as Descartes, Malebranche, Spinoza, and Leibniz, and even those of some earlier empiricists such as Hobbes and Locke. Further, while they saw the scientific method as the best way to compensate for the limits of the human mind, they denied that it could provide conclusive or complete knowledge of the natural world. They certainly welcomed the practical advances that the natural sciences afford, but by no means did they think science could solve all human problems. Finally, while these thinkers all rejected the claims of revealed religion and devoted great amounts of intellectual energy to condemning religious fanaticism and intolerance, their basic stance toward religion was actually quite moderate, especially in comparison with the more radical philosophes such as La Mettrie and d'Holbach. They all regarded the inclination to believe in a higher power as natural in some sense, and they aimed to moderate or "liberalize" religion – to restrain its most dangerous impulses and consequences and to encourage its more beneficial ones – rather than to eradicate it altogether. Nor did they believe that reason could conclusively *disprove* the claims of revealed religion; on the

Introduction 21

contrary, their skepticism regarding religion was simply a manifestation of their general skepticism regarding *any* claims of absolute certainty. In all of these ways, the pragmatic Enlightenment was decidedly a limits-of-reason movement – hence my reversal of the traditional moniker of this period in the title of the chapter.

Chapter 4, "The Perils of Political Rationalism," extends the argument of Chapter 3 to the political sphere. It is widely claimed that Enlightenment thinkers embraced a kind of political rationalism, meaning that they advocated subjecting all laws, institutions, and practices to the withering light of reason, and discarding those found wanting by its standards. I show, however, that Hume, Smith, Montesquieu, and Voltaire all adopted a practical, pragmatic outlook that supports the reform of existing institutions but opposes efforts to form a wholly new "rational" order from scratch. To be sure, none of these thinkers was simply an advocate of the status quo. They *did* want to "change men's common way of thinking," to borrow Diderot's famous line from the *Encyclopédie*,[46] and to push their societies in a broadly liberal direction, but they did not insist that these reforms must be made all at once, or that the political and legal slates must be wiped clean in order to make room for a more liberal order. Further, these thinkers were deeply and manifestly – one wants to say instinctually – antiutopian. None of them believed that progress toward liberal practices and institutions was in any way inevitable or could possibly be endless or uniform. They believed in progress in the sense that they thought the Europe of their time constituted an improvement in many respects over what had gone before it, but they did not believe in any kind of supernatural agency, transcendent design, or Hegelian dialectic that meant that it *had to be* better than what preceded it, or that the future would be better still. They were far too realistic, too alive to the shortcomings of even their comparatively enlightened age, to be dupes of the sort of faith in the "historical process" that came to enthrall later generations of thinkers.

The fifth chapter, "The Social and Encumbered Self," shows that these thinkers did not adopt the individualistic and reductive assumptions about human nature that communitarian critics often attribute to the Enlightenment. First of all, Hume, Smith, Montesquieu, and Voltaire were unequivocal in affirming that human beings are inherently social – drawn to others not just for instrumental reasons but also out of an innate desire

---

[46] Denis Diderot, "Encyclopedia," in *Rameau's Nephew and Other Works*, trans. Jacques Barzun and Ralph H. Bowen (Indianapolis: Hackett, [1755] 1956), 296.

for companionship. Hence, they all rejected the idea of a social contract made by otherwise isolated individuals: they denied that there ever was a presocial state of nature, and they envisioned political institutions as having arisen spontaneously and gradually over time, more from necessity and habit than consent or contract. Moreover, they concurred that people's characters, beliefs, and values are fundamentally shaped by their circumstances and their communities, rather than somehow developed in a vacuum. (To use Michael Sandel's terms, they saw human beings as invariably "encumbered" rather than "unencumbered" selves.) Far from demanding a strong form of moral autonomy, they argued that it is only in and through society that people become moral beings at all. In short, these thinkers did not see people as abstract, self-interested atoms at their core; on the contrary, they consistently saw people as fundamentally interdependent, not only economically and politically, but also morally and psychologically.

Chapter 6, "Negative Liberty for a Positive Community," demonstrates not only that Hume, Smith, Montesquieu, and Voltaire did not seek to promote atomistic individualism with their political and economic ideals, but that they sought to do precisely the opposite. They did, of course, adopt a largely "negative" conception of liberty, where liberty means protecting the individual from interference from and dependence on others. They did so, however, not because they held an implausibly "unencumbered" view of the self, because they dogmatically insisted on the inviolability of natural rights, or because they wanted to reduce people to self-interested atoms who have no connection to others or to the community at large. Rather, they advocated negative liberty because they saw clearly the dangers inherent in communities that are dedicated to shared ends and "higher" purposes, above all coercion, exclusion, and intolerance. For this reason, these thinkers would see the pitting of the individual *against* the community as a false dichotomy: by focusing on the protection of the individual, they were seeking to reduce the conflict produced by the pursuit of consensus and thereby *safeguard* the community. Similarly, these thinkers supported commerce and economic freedoms not in order to encourage unbridled greed and selfishness, but rather in hopes of finding a healthier way to unite people than the traditional bonds of blood, religion, and nationalism. They recognized that extensive commerce might be incompatible with strict republican virtue, but they also believed that a focus on material self-interest would help to replace dangerous and divisive passions such as xenophobia, religious intolerance, and the thirst for military glory. In their view, rather than

Introduction 23

atomizing people, commerce draws them together, leading not only to greater prosperity but also to greater concord and civility by making people and nations interdependent. In a word, their support of negative liberty and commerce was *not* a support of atomism and selfishness; on the contrary, they supported negative liberty and commerce precisely because they saw them as prerequisites of a healthy community.

The Conclusion summarizes some of the lessons, both historical and normative, that emerge from an examination of the pragmatic Enlightenment of Hume, Smith, Montesquieu, and Voltaire. On the interpretive front, such an examination serves to challenge not only those who criticize the Enlightenment for being overly universalist, rationalist, or individualist, but also those who would posit a deep divergence – even diametrical opposition – between the French and Scottish Enlightenments, as well as Jonathan Israel's recent defense of the "Radical Enlightenment," over and against the "moderate mainstream." Most of all, though, it serves to remind us that the types of liberalism that we have inherited from Locke, Kant, Bentham, and other "idealistic" Enlightenment thinkers were not the only ones to emerge from this period, and that a more moderate, flexible variety of liberalism too is as old as the Enlightenment. The book concludes with some reflections about why I find this latter strand of the liberal tradition to be a particularly attractive one.

HEGEMONIC UNIVERSALISM?

I

Morality in Context

The term "the Enlightenment project" seems to have been popularized by Alasdair MacIntyre, who identifies the "project" as that of finding "an independent rational justification for morality," or of going beyond tradition and authority to discover universally valid moral principles, grounded in enduring features of human nature.[1] The Enlightenment's goal, according to MacIntyre, was to find moral principles that would be "undeniable by any rational person and therefore independent of all those social and cultural particularities which the Enlightenment thinkers took to be the mere accidental clothing of reason in particular times and places."[2] The idea that the Enlightenment sought or promulgated an objective, eternal, transcultural standard of right and wrong, one that would apply to all people (and peoples) in all times and places, has become a commonplace of contemporary political theory – particularly among postmodernists and communitarians, but they are far from alone.[3]

[1] See Alasdair MacIntyre, *After Virtue*, second edition (Notre Dame, IN: University of Notre Dame Press, [1981] 1984), chapter 4. For a compelling argument that MacIntyre's portrait of the Enlightenment project in *After Virtue* is profoundly misleading, see Robert Wokler, "Projecting the Enlightenment," in *After MacIntyre: Critical Perspectives on the Work of Alasdair MacIntyre*, ed. John Horton and Susan Mendus (Notre Dame, IN: University of Notre Dame Press, 1994).

[2] Alasdair MacIntyre, *Whose Justice? Which Rationality?* (Notre Dame, IN: University of Notre Dame Press, 1988), 6; see also 353; and MacIntyre, *After Virtue*, 51–2.

[3] The Enlightenment and its alleged universalism are *the* main antagonists of most postmodernist thinkers. As Daniel Gordon writes, "'Enlightenment' is to postmodernism what 'Old Regime' was to the French Revolution. The Enlightenment, that is to say, symbolizes the modern that postmodernism revolts against. It is the other of postmodernism: not only that which preceded postmodernism but that in opposition to which postmodernism defines itself." Daniel Gordon, "Introduction: Postmodernism and the

Isaiah Berlin, for instance, claims that this is the one belief that unified an otherwise diverse movement:

One set of universal and unalterable principles governed the world for theists, deists and atheists, for optimists and pessimists, puritans, primitivists and believers in progress and the richest fruits of science and culture; these laws governed ... means and ends, private life and public, all societies, epochs, and civilisations; it was solely by departing from them that man fell into crime, vice, misery. Thinkers might differ about what these laws were, or how to discover them, or who were qualified to expound them; that these laws were real, and could be known, whether with certainty, or only probability, remained the central dogma of the entire Enlightenment.[4]

Recent scholars of eighteenth-century thought have also frequently embraced this view. Thus, Jonathan Israel asserts that "universalism was one of the quintessential characteristics of the Enlightenment,"[5] and Roy Porter writes, in his overview of the period, that "amongst the values dearest to the Enlightenment" was the idea that since "reason, like the Sun, shed the same light all the world over," there must be "a single universal standard of justice, governed by one normative natural law – and indeed ... a single uniform human nature, all people being endowed with fundamentally the same attributes and desires, 'from China to Peru'."[6]

There are, of course, potential advantages to this kind of view: a universal standard of right and wrong would provide a way to surmount the contingencies of time and place, to move beyond mere received tradition and arbitrary authority, to unite human beings around the world under a common set of shared ideals, and to condemn unequivocally practices that one sees as appalling. Thus, it comes as no surprise that so many eminent philosophers – before, during, and after the Enlightenment – have embraced such a standard. Locke, to take one of the leading predecessors of Hume, Smith, Montesquieu, and Voltaire, claimed that "the measures of right and wrong might be made out" from "self-evident Propositions, by necessary Consequences, as incontestable as those in

---

French Enlightenment," in *Postmodernism and the Enlightenment: New Perspectives in Eighteenth-Century French Intellectual History*, ed. Daniel Gordon (New York: Routledge, 2001), 1. The communitarian critique of the Enlightenment will be treated in more detail in Chapters 5 and 6.

[4] Isaiah Berlin, "The Counter-Enlightenment," in *The Proper Study of Mankind: An Anthology of Essays*, ed. Henry Hardy and Roger Hausheer (New York: Farrar, Straus & Giroux [1973] 1998), 245–6.

[5] Jonathan I. Israel, *Democratic Enlightenment: Philosophy, Revolution, and Human Rights, 1750–1790* (Oxford: Oxford University Press, 2011), 5.

[6] Roy Porter, *The Enlightenment*, second edition (New York: Palgrave, 2001), 47.

Morality in Context

Mathematicks."[7] Similarly, Kant would later *define* morality in terms of its universality.[8] Numerous critics have claimed, however, that the promotion of a universal moral standard is both implausible and dangerous – implausible because it requires ignoring the historical and cultural differences among peoples and beliefs, and dangerous because it requires excluding, coercing, or condemning those who do not live up to its ideals. Moral universalism, in short, is necessarily "hegemonic."

Whatever the advantages and drawbacks of a universal moral standard may be, we will see in this chapter that Hume, Smith, Montesquieu, and Voltaire all in fact accepted that moral standards can, do, and should vary according to context. While there were some differences among them, each of these thinkers held that morality is ultimately derived from people's sentiments or desires and that binding moral standards emerge as these sentiments are developed and generalized through social interaction. Thus, the way in which moral standards are *formulated* may be the same everywhere and always, for these thinkers, but the *content* of these standards – what actually counts as moral – is in large part socially determined, and so varies with varied circumstances. My aim in this chapter is less to prove that the moral theories of these thinkers are ultimately true or valid than to demonstrate that they were far from embracing the kind of hegemonic moral universalism that is so often ascribed to the Enlightenment.[9] However, it is perhaps worth noting at the outset the inherent attractiveness of the sort of theory they proposed, insofar as it is far less rigid and sweeping than the deontological and utilitarian approaches that have dominated much of the philosophical debate over the last fifty years, while also avoiding the moral relativism to which postmodernists have proven so susceptible.[10] Given that Hume and Smith

---

[7] John Locke, *An Essay Concerning Human Understanding*, ed. Peter H. Nidditch (Oxford: Oxford University Press, [1689] 1975), IV.iii.18, 549; see also I.3.1, 66; III.11.16, 516; IV.iv.7, 565; IV.xii.8, 643–4; and John Locke, *Two Treatises of Government*, ed. Peter Laslett (Cambridge: Cambridge University Press, [1689] 1988), II.2.6, 271.

[8] See, for instance, Immanuel Kant, *Fundamental Principles of the Metaphysics of Morals*, in *Basic Writings of Kant*, ed. Allen W. Wood (New York: Modern Library, [1785] 2001), 160 ff. and 178 ff.

[9] For a detailed defense of the sentimentalist moral theories of Hume, Smith, and J. G. Herder, see Michael Frazer, *The Enlightenment of Sympathy: Justice and the Moral Sentiments in the Eighteenth Century and Today* (Oxford: Oxford University Press, 2010). Frazer reads both Hume and Smith as moral universalists, and so turns to Herder to introduce a dose of pluralism and contextual sensitivity into Enlightenment sentimentalism. I argue in this chapter that in fact Hume and Smith were moral pluralists and contextualists, as well.

[10] The moral theories of Hume, Smith, Montesquieu, and Voltaire bear a somewhat greater resemblance to virtue ethics, the approach that has become the main contemporary rival

The Pragmatic Enlightenment

explored the nature and source of morality in much greater detail than did Montesquieu and Voltaire, we will examine the moral theories of the Scots at somewhat greater length, although we will see in the later sections of the chapter that their French counterparts adopted broadly similar views.

THE IMPORTANCE OF CONTEXT IN HUME'S EMPIRICAL SENTIMENTALISM

One of the chief purposes and effects of Hume's moral philosophy, as outlined in book 3 of *A Treatise of Human Nature* and *An Enquiry Concerning the Principles of Morals*, is one to which he does not draw much explicit attention: the rejection of the idea that morality has any transcendent basis. Hume does not overtly attack the idea of a transcendent standard of right and wrong, as he does the claim that morality is derived from reason alone; rather, he simply and quietly dismisses the notion that morality is based on anything outside the human mind and human relations.[11] This is evident in the inductive, empirical method that he adopts, whereby right and wrong are ascertained through "experience and observation" of human actions and sentiments in "different circumstances and situations" (THN intro.7, 4; intro.8, 5; see also EPM 1.10, 6–7). The only sensible way to philosophize about moral subjects, he maintains, is to "glean up our experiments … from a cautious observation of human life, and take them as they appear in the common course of the world, by men's behaviour in company, in affairs, and in their pleasures" (THN intro.10, 6). For Hume, morality is an eminently practical phenomenon, embedded in common human concerns, rather than one based on any kind of sacred, mysterious, or otherworldly authority. As Sharon Krause notes, Hume's claim that morality is "a human artifact that grows

---

of deontology and utilitarianism, although these thinkers largely eschewed the teleological conception of nature that is often associated with the virtue ethics tradition. For arguments that Hume and Smith belong to the virtue ethics tradition broadly conceived, see Christine Swanson, "Can Hume Be Read as a Virtue Ethicist?" *Hume Studies* 33.1 (2007): 91–113; and Ryan Patrick Hanley, *Adam Smith and the Character of Virtue* (Cambridge: Cambridge University Press, 2009), chapter 2.

[11] Hume also dismisses the idea that the lack of a transcendent basis for morality means that there *is* no real morality; see especially EPM 1.2, 3. It was once commonly asserted that Hume's skepticism effectively undermined any genuine basis for morality, but there is now widespread agreement among Hume scholars that his skepticism regarding metaphysics did not extend to morality itself. An influential argument to this effect can be found in David Fate Norton, *David Hume: Common-Sense Moralist, Sceptical Metaphysician* (Princeton, NJ: Princeton University Press, 1982).

Morality in Context

out of and answers to familiar needs and purposes" was meant in part to "undercut the force of religious convictions oriented to otherworldly ends and authorities, and so to neutralize the sources of zealotry."[12]

The main rhetorical thrust of Hume's writings on morality, however, is directed at demonstrating that right and wrong are ultimately derived from the sentiments rather than reason. Thus, his most obvious antagonists are the moral rationalists who hold that human reason can apprehend or deduce eternal, objective standards of right and wrong, such as Samuel Clarke, William Wollaston, Ralph Cudworth, and Nicolas Malebranche, although Hume's criticisms would also apply to the kind of moral rationalism later adopted by Kant and his many contemporary followers.[13] Hume argues, first, that morality moves people to act in certain ways, and since reason itself is not a motive to action – since, as he famously puts it, "reason is, and ought only to be the slave of the passions" (THN 2.3.3.4, 266) – morality cannot be wholly rational (see THN 3.1.1.5–7, 294). He maintains, further, that virtue and vice are not objective matters of fact "out there," inherent in actions or objects themselves, waiting to be discovered by reason:

Take any action allow'd to be vicious: Wilful murder, for instance. Examine it in all lights, and see if you can find that matter of fact, or real existence, which you call *vice*. In which-ever way you take it, you find only certain passions, motives, volitions, and thoughts. There is no other matter of fact in the case. The vice entirely escapes you, as long as you consider the object. You never can find it, till you turn your reflection into your own breast, and find a sentiment of disapprobation, which arises in you, towards this action. Here is a matter of fact; but 'tis the object of feeling, not of reason. It lies in yourself, not in the object. (THN 3.1.1.26, 301)

Since morality is inextricably connected to human sentiments, Hume has little truck with the idea that "there are eternal fitnesses and unfitnesses of things, which are the same to every rational being that considers them" (THN 3.1.1.4, 294; see also EPM 1.3, 3). These two aspects of his moral philosophy – his denial that morality has either a transcendent or a rational basis – effectively undermined the fundamental premises of much of the natural law tradition.[14]

---

[12] Sharon R. Krause, "Frenzy, Gloom, and the Spirit of Liberty in Hume," in *The Arts of Rule: Essays in Honor of Harvey C. Mansfield*, ed. Sharon R. Krause and Mary Ann McGrail (Lanham, MD: Lexington, 2009), 293, 289.

[13] See Donald W. Livingston, *Philosophical Melancholy and Delirium: Hume's Pathology of Philosophy* (Chicago: University of Chicago Press, 1998), 122–3.

[14] Hume does allow that certain rules of justice may be called "laws of nature," of course, but he insists that these laws are entirely artificial or conventional: they arise spontaneously

Hume's basic claim is that some human qualities and actions give rise to the sentiment of approval, and consequently come to be identified as moral or virtuous, while others give rise to disapproval, and consequently are identified as immoral or vicious. Here we run into an issue that will emerge in our examination of Smith, Montesquieu, and Voltaire as well: in deriving morality (an "ought") from people's sentiments (an "is"), Hume combines the empirical with the normative, the descriptive with the prescriptive.[15] This move would seem to contradict what has become known as "Hume's law," which states that it is *impossible* to derive an "ought" from an "is." While this "law" springs from a passage in Hume's *Treatise* (see THN 3.1.1.27, 302), it is not one that he accepts himself. Hume's point in the famous is-ought paragraph is not that it is never valid to move from "is" to "ought," but rather that an "ought" cannot be logically or rationally *deduced* from an "is." This paragraph is found at the end of the section in which Hume attacks the moral rationalists, and it is directed at their attempts to derive morality from reason alone. He leaves open the possibility that an "ought" could be derived in some nonrational way from an "is," and this is precisely what he proceeds to do in the following section when he shows that morality ultimately springs from the sentiments.[16] Thus, if "Hume's law" is understood to deny altogether

over time as people coordinate their actions and sentiments in response to others (THN 3.2.2.19, 311; see also 3.2.6.10, 342). On the divergences between Hume's thought and the natural law tradition, see Pauline C. Westerman, "Hume and the Natural Lawyers: A Change of Landscape," in *Hume and Hume's Connexions*, ed. M. A. Stewart and John P. Wright (University Park: Pennsylvania State University Press, 1994). For works that stress the continuities between Hume and this tradition, in large part by arguing that the later natural law thinkers were in fact more empirical, and less metaphysical and rationalistic, than is often supposed, see Duncan Forbes, *Hume's Philosophical Politics* (Cambridge: Cambridge University Press, 1975), chapters 1–2; and Stephen Buckle, *Natural Law and the Theory of Property: Grotius to Hume* (Oxford: Oxford University Press, 1991), chapter 5. Hume's approach to natural law will be examined in greater detail in Chapter 2.

[15] This should make it clear that Hume's empiricism is not a form of positivism; as we will see throughout this study, his "science of man" is anything but value-free. On this point, see also Donald W. Livingston, *Hume's Philosophy of Common Life* (Chicago: University of Chicago Press, 1984), 31, 272; and Stephen G. Salkever, "'Cool Reflexion' and the Criticism of Values: Is, Ought, and Objectivity in Hume's Social Science" *American Political Science Review* 74.1 (March 1980): 70–7. For a recent work that takes a different view, championing the "social scientific" character of Hume's writings and downplaying the normative elements, see Russell Hardin, *David Hume: Moral and Political Theorist* (Oxford: Oxford University Press, 2007).

[16] See Annette C. Baier, *A Progress of Sentiments: Reflections on Hume's Treatise* (Cambridge, MA: Harvard University Press, 1991), 176–7; and Frederick G. Whelan, *Order and Artifice in Hume's Political Philosophy* (Princeton, NJ: Princeton University Press, 1985), 79–80, 207–8, 306.

Morality in Context

33

the possibility of moving from "is" to "ought," then "the first breach of Hume's law was committed by Hume."[17]

Hume's claim, to repeat, is that morality arises from the sentiments of approval and disapproval. He devotes much of *An Enquiry Concerning the Principles of Morals* to cataloging what people *do* in fact approve of, and he finds that all of the qualities and actions that give rise to this sentiment can be categorized as either useful or agreeable, either to oneself or to others (see EPM 9.1, 72; 9.12, 78; THN 3.3.1.30, 377). This emphasis on usefulness has led some commentators to consider Hume a moral utilitarian, but such a reading is clearly erroneous. First of all, Hume devotes two full sections of the *Enquiry* (sections 7 and 8) to delineating the many qualities and actions that are approved of (and hence moral) not because they are useful in any way, but rather because they are immediately "agreeable." Further, even the "useful" qualities and actions are moral because of people's tendency to approve of them, not because of their usefulness itself; it is the approval, not the utility, that gives these qualities and actions a moral character. As Hume stresses in the first appendix, "utility is only a tendency to a certain end; and were the end totally indifferent to us, we should feel the same indifference towards the means. It is requisite a *sentiment* should here display itself, in order to give a preference to the useful above the pernicious tendencies" – namely, the sentiment of approval (EPM App. 1.3, 84). Thus, he never claims that morality can be measured by the maximization of utility, or that morality is simply the greatest good for the greatest number. Bentham's conviction that ethics could be made into an exact science, like the zeal with which he sought to promote and apply this science, could hardly be further from the spirit of Hume's thought.[18]

While Hume claims that morality is derived from the sentiments, he does *not* claim that it is simply a matter of individual sentiment, or that

---

[17] Alasdair MacIntyre, "Hume on 'Is' and 'Ought,'" in *Hume*, ed. V. C. Chappell (Garden City: Anchor Books, 1966), 242. MacIntyre defends the philosophical propriety of this "breach."

[18] There is now widespread agreement among Hume scholars that Hume was not in fact a utilitarian, despite his earlier reputation as one, and despite the inspiration that Bentham would claim from him. See especially Aryeh Botwinick, "A Case for Hume's Nonutilitarianism" *Journal of the History of Philosophy* 15.4 (October 1977): 423–35; Knud Haakonssen, *The Science of a Legislator: The Natural Jurisprudence of David Hume and Adam Smith* (Cambridge: Cambridge University Press, 1981), 8, 39–41; David Miller, *Philosophy and Ideology in Hume's Political Thought* (Oxford: Clarendon Press, 1981), 190–1; and Geoffrey Sayre-McCord, "Hume and the Bauhaus Theory of Ethics" *Midwest Studies in Philosophy* 20 (1995): 280–98.

whatever "feels right" to me *is* right for me. Such a view would be tantamount to complete moral relativism. According to Hume, what makes a sentiment a *moral* sentiment is that it has been properly generalized (see THN 3.1.2.4, 303). Distinguishing right from wrong requires that we correct for biases due to our particular circumstances and interests, and Hume claims that we are able to make such corrections through sympathy, the faculty that communicates to us the feelings and sentiments of others. Sympathy enables us to experience the effects of a person's character traits or actions not just on ourselves but also on "those, who have any commerce with the person we consider" (THN 3.3.1.18, 373; see also 3.3.1.30, 377). This, in turn, allows us to view such traits and actions from a broader standpoint – to adopt what Hume refers to as the "general point of view" or the "common point of view" (e.g., THN 3.3.1.15, 371–2; 3.3.1.30, 377; EPM 9.6, 75). This is not to say that all people always *do* adopt the general point of view – Hume acknowledges that it is difficult to overcome self-interest entirely and continually – but rather that this is what moral judgment requires. It is important to note here that while the general point of view entails a degree of impartiality, insofar as it obliges us to correct for our own prejudices and interests, it is a human viewpoint rather than a transcendent one, and it rests on generalized sentiment rather than perfect rationality. As Annette Baier writes, Hume's general point of view "is not a 'view from nowhere'; it is a view from a common *human* viewpoint.... It aims not at detachment from human concerns but at impartiality, and interpersonal agreement."[19]

Despite Hume's insistence that morality cannot be derived from reason and his language about reason's being a mere slave of the passions, he does accord reason an important role in the determination of moral standards, namely, that of *informing* the sentiments. The sentiments that we feel depend in part on how we understand the world around us and our place in it, and reason can help us to ascertain relevant matters of fact and to predict the possible consequences of a given action.[20] For instance, luxury was long regarded as vicious because it was seen as "the source

[19] Baier, *A Progress of Sentiments*, 182. Similarly, Geoffrey Sayre-McCord writes that the general point of view "supposes neither an impossible omniscience nor an angelic equisympathetic engagement with all of humanity. Hume's is a standard both more human in scope and more accessible in practice than any set by an Ideal Observer." Geoffrey Sayre-McCord, "On Why Hume's 'General Point of View' Isn't Ideal – and Shouldn't Be" *Social Philosophy and Policy* 11.1 (winter 1994), 203.

[20] See Sharon R. Krause, "Passion, Power, and Impartiality in Hume," in *Bringing the Passions Back In: The Emotions in Political Philosophy*, ed. Rebecca Kingston and Leonard Ferry (Vancouver: UBC Press, 2008), especially 136, 139–40.

Morality in Context   35

of every corruption in government, and the immediate cause of faction, sedition, civil wars, and the total loss of liberty"; Hume notes that those "who prove, or attempt to prove, that such refinements rather tend to the encrease of industry, civility, and arts, regulate anew our *moral* as well as *political* sentiments" (EPM 2.21, 11). In other words, we may revise our moral sentiments when shown to be in factual error (see also EPM App. 1.11, 86). Similarly, Hume accepts that reason "must enter for a considerable share" in the determination of the "useful" virtues, "since nothing but that faculty can instruct us in the tendency of qualities and actions, and point out their beneficial consequences to society and to their possessor" (EPM App. 1.2, 83; see also 1.9, 5). While it is the sentiment of approval (properly generalized) that imparts a moral character to a quality or action, then, this sentiment can be informed and revised through reflection. Yet there are important limits to the corrective role that reason can play. As Rachel Cohon observes, reason may be able to inform people's sentiments by correcting false causal beliefs – say, beliefs about the harmful effects that homosexuality has on its possessor, his or her associates, or society at large – but it cannot do much more than this. Thus, if people were to regard homosexuality as vicious or immoral not because of its consequences but because they find it immediately "disagreeable," then it is difficult to see how reason could alter their views.[21]

Given what we have seen thus far, it is clear that Hume rules out the possibility of a universal morality based on transcendent, rational, or utilitarian grounds: right and wrong are determined through generalized sentiment, not any of these other sources. If he believed in the uniformity of sentiments across time and space, however – that is, if he believed in a "strong" human nature or innate moral sense – then presumably he would see morality as universal, as well. Hume is sometimes interpreted as having held precisely this view, on the basis of passages such as this famous one from *An Enquiry Concerning Human Understanding*:

It is universally acknowledged, that there is a great uniformity among the actions of men, in all nations and ages, and that human nature remains still the same, in its principles and operations. The same motives always produce the same actions: The same events follow from the same causes. Ambition, avarice, self-love, vanity, friendship, generosity, public spirit; these passions, mixed in various degrees, and

---

[21] See Rachel Cohon, *Hume's Morality: Feeling and Fabrication* (Oxford: Oxford University Press, 2008), 248, 252. Chapter 9 of Cohon's book provides a thorough and thoughtful exploration of the question of whether (or to what extent) there is a basis in Hume's moral philosophy for criticizing or revising a moral sentiment that is widely held in a given age or society.

distributed through society, have been, from the beginning of the world, and still are, the source of all the actions and enterprizes, which have ever been observed among mankind. Would you know the sentiments, inclinations, and course of life of the GREEKS and ROMANS? Study well the temper and actions of the FRENCH and ENGLISH: You cannot be much mistaken in transferring to the former *most* of the observations, which you have made with regard to the latter. Mankind are so much the same, in all times and places, that history informs us of nothing new or strange in this particular. Its chief use is only to discover the constant and universal principles of human nature, by showing men in all varieties of circumstances and situations, and furnishing us with materials, from which we may form our observations, and become acquainted with the regular springs of human action and behaviour. (EHU 8.7, 64)[22]

However, Hume's main point in this passage, as in the analogous passage in the *Treatise* (see THN 2.3.1.5, 258), is that there is a regularity between human motives and human actions, or that like causes generally produce like effects, *not* that all such motives and actions are identical.[23] Even in this passage, Hume notes that the passions that all people share are "mixed in various degrees" in different societies, and that only "*most* of the observations" (Hume's italics) one makes of the temper and actions of the French and English would also apply to the Greeks and Romans. Further, on the next page he cautions that "we must not, however, expect, that this uniformity of human actions should be carried to such a length, as that all men,

---

[22] On the basis of passages like this one, MacIntyre argues that Hume believed in a universal morality derived from universally held sentiments, but that the sentiments that he took to be universal were in fact little more than the prejudices of his age: "What Hume identifies as the standpoint of universal human nature turns out in fact to be that of the prejudices of the Hanoverian ruling elite," or "of a complacent heir of the revolution of 1688." MacIntyre, *After Virtue*, 231, 49; see also MacIntyre, *Whose Justice? Which Rationality?* 295. Christopher Berry too claims that Hume derived a universal morality from the fact that "humans have universally felt the same about the same kinds of things." Christopher J. Berry, "Hume's Universalism: The Science of Man and the Anthropological Point of View" *British Journal for the History of Philosophy* 15.3 (August 2007), 549.

[23] As Richard Dees points out, these passages were intended to offer a methodological principle rather than an empirical observation: "In both the *Treatise* and the first *Enquiry*, Hume argues that we operate every day on the assumption that human behavior is, on the whole, regular and predictable.... Without some kind of predictability, the human sciences – history, politics, and aesthetics – would be impossible.... [But] even if we must assume that all humans are somewhat alike as a methodological presumption, we are not thereby forced to claim that they will always act in the same ways we do.... We only assume that their behavior is *explainable*, that we can find a system of desires and beliefs that will make their actions understandable. In other words, we assume that the *structure* of human motivations remains the same, even when the content of those motivations is quite different." Richard H. Dees, "Hume and the Contexts of Politics" *Journal of the History of Philosophy* 30.2 (April 1992), 226–7.

Morality in Context

37

in the same circumstances, will always act precisely in the same manner, without making any allowance for the diversity of characters, prejudices, and opinions. Such a uniformity in every particular, is found in no part of nature" (EHU 8.10, 65). He goes on to point to a number of sources of this diversity of characters, prejudices, and opinions, including the influence of historical and cultural context: "Are the manners of men different in different ages and countries? We learn thence the great force of custom and education, which mould the human mind from its infancy, and form it into a fixed and established character" (EHU 8.11, 66).

There is no question that Hume believed in a common human nature; after all, he wrote an entire *Treatise* on the subject. As he rightly points out, the outright denial that there are general principles of human nature, ahead of any empirical investigation, would be every bit as "rash, precipitate, and dogmatical" as the a priori insistence that there *must* be such general principles (EHU 1.15, 12). And, indeed, Hume's empirical investigations left him convinced that there are certain "primary expression[s] of nature, such as ... self-love, affection between the sexes, love of progeny, gratitude, [and] resentment" that have "been found absolutely universal in all nations and ages."[24] Yet even if these "primary" passions are "absolutely universal," he emphasizes that many others are not, and that even the primary passions can be generated and expressed in many different ways. All people experience the same kinds of feelings – joy and sorrow, pride and shame, approval and disapproval, and so on – but what *prompts* these feelings often varies greatly across different cultures. As Duncan Forbes notes, "Hume is quite explicit on this point: the same object will not arouse the same passions, nor the same passions produce the same actions, in different societies.... Men always and everywhere value certain qualities [such as] love, friendship, honour, courage, etc ... [but] these primary sentiments of morals will take different forms, and the quality of actions and general pattern of behaviour will vary."[25] Thus, there is a growing scholarly consensus that Hume in fact saw human nature as highly flexible and adaptable, such that even if human beings are *structurally* alike in all ages and cultures, they are not also *substantively* alike.[26]

---

[24] David Hume, *The Natural History of Religion*, in *A Dissertation on the Passions and The Natural History of Religion*, ed. Tom L. Beauchamp (Oxford: Clarendon Press, [1757] 2007), 33. See also THN 2.1.11.5, 207.

[25] Forbes, *Hume's Philosophical Politics*, 109.

[26] See especially Dees, "Hume and the Contexts of Politics," 224–31; Forbes, *Hume's Philosophical Politics*, chapter 4; Livingston, *Hume's Philosophy of Common Life*,

There is no shortage of passages in which Hume demonstrates a keen awareness of the importance of culture and custom in shaping people's sentiments, beliefs, and actions, but given that he is sometimes thought to have believed in a "strong," uniform human nature, it is perhaps worth reproducing a few of these passages here. In the *Treatise*, he asserts that "the common principles of human nature ... accommodate themselves to circumstances, and have no stated invariable method of operation" (THN 3.2.6.9, 341). On the first page of the second *Enquiry*, he writes that "the difference, which nature has placed between one man and another, is so wide, and this difference is still so much farther widened, by education, example, and habit, that ... there is no scepticism so scrupulous ... as absolutely to deny all distinction between them" (EPM 1.2, 3). Later in this work, he highlights the great chasm that separates the ancients from the moderns, noting that the ancient heroes "have a grandeur and force of sentiment, which astonishes our narrow souls, and is rashly rejected as extravagant and supernatural. They, in their turn, I allow, would have had equal reason to consider as romantic and incredible, the degree of humanity, clemency, order, tranquillity, and other social virtues, to which ... we have attained in modern times" (EPM, 7.18, 63). Similarly, in his *Essays* he returns again and again to the theme of human diversity across time and space: "Those, who consider the periods and revolutions of human kind, as represented in history, are entertained with a spectacle full of pleasure and variety, and see, with surprize, the manners, customs, and opinions of the same species susceptible of such prodigious changes in different periods of time" (EMPL, 97). "The prodigious effects of education may convince us, that the mind ... will admit of many alterations from its original make and structure" (EMPL, 170). "The manners of a people change very considerably from one age to another; either by great alterations in their government, by the mixtures of new people, or by that inconstancy, to which all human affairs are subject" (EMPL, 205–6). "The great variety of Taste, as well as opinion, which prevails in the world, is too obvious not to have fallen under every one's observation" (EMPL, 226). "Man is a very variable being, and susceptible of many different opinions, principles, and rules of conduct" (EMPL, 255–6).

214–25; Claudia M. Schmidt, *David Hume: Reason in History* (University Park: Pennsylvania State University Press, 2003), chapter 7; and S. K. Wertz, "Hume, History, and Human Nature" *Journal of the History of Ideas* 36.3 (July–Sept. 1975): 481–96. For an exception to this trend, which attempts to demonstrate that Hume in fact sees human nature as constant and uniform, see Christopher J. Berry, *Hume, Hegel and Human Nature* (The Hague: Martinus Nijhoff, 1982), part 2; and Berry, "Hume's Universalism."

Morality in Context

Hume's appreciation of historical and cultural diversity should not be surprising, given his emphasis on the importance of sympathy in shaping people's sentiments. Indeed, he claims that sympathy, which "causes like passions and inclinations to run, as it were, by contagion" throughout neighborhoods, groups, and even entire nations, is the key source of variation in "national characters" (EMPL, 202; see also THN 2.1.11.2, 206). As Jacqueline Taylor observes, this emphasis on sympathy also marks a key point of divergence between Hume and "moral sense" theorists such as Francis Hutcheson and the Third Earl of Shaftesbury: "Our moral sentiments, Hume suggests, do not derive from an innate moral sense, but are forms of the natural sympathetic responses that we cultivate and correct in conversation with one another."[27] In other words, whereas Hutcheson posits a moral sense that is built into human nature by God, and Shaftesbury posits one that corresponds to a teleological natural order, Hume's sentimentalism does not depend on morality being "written into" human nature.[28] Indeed, he proclaims explicitly that it is "absurd to imagine" that our moral sentiments "are produc'd by an *original* quality and *primary* constitution. For as the number of our duties is, in a manner, infinite, 'tis impossible that our original instincts shou'd extend to each of them, and from our very first infancy impress on the human mind all that multitude of precepts, which are contain'd in the compleatest system of ethics" (THN 3.1.2.6, 304). Rather, as we have seen, Hume holds that moral standards emerge over time, spontaneously and intersubjectively, through the coordination and generalization of people's sentiments. Thus, while he believes that moral sentiments arise and evolve through natural processes, he does not believe that nature or human nature determines our ends directly. As he tells Hutcheson in an oft-quoted letter, "I cannot agree to your Sense of *Natural*. Tis founded on final Causes; which is a Consideration, that appears to me pretty uncertain & unphilosophical. For pray, what is the End of Man? Is he created for Happiness or for Virtue? For this Life or for the next? For himself or for his Maker?"[29]

Given that Hume is well aware that people's moral sentiments vary widely in different historical and cultural settings, the only remaining

---

[27] Jacqueline Taylor, "Hume's Later Moral Philosophy," in *The Cambridge Companion to Hume*, ed. David Fate Norton and Jacqueline Taylor, second edition (Cambridge: Cambridge University Press, 2009), 329.

[28] See Frazer, *The Enlightenment of Sympathy*, 16, as well as chapters 1–2 more generally.

[29] David Hume, letter to Francis Hutcheson, 17 September 1739, in *The Letters of David Hume*, ed. J. Y. T. Greig, vol. 1 (Oxford: Clarendon Press, 1932), 33.

question is whether he accepts all of this variation as legitimate, or whether he proposes a way to rule out or reject the generalized sentiments of some societies. Hume walks a fine line and offers some ambiguous statements on this score, but ultimately he appears to be a moral and cultural pluralist without being a complete moral or cultural relativist. That is, he sees context as playing a crucial role in the formation of moral standards and allows for a great deal of variation in these standards, but there are a few "virtues" and ways of life that he appears to deem beyond the pale.

To begin with, it is clear that Hume is a moral pluralist, insofar as he identifies a number of different moral ends: the virtues that are useful to oneself, useful to others, agreeable to oneself, and agreeable to others.[30] He also recognizes that these ends can and do conflict with one another: certain virtues (such as pride) are often agreeable to oneself but disagreeable to others, while others (such as justice) are often useful but disagreeable, and so on.[31] Thus, for Hume there is no conceivable social order or way of life that could maximize all moral ends or virtues at once; choices and compromises are inevitable, and there are many different forms of human flourishing.[32] Further, Hume allows unambiguously that moral right and wrong can vary according to what people find useful and agreeable in their particular circumstances: "Particular customs and manners alter the usefulness of qualities: They also alter their merit" (EPM 6.20, 52). To take a specific example from one of Hume's *Essays*, he posits that luxury "may be innocent or blameable, according to the age, or country, or condition of the person. The bounds between the virtue and the vice cannot here be exactly fixed, more than in other moral

---

[30] See Michael B. Gill, "Humean Moral Pluralism" *History of Philosophy Quarterly* 28.1 (January 2011), especially 45–7; and Andrew Sabl, "When Bad Things Happen from Good People (and Vice-Versa): David Hume's Political Ethics of Revolution" *Polity* 35.1 (autumn 2002), 82–3.

[31] See Gill, "Humean Moral Pluralism," 47–9. As John Danford writes, Hume would surely hold that "any theory which pretended to eliminate such tensions – which are inherent in common life and obvious to common sense – would be guilty of precisely the kind of systematizing distortion to which philosophical theories not grounded in common life are so prone." John W. Danford, *David Hume and the Problem of Reason: Recovering the Human Sciences* (New Haven, CT: Yale University Press, 1990), 160. See also Richard Dees, "Hume on the Characters of Virtue" *Journal of the History of Philosophy* 35.1 (January 1997): 45–64.

[32] In the dialogue that Hume appended to the second *Enquiry*, the narrator proclaims that "we must sacrifice somewhat of the *useful*, if we be very anxious to obtain all the *agreeable* qualities; and cannot pretend to reach alike every kind of advantage" (EPM D.47, 120). See also Livingston, *Philosophical Melancholy and Delirium*, 390.

Morality in Context

subjects" (EMPL, 268). Indeed, in a few passages he suggests not only that right and wrong are established by the prevailing sentiments of a given society, but that these sentiments are essentially *infallible*. On moral questions, he writes,

the opinions of men ... carry with them a peculiar authority, and are, in a great measure, infallible. The distinction of moral good and evil is founded on the pleasure or pain, which results from the view of any sentiment, or character; and as that pleasure or pain cannot be unknown to the person who feels it, it follows, that there is just so much vice or virtue in any character, as every one places in it, and that 'tis impossible in this particular we can ever be mistaken. (THN 3.2.8.8, 350; see also 3.2.9.4, 354)

Again: "though an appeal to general opinion may justly, in the speculative sciences of metaphysics, natural philosophy, or astronomy, be deemed unfair and inconclusive, yet in all questions with regard to morals ... there is really no other standard, by which any controversy can ever be decided" (EMPL, 486).

On the other hand, Hume suggests that people's moral sentiments *can* be mistaken when they are colored by "the delusive glosses of superstition and false religion" (EPM 9.3, 73). He claims that certain forms of religious belief lead people to approve of qualities and actions that are neither useful *nor* agreeable, and thus to make erroneous moral judgments. "Celibacy, fasting, penance, mortification, self-denial, humility, silence, solitude, and the whole train of monkish virtues" are "every where rejected by men of sense," he writes, "because they serve to no manner of purpose; neither advance a man's fortune in the world, nor render him a more valuable member of society; neither qualify him for the entertainment of company, nor encrease his power of self-enjoyment" (EPM 9.3, 73). In fact, "they cross all these desirable ends; stupify the understanding and harden the heart, obscure the fancy and sour the temper. We justly, therefore, transfer them to the opposite column, and place them in the catalogue of vices" (EPM 9.3, 73). Hume's statements in this paragraph surely do not encompass *all* religiously motivated qualities and actions, but he does suggest that some extreme religious "virtues" are actually vices.

It is unclear, however, whether this conclusion in fact follows from Hume's premises.[33] Hume seems to be convinced that the extreme

---

[33] For discussions of this question, see William Davie, "Hume on Monkish Virtue" *Hume Studies* 25.1–2 (April/November 1999): 139–54; and Hans Lottenbach, "Monkish Virtues, Artificial Lives: On Hume's Genealogy of Morals" *Canadian Journal of Philosophy* 26.3 (September 1996): 367–88.

"monkish virtues" will never be widely embraced: "A gloomy, hair-brained enthusiast, after his death, may have a place in the calendar; but will scarcely ever be admitted, when alive, into intimacy and society, except by those who are as delirious and dismal as himself" (EPM 9.3, 73). Yet it is obvious that many societies *have* approved of some or all of these virtues – whether because they found them useful (say, as a means to promote social cohesion) or agreeable (say, because they found them awe-inspiring) or indeed precisely because they are *not* merely useful or agreeable, but serve other, higher ends. As we have seen, Hume allows that reason can play an informational role in correcting factual errors and helping us to predict the possible consequences of a given action, but it cannot determine people's sentiments or establish right and wrong on its own. Recall also that taking the general point of view does not require us to take a completely detached or global perspective; rather, it requires us to reflect on the effects of a person's character traits or actions on "those, who have any commerce with the person we consider" (THN 3.3.1.18, 373; see also 3.3.1.30, 377).[34] Thus, if Hume were to adhere strictly to his empirical method and examine what societies around the world and throughout history *have* in fact approved of, rather than what he would prefer them to approve of, he may be forced to accept that even the "monkish virtues" can in fact be virtues.

Hume continues to walk this fine (or ambiguous) line in the most extensive discussion of the relationship between morality and cultural diversity in his corpus, namely, the fictional dialogue that he appended to *An Enquiry Concerning the Principles of Morals*.[35] The dialogue opens with the narrator's "friend," Palamedes, describing in some detail an imaginary country named Fourli "whose inhabitants have ways of thinking, in many things, particularly in morals, diametrically opposite to ours" (EPM D.2, 110). After recounting how the Fourlians condoned practices such as tyrannicide, infanticide, suicide, incest, and pederasty, all in stark opposition to the mores of eighteenth-century Europe, Palamedes reveals that only the names he used were fictitious, since all of the sentiments and customs that he ascribed to the Fourlians were in fact upheld by the

---

[34] Although Hume does not explore this point, it would seem that if this is what the general point of view requires, we may end up with the interesting result that morality would become *more* universal over time, as the world becomes more connected and people have more "commerce" with different individuals and cultures, although it is questionable whether it could ever be truly universal.

[35] This dialogue has received surprisingly little scholarly attention. For one helpful discussion, see Kate Abramson, "Hume on Cultural Conflicts of Values" *Philosophical Studies* 94.1/2 (May 1999): 173–87.

Morality in Context

ancient Greeks and Romans. Thus, he declares, "an ATHENIAN man of merit might be such a one as with us would pass for incestuous, a parricide, an assassin, an ungrateful, perjured traitor, and something else too abominable to be named" (presumably, a pederast) (EPM D.17, 113). The narrator admonishes his friend that "you have no indulgence for the manners and customs of different ages. Would you try a GREEK or ROMAN by the common law of ENGLAND? Hear him defend himself by his own maxims; and then pronounce. There are no manners so innocent or reasonable, but may be rendered odious or ridiculous, if measured by a standard, unknown to the persons" (EPM D.18–19, 114). He then goes on to show that many of the customs of eighteenth-century France – such as open adultery, reverence for monarchs, dueling, routine judicial torture, the practice of primogeniture, and deference to women – would be equally abhorrent to an ancient Athenian. Given these stark differences even between two "civilized, intelligent people," Palamedes concludes that "fashion, vogue, custom, and law" must be "the chief foundation of all moral determinations" (EPM D.25, 116).

All of this might seem to imply complete cultural relativism with respect to morality. The narrator, however, goes on to suggest that these diverse moral norms all spring from the same source, just as "the RHINE flows north, the RHONE south; yet both spring from the *same* mountain, and are also actuated, in their opposite directions, by the *same* principle of gravity. The different inclinations of the ground, on which they run, cause all the difference of their courses" (EPM D.26, 116). In other words, the moral standards of the ancient Greeks and Romans and the modern Europeans were both derived from the same source – what people found useful or agreeable, to them or to others – and the differences between them arose because of their different circumstances (see EPM D.37, 118). The narrator states explicitly that it is "custom" that determines not only what people find useful and agreeable, but whether it is the useful qualities or the agreeable ones, the selfish ones or the social ones, that dominate in their society: "Different customs ... by giving an early biass to the mind, may produce a superior propensity, either to the useful or the agreeable qualities; to those which regard self, or those which extend to society" (EPM D.42, 119).[36] Thus, while the sentimental *source* of morality may be universal, the actual *morals* of a given society – the conclusions that people draw from their sentiments – can vary according to a host of factors, including whether their government is

---

[36] See also Dees, "Hume and the Contexts of Politics," 228–30.

monarchial or republican, whether women have a place in their public life, whether their society is rich or poor, united or divided, learned or ignorant, at peace or at war, and so on (see EPM D.28–51, 117–21). For instance, "a degree of luxury may be ruinous and pernicious in a native of SWITZERLAND, which only fosters the arts, and encourages industry in a FRENCHMAN or ENGLISHMAN. We are not, therefore, to expect, either the same sentiments, or the same laws in BERNE, which prevail in LONDON or PARIS" (EPM D.41, 119).

Once again, however, Hume goes on to suggest that people's moral sentiments can sometimes be mistaken. In the closing paragraphs of the dialogue, Palamedes and the narrator turn to ways of life that depart significantly from "the maxims of common life and ordinary conduct," which they dub *"artificial* lives" (EPM D.52, 122).[37] They discuss two chief examples of such lives, namely, those of Diogenes the Cynic and Blaise Pascal. Diogenes, they note, sought complete independence from worldly needs and especially from other people and their opinions, to the point where he "indulged himself in the most beastly pleasures, even in public" (EPM D.55, 123). Pascal, in contrast, "made constant profession of humility and abasement, of the contempt and hatred of himself" and "refused himself the most innocent [pleasures], even in private" (EPM D.55, 122–3). (Here we see that it is not only "the illusions of religious superstition" that Hume finds problematic, as with Pascal, but also those of "philosophical enthusiasm," as with Diogenes [EPM D.57, 123].) The narrator is at a loss about how to account for such lives, given the Humean criteria that they had been using to explain moral norms – the useful and the agreeable, to oneself and to others – and simply concludes that "an experiment ... which succeeds in the air, will not always succeed in a vacuum. When men depart from the maxims of common reason, and affect these *artificial* lives ... no one can answer for what will please or displease them" (EPM D.57, 123).

As with the "monkish virtues," though, it is not entirely clear on what basis Hume deems these ways of life beyond the pale. It cannot be simply that they are "artificial" rather than "natural" in some sense; remember that Hume famously argues in the *Treatise* that justice itself is an artificial virtue (see THN 3.2.1, 307–11). Nor can it be simply that these are individual lives, not generalized sentiments, since Hume himself seems to acknowledge (in the voice of Palamedes) that Diogenes and Pascal both

---

[37] For an examination of these closing paragraphs, see James King, "Hume on Artificial Lives, with a Rejoinder to A. C. MacIntyre" *Hume Studies* 14.1 (April 1988): 53–92.

Morality in Context

"met with general admiration in their different ages, and have been proposed as models of imitation" (EPM D.56, 123). These ways of life may depend on false beliefs of some kind – say, about God or the afterlife or the possibility of complete self-sufficiency – but given the severe limits that Hume places on the capacity of reason to reach definitive conclusions about such questions (a topic that will be examined in Chapter 3), it is doubtful that he thought reason could effectively correct the sentiments of Diogenes, Pascal, or their followers.

Fortunately, we need not resolve this issue in order to determine whether Hume adopted the kind of "hegemonic" moral universalism that is so often ascribed to the Enlightenment. Even if his moral philosophy does effectively rule out certain "monkish virtues" and "artificial lives" as immoral, it is clear that he accords context a central role in the determination of right and wrong, and that he recognizes that there are many different (and incommensurable) virtues and ways of life that could qualify as "moral."[38] He holds that morality has the same *source* in all times and places – the sentiment of approval, properly generalized – but that the *content* of morality can vary widely, even if not infinitely. Indeed, it is not too much to say, with Emma Rothschild, that for the empiricist Hume "the universal was something to be considered with the greatest circumspection, something insidious, almost ecclesiastical."[39]

SMITH, THE IMPARTIAL SPECTATOR, AND THE INFLUENCE OF "CUSTOM AND FASHION"

Smith's moral philosophy diverges from Hume's in several very real respects, but ultimately their similarities are far broader and more fundamental. To begin with, Smith follows Hume in quietly rejecting the idea of a transcendent standard of right and wrong and in adopting a basically empirical approach to the subject. In *The Theory of Moral Sentiments*, he asserts that moral philosophy addresses two basic questions, namely, "wherein does virtue consist?" and "by what power or faculty in the

---

[38] As Michael Gill points out, Hume's apparent condemnation of the "artificial lives" of Diogenes and Pascal "comes *after* and *in contrast to* his discussion of the different ways different cultures have resolved conflicts between usefulness and agreeability," which suggests that "the differences between the relative priorities different cultures give to the same set of moral principles do not always admit of principled adjudication." Gill, "Humean Moral Pluralism," 58.

[39] Emma Rothschild, "The Atlantic Worlds of David Hume," in *Soundings in Atlantic History: Latent Structures and Intellectual Currents, 1500–1830*, ed. Bernard Bailyn and Patricia L. Denault (Cambridge, MA: Harvard University Press, 2009), 425.

mind is it, that this [virtuous] character ... is recommended to us?" (TMS VII.i.2, 265; see also VII.iii.intro.1, 314–15). Throughout the book, his discussions of both of these topics – the character of virtue and what we would call moral psychology – are resolutely practical and this-worldly, drawing on everyday observation and experience rather than abstract or a priori reasoning. As Samuel Fleischacker writes, Smith "tries to develop moral theory out of ordinary moral judgments, rather than beginning from a philosophical vantage point 'above' or 'beyond' those judgments.... He brings out the rationality already inherent in common life, mapping it from within and correcting it, where necessary, with its own tools, rather than trying either to justify or to criticize it from an external standpoint."[40] Thus, in *The Wealth of Nations* Smith describes moral philosophy as the attempt to show how "the maxims of common life" are "connected together by a few common principles" (WN V.i.f.25, 769).

Smith also joins Hume in positing that morality is ultimately based on the sentiments rather than reason. Whereas Hume devotes a good deal of intellectual energy to debunking moral rationalism, however, Smith seems to take for granted that it had already been effectively dismantled by the efforts of Hume and Hutcheson. Hence, he dismisses it out of hand rather briskly, writing that "it is altogether absurd and unintelligible to suppose that the first perceptions of right and wrong can be derived from reason" (TMS VII.iii.2.7, 320). Instead, he argues, the rightness or wrongness of an action – what Smith dubs its "merit" or "demerit" – is derived from "the sentiment or affection of the heart from which [that] action proceeds," and particularly from "the beneficial or hurtful nature of the effects which the affection aims at, or tends to produce" (TMS I.i.3.5–7, 18; see also II.i.intro.2, 67). Thus, Smith too holds that morality (an "ought") springs from people's sentiments (an "is") and so combines empirical and normative modes of inquiry. Some prominent Smith scholars have argued that his moral theory was "scientific" or value-neutral, concerned to observe and explain the formation of moral norms but not to judge them or to say what morality actually *is* – that is, that he sought to answer the second question of moral philosophy (how people make moral judgments) rather than the first (what virtue actually consists of).[41]

---

[40] Samuel Fleischacker, "Adam Smith," in *A Companion to Early Modern Philosophy*, ed. Steven Nadler (Oxford: Blackwell, 2002), 506.

[41] See, for example, T. D. Campbell, *Adam Smith's Science of Morals* (London: Allen & Unwin, 1971), 46–52 and passim; Andrew S. Skinner, *A System of Social Science: Papers Relating to Adam Smith*, second edition (Oxford: Clarendon Press, 1996), chapter 3; and Knud Haakonssen and Donald Winch, "The Legacy of Adam Smith," in *The Cambridge*

Morality in Context 47

However, I follow the majority of recent scholarship in interpreting Smith as having adopted a self-consciously normative position.[42] After all, Smith gives explicit precedence to the question of what virtue actually consists of, going so far as to say that the question of how people make moral judgments, "though of the greatest importance in speculation, is of none in practice," and thus that it is "a mere matter of philosophical curiosity" (TMS VII.iii.intro.3, 315).

Yet again like Hume, Smith holds that the faculty of sympathy plays a critical role in the formation of moral standards. However, sympathy is a rather more complicated process for Smith than it was for Hume. According to Hume, sympathy simply transmits the sentiments or passions of one person to another, more or less vividly depending on the circumstances (see THN 2.1.11.2–3, 206; 3.3.1.7, 368). In the second *Enquiry*, he goes so far as to refer to it as a kind of "contagion" (EPM 7.2, 59; 7.21, 64). Smith accepts that sympathy does sometimes occur in this straightforward manner, such as when a smiling face cheers a spectator (see TMS I.i.1.6, 11), but in general he describes it in terms of a much fuller imaginative identification with, or projection into, the situation of another person (see TMS I.i.1.10, 12). For instance, we do not generally feel anger upon seeing an angry person; rather, we have to take into account what provoked him in order to "bring his case home to ourselves" and decide whether his anger is proper (TMS I.i.1.7, 11). Importantly, Smith builds this kind of imaginative identification into his moral philosophy, claiming that the sense of merit and demerit (or right and wrong) is a compound sentiment, made up of a "direct sympathy" with an individual's actions as well as an "indirect sympathy" with those who are either benefited or harmed by those actions (TMS II.i.5.2, 74). In other words, moral judgment requires not just an external or observer's point of view, as in Hume's theory, but the imaginative adoption of the perspective of each person involved in a given situation.[43]

 Companion to Adam Smith, ed. Knud Haakonssen (Cambridge: Cambridge University Press, 2006), especially 380–8.

[42] See, for example, Charles L. Griswold, *Adam Smith and the Virtues of Enlightenment* (Cambridge: Cambridge University Press, 1999), 49–58, 71–3; James R. Otteson, *Adam Smith's Marketplace of Life* (Cambridge: Cambridge University Press, 2002), chapter 6; Samuel Fleischacker, *On Adam Smith's Wealth of Nations: A Philosophical Companion* (Princeton, NJ: Princeton University Press, 2004), 36, 52–4; and Hanley, *Adam Smith and the Character of Virtue*, 55–9.

[43] See Stephen Darwall, "Sympathetic Liberalism: Recent Work on Adam Smith" *Philosophy & Public Affairs* 28.2 (April 1999), 141–4; and Samuel Fleischacker, "Sympathy in Hume and Smith: A Contrast, Critique, and Reconstruction," in *Intersubjectivity and*

Another point of divergence between Hume and Smith is that Smith accords an even slighter role to utility or usefulness in his moral philosophy than does Hume. It is true that according to Smith we judge the merit (as opposed to propriety) of an action by its result – "the beneficial or hurtful nature of the effects which the affection aims at, or tends to produce" (TMS I.i.3.5–7, 18; see also II.i.intro.2, 67) – rather than by what motivated it, but that result is judged by sympathetic identification with those involved, not any kind of measure of overall utility. For Smith, utility or usefulness always enters our moral judgments as a kind of afterthought, rather than as the initial ground of our approval of an action (see TMS II.ii.3.8–9, 89). Indeed, he explicitly differentiates himself from Hume on this point. Whereas Hume holds that many qualities – the "useful" as opposed to "agreeable" virtues – are approved of as a result of reflection on their utility, Smith counters that "it is not the view of this utility or hurtfulness which is either the first or principal source of our approbation and disapprobation. These sentiments are no doubt enhanced and enlivened by the perception of the beauty or deformity which results from this utility or hurtfulness. But still, I say, they are originally and essentially different from this perception" (TMS IV.2.3, 188; see also VII.ii.3.21, 306). Like many contemporary Hume scholars, Smith tends to overlook the "agreeable" virtues in his discussions of Hume's outlook, and so paints him as more of a utilitarian than he really was (see especially TMS VII.iii.3.17, 327).[44] However, even on a more complete reading of Hume's moral philosophy, Smith stands still further from utilitarianism than does Hume.[45]

Nevertheless, the basic structure of Smith's moral philosophy is quite similar to Hume's: for both, moral standards arise as people coordinate their sentiments and behavior in response to others, above all through sympathetic observation and interaction. This is how it is possible to move from individual sentiments to general norms without relying on

---

Objectivity in Adam Smith and Edmund Husserl: A Collection of Essays, ed. Christel Fricke and Dagfinn Føllesdal (Frankfurt: Ontos Verlag, 2012).

[44] As David Raynor points out, Hume seems to have noticed this oversimplification of his views and silently corrected it in an anonymous (and extremely favorable) review of *The Theory of Moral Sentiments*. See David R. Raynor, "Hume's Abstract of Adam Smith's Theory of Moral Sentiments" *Journal of the History of Philosophy* 22.1 (January 1984), 59–60.

[45] Another, related point of divergence between the two is that Smith, unlike Hume, understands justice as a natural rather than an "artificial" virtue, one that springs from the sentiment of resentment rather than from a recognition of the utility of rules of justice. Their respective views of justice will be examined in Chapter 2.

Morality in Context 49

any transcendent source, according to Smith: moral standards arise spontaneously over time from a great multitude of individual actions and interactions, similarly to the way markets function in the economic sphere. Of course, like Hume – perhaps even more than Hume – Smith strives to show that impartiality is possible within a moral theory that relies on the sentiments. To this end, he introduces the famous "impartial spectator," which plays an analogous role in his theory to the one played by the general point of view in Hume's, namely, that of correcting for an individual's particular biases and interests. Smith's fundamental claim in *The Theory of Moral Sentiments* is that the impartial spectator sets the ultimate standard for moral judgment: sentiments, qualities, and actions that earn such a spectator's sympathy or approval are morally right, and those that earn his disapproval or resentment are morally wrong (see TMS II.i.2.2, 69).[46] According to Smith, it is the idea of the impartial spectator that enables us to distinguish between what people happen to praise and what is truly praise*worthy*, and between what they blame and what is truly blame*worthy* (see TMS III.2.3, 114; III.2.32, 130–1).

What, then, is the impartial spectator like? What does his "impartiality" consist of? Smith's explanation is actually quite simple: an impartial spectator is just like any other spectator except that he is both fully informed and disinterested, meaning that he knows all of the relevant circumstances and "has no particular connexion" to any of the individuals involved in a given situation (TMS III.3.3, 135). In other words, adopting the perspective of the impartial spectator – like Hume's general point of view – does not require perfect rationality or the ability to take a "God's-eye view"; the impartial spectator is far more humanly and emotionally engaged than the kind of "ideal observer" associated with Roderick Firth.[47] Indeed, it is precisely the impartial spectator's *feelings* of approval and disapproval that set the moral standard.

Amartya Sen has recently argued that Smith associated impartiality with universality, and so sought to incorporate the views and sentiments of many different cultures into the impartial spectator as a way to

---

[46] While I follow Smith in using the masculine pronoun here, I agree with Henry Clark that Smith's conception of the impartial spectator is not inherently gendered. See Henry C. Clark, "Women and Humanity in Scottish Enlightenment Social Thought: The Case of Adam Smith" *Historical Reflections/Réflexions Historiques* 19.3 (summer 1993): 335–61.

[47] See Campbell, *Adam Smith's Science of Morals*, 127–41; Griswold, *Adam Smith and the Virtues of Enlightenment*, 135–46; Otteson, *Adam Smith's Marketplace of Life*, 58–64; and D. D. Raphael, *The Impartial Spectator: Adam Smith's Moral Philosophy* (Oxford: Clarendon Press, 2007), 43–5.

50   *The Pragmatic Enlightenment*

surmount "the impact of entrenched tradition and custom," and thereby
to achieve what Sen calls "open" rather than "closed" impartiality.[48] This
is not a claim that Smith makes explicitly, however, and it is at odds with
the tenor of his account. In referring to the idea of the impartial spectator,
Smith frequently replaces or supplements the adjective "impartial" with
other terms; by far the most common of these substitutions is "indifferent," but he also uses terms such as "cool," "fair," "well-informed," "candid," and even "generous" and "intelligent."[49] He never, however, uses
terms that imply universality or the ability to transcend one's culture.[50]
On the contrary, he alludes constantly to the fact that the impartial spectator is built out of actual spectators – out of what "we" approve or "we"
sympathize with. As T. D. Campbell writes, it seems that for Smith the
impartial spectator "is simply a short-hand way of referring to the normal reaction of a member of a particular social group, or of a whole society, when he is in the position of observing the conduct of his fellows."[51]
In other words, Smith's impartial spectator is much more rooted in time
and place – much more culture-bound – than Sen suggests.[52]

   To say that the impartial spectator is culture-bound, however, is not
to say that Smith advocates that we confine our moral judgments to a
narrow social group. After all, the entire *point* of the impartial spectator

---

[48] Amartya Sen, *The Idea of Justice* (Cambridge, MA: Belknap Press, 2009), 45, and chapter 6 more generally. See also Amartya Sen, "Introduction," in Adam Smith, *The Theory
of Moral Sentiments* (New York: Penguin, 2009), vii–viii, xvii–xxi.

[49] References to the impartial spectator as "indifferent" can be found at TMS I.ii.4.1, 39;
II.i.2.2, 69; II.ii.2.4, 85; III.3.33, 151; III.3.42, 154; III.4.3, 157; III.4.5, 158; and VI.iii.5,
238. "Cool": TMS I.ii.3.8, 38. "Fair": TMS III.1.2, 110. "Well-informed": TMS III.2.32,
130; and VII.ii.1.49, 294. "Candid": TMS III.3.28, 148. "Generous": TMS II.ii.1.7, 81.
"Intelligent": TMS VI.iii.27, 249; and VII.ii.1.28, 283.

[50] The one potential exception that I am aware of is TMS III.2.32, 131, where Smith refers
to the impartial spectator as a "demigod within the breast" that "appears, like the demi-
gods of the poets, though partly of immortal, yet partly too of mortal extraction." This
reference appears in a discussion of a particularly thorny and delicate issue for Smith,
namely, the question of how (or whether) it is possible to retain a sense of our own
deserved merit even when "all our brethren appear loudly to condemn us." This is essentially Glaucon's age-old challenge to Socrates, to show that a just person can be content
even if he has "the greatest reputation for injustice." Plato, *The Republic*, trans. Allan
Bloom (New York: Basic Books, 1968), 361b–d, 39. Smith more or less admits that he
cannot meet this challenge within the parameters of his moral theory, and that "the only
effectual consolation" in these cases may lie in "the humble hope and expectation of a
life to come." TMS III.2.33, 131–2.

[51] Campbell, *Adam Smith's Science of Morals*, 145.

[52] For an extended argument along these lines, see Fonna Forman-Barzilai, *Adam Smith and
the Circles of Sympathy: Cosmopolitanism and Moral Theory* (Cambridge: Cambridge
University Press, 2010), 166–92.

Morality in Context 51

is that it enables us to overcome our natural favoritism for ourselves and our associates and the kind of prejudices that are frequently found in narrow groups. In fact, Smith claims explicitly that "of all the corrupters of moral sentiments ... faction and fanaticism have always been by far the greatest" (TMS III.3.43, 156). Yet the focus of *The Theory of Moral Sentiments* is squarely on *individual* moral self-correction – using the "mirror" of society to correct for one's individual or group biases (TMS III.1.3, 110) – rather than on the reform of societal or cultural standards more broadly. Recall that for Smith there simply *is* no transcendent or independent standard of moral judgment, no Platonic Form of morality to which the impartial spectator could appeal in order to correct the broadly held sentiments and judgments of a given society.[53] Moreover, Smith describes the impartial spectator in terms of "set[ting] up in our own minds a judge between ourselves and *those we live with*" – not a judge between different societies or cultures (TMS, 129, emphasis added). Hence, as Fleischacker remarks, "there is little in Smith's construction of the idealized spectator to correct for the surrounding society's standards of judgment"; rather, the impartial spectator "takes over those standards and corrects merely for their partial or ill-informed *use*."[54]

In addition to the impartial spectator, Smith describes a second means of correcting for individual and group bias, namely, the formation of "general rules" of morality. On the basis of "our continual observations upon the conduct of others," he writes, we are "insensibly [led] to form to ourselves certain general rules concerning what is fit and proper either to be done or to be avoided" (TMS III.4.7, 159). For instance, given that we (and those around us) generally disapprove of lying, we make a general rule that lying is wrong. This rule can then be used to check our selfish impulses and biases – to make us stop and think, before we tell a lie, whether an impartial spectator would approve of our actions. Yet Smith emphasizes that these rules are collectively derived from particular sentiments in response to particular actions; as he succinctly puts it, "the general maxims of morality are formed, like all other general maxims, from experience and induction" (TMS VII.iii.2.6, 319). Thus, he insists that these rules should not themselves be taken as the ultimate arbiter of right and wrong, as if this kind of determination could be made "like the decisions of a court of judicatory, by considering first the general rule,

---

[53] See Griswold, *Adam Smith and the Virtues of Enlightenment*, 145.
[54] Samuel Fleischacker, "Adam Smith and Cultural Relativism" *Erasmus Journal for Philosophy and Economics* 4.2 (autumn 2011), 28.

and then, secondly, whether the particular action under consideration fell properly within its comprehension" (TMS, III.4.11, 160). While rigid general rules, such as the rule that lying is wrong, are normally adequate for everyday use, Smith says, we should bear in mind that in fact "the general rules of almost all the virtues ... are in many respects loose and inaccurate, admit of many exceptions, and require so many modifications, that is scarce possible to regulate our conduct entirely by a regard to them" (TMS III.6.9, 174).[55] So, for example, it is true that lying is *generally* wrong – that is, that the impartial spectator would generally disapprove of it – but there are situations in which it may *not* be wrong, such as a lie to save a person's life, or the breaking of a promise extorted by force (see TMS VII.iv.12, 331–2).[56]

Given the impossibility of formulating general moral rules that apply under all circumstances, without exception, Smith protests vigorously against the idea that the function of moral philosophy is to lay down rigid or universal rules for how to act. He praises the "ancient" moralists who wrote about morality in a "loose" way, without "affect[ing] to lay down many precise rules that are to hold good unexceptionally in all particular cases" (TMS VII.iv.2–3, 327–8). He contrasts this method with that of "the casuists of the middle and latter ages of the christian church, as well as all those who in this and in the preceding century have treated of what is called natural jurisprudence," who "endeavour to lay down exact and precise rules for the direction of every circumstance of our behaviour" (TMS VII.iv.7, 329). "That frivolous accuracy which they attempted to introduce into subjects which do not admit of it, almost necessarily betrayed them into ... dangerous errors," he writes (TMS VII. iv.33, 340). Indeed, for Smith one of the great advantages of his moral philosophy, with its basis in impartial spectatorship, is that it avoids these hard and fast rules:

[55] The one exception to this rule, according to Smith, is the virtue of justice, whose rules "are accurate in the highest degree, and admit of no exceptions or modifications" (TMS III.6.10, 175). As Fleischacker notes, Smith does not make clear whether justice is a "naturally" precise virtue or whether we need to *impose* precision on it in order to make it more effective and enforceable, but he seems to lean toward the latter alternative. See Fleischacker, *On Adam Smith's Wealth of Nations*, 153–67, especially 155, as well as TMS VII.iv.12, 331–2. To repeat, Smith's conception of justice will be examined in greater detail in Chapter 2.

[56] The flexibility of Smith's outlook here, of course, stands in stark contrast to Kant's stance on the same issue. See Kant, *Fundamental Principles of the Metaphysics of Morals*, 160–1; and Immanuel Kant, "On a Supposed Right to Lie Because of Philanthropic Concerns," in *Ethical Philosophy*, trans. James W. Ellington, second edition (Indianapolis: Hackett, [1799] 1994).

Morality in Context   53

If we place ourselves completely in [the impartial spectator's] situation, if we really view ourselves with his eyes, and as he views us, and listen with diligent and reverential attention to what he suggests to us, his voice will never deceive us. We shall stand in need of no casuistic rules to direct our conduct. These it is often impossible to accommodate to all the different shades and gradations of circumstance, character, and situation, to differences and distinctions which, though not imperceptible, are, by their nicety and delicacy, often altogether undefinable. (TMS VI.ii.1.22, 227)

In short, neither of the two chief means of attaining impartiality in Smith's moral philosophy, the impartial spectator or the formation of general rules, requires that right and wrong are the same in all times and places. On the contrary, both of them seem to push in the opposite direction, and to suggest that morality *will* vary according to context and circumstance.

The major outstanding question regarding Smith's outlook, at this point, is one that was also central in our examination of Hume, namely, that of whether he believed in a "strong" human nature that would ensure that people have the same sentiments or approve of the same things in all times and places. While Smith is occasionally thought to have held such a view,[57] his stance is in fact quite similar to Hume's. He does not, any more than Hume, envision human nature as a mere "blank slate" to be filled in by society; indeed, he refers occasionally to the existence of certain "original passions" or "original principles" of human nature (e.g., TMS I.i.1.1, 9; WN I.ii.2, 25). Yet he categorically rejects the notion that there is an innate "moral sense" of the kind posited by Hutcheson and Shaftesbury (see TMS VII.iii.3.4–16, 321–7), and he recognizes that the "original" passions and principles of human nature can be modified and channeled in substantially different ways. For instance, in the famous passage on the philosopher and the street porter in *The Wealth of Nations*, he points to the great effects of environmental influences on people's characters:

The difference between the most dissimilar characters, between a philosopher and a common street porter, for example, seems to arise not so much from nature,

---

[57] For instance, Richard Teichgraeber writes that Hutcheson, Hume, and Smith all "by and large assumed human nature was fixed and universal. Understanding man's nature was a matter of deducing a single set of principles of conduct which were universally true." Richard F. Teichgraeber III, *'Free Trade' and Moral Philosophy: Rethinking the Sources of Adam Smith's Wealth of Nations* (Durham: Duke University Press, 1986), 21. More recently, Michael Frazer contends that Hume and Smith both held that "all human beings share a psychology from which, with sufficient reflection, the same moral sentiments will develop," and that they "thus seek to explain away rather than to understand the full scope of human diversity." Frazer, *The Enlightenment of Sympathy*, 141; see also 142–7.

as from habit, custom, and education. When they came into the world, and for the first six or eight years of their existence, they were, perhaps, very much alike, and neither their parents nor play-fellows could perceive any remarkable difference. About that age, or soon after, they come to be employed in very different occupations. The difference of talents comes then to be taken notice of, and widens by degrees, till at least the vanity of the philosopher is willing to acknowledge scarce any resemblance. (WN I.ii.4, 28–9)

Moreover, as with Hume, Smith's emphasis on the role of sympathy – on people's tendency to fashion and coordinate their sentiments, beliefs, and behavior through social interaction – indicates that there is a good deal of flexibility in his conception of human nature. As Ryan Hanley writes, "insofar as sympathy is natural, Smith suggests that it is natural for our natures to be shaped by convention."[58]

In addition, nearly all of Smith's writings show him to be highly attuned to historical and cultural diversity. According to the "four stages" theory of history that he was one of the first to adopt, there is a great deal of variation among the hunting, shepherding, agricultural, and commercial stages of society, in terms of not only modes of subsistence and political institutions but also manners, beliefs, and sentiments.[59] Smith places a particular emphasis on the considerable differences between primitive and civilized societies. He reports, for example, that "the savages of North America, we are told, assume upon all occasions the greatest indifference, and would think themselves degraded if they should ever appear in any respect to be overcome, either by love, or grief, or resentment. Their magnanimity and self-command, in this respect, are almost beyond the conception of Europeans" (TMS V.2.9, 205). It is with obvious admiration and amazement that he relates the "heroic and unconquerable firmness" with which American Indian prisoners of war bear even "the most dreadful torments" (TMS V.2.9–10, 206–7). Moreover, Smith suggests that there is often quite a bit of variation *within* societies in terms of manners and sentiments. In his discussion of religion in *The Wealth of Nations*, he claims that "in every civilized society" there are "always two different schemes or systems of morality current at the same

---

[58] Hanley, *Adam Smith and the Character of Virtue*, 145.

[59] The roots of this theory can be found in Montesquieu, and a similar theory can be found in the works of many of Smith's contemporaries, including Adam Ferguson, Lord Kames, John Millar, and William Robertson. For an extensive analysis of the precursors and exponents of the "four stages" theory, one that concludes that the fully developed theory was probably conceived by Smith and Turgot independently and around the same time, see Ronald L. Meek, *Social Science and the Ignoble Savage* (Cambridge: Cambridge University Press, 1976).

Morality in Context

time": the "strict or austere" system that is prevalent among "the common people," which sets firm limits on luxury, levity, and intemperance, and the "liberal or loose" system, which is prevalent among "what are called people of fashion," which is much more indulgent on these scores (WN V.i.g.10, 794).

Smith's most extensive discussion of the relationship between morality and cultural diversity appears in part 5, chapter 2, of *The Theory of Moral Sentiments*, entitled "Of the Influence of Custom and Fashion upon Moral Sentiments." He opens part 5 by noting that "custom and fashion" have "a considerable influence upon the moral sentiments of mankind, and are the chief causes of the many irregular and discordant opinions which prevail in different ages and nations concerning what is blameable or praise-worthy" (TMS V.1.1, 194). After discussing the enormous historical and cultural variation in people's notions of physical beauty in chapter 1, he introduces chapter 2 by suggesting that moral sentiments do not vary quite this much: "the characters and conduct of a Nero, or a Claudius," for example, "are what no custom will ever reconcile us to, what no fashion will ever render agreeable" (TMS V.2.1, 200). Yet he suggests that even if the influence of custom and fashion on moral sentiments is "not altogether so great" as it is on notions of physical beauty, it is still "perfectly similar" (TMS V.2.2, 200). He goes on to discuss many different factors that influence people's moral sentiments, including their education and upbringing, what the "great" in their society are like, how old they are, and their profession (see TMS V.2.2–6, 200–4). Importantly, he also highlights the effects of "the different situations of different ages and countries," noting, for instance, that "that degree of politeness, which would be highly esteemed, perhaps would be thought effeminate adulation, in Russia, would be regarded as rudeness and barbarism at the court of France," while "that degree of order and frugality, which, in a Polish nobleman, would be considered as excessive parsimony, would be regarded as extravagance in a citizen of Amsterdam" (TMS V.2.7, 204). Again, he draws particular attention to the differences between civilized societies, where "the virtues which are founded upon humanity, are more cultivated than those which are founded upon self-denial and the command of the passions," and primitive societies, where the reverse is the case (TMS V.2.8–9, 204–5). He offers a detailed discussion of the contrasting manners and sentiments of civilized and primitive peoples, calling the differences between them "wide" and "essential" (TMS V.2.10–11, 208).

Moreover, it is clear that Smith sees this kind of cultural variation in people's moral sentiments as perfectly fitting and legitimate – even necessary. After all, different circumstances do not just *promote* different manners and sentiments, they *require* them: "In general, the style of manners which takes place in any nation, may commonly upon the whole be said to be that which is most suitable to its situation. Hardiness is the character most suitable to the circumstances of a savage; sensibility to those of one who lives in a very civilized society" (TMS V.2.13, 209). Thus, Smith too embraces a form of moral pluralism, insofar as he accepts that there are multiple (and incommensurable) genuine moral goods and ways of life, from the "gentle" virtues of humanity to the "awful" virtues of self-command. In fact, Smith seems to join Hume in regarding widely held moral sentiments as nearly incontrovertible: while "a system of natural philosophy may appear very plausible, and be for a long time very generally received in the world, and yet have no foundation in nature, nor any sort of resemblance to the truth," he remarks, "it is otherwise with systems of moral philosophy." Since our sentiments of approval and disapproval are so intimately connected to ourselves and to "the very parish that we live in," we cannot be too grossly deceived regarding what is morally right and wrong (TMS VII.ii.4.14, 313–14). As Fleischacker observes, "for Smith, morality just *is* the social practice by which people correct one another for not adequately living up to their society's standards of conduct ... this definition is neutral as to what the society's standards of conduct might be, and according to it, the thought that societies might entirely misunderstand the nature of morality is quite literally unintelligible."[60]

However, Smith joins Hume in placing *some* limits on the range of moral sentiments and actions that can be deemed acceptable. Whereas Hume draws the line at certain "monkish virtues" and "artificial lives" that are inspired by religious superstition and philosophical enthusiasm, Smith's main concern is with customs or "particular usages" that are relics of previous eras, and so are no longer suitable or necessary in a given society (TMS V.2.14, 209). Smith's chief example is the practice of infanticide in ancient Greece; he concludes part 5 of *The Theory of Moral Sentiments* with a discussion of this topic. He notes that "the exposition, that is, the murder of new-born infants, was a practice allowed of in almost all the states of Greece, even among the polite and civilized Athenians; and whenever the circumstances of the parent rendered it inconvenient to bring up the child, to abandon it to hunger, or to wild beasts, was regarded without blame or censure" (TMS V.2.15, 210).

---

[60] Fleischacker, "Adam Smith and Cultural Relativism," 24–5.

Morality in Context 57

Smith laments that "this barbarous prerogative" was tolerated not only by "the loose maxims of the world" but also by philosophers like Plato and Aristotle, who "supported the horrible abuse, by far-fetched considerations of public utility" (TMS V.2.15, 210). He concludes that "when custom can give sanction to so dreadful a violation of humanity, we may well imagine that there is scarce any particular practice so gross which it cannot authorize" (TMS V.2.15, 210).

Yet Smith also suggests that in cases of dire necessity infanticide may in fact be morally acceptable. In contrast to "the latter ages of Greece," when this practice "was permitted from views of remote interest or conveniency," he says, in more primitive times it was all but inevitable:

The extreme indigence of a savage is often such that he himself is frequently exposed to the greatest extremity of hunger, and he often dies of pure want, and it is frequently impossible for him to support both himself and his child. We cannot wonder, therefore, that in this case he should abandon it. One who, in flying from an enemy, whom it was impossible to resist, should throw down his infant, because it retarded his flight, would *surely be excusable*; since, by attempting to save it, he could only hope for the consolation of dying with it. That in this state of society, therefore, a parent should be allowed to judge whether he can bring up his child, ought not to surprise us so greatly. (TMS V.2.15, 210, emphasis added; see also WN intro.4, 10)

As Jennifer Pitts observes, in cases of dire necessity the impartial spectator would "enter imaginatively into the situation of the burdened parent and concur with a judgment that abandoning the child is preferable to dying with it. The moral wrong occurs in the preservation of this practice in societies such as ancient Greece, where only 'remote interest or conveniency', not necessity, motivated infanticide."[61] In other words, Smith does not propose a *universal* prohibition on even this barbaric practice. Nonetheless, he plainly sees it as a moral abomination in all but the most dire circumstances. As Charles Griswold rightly points out, Smith's moral philosophy provides a clear basis from which to contest and condemn the practice of infanticide, insofar as the impartial spectator would (by definition) sympathize fully with each individual involved in a situation, including an unwanted infant.[62] Taking a more comprehensive or

---

[61] Jennifer Pitts, *A Turn to Empire: The Rise of Imperial Liberalism in Britain and France* (Princeton, NJ: Princeton University Press, 2005), 48.

[62] As Griswold notes, Smith "conjures up for us the terrible situation of the helpless victim" in an effort to show that the impartial spectator would plainly disapprove of this practice. Griswold, *Adam Smith and the Virtues of Enlightenment*, 201–2. Griswold makes a similar case with respect to slavery, which Smith also condemns. See ibid., 199–201; and TMS V.2.9, 206–7.

disinterested view of a situation provides an important means of correcting for defects and inconsistencies in a society's moral code. Again, Smith is no mere moral or cultural relativist.

Still, as with Hume's condemnation of the "artificial lives" of Diogenes and Pascal, Smith's condemnation of infanticide in all but the most dire circumstances stands as an explicit exception to the general contours of his moral theory, which accords context a central role. Societies may sometimes be misguided in their acceptance of certain "particular usages," as civilized Athens was in the case of infanticide, he holds, but not in their "general style of character and behaviour" (TMS V.2.12, 209). The vast majority of the cultural variation in people's moral sentiments is, in other words, perfectly appropriate. Like Hume, Smith accepts that there are multiple, incommensurable forms of human flourishing, from the gentle virtues of humanity to the awful virtues of self-command. Also like Hume, he presents a means of attaining impartiality on moral questions that allows – indeed, *requires* – that morality will vary according to context and circumstance. Thus, I am disinclined to read Smith as a kind of proto-Kantian, as several recent commentators have done.[63] Indeed, in many respects Smith and Kant are near-opposites: whereas Kant's moral philosophy derives rigid and universally applicable moral standards from a priori reason, Smith's derives flexible and contextual moral standards from empirically observed sentiments.

MONTESQUIEU AND THE INDETERMINATE NATURE OF
NATURAL LAW

As we turn from Hume and Smith to Montesquieu and Voltaire, the question of moral universalism becomes a bit more difficult to assess.

---

[63] Among the most prominent recent works to link Smith to Kant are Darwall, "Sympathetic Liberalism," 149, 152–4; Samuel Fleischacker, "Philosophy in Moral Practice: Kant and Adam Smith" *Kant-Studien* 82.3 (1991), especially 261–4; Knud Haakonssen, *Natural Law and Moral Philosophy: From Grotius to the Scottish Enlightenment* (Cambridge: Cambridge University Press, 1996), 148–53; Leonidas Montes, *Adam Smith in Context: A Critical Reassessment of Some Central Components of His Thought* (New York: Palgrave Macmillan, 2004), 114, 118–22; and Sen, *The Idea of Justice*, chapter 6. These scholars tend to view Smith's impartial spectator as a kind of precursor to Kant's categorical imperative because of its implied assumption of the basic dignity of all human beings and its aim of preventing us from preferring ourselves or our kind over others. There is certainly something to this line of reasoning; it is this aspect of Smith's outlook that leads him to condemn infanticide in all but the most dire circumstances. However, I have argued that Smith self-consciously avoids drawing the kind of rigidly universalistic conclusions from these premises that Kant does.

Morality in Context 59

For a variety of reasons, the debate over the nature and basis of morality received far less attention in France than in Britain in the eighteenth century,[64] and there is no equivalent, in the writings of Montesquieu or Voltaire, to Hume's *Enquiry Concerning the Principles of Morals* or Smith's *The Theory of Moral Sentiments*. That is, these thinkers never spell out in a detailed way what underlies the normative claims they make, or where morality ultimately originates. Given that they have both been depicted as moral universalists, however, it will be necessary to consider their views on these issues on the basis of hints that can be found scattered throughout their writings.[65] As we will see in this section and the following one, the available evidence suggests that Montesquieu and Voltaire concurred with Hume and Smith not only that the ultimate basis of morality is human and sentimental rather than transcendent or rational, but also that morality can and does vary according to context.

While some scholars contend, against the view that I have put forward, that Hume and Smith had little appreciation for true cultural diversity, assuming that people must be substantively alike in all times and places, it would be difficult indeed to make such a case regarding Montesquieu. His masterpiece, *The Spirit of the Laws*, gives its reader a vivid sense of the extraordinary diversity of laws, customs, and beliefs in different societies. In fact, he announces in the preface that he will examine the "*infinite* diversity of laws and mores" around the world and throughout history (SL, xliii, emphasis added).[66] He famously emphasizes the

---

[64] The lack of extensive debate on this topic in France seems to have been due in part to greater fears of censorship and persecution, and in part to the philosophes' comparatively greater emphasis on practical reform over philosophical disputes. See David Fate Norton and Manfred Kuehn, "The Foundations of Morality," in *The Cambridge History of Eighteenth-Century Philosophy*, ed. Knud Haakonssen, vol. 2 (Cambridge: Cambridge University Press, 2006), 971–4; and J. B. Schneewind, *The Invention of Autonomy: A History of Modern Moral Philosophy* (Cambridge: Cambridge University Press, 1998), chapter 21.

[65] This depiction can be traced back at least to Ernst Cassirer, who singles out Montesquieu and Voltaire as prime examples of the Enlightenment's moral universalism. See Ernst Cassirer, *The Philosophy of the Enlightenment*, trans. Fritz C. A. Koelln and James P. Pettegrove (Princeton, NJ: Princeton University Press, [1932] 1979), 242–6.

[66] As every reader of the work soon discovers, it virtually overflows with examples drawn not only from modern Europe and ancient Greece and Rome but also from such then far-flung places as Persia, China, Japan, India, Muscovy, Tartary, and various nations and tribes in Africa and the Americas. Montesquieu later asserted that the subject of the work was nothing less than "the laws, customs, and diverse manners of all the peoples on earth." Charles de Secondat, baron de Montesquieu, *Défense de l'Esprit des lois*, in *Oeuvres complètes*, ed. Roger Caillois, vol. 2 (Paris: Gallimard, [1750] 1951), 1137. Hence, one of his modern editors claims that "Montesquieu was the first major political

great variation in the "spirit" or character of different nations, due to a host of physical and nonphysical factors. One of his lists of these factors includes "climate, religion, laws, the maxims of the government, examples of past things, mores, and manners" (SL 19.4, 310), and elsewhere he also discusses factors like terrain, geographical size, the size of the population, the predominant occupations, the manner of education, and the levels of commerce, wealth, and technology. Throughout the work Montesquieu points to laws, customs, and moral and religious beliefs that are wildly different from those of eighteenth-century Europe. For instance, he cites a travel account that attributes to the Formosans the belief that a place in hell is reserved for those "who have failed to go naked in certain seasons, who have worn clothing of linen and not of silk, who have gathered oysters, and who have acted without consulting the songs of birds" (SL 24.14, 469). Similarly, in Montesquieu's first book, *The Persian Letters*, the worldviews of the protagonists Usbek and Rica are so different from those of the Europeans they encounter that what seems entirely ordinary in one culture seems outlandish and inexplicable in the other. Such was Montesquieu's sensitivity to the great variety of institutions, customs, and mores around the world that Robert Wokler suggests that *The Spirit of the Laws* "might well have been subtitled 'A Study of Difference'" and that *The Persian Letters* "ought to be required reading in any course of comparative literature devoted to the subject of 'Otherness'."[67]

Although Montesquieu regards human diversity as "infinite," he does not infer that it is simply arbitrary: even "amidst the infinite diversity of laws and mores," he persists in believing that people are "not led by their fancies alone" (SL, xliii). Like Hume and Smith, he maintains that beneath all the variation in laws, customs, and beliefs there is a human nature, one that can be concealed or obscured but never effaced entirely (see SL, xlv). Also like Hume and Smith, however, he understands this human nature to be indeterminate and highly flexible.[68] In the preface

---

philosopher who defined his subject matter as truly global." See the editor's introduction in Montesquieu, *Selected Political Writings*, ed. Melvin Richter (Indianapolis: Hackett, 1990), 16.

[67] Robert Wokler, "Isaiah Berlin's Enlightenment and Counter-Enlightenment," in *Isaiah Berlin's Counter-Enlightenment*, ed. Joseph Mali and Robert Wokler (Philadelphia: American Philosophical Society, 2003), 19.

[68] Isaiah Berlin goes so far as to claim that "Montesquieu abhors the concept of man in general, no less than do later thinkers like Burke and Herder, or the cultural anthropologists of our own time." Isaiah Berlin, "Montesquieu," in *Against the Current: Essays in the History of Ideas*, ed. Henry Hardy (New York: Viking, [1955] 1980), 139.

Morality in Context

of *The Spirit of the Laws* he speaks of "man, that flexible being who adapts himself in society to the thoughts and impressions of others" (SL, xliv–xlv). Similarly, in his *Pensées* he proclaims that "nature acts at all times; but it is greatly outweighed by mores" (Pensées #1296, 356) and that "certain circumstances that do not at first seem weighty have such an influence on [people] and act so forcefully and persistently that they can impart a certain cast of mind to human nature itself" (Pensées #1622, 470). Even where Montesquieu seems to point to a specific trait that is consistent across all ages and cultures, he generally goes on to cast doubt on its actual universality: immediately after claiming that feelings of horror toward incest "are so strong and so natural that they have acted almost everywhere on earth, independent of any communication," he notes that these "natural" feelings have often been overridden by local customs and religious beliefs (SL 26.14, 508). In fact, this belief in a common yet flexible human nature is, as Sharon Krause points out, implicit in Montesquieu's comparative method itself:

> If eighteenth-century Frenchmen were altogether different from ancient Spartans or modern Persians, then all Montesquieu's ruminations on the civilizations of past and distant peoples would be worthless to us. In order for his readers to learn from his examples there must be some continuities. At the same time, if human nature were always and everywhere the same, then there would be no need for Montesquieu's comparative method. It is the variations in human nature that make a comparative approach to the study of politics necessary, and it is the consistencies that make such an approach possible.[69]

In short, Montesquieu too sees human beings as structurally alike in all ages and cultures but not also *substantively* alike.

As noted previously, Montesquieu devotes far less explicit attention to the nature and basis of morality than do Hume and Smith. In fact, he himself notes that in *The Spirit of the Laws* he focuses mostly on politics and says much less about morality per se (see SL, xli; 3.5, 25n; 19.11, 314). However, he refers far *more* often than his Scottish counterparts to the time-honored concept of natural law. This concept is, of course, a notoriously slippery one. Roughly speaking, in the ancient and medieval worlds natural law was generally understood as a universal, transcendent standard of justice that is discoverable a priori through what was often referred to as "right reason," while in the seventeenth and eighteenth centuries this concept began to shift from the transcendent plane to the

---

[69] Sharon R. Krause, "History and the Human Soul in Montesquieu" *History of Political Thought* 24.2 (summer 2003), 251.

62   *The Pragmatic Enlightenment*

human one and from an a priori basis to an empirical one.[70] Montesquieu
not only continued this shift toward understanding natural law in human
and empirical terms but also added another shift of his own, describing it
in terms of the sentiments rather than reason.

The second chapter of book 1 of *The Spirit of the Laws* is dedicated to
the subject of the "laws of nature" (*lois de la nature*), which Montesquieu
says are "so named because they derive uniquely from the constitution
of our being" (SL 1.2, 6).[71] Whereas most of his predecessors defined
natural laws as laws of reason,[72] Montesquieu describes them instead in
terms of people's natural inclinations or sentiments – specifically, their
desire for self-preservation (and hence peace), nourishment, sex or companionship, and society with others (see SL 1.2, 6–7). Although he does
not make the point explicitly, Montesquieu seems to believe that these
kinds of desires or sentiments form the ultimate basis of morality.[73] Some
commentators assume that since Montesquieu's natural laws consist of
desires, they must be purely descriptive rather than normative, concerned
with what people *do* (or are inclined to do) rather than with what they
are *obliged* to do.[74] As Krause has shown, however, Montesquieu understands these natural laws to embody both the ends that are most important *to* human beings (psychologically) and those that are most important

---

[70] For helpful overviews of this shift, see Haakonssen, *Natural Law and Moral Philosophy*,
chapter 1; and Richard Tuck, "The 'Modern' Theory of Natural Law," in *The Languages
of Political Theory in Early-Modern Europe*, ed. Anthony Pagden (Cambridge: Cambridge
University Press, 1987).

[71] Montesquieu also speaks of certain "natural laws" (*lois naturelles*) in the famously enig-
matic first chapter of book 1, but it is fairly clear that here he is referring to physical
rather than moral laws, as he attributes them to animals and plants but not to human
beings (see SL 1.1, 5).

[72] For some prominent examples, see Hugo Grotius, *The Rights of War and Peace*, ed.
Richard Tuck (Indianapolis: Liberty Fund, [1625] 2005), I.1.10, 150–1; Thomas Hobbes,
Leviathan, ed. Edwin Curley (Indianapolis: Hackett, [1651] 1994), I.14.3, 79; Samuel
Pufendorf, *The Whole Duty of Man, According to the Law of Nature*, ed. Ian Hunter and
David Saunders (Indianapolis: Liberty Fund, [1673] 2003), I.2.16, 52; and Locke, *Two
Treatises of Government*, II.2.6, 271.

[73] Montesquieu regularly speaks of morality in terms of the sentiments. See, for instance,
his claim that in their hearts people "love morality," and that this fact becomes "remarkably clear in the theaters: one is sure to please people by the sentiments that morality
professes, and one is sure to offend them by those that it disapproves" (SL 25.2, 481). See
also the introduction to the story of the Troglodytes in *The Persian Letters*, where Usbek
states: "There are certain truths of which one must not only be persuaded but must feel;
such are the truths of morality" (PL #11, 22).

[74] For two prominent examples, see Melvin Richter, *The Political Theory of Montesquieu*
(Cambridge: Cambridge University Press, 1977), 67; and Robert Shackleton, *Montesquieu:
A Critical Biography* (Oxford: Oxford University Press, 1961), 251–61.

Morality in Context

for them (normatively): for Montesquieu, "natural laws have normative significance because they embody the most important human ends rather than simply describing human psychology.... There is an original coincidence of facts and norms here, in view of which Montesquieu's account of natural laws brings together normative standards and the psychological springs of action without compromising the distinctive force of either one."[75]

In the remainder of the book, Montesquieu frequently derives moral judgments and standards from people's desires or sentiments. For instance, in book 26 he claims that civil laws that violate the desire to preserve the self and family – or what he there calls "natural defense" – are "contrary to natural law" (SL 26.3–4, 496–7).[76] Likewise, in arguing against those who continue to maintain that "it would be good if there were slaves among us," he proposes that the matter should be viewed from the standpoint of something like a Rawlsian veil of ignorance: "I do not believe," he writes, "that any one ... would want to draw lots to know who was to form the part of the nation that would be free and the one that would be enslaved" (SL 15.9, 253). The way to determine whether or not slavery is morally legitimate, he concludes, is to "examine the desires [*désirs*] of all" (SL 15.9, 253). Similar statements can be found throughout the book; as Krause notes, "Montesquieu's preferred method of making moral and political judgments consists in looking to the desires of human beings as feeling creatures.... The normative judgments one finds in *The Spirit of the Laws* demonstrate above all respect for the natural human desires for security, society, and knowledge."[77] None of this is to suggest that Montesquieu considers morality to be simply a matter of individual feeling or desire. Rather, he seems to hold, with Hume and Smith, that morality is socially rather than individually determined, and thus that an individual's sentiments must be properly generalized to qualify as *moral* sentiments. In one of his *Pensées* he proposes a standard that is reminiscent of Hume's general point of view and Smith's impartial spectator: "We can gauge what our fellow citizens should demand of us by that which we ourselves demand of those with whom we want to live in any kind of close liaison – and which we derive, for this purpose, from the

---

[75] Sharon R. Krause, "Laws, Passion, and the Attractions of Right Action in Montesquieu" *Philosophy and Social Criticism* 32.2 (March 2006), 218.

[76] We will return to this passage in Chapter 2, when considering whether this represents an instance of political universalism in Montesquieu's thought. For now, the important point is that he takes these basic feelings or desires to carry normative weight.

[77] Ibid., 220.

64 *The Pragmatic Enlightenment*

bosom of society as a whole" (Pensées #1270, 348).[78] Hence, reason or critical reflection plays an important role in *ascertaining* what is right and wrong, even if it is the sentiments that ultimately determine the content; as Montesquieu indicates in the preceding quotation, we must *examine* the desires of *all* to determine what is morally right.

Montesquieu is not generally regarded as a moral sentimentalist,[79] but this reading helps to explain an aspect of his thought that Montesquieu's contemporaries and modern scholars alike have found endlessly puzzling, namely, his frequent blending of empirical and normative concerns.[80] Nearly every examination of *The Spirit of the Laws* notes Montesquieu's apparent ambiguity on this point, not only in the discussion of natural law but throughout the book. In fact, the ambiguity is present in the very definition of "law" that opens the first chapter: rather than defining laws as rules or commands, as earlier philosophers and jurists had done, Montesquieu describes them as "the necessary *relations* [*rapports*] deriving from the nature of things" (SL 1.1, 3, emphasis added). Further, as Judith Shklar notes, throughout the work Montesquieu uses "the word *devoir* ... to mean 'must' (as a natural necessity), 'should' (in order to bring about some end), and 'ought' (because it is right). Even the subtitle to his final edition is ambiguous: 'The relation that the laws *doivent* (must, should, ought to?) have with the constitution of every government, with mores, the climate, religion, commerce, etc.'"[81] While there has long been confusion on this point, if Montesquieu was in fact a moral sentimentalist, as Krause and I have argued, then the puzzle disappears: if morality (an "ought") is ultimately derived from people's sentiments (an

---

[78] This entry also calls to mind Hume's emphasis on the useful and the agreeable: Montesquieu writes that "it is just in general for men to have consideration for each other – not only in the things that can make society more useful to them, but also in the things that can make it more agreeable" (Pensées #1270, 348).

[79] Krause is a clear exception here. In fact, Hume himself seems to have interpreted Montesquieu as a moral rationalist: see EPM 3.34, 22.

[80] For the reaction of some of Montesquieu's contemporaries on this point, see Shackleton, *Montesquieu*, 244–5. There have been a few attempts to recruit Montesquieu into the ranks of sociology by claiming that his work is purely empirical or descriptive – see, for example, Auguste Comte, *Cours de philosophie positive*, vol. 4 (Paris: Bechelier, 1852), 243–64; and Emile Durkheim, *Montesquieu and Rousseau: Forerunners of Sociology*, trans. Ralph Manheim (Ann Arbor: University of Michigan Press, 1960), 1–64 – but there is now a near-consensus among Montesquieu scholars that this reading is ultimately inadequate, and that he addressed normative concerns as well.

[81] Judith N. Shklar, *Montesquieu* (Oxford: Oxford University Press, 1987), 69. See also Stuart D. Warner, "Montesquieu's Prelude: An Interpretation of Book I of *The Spirit of the Laws*," in *Enlightening Revolutions: Essays in Honor of Ralph Lerner*, ed. Svetozar Minkov (Lanham, MD: Lexington, 2006), 181–2.

Morality in Context 65

"is"), then a discussion of moral issues *must* combine empirical and normative modes of inquiry. Rather than positing a sharp and unbridgeable divide between "is" and "ought" – either for the sake of the "ought" (as Kant would later do) or for the sake of the "is" (as many nineteenth-century positivists and contemporary social scientists would later do) – Montesquieu joins Hume and Smith in holding that the two are deeply interdependent.

Given that Montesquieu believes both that morality is ultimately derived from the sentiments and that human nature is highly flexible, it should come as no surprise that he too holds that morality can and does vary according to context.[82] Throughout *The Spirit of the Laws*, he treats each type of regime as providing a different framework for moral as well as political life. Each regime has its own "principle" or motivating force – honor for monarchies, virtue for republics, and fear for despotisms – which means that each regime necessarily has its own moral standards. For instance, luxury is generally beneficial (and so morally acceptable) in monarchies since it encourages commerce and hence prosperity, but it is harmful (and so morally objectionable) in democratic republics since it detracts from public-spiritedness (see SL 7.2–4, 98–100). Elsewhere, Montesquieu states explicitly that "the terms beautiful, good, noble, great, perfect are attributes of objects that are relative to the beings who consider them. It is essential to put this principle in one's head: it is a sponge for handling most prejudices" (Pensées #410, 155; see also #764, 226–7; #799, 234; #911, 261).[83]

As the term "prejudices" alerts us, however, Montesquieu is not simply a moral relativist, as is sometimes claimed. Many scholars – particularly those who would turn Montesquieu into a kind of sociologist

---

[82] Scholars often cite Montesquieu as claiming, "I think that justice is eternal and independent of human conventions. Were it dependent on them, this would be such a terrible truth that we would have to hide it from ourselves" (PL #83, 140). But this statement appears in a letter by the character Usbek rather than in Montesquieu's own name, and the context suggests that Montesquieu may have meant it ironically – a proclamation of eternal justice put in the mouth of a despotic ruler of a harem. Here I agree with Michael Mosher, who claims that "if anything, the figure of Usbek is a better satire on the foibles of the cruel universalizing philosopher than anything contemporary postmodernists have written." Michael A. Mosher, "The Judgmental Gaze of European Women: Gender, Sexuality, and the Critique of Republican Rule" *Political Theory* 22.1 (February 1994), 35.

[83] Montesquieu makes a similar point in the last work he ever published, the essay "Taste" for the *Encyclopédie*. See Charles de Secondat, baron de Montesquieu, *Essai sur le goût*, in *Oeuvres complètes*, ed. Roger Caillois, vol. 2 (Paris: Gallimard, [1757] 1951), 1240, as well as the note on 1556.

who deals with descriptive but not normative concerns – have taken at face value his claim, in the preface of *The Spirit of the Laws*, that "I do not write to censure that which is established in any country whatsoever" (SL, xliv). While this statement does indeed reveal something of Montesquieu's moderate and moderating spirit, it should not be read as a complete disavowal of all moral judgment. After all, on the same page he goes on to announce his aspiration to help people "cure themselves of their prejudices" (SL, xliv). No reader could come away from the book unsure about whether Montesquieu approves of slavery, religious persecution, and harsh criminals laws; as Vickie Sullivan stresses, one of Montesquieu's key aims is to identify and root out the kinds of prejudices that lead to such practices.[84] Still, it is not immediately clear whether – or on what basis – Montesquieu would deem even these practices as *universally* wrong, especially given that each of them has been widely practiced and accepted throughout much of human history.

While some scholars contend that Montesquieu conceived of the laws of nature as substantive and universally applicable commands that would rule out much of the cultural and historical diversity that he catalogs as unjust or illegitimate,[85] I would side with those who maintain that his account is instead meant "to combat the universalism or doctrinairism of previous natural law teachings"[86] and that he in fact "resisted the idea of a single, universal standard of right derived directly from nature."[87] This is because, in addition to being human rather than transcendent, empirical rather than a priori, and sentimental rather than rational, Montesquieu's natural laws are fairly minimal and indeterminate: as

---

[84] See Vickie B. Sullivan, "Montesquieu's Philosophical Assault on Despotic Ideas in *The Spirit of the Laws*" (unpublished manuscript), chapter 1. I would like to thank Sullivan for sharing this work with me prior to publication.

[85] See, for example, C. P. Courtney, "Montesquieu and Natural Law," in *Montesquieu's Science of Politics: Essays on The Spirit of Laws*, ed. David W. Carrithers, Michael A. Mosher, and Paul A. Rahe (Lanham, MD: Rowman & Littlefield, 2001); and Mark H. Waddicor, *Montesquieu and the Philosophy of Natural Law* (The Hague: Martinus Nijhoff, 1970). Other scholars claim that Montesquieu was simply confused as to the status of the laws of nature. Melvin Richter, for instance, claims that Montesquieu's "relativism" about regimes and laws sat uneasily with his "untroubled certainty about the existence and applicability of a universal law of nature valid everywhere ... such simultaneous relativism and universalism created a tension that Montesquieu was never to resolve." Richter, *The Political Theory of Montesquieu*, 32.

[86] Thomas L. Pangle, *Montesquieu's Philosophy of Liberalism: A Commentary on The Spirit of the Laws* (Chicago: University of Chicago Press, 1973), 259; see also 43.

[87] Sharon R. Krause, *Liberalism with Honor* (Cambridge, MA: Harvard University Press, 2002), 210; see also 53.

Morality in Context

Stuart Warner writes, "the laws of nature set down by Montesquieu ... are not the substantive moral laws typically associated with natural law theory."[88] While Montesquieu holds that we should, as much as possible, recognize and respect people's elemental desires – their desire for security, nourishment, companionship, and the like – he also acknowledges that these desires will take different forms, that respecting them will require different arrangements, and that it will be *possible* to respect them to different degrees in societies with different institutions, customs, mores, climates, and so on. In short, the laws of nature must, like positive laws, be mediated by the particular circumstances of a given society.[89]

Let us take, as a test case, the one that lends the most support to a universalist reading: the issue of slavery. Throughout his corpus, Montesquieu denounces slavery in the most trenchant and excoriating terms imaginable; as Melvin Richter writes, he "spoke out against slavery as no previous political philosopher had done."[90] Some of his statements on this issue seem to be unambiguously universal. For instance, he says that slavery "is not good by its nature" (SL 15.1, 246), that it is "opposed ... to natural right" (SL 15.2, 248), and that "as all men are born equal, one must say that slavery is against nature" (SL 15.7, 252). While such statements are often presented on their own, divorced from their context, it is important to note that they are found in the middle of an extremely complex, almost dialectical set of chapters.[91] Montesquieu begins book 15 of *The Spirit of the Laws* with a series of chapters designed to refute

---

[88] Warner, "Montesquieu's Prelude," 175.

[89] In the first chapter of the book – the one that immediately precedes the discussion of the laws of nature – Montesquieu asserts (rather cryptically) that "to say that there is nothing just or unjust but what positive laws ordain or prohibit is to say that before a circle was drawn, all its radii were not equal" (SL 1.1, 4). To say that there is *something* just or unjust other than what positive laws ordain or prohibit, however, is not necessarily to say that there is a substantive and universally applicable standard of justice; Montesquieu's indeterminate laws of nature, whose application varies according to context, would certainly meet this criterion. Also telling is his first example of the "relations of fairness" that precede positive laws: "assuming that there were societies of men, it would be just to conform to their laws" (SL 1.1, 4). As Werner Stark notes, "our philosopher teaches no more here than an absolute duty to obey relative enactments." Werner Stark, *Montesquieu, Pioneer of the Sociology of Knowledge* (Toronto: University of Toronto Press, 1961), 206.

[90] Richter, *The Political Theory of Montesquieu*, 59. Montesquieu's thought did much to encourage the antislavery movement in France and Britain; see Thomas L. Pangle, *The Theological Basis of Liberal Modernity in Montesquieu's Spirit of the Laws* (Chicago: University of Chicago Press, 2010), 174, n. 29, and the works cited there.

[91] For a careful reading of these chapters, see Diana J. Schaub, "Montesquieu on Slavery" *Perspectives on Political Science* 34.2 (spring 2005): 72–7.

68   *The Pragmatic Enlightenment*

the traditional justifications for slavery, such as those based on the right of
the conqueror or on cultural, religious, or racial prejudice (see SL 15.2–5,
247–50). However, he then devotes chapters 6 through 8 to investigating
what he calls "the true origin of the right of slavery," one that would be
"founded on the nature of things" (SL 15.6, 251). He begins, in chapter 6, by noting that in despotic governments individuals frequently seek
to sell themselves (since the government has taken away most of their liberty anyway) and says that "here lies the just origin, the one conforming
to reason" of a kind of slavery – but only a very "gentle" kind, since it
is founded on the free choice of a master, which ensures a degree of reci-
procity (SL 15.6, 251).

Next, in chapter 7, Montesquieu considers whether there is a similarly
"just" or "true" origin of the *cruel* kind of slavery that he himself so forcefully condemns. He observes that in some nations the heat enervates people's bodies and spirit to the point that fear of punishment is the only way
to induce them to work hard, and says that for that reason slavery "runs
less counter to reason" in such nations (SL 15.7, 251). In the subsequent
discussion, he appears to waver about whether this provides a sanction
or justification of the institution. For instance, he says in almost the same
breath that slavery is "against nature" and that "in certain countries it
may be founded on a natural reason" (SL 15.7, 252). Then, in chapter 8,
he says both that "natural slavery must be limited to certain particular
countries of the world" and that "*perhaps* there is no climate on earth
where one could not engage freemen to work" – but even here he admits,
"I do not know if my mind [*esprit*] or my heart dictates this point" (SL
15.8, 252–3, emphasis added).[92] After this rather inconclusive discussion,
he spends most of the rest of book 15 discussing not how slavery might
be universally abolished, but rather how its dangers and abuses might be
mitigated. At one point during this discussion, he says that in despotic
states "it is almost indifferent whether few or many people ... live in
slavery" since "political slavery ... makes civil slavery little felt," while
"in moderate states, it is very important not to have *too many* slaves" (SL
15.13, 256, emphasis added). Despite his abhorrence of slavery and his

---

[92] A similar ambivalence can be found in book 6, chapter 17, where Montesquieu begins
to suggest that the practice of torture "might be suitable for despotic government, where
everything inspiring fear enters more into the springs of government," but then stops
himself, proclaiming that "I hear the voice of nature crying out against me" (SL 6.17,
93). Rather than simply asserting that torture is against nature and therefore universally
unjust, Montesquieu reveals to the reader how his "head" and "heart" pull in opposite
directions on this question.

Morality in Context 69

insistence that it is immoral in modern Europe, then, Montesquieu goes out of his way to refrain from positing a standard of justice that would unequivocally condemn it under all circumstances.[93] As Thomas Pangle writes, while Montesquieu believes that "slavery is bad or unhealthy for human nature," this "does not prove that it is always to be avoided. In some times and places human nature is in so miserable a state that a man has a better chance for life and minimal comfort as a slave than as a free man."[94]

In short, the available evidence suggests that Montesquieu, like Hume and Smith, holds both that morality ultimately springs from people's sentiments or desires and that the content of morality will be different in different circumstances. We should, so far as possible, respect people's elemental desires – Montesquieu's empirical *and* normative natural laws – but what this entails or requires will vary according to context: the laws of nature, no less than positive laws, must be mediated by the institutions, customs, mores, and other characteristics of a society. In other words, while Montesquieu does adopt a kind of natural standard of right, that standard is flexible indeed, to the point where even slavery cannot be judged universally wrong. Far from adopting a "hegemonic" moral universalism, then, Montesquieu makes allowances for context to an extent that would make many contemporary liberals more than a little uneasy, our extreme wariness of anything that smacks of "hegemony" notwithstanding.

CULTURE AND CIRCUMSTANCE IN VOLTAIRE'S *TREATISE ON METAPHYSICS*

Montesquieu is sometimes thought to have been an exception among the philosophes in his keen appreciation of historical and cultural diversity, but in fact such appreciation was rather more the rule than the exception.[95] Voltaire, for one, frequently emphasizes the immense variety

[93] Montesquieu's argument against slavery in modern Europe (quoted previously) was that no one would want to draw lots to see who would be enslaved and who would be free, and hence that "the desires of all" would rule against the institution. The title of this chapter makes clear, however, that he is making this argument in reference to "nations among whom civil liberty is generally established" (SL 15.9, 253). In other words, this argument may not be universally applicable, even if it does apply to modern Europe.

[94] Pangle, *Montesquieu's Philosophy of Liberalism*, 171; see also 170–2 more generally, as well as Thomas L. Pangle, "The Liberal Critique of Rights in Montesquieu and Hume" *Tocqueville Review* 13.2 (1992), 40; and Shklar, *Montesquieu*, 96–7.

[95] Henry Vyverberg provides a useful overview of the philosophes' views on this score and concludes that "the French Enlightenment did indeed repeatedly note the differences in human beings around the globe and across the centuries." Henry Vyverberg, *Human*

70   *The Pragmatic Enlightenment*

of customs and beliefs that have prevailed in different ages and different lands, particularly in his historical works such as the *Essay on the Mores and Spirit of Nations*.[96] This lengthy tome, which spans the entire globe and all of recorded history, was written in part as an attack on the then-authoritative *Discourse on Universal History* of Jacques-Bénigne Bossuet (1681), which Voltaire ranks among the "pretended universal histories" that in fact "forget three-quarters of the earth" (EM I.intro.15, 55).[97] At the end of the *Essay*, he summarizes the many divergences he had cataloged between the East and West throughout the book, writing that "everything is different between them and us: religion, policy, government, mores, food, clothing, and the manner of writing, expressing, and thinking. The way in which we bear the greatest resemblance to them is in our propensity to war, murder, and destruction" – although even here he notes that "this furor is much less a part of the character of the people of India or China than of ours" (EM II.197, 808). Similarly, in his *Philosophical Dictionary* he asserts that "ancient oriental customs are so prodigiously different from ours that nothing can appear extraordinary to anyone who has some reading" (PD, 149).

As might be expected, given his alertness to historical and cultural diversity, Voltaire too regards human nature as quite flexible. Like Hume, Smith, and Montesquieu, he posits that there are a few basic passions that all people share: "When nature formed our species," he writes, "she

---

    Nature, Cultural Diversity, and the French Enlightenment (Oxford: Oxford University Press, 1989), 55.

[96] The title of the *Essai sur les moeurs et l'esprit des nations* is usually translated as the *Essay on the Manners and Spirit of Nations* or simply as the *Essay on Customs*, but I have rendered it this way throughout since the term in question is *moeurs*, not *manières* or *coutumes*. For studies of this *Essay* and Voltaire's many other historical works, see J. H. Brumfitt, *Voltaire: Historian* (Oxford: Oxford University Press, 1958); Karen O'Brien, *Narratives of Enlightenment: Cosmopolitan History from Voltaire to Gibbon* (Cambridge: Cambridge University Press, 1997), chapter 2; and J. G. A. Pocock, *Barbarism and Religion*, vol. 2: *Narratives of Civil Government* (Cambridge: Cambridge University Press, 1999), 72–159.

[97] Whereas most of his predecessors devoted virtually all of their attention to Europe, Voltaire begins his work with a series of chapters on ancient China and India, which he takes to be the first nations to have become civilized, and on the flourishing Islamic civilization of the medieval world. Only *then* does he turn to Europe. He also includes separate chapters (in some cases several chapters) on the more recent history of Turkey, Persia, Russia, India, Tartary, China, Japan, Ethiopia/Abyssinia, the Barbary Coast, Morocco, the discovery and exploration of the Americas, and the Inca civilization in Peru. J. H. Brumfitt claims that it was Voltaire "who, more than any other individual, [brought] about the Copernican revolution in historiography, displacing the Christian European from his comfortable seat at the centre of the universe." Brumfitt, *Voltaire*, 165.

Morality in Context 71

gave us a few instincts: self-love for our preservation, benevolence for the preservation of others, the love which is common to all species, and the inexplicable gift of being able to combine more ideas than all animals put together. After thus giving us our portion she said to us: 'Do what you can'" (PD, 287–8). As the latter part of this statement intimates, however, Voltaire also holds that these passions can be modified and channeled in substantially different ways in different circumstances. Hence, he proclaims that "every man is formed by his age" (EM I.82, 774) and that "men's inclinations and natures differ as much as their climates and their governments."[98] Scholars seeking to prove that Voltaire saw human nature as substantially alike in all times and places frequently cite the conclusion of the *Essay on the Mores and Spirit of Nations*, where he proclaims that "everything closely connected to human nature looks the same from one end of the universe to the other"; less frequently quoted is the statement that immediately follows, declaring that "the empire of custom is much vaster than that of nature; it extends over all mores, over all usages; it spreads variety over the face of the universe ... the soil is everywhere the same, but culture produces diverse fruits" (EM II.197, 810). Similarly, in his *Philosophical Dictionary* Voltaire counsels that "we must get rid of all our prejudices when we read ancient authors and travel in distant nations. Nature is the same everywhere and customs are everywhere different" (PD, 199–200).

If Voltaire resembles Montesquieu in his awareness of historical and cultural diversity and his belief in the flexibility of human nature, he also resembles him in his lack of a comprehensive moral theory. Among the most persistent themes of Voltaire's writings are his mocking and undermining of metaphysical "certainties" and abstract system building; thus, he is generally much more concerned to show that revealed religion and a priori reason are *not* the ultimate bases of morality than to examine what the actual basis is. However, he too frequently uses the language of the moral sentiments, such as when he proclaims that "we all have two sentiments which form the foundation of society: sympathy [*commisération*] and justice" (EM I.intro.7, 27).[99] Much as a child senses that he will be able to jump over a ditch more easily if he gets a running start, even

---

[98] Voltaire, "Man," in *Questions on the Encyclopedia*, in *Political Writings*, trans. David Williams (Cambridge: Cambridge University Press, [1771] 1994), 67.

[99] Voltaire also concurs with Hume, Smith, and Montesquieu that "the passions are the wheels that drive" human beings (TM, 92) and that "instinct, more than reason, conducts human life." Voltaire, *Notebooks*, vol. 2, ed. Theodore Besterman, in *The Complete Works of Voltaire*, vol. 82 (Geneva: Institut et Musée Voltaire, 1968), 489.

72   *The Pragmatic Enlightenment*

if he does not know that force equals mass times acceleration, Voltaire maintains, similarly we all have a basic sense of right and wrong that "precedes all reflection" (EM I.intro.7, 27).[100] Elsewhere, he declares that we all have a "crude [*grossière*] notion of justice and injustice" that is "independent of all law, of all compact, of all religion."[101] Given how rudimentary this instinctive sense of morality is, however, he also sees critical reflection as having an important role to play: we need reason, he says, "to discern the shades of goodness and badness. Good and bad are often neighbors; our passions fail to distinguish between them. Who will enlighten us? We ourselves, when we are calm" (PD, 272–3).

While Voltaire harbored a lifelong aversion to the rationalist natural law tradition associated with Grotius and Pufendorf, he does periodically employ the language of natural law.[102] In his most explicit definition of the concept, he writes: "I call *natural laws* those laws that nature points to in all ages to all men for the maintenance of that sense of justice which nature, whatever one might say, has engraved in our hearts."[103] This use of the concept bears a certain resemblance to Montesquieu's, insofar as they both link natural laws to the sentiments, but whereas Montesquieu identifies natural laws as *themselves* sentiments – which he treats both empirically and normatively – Voltaire more often conceives of them as rules or norms that are developed to *support* and *protect* people's basic needs and desires, such as prohibitions on murder, violence, theft, and the

---

[100] Voltaire frequently suggests not only that our moral sentiments precede all reflection but also that they have been instilled in us by God himself. In keeping with his empiricist outlook, however, he still insists that these sentiments are acquired and developed through experience: "nothing is what is called innate, that is, born developed," he writes, "but ... God caused us to be born with organs which, as they grow, make us feel all that our species must feel in order to preserve this species" (PD, 272).

[101] Voltaire, *The Ignorant Philosopher*, in *Voltaire: Selections*, ed. Paul Edwards (New York: Macmillan [1766] 1989), 172–3. Hence, Voltaire responds to Hobbes's argument that all justice arises from contracts and positive laws by way of an appeal to moral intuition: "If you [Hobbes] found yourself alone with Cromwell on a desert island, and Cromwell killed you for having been a supporter of your king in England, would not such an offense have seemed as unjust on your new island as in England?" Ibid., 180. On Voltaire's ambivalent relationship to Hobbes more generally, see Leland Thielemann, "Voltaire and Hobbism" *Studies on Voltaire and the Eighteenth Century* 10 (1959): 237–58.

[102] See Merle L. Perkins, "Voltaire's Principles of Political Thought" *Modern Language Quarterly* 17.4 (December 1956), 290–1; Merle L. Perkins, *Voltaire's Concept of International Order* (Geneva: Institut et Musée Voltaire, 1965), 81–3; and Peter Gay, *Voltaire's Politics: The Poet as Realist* (New Haven, CT: Yale University Press [1959] 1988), 345–6.

[103] Voltaire, "Commentary on the Book *On Crimes and Punishments*," in *Political Writings*, trans. David Williams (Cambridge: Cambridge University Press, [1766] 1994), 263.

Morality in Context 73

like. In his poem on the topic, Voltaire suggests that the laws of nature are ultimately derived from – or perhaps just another name for – the conscience that God has instilled in all human beings.[104] However, in the entry "Conscience" in his *Questions on the Encyclopedia*, he casts doubt on both the divine origins and the innateness of the conscience, concluding that in fact we have no other conscience except "that which is inspired by the times, by example, by our temperament, by our reflections. Man is not born with any principle, but with the faculty of receiving them all."[105] Thus, just as Montesquieu holds that natural law must be mediated by a society's particular circumstances, Voltaire indicates here that the directives of the conscience depend in large part on an individual's particular makeup and on the context in which he finds himself.

On the other hand, Voltaire suggests elsewhere that even though there is no innate moral sense, people have ultimately developed the same moral norms in all times and places, such that cultures as disparate as the Greeks, Romans, Confucians, Hindus, Jews, and Christians have all shared the same notions of right and wrong. In the entry "Morality" in his *Philosophical Dictionary*, for instance, he writes:

> There is but one morality … just as there is but one geometry. But, I shall be told, most men know nothing of geometry. Yes, but as soon as it is studied a little everyone agrees. Farmers, artisans, artists have not taken a course in morality. They have read neither Cicero's *De finibus* nor Aristotle's *Ethics*, but as soon as they reflect they are unwittingly Cicero's disciples. The Indian dyer, the Tartar shepherd, and the English sailor know justice and injustice. Confucius did not invent a system of morality as one constructs a system in natural philosophy. He found it in the hearts of all men. (PD, 322)

Similarly, in the entry "On Right and Wrong," he asserts that all people everywhere "feel equally that it is better to give your extra bread, rice, and manioc to the poor person who humbly asks you for it, than to kill him or put out his two eyes. It is obvious to the whole world that a service is better than an injury, that gentleness is preferable to acting out of

---

[104] See Voltaire, *Poème sur la loi naturelle*, in *Mélanges de Voltaire*, ed. Jacques Van Den Heuvel (Paris: Gallimard, [1756] 1961). Patrick Henry suggests that Voltaire "adopts the Rousseauistic position that God is found in our hearts" in this work, even though he does not really hold it himself, "in order to undo the atheistic influence of La Mettrie on Frédéric" – that is, Frederick II, to whom Voltaire sent an early version of the poem. Patrick Henry, "Voltaire as Moralist" *Journal of the History of Ideas* 38.1 (January–March 1977), 144.

[105] Voltaire, "Conscience," in *Questions sur l'Encyclopédie*, vol. 4, ed. Nicholas Cronk and Christiane Mervaud, in *The Complete Works of Voltaire*, vol. 40 (Oxford: Voltaire Foundation, [1771] 2009), 191.

74   *The Pragmatic Enlightenment*

anger" (PD, 272).[106] Given passages like these, it is understandable why Voltaire is often thought to have been a determined moral universalist. Strikingly, however, the argument of these passages is not that there are universally valid moral norms, whether or not all individuals and cultures acknowledge them or obey them, but rather that as a matter of empirical fact all individuals and cultures *do* share the same moral norms – those on which "everyone agrees," that are "found in the hearts of all men," that all people "feel equally," that are "obvious to the whole world." Yet, as we have seen, in other works Voltaire evinces an awareness of deep moral diversity in different times and places. In fact, he allows that "what is called virtue in one climate may be precisely what is called vice in another" and that "the majority of rules on good and evil vary as much as languages and clothes" (TM, 93).

It is possible that Voltaire simply changed his mind on this question repeatedly throughout his life, and on occasion multiple times within a single work. It seems more likely, however, that his claims regarding a universal moral consensus were less genuine empirical conclusions than thinly veiled attempts to promote peace and toleration; if the differences among cultures and religions are illusory or superficial, after all, then it is absurd to fight over them. In both of the *Philosophical Dictionary* entries cited earlier, this intention is made explicit. In "On Right and Wrong," Voltaire draws on the supposed universal agreement on what morality entails to ask, "Of what use to virtue are theological distinctions, dogmas based on these distinctions, persecutions based on these dogmas?" (PD, 273). In "Morality," a response to a Christian "harangue" about the immorality of the pagans, he reiterates that "there is no morality in superstition, it is not in ceremonies, it has nothing in common with dogmas" (PD, 322).[107] In fact, in a letter to Frederick II in which he discusses an early version of his poem on natural law, Voltaire admits that "the true goal of this work is tolerance" and that the idea of a universal, God-given conscience was only "the pretext."[108] As Norman Torrey writes in a closely related context, "Voltaire may have been naive in some respects,"

---

[106] See also Voltaire, *The A B C, or Dialogues between A B C*, in *Political Writings*, trans. David Williams (Cambridge: Cambridge University Press, [1768] 1994), 115–16.

[107] In the *Treatise on Tolerance* too Voltaire derives a call for tolerance from a moral law that nature discloses to "all men"; see Voltaire, *Treatise on Tolerance*, in *Treatise on Tolerance and Other Writings*, ed. Simon Harvey and trans. Brian Masters (Cambridge: Cambridge University Press, [1763] 2000), 28.

[108] Voltaire, letter to Frederick II, king of Prussia, 25 August 1752, in *The Complete Works of Voltaire*, ed. Theodore Besterman, vol. 97 (Geneva: Institut et Musée Voltaire, 1971), 166.

Morality in Context

but "in the interests of human happiness and the betterment of society, he was willing to appear much more naive than he truly was."[109]

Given the inconsistencies – or at least apparent inconsistencies – that pervade Voltaire's corpus on the question of moral universalism, it will be useful to turn to a more detailed examination of his most sustained discussion of the ultimate source of morality, which appears in the final chapter of his *Treatise on Metaphysics*, entitled "On Virtue and Vice."[110] He begins the chapter by noting that while laws and moral standards are necessary for any society to survive, the content of the laws and moral standards that one finds around the world varies greatly. Some cultures strongly disapprove of alcohol, adultery, premarital sex, polygamy, and disobedience to parents, for instance, while others condone any or all of these things (TM, 92–3). Voltaire goes on to explore what underpins all of these norms, or how it is that virtue and vice are determined, and he seems to offer two different answers. First, he posits a utilitarian standard: "Virtue and vice, moral good and evil, are in every country what is useful or harmful in that society" (TM, 93). A few sentences later, however, he proposes a sentimentalist standard that bases morality on feelings of approval: "Virtue is the habit of doing those things that please men, and vice is the habit of doing those things that displease them" (TM, 93). Obviously, these standards could easily be reconciled in a Humean fashion: if people generally approve of (or are pleased by) things that are useful, then the two standards will point in the same direction.[111]

---

[109] Norman L. Torrey, *The Spirit of Voltaire* (New York: Russell and Russell, [1938] 1968), 243–4.

[110] For brief but useful summaries of Voltaire's moral theory in the *Treatise*, see Rosemary Z. Lauer, *The Mind of Voltaire: A Study of His "Constructive Deism"* (Westminster, MD: Newman Press, 1961), 70–3; and Schneewind, *The Invention of Autonomy*, 459–60. Ira Wade shows that this chapter of the *Treatise* was heavily influenced by Voltaire's reading of Bernard Mandeville's *An Enquiry into the Origin of Moral Virtue*, noting that "both men regard virtue and vice as a social matter, both stress its relative character, both reject the idea of a religious, absolute, God-given code of conduct." Ira O. Wade, *Studies on Voltaire* (Princeton, NJ: Princeton University Press, 1947), 47; see also 43–8. See also the editor's introduction in Voltaire, *Traité de métaphysique*, ed. W. H. Barber, in *The Complete Works of Voltaire*, vol. 14 (Oxford: Voltaire Foundation, 1989), 378–81.

[111] While Hume is explicit that it is the approval, not the utility, of a quality or action that gives it a moral character, Voltaire does not clarify whether he regards utility or approval as more significant. However, we will see that most of the examples he offers in this chapter appeal to people's feelings or sentiments – whether they would be *covered in shame* if they did not lie to save their friend, whether they are *horrified* by incest, and so on – rather than to abstract calculations of usefulness. As with Hume and Smith, Voltaire's emphasis on usefulness in this passage should not be taken to imply that he was simply a utilitarian with respect to morality. As Mark Hulliung writes, "nothing

Importantly, *both* of these formulations suggest that virtue and vice consist in conforming to the widely divergent norms that one finds around the world, and thus to make morality deeply dependent on context – on what people find useful or harmful in their particular circumstances, or on what they find pleasing or displeasing in their particular circumstances.

At this point, however, Voltaire appears to reverse course, declaring that "it seems certain to me that there are natural laws which men are obliged to acknowledge throughout the universe, whatever they might say" (TM, 93). As we have seen, he generally conceives of natural laws as norms or principles that are developed to support and protect people's basic natural desires, rather than as transcendent commands or dictates of a priori reason, and this is plainly the case here as well. In explaining the character of these natural laws, Voltaire writes:

> It is true that God did not say to men: Look, here are laws which I am giving to you directly from my mouth, by which I want you to govern yourselves. But he has done for men what he has done for many other animals. He gave bees a powerful instinct which makes them work and feed together, and he gave man certain sentiments which he can never shake off and which are the permanent ties and first laws of society in which he foresaw that man would live. (TM, 93; see also 95)

While Voltaire insists that we can "never shake off" these sentiments and that we are obliged to acknowledge these natural laws "throughout the universe," it is notable that he goes on to identify exceptions and modifications to every one of the moral norms that he discusses. Our natural sense of benevolence should lead us to help others, he claims – "unless it conflicts with self-love, which must always prevail" (TM, 93). Lying is wrong, since it is impossible for society to survive among people who constantly deceive one another – although if it were necessary to lie in order to save a friend's life, "someone who told the truth on that occasion would be covered in shame" (TM, 94). Theft is "contrary to society and consequently ... unjust" – as long as there is a system of private property: "petty theft was held in honor in Sparta because all goods were held in

---

was more important to Bentham than that we should take our utilitarianism pure, simple, undiluted, without a trace of sentimentality or embarrassment; nothing was more important to the French philosophes than to avoid all-out utilitarianism, despite their constant and enthusiastic recourse to the notions of interest, self-love, and usefulness." Hence, he claims that throughout the French Enlightenment, "one finds utilitarian arguments everywhere, utilitarianism nowhere." Mark Hulliung, *The Autocritique of Enlightenment: Rousseau and the Philosophes* (Cambridge, MA: Harvard University Press, 1994), 9, 19.

Morality in Context 77

common" (TM, 94). Incest is horrifying – but "we would consider it a very good action" if it were necessary to keep the species alive (TM, 94). A murderer is a "monster" – "but a man who had no other means to save his country than by sacrificing [even] his brother would be an admirable man" (TM, 94). So important are specific circumstances and cultural context in determining right and wrong, in fact, that Voltaire allows that "we are forced to change, according to need, *all* the ideas we have formed for ourselves regarding justice and injustice" (TM, 94, emphasis added).[112]

There is no question that Voltaire regards the moral norms or "natural laws" that we develop to support and protect our basic desires as real and binding in the sense that we use them as guides in our own lives, cultivate them in our children, and sanction those who violate them, whether through physical punishment or social disapproval (see TM, 95–7).[113] It is also clear that he thinks there are a number of moral norms that should be followed in the vast majority of situations, such as the prohibitions on murder, violence, theft, and the like. Yet he makes it equally clear that in his view "moral good and evil … exist only in relation to us" and thus there is "no good which exists by itself, independent of man," any more than there is hot or cold, sweet or sour, good or bad smells independent of human sensations (TM, 94). As J. B. Schneewind succinctly expresses it, for Voltaire "it is our reaction that introduces morality into a world of fact."[114] And given that our reactions – what we find useful, what we find pleasing – can vary according to culture and circumstance, Voltaire ultimately accepts, at least in the *Treatise on Metaphysics*, that no moral norms are truly *universally* applicable.

[112] While most of Voltaire's examples highlight individual exceptions to moral norms, where breaking these norms is necessary for some greater good, such as saving a friend's life or one's country or repopulating a decimated society, he also suggests that cultural context can affect what is right and wrong, as in the case of petty theft in Sparta. Likewise, in the midst of these examples he notes that adultery and homosexuality are "allowed by many nations" and suggests that there are no valid grounds on which to find such norms objectionable since "society can well exist among adulterers or homosexuals" (TM, 94).

[113] As Gustave Lanson, the great early twentieth-century literary critic, writes, since Voltaire held that "there was no absolute good and evil, no innate moral ideas," he reasoned that "we must be content with human and social sanctions: fear of punishment and a respect for public opinion which holds the power of approval and disapproval. Let us also take into account that the well-bred person has a natural inclination for virtue, that is, that in the normal development of a healthy individual, social sentiments play a very strong role. And let us also count upon education to cultivate and fortify these feelings." Gustave Lanson, *Voltaire*, trans. Robert A. Wagoner (New York: John Wiley & Sons, [1906] 1966), 61–2.

[114] Schneewind, *The Invention of Autonomy*, 462.

78   *The Pragmatic Enlightenment*

Indeed, at one point he goes so far as to claim that "it hardly matters by which laws a state governs itself" as long as "once the laws are established, they are enforced" (TM, 93).

Voltaire never lays out a moral theory anywhere near as developed or nuanced as those of Hume and Smith; nor is he entirely consistent on the question of the nature of morality in his scattered writings on the subject. As we have seen, he both highlights the deep moral diversity that exists in different ages and cultures *and* states that all ages and cultures have shared the same basic moral norms. I have argued that the latter statements were intended less as genuine empirical observations or claims about moral truth than as appeals for toleration. In any case, in his most extensive treatment of the subject Voltaire argues that context is in fact crucial in distinguishing right from wrong. On balance, then, he seems to hold, with Hume, Smith, and Montesquieu, not only that morality is a this-worldly phenomenon, derived from human sentiments, but also that what counts as moral varies with varied circumstances.

CONCLUSION

While the Enlightenment is widely associated in the scholarly mind with moral universalism, we have seen that such leading Enlightenment figures as Hume, Smith, Montesquieu, and Voltaire all moved away from the idea that right and wrong are identical in all times and places, or that morality consists of a set of unalterable commands that are somehow written into human nature or the nature of the universe. Instead, they each posit that right and wrong are derived from people's sentiments and embodied in evolving communal norms: Hume holds that morality varies according to what people find useful or agreeable in their particular circumstances; Smith holds that the impartial spectator's judgments are to a large degree dependent on the "custom and fashion" of his society; Montesquieu holds that natural laws, no less than positive laws, must be mediated by the institutions, customs, mores, and other characteristics of a given society; and Voltaire holds, at least in the *Treatise on Metaphysics*, that right and wrong can change according to context and circumstance. Once again, none of this is to suggest that these thinkers are simply moral relativists: they see the morality that originates in people's sentiments as "real" and binding, which means that individuals are subject to moral standards that they do not choose in any direct or immediate sense. To state it another way, they understand morality to be not subjective but *intersubjective*. Thus, they propose a contextual basis

Morality in Context 79

for normative judgments that avoids both the Scylla of universalism and the Charybdis of relativism.

In this, these thinkers provide a welcome alternative to the dominant neo-Kantian and utilitarian paradigms in contemporary moral philosophy.[115] Even the leading alternative to these paradigms, virtue ethics, seeks (at least in many of its formulations) to establish universally valid criteria for what constitutes a virtuous character. Compared to these approaches, the contextually sensitive moral theories of Hume, Smith, Montesquieu, and Voltaire are arguably both more realistic, insofar as they are more consistent with recent research by psychologists and neuroscientists on the central role of emotion and empathy in the process of moral judgment,[116] as well as more liberal, tolerant, and humane, insofar as they are better able to account for and embrace the historical and cultural differences among peoples, norms, and beliefs. In other words, the moral theories of these thinkers may in fact offer a remedy to the very ill ascribed to the Enlightenment by its critics – that of being "hegemonic" – while also avoiding the dangers of outright moral relativism. Substantiating these suggestions fully would, of course, require at least another book. For present purposes, the critical point is that, far from pursuing MacIntyre's "Enlightenment project" of finding "an independent rational justification for morality," these leading Enlightenment figures all saw context as crucial in the formulation of moral standards and accepted that what constitutes right and wrong can and does change with changing circumstances.

[115] Several scholars have drawn on Hume, in particular, to challenge these paradigms. For a few prominent examples, see Annette C. Baier, *Moral Prejudices: Essay on Ethics* (Cambridge, MA: Harvard University Press, 1994); Simon Blackburn, *Ruling Passions: A Theory of Practical Reasoning* (Oxford: Oxford University Press, 1998); Allan Gibbard, *Wise Choices, Apt Feelings: A Theory of Normative Judgment* (Cambridge, MA: Harvard University Press, 1990); J. L. Mackie, *Ethics: Inventing Right and Wrong* (New York: Penguin, 1977); Michael Smith, *The Moral Problem* (Malden, MA: Blackwell, 1994); Bernard Williams, *Ethics and the Limits of Philosophy* (Cambridge, MA: Harvard University Press, 1985); and Bernard Williams, *Moral Luck* (Cambridge: Cambridge University Press, 1981).

[116] For a useful overview of this literature that explores potential links between it and Enlightenment era moral sentimentalism, see Frazer, *The Enlightenment of Sympathy*, chapter 7.

2

Pragmatic Liberalism

While Alasdair MacIntyre identifies "the Enlightenment project" as the search for universal moral principles, John Gray describes it as the attempt to forge what he calls a "universal civilization," meaning the global realization of an ideal political order – a civilized, secular ideal that is based on rational principles and hence the same for all of humanity.[1] According to Gray, it was the Enlightenment's central hope and belief that the spread of reason would lead to a universal consensus on what the good life entails and on what kind of society or regime would best promote such a life. While Gray is perhaps the most vociferous of the Enlightenment's recent critics, this view of the Enlightenment's project is hardly unique to him: the idea that Enlightenment thinkers adopted a universal standard of political right and wrong, like the related idea that they adopted a universal standard of *moral* right and wrong, is widespread among contemporary political theorists and philosophers of many ideological stripes. Crucially, this is perhaps the main reason why the Enlightenment is criticized or rejected even by most contemporary liberals, who would seem to be its natural allies. John Rawls, for instance, insists that his own political liberalism "is sharply different from and rejects Enlightenment Liberalism," which he describes as "a comprehensive liberal and often secular doctrine founded on reason" according to which politics should be directed

---

[1] See John Gray, *Enlightenment's Wake: Politics and Culture at the Close of the Modern Age* (New York: Routledge, 1995). Gray manages to collect almost all of the currently fashionable criticisms of the Enlightenment into this single book, but his central line of argument revolves around the Enlightenment's alleged search for universal grounds on which to base their liberal political principles.

80

Pragmatic Liberalism

toward a single understanding of the good life, one that is the same for all people everywhere.[2] Rawls reproaches this comprehensive or "Enlightenment" form of liberalism for failing to accommodate the moral, political, and religious diversity that exists among and within modern societies. Numerous contemporary liberals have followed Rawls on this score, although many others – such as his pluralist critics – go even *further* than he does in insisting that the Enlightenment, with its pursuit of a universal political consensus, does not sufficiently "give diversity its due."[3] Hence, Gerald Gaus proclaims in his survey of the field that "the main current of contemporary liberal political theory seeks to develop a post-Enlightenment account of politics," having advanced far beyond the "Enlightenment faith" that "progress in the moral and political sciences will bring about increased convergence on the moral and political truth."[4]

As we saw in the previous chapter, there is a kernel of truth in the claim that Hume, Smith, Montesquieu, and Voltaire were universalists with respect to morality: they all believed that the way in which moral standards are *formulated* is the same everywhere and always, although the *content* of these standards – what actually counts as moral – is in large part socially determined, and so varies with varied circumstances. There is an even bigger grain of truth in the claim that these thinkers were universalists with respect to politics, insofar as they were all, broadly speaking, liberals. That is, they all embraced what Peter Gay has called "the politics of decency," which includes liberal political ideals such as limited government, religious toleration, freedom of expression, commerce, and

---

[2] John Rawls, *Political Liberalism*, expanded edition (New York: Columbia University Press, [1993] 2005), 486, xxxviii. Of course, this represented something of a shift from Rawls's earlier work, in which he articulated a theory of justice that appealed explicitly to figures such as Kant and Hume. See John Rawls, *A Theory of Justice* (Cambridge, MA: Harvard University Press, 1971). For commentary on Rawls's debt to the Enlightenment in *A Theory of Justice*, see Michael L. Frazer, "John Rawls: Between Two Enlightenments" *Political Theory* 35.6 (December 2007): 756–80.

[3] The quotation is from William A. Galston, *Liberal Pluralism: The Implications of Value Pluralism for Political Theory and Practice* (Cambridge: Cambridge University Press, 2002), 23. Galston argues that liberals should take their bearings not from the Enlightenment, which he associates with an emphasis on autonomy and self-directedness, but rather from what he calls the "post-Reformation project" of dealing with religious differences, which emphasized toleration of diversity rather than autonomy. "To the extent that many liberals identify liberalism with the Enlightenment," he writes, "they limit support for their cause and drive many citizens of goodwill – indeed, many potential allies – into opposition." Ibid., 24–6.

[4] Gerald F. Gaus, *Contemporary Theories of Liberalism: Public Reason as a Post-Enlightenment Project* (London: Sage, 2003), x.

82   *The Pragmatic Enlightenment*

humane criminal laws.[5] Yet, as we will see in this chapter, their liberalism was quite pragmatic and flexible in terms of both its basis and its implications.

Hume, Smith, Montesquieu, and Voltaire all adopted what today would be called an antifoundationalist (or, even better, nonfoundationalist) approach to politics. They rejected the leading foundationalist political theories of the seventeenth and early eighteenth centuries, social contract theory and the rationalist natural law tradition, and instead turned once again to empirical observation. These thinkers concluded that liberal practices and institutions are preferable not because they are in accord with Reason or Nature – as Locke, for instance, had done – but because historical and comparative analysis revealed them to be relative improvements on the alternatives. This is why their political theories, like their moral theories, tended to combine or blend empirical and normative concerns: their approach to justification requires an examination of the available alternatives. Nor did they rely on a single standard or benchmark in making these comparisons: sometimes they lauded liberal regimes and practices for the personal freedom they afforded, while at other times they lauded the security they provided, the happiness they produced, the prosperity they made possible, and/or the character traits they encouraged. In this respect, these thinkers could be seen as precursors of the liberal pluralism that has more recently been advocated by Isaiah Berlin and his followers: they all concur that there are a number of important political ends or goods, that there is no simple or foolproof means by which to rank them or adjudicate among them, and that balance and compromise will always be necessary – but also that liberal regimes generally provide a greater degree of a greater number of these goods than illiberal regimes.

The "Enlightenment liberalism" of Hume, Smith, Montesquieu, and Voltaire was also, pace Gray and Rawls, quite flexible in terms of its implications. For these thinkers, there is simply no such thing as a perfect, single best, or uniquely legitimate form of government or set of political institutions and practices. They all expressed a good deal of admiration for the government and society of eighteenth-century Britain, given that it embodied many of their liberal ideals to a greater degree than those of other European nations of the time, but they did not believe that British institutions and practices were appropriate for all societies.

---

[5] Peter Gay, *The Enlightenment: An Interpretation*, vol. 2: *The Science of Freedom* (New York: W. W. Norton, 1969), chapter 8.

Pragmatic Liberalism

83

On the contrary, they stressed that different institutions and practices are appropriate for societies with different circumstances, histories, customs, and so on. Thus, they were all cautious about making general political claims and positing abstract political ideals, and they essentially set aside the time-honored notion that there is a specific set of criteria that all regimes must meet in order to attain legitimacy. To repeat, this does not mean that these thinkers had no political principles or preferences, but rather that their liberal principles and preferences were sufficiently flexible that they did not insist on (or even allow for) a single set of institutions and practices or a comprehensive view of the good life that would be applicable in all times and places. Insofar as they *did* adopt a substantively universalist view, it was a kind of "negative universalism" that was more concerned to prevent certain ills than to attain certain goods. In all of these respects, their political theories, like their moral theories, were far from "hegemonic."

THE MODERATE SPIRIT OF MONTESQUIEU'S LIBERALISM

Montesquieu's political thought falls squarely within the liberal tradition.[6] Like earlier liberals such as Locke, he advocates limited government, religious toleration, freedom of expression, the protection of property and commerce, and above all liberty understood in terms of living under laws that provide security for each individual, and self-determination within the limits of these laws (see SL 11.3, 155; 12.2, 188). Among Montesquieu's main substantive contributions to the liberal tradition were his conception of the separation of powers, his advocacy of the decentralization of power, and his call for humane criminal laws. Montesquieu's name has long been nearly synonymous with the idea that political power should be separated into legislative, executive, and judicial functions; James Madison calls him "the oracle who is always consulted and cited on this subject."[7] In the France of his time,

---

[6] For a recent essay questioning this widely accepted view of Montesquieu's thought, see Céline Spector, "Was Montesquieu Liberal? *The Spirit of the Laws* in the History of Liberalism," in *French Liberalism from Montesquieu to the Present Day*, ed. Raf Geenans and Helena Rosenblatt (Cambridge: Cambridge University Press, 2012).

[7] James Madison, *The Federalist* #47, ed. George W. Carey and James McClellan (Indianapolis: Liberty Fund [1788] 2001), 250. Of course, Locke too advocates a separation of powers, but instead of calling for an independent judiciary he divides government into legislative, executive, and "federative" powers, the latter being the power over foreign affairs. See John Locke, *Two Treatises of Government*, ed. Peter Laslett (Cambridge: Cambridge University Press, [1689] 1988), II.12, 364–6.

84   *The Pragmatic Enlightenment*

however, Montesquieu was more closely connected with the claim that "intermediary institutions" such as the nobility, clergy, and *parlements*[8] were the chief guardians of the people's liberty, since they served as bulwarks against royal despotism.[9] Yet in terms of rhetorical emphasis, even Montesquieu's advocacy of decentralizing power away from the king and his council cannot match his stress on the importance of humanity, fairness, and restraint in executing criminal laws. Given that the nexus of the police, the courts, and the accused is the point at which people's freedom and security are most directly threatened or safeguarded by the state, he maintains that "the citizen's liberty depends principally on the goodness of the criminal laws" and that "knowledge ... concerning the surest rules one can observe in criminal judgments, is of more concern to mankind than anything else in the world" (SL 12.2, 188; see also 6.2, 74).[10]

While Montesquieu's politics largely resembled those of earlier liberals, he was arguably one of the first thinkers to propose a liberalism without foundations – that is, to advocate liberal practices and institutions without insisting that these are the only practices and institutions that are in accordance with Nature or Reason or God's wishes. Locke, to take a paradigmatic case, had claimed that the law of nature, which protects people's rights to life, liberty, and property, "stands as an Eternal Rule to all Men, Legislators as well as others. The Rules that they make for other Mens Actions, must ... be conformable to the Law of Nature, i.e.

---

[8] The French *parlements* were, of course, very different from the British Parliament: they were more judicial than legislative bodies, responsible for approving and applying on a local level the laws enacted by the royal government at Versailles.

[9] Early in *The Spirit of the Laws*, Montesquieu proclaims that "the nobility is of the essence of monarchy, whose fundamental maxim is: *no monarch, no nobility: no nobility, no monarch*; rather, one has a despot" (SL 2.4, 18).

[10] Judith Shklar maintains that "Montesquieu's claim to being one of the greatest of liberal thinkers rests not on his famous homage to the English constitution, but on his theory of the criminal law and punishment." Judith N. Shklar, *Montesquieu* (Oxford: Oxford University Press, 1987), 89. Detailed examinations of Montesquieu's views regarding the proper role of the judiciary and criminal law can be found in Paul O. Carrese, *The Cloaking of Power: Montesquieu, Blackstone, and the Rise of Judicial Activism* (Chicago: University of Chicago Press, 2003), part 1; David W. Carrithers, "Montesquieu's Philosophy of Punishment" *History of Political Thought* 19.2 (summer 1998): 213–40; David W. Carrithers, "Montesquieu and the Liberal Philosophy of Jurisprudence," in *Montesquieu's Science of Politics: Essays on The Spirit of Laws*, ed. David W. Carrithers, Michael A. Mosher, and Paul A. Rahe (Lanham, MD: Rowman & Littlefield, 2001); and Vickie B. Sullivan, "Against the Despotism of a Republic: Montesquieu's Correction of Machiavelli in the Name of the Security of the Individual" *History of Political Thought* 27.2 (summer 2006): 263–89.

Pragmatic Liberalism

to the Will of God, of which that is a Declaration."[11] While neither the law of nature nor the idea of the social contract dictates a specific form of government, in Locke's view, they do require that every regime must operate through "settled standing Laws" that are passed with the people's consent, that apply equally to all citizens, and that are adjudicated by "known authorized judges."[12] They also require some specific policies, such as that no government can levy taxes without the consent of the majority of the citizens (or their representatives).[13] Locke deems any government that violates these requirements illegitimate; indeed, it is not too much to say that the question of political legitimacy is *the* central question of the *Second Treatise*. Thus, he concludes that absolute monarchy is not just a bad or undesirable form of government; it "is inconsistent with Civil Society, and so can be no Form of Civil Government at all."[14]

Montesquieu's political pronouncements are far less sweeping and uncompromising. To begin with, while the idea of the social contract was common in the seventeenth and early eighteenth centuries – Hume calls it the "fashionable system" of accounting for political obligation (THN 3.2.8.3, 347) – Montesquieu mocks this idea in *The Persian Letters* and then all but ignores it in *The Spirit of the Laws*. In the former, Usbek finds it "ridiculous" that philosophers always feel obliged to have recourse to the origins of society in any discussion of political right (PL #94, 155), and the futile attempt to form a social contract among the Troglodytes is subverted almost immediately by a violent reaction against the rulers thus instituted (see PL #11, 23). In the latter book Montesquieu does speak of a state of nature, but he depicts the move into society as natural and immediate, such that it is questionable whether a presocial state really existed in the first place.[15] The term "social contract" does not appear anywhere in the book, and it is evident from Montesquieu's extensive examination of French constitutional history in books 28, 30, and 31 that he recognizes that governments generally emerge and develop gradually over many centuries, rather than arising in a single founding moment. Accordingly, he firmly rejects the idea that a social contract is the only valid basis for political legitimacy.[16]

---

[11] Locke, *Two Treatises of Government*, II.11.135, 358; see also II.2.12, 275; and II.11.134, 355–6.

[12] Ibid., II.11.134–7, 355–60.

[13] See ibid., II.11.138–9, 360–1.

[14] Ibid., II.7.90, 326.

[15] This question will be considered in some detail in Chapter 5.

[16] See the chapter on Montesquieu in C. E. Vaughan's classic overview of the history of political philosophy, which is entitled "The Eclipse of Contract." C. E. Vaughan, *Studies in The History of Political Philosophy Before and After Rousseau*, vol. 1 (New York:

86   *The Pragmatic Enlightenment*

Montesquieu also rejects the idea that natural law provides a rigid standard by which to measure regimes and positive laws. As we saw in the previous chapter, he identifies the "laws of nature" not as rules or commands but rather as natural inclinations or desires – specifically, the desires for self-preservation, nourishment, sex or companionship, and society with others (see SL 1.2, 6–7) – and suggests that the implementation of these "laws" must be mediated by the institutions, customs, mores, and other characteristics of a society. To be sure, he devotes two chapters of book 26 of *The Spirit of the Laws* to the subject of "civil laws that are contrary to natural law," where he suggests that certain laws and practices violate the right of "natural defense" (SL 26.3–4, 496–7). Montesquieu certainly disapproves of infringements on people's basic desires, above all the desire to preserve the self and family. But he does not use these desires to formulate inalienable natural rights that individuals can assert against their government, or to judge all nonliberal regimes to be illegitimate.[17] Recall that even after asserting that slavery is "opposed … to natural right" (SL 15.2, 248) he goes on to suggest that this institution is understandable, perhaps even necessary, in certain situations. Further, immediately after the chapters that discuss "civil laws that are contrary to natural law," Montesquieu devotes a chapter to showing that it is sometimes necessary to *modify* the principles of natural law in judging civil laws (SL 26.5, 498). While natural laws – people's basic desires – play a role in Montesquieu's judgments of positive laws and regimes, then, they are not specific requirements that must be met by all regimes so much as general ends or goals that must be adapted to different circumstances.[18] It

---

Russell & Russell, [1925] 1960), chapter 5. For a different view, see Mark H. Waddicor, *Montesquieu and the Philosophy of Natural Law* (The Hague: Martinus Nijhoff, 1970), 91–9.

[17] On Montesquieu's opposition to the Lockean conception of natural rights, see Thomas L. Pangle, "The Liberal Critique of Rights in Montesquieu and Hume" *Tocqueville Review* 13.2 (1992): 31–42.

[18] Thomas Pangle remarks that for Montesquieu, unlike for Hobbes and Locke, "the principles of justice deducible from the natural law describing men's fundamental needs must be adjusted or diluted, often drastically, before they can be applied to civilized political life. This thought in all its profound ramifications is the key to Montesquieu's political philosophy." Thomas L. Pangle, *Montesquieu's Philosophy of Liberalism: A Commentary on The Spirit of the Laws* (Chicago: University of Chicago Press, 1973), 43. Similarly, Aurelian Craiutu writes: "While natural law may sometimes provide effective standards for judging political and civil matters, it cannot be applied uniformly, without giving due consideration to particular circumstances and contexts." Aurelian Craiutu, *A Virtue for Courageous Minds: Moderation in French Political Thought, 1748–1830* (Princeton, NJ: Princeton University Press, 2012), 57. See also Sharon R. Krause, *Liberalism with Honor* (Cambridge, MA: Harvard University Press, 2002), 53; and Michael Zuckert, "Natural

Pragmatic Liberalism

is perhaps also worth noting that, in stark contrast to Locke's works, the very idea of natural law recedes into the background in Montesquieu's extensive analysis of positive laws and their relationship to the context in which they arise; indeed, by my count he refers to natural law or natural right in only 17 of the book's 605 chapters.[19]

Thus, as Maurice Cranston writes, while Montesquieu is sometimes depicted as "the Whig of the French Enlightenment," in truth "he subscribed to very little of what might be called the metaphysics of Whiggery. For Montesquieu there were no natural rights to life, liberty, and property; no social contract; no radical individualism, and certainly no hints of revolution."[20] In fact, Montesquieu essentially dispenses with the entire notion that there is a set of criteria that every regime must meet in order to be considered legitimate.[21] In his view, the variation in the "spirit" of different nations is simply too great to impose a single rule or standard on them all. Whereas Locke insisted that absolute monarchy could not properly be considered a form of civil government, Montesquieu allows that even despotism may be the best (or only) form of government possible under certain circumstances – for instance, in large, populous nations with hot climates and no tradition of liberty or self-rule.[22] This is why, in addition to the evils of despotism, he discusses why despotic regimes

---

Law, Natural Rights, and Classical Liberalism: On Montesquieu's Critique of Hobbes" *Social Philosophy and Policy* 18.1 (winter 2001), 246.

[19] Namely, in chapters 1.1, 1.2, 3.10, 10.3, 15.2, 15.12, 15.17, 16.12, 21.21, 25.13, 26.1, 26.3–7, and 26.14. Pangle counts references in 16 chapters, but his list differs from mine in that he misses 3.10, 15.2, 16.12, 21.21, 25.13, and 26.1 but includes chapters that refer not to natural law (*loi*) or natural right (*droit*) but to "natural defense" (6.13, 10.2, 24.6), "natural reason" (15.7), and a "paternal power established by nature" (6.20). See Pangle, *Montesquieu's Philosophy of Liberalism*, 309–10.

[20] Maurice Cranston, *Philosophers and Pamphleteers: Political Theorists of the Enlightenment* (Oxford: Oxford University Press, 1986), 34.

[21] On this point, see Pierre Manent, *An Intellectual History of Liberalism*, trans. Rebecca Balinski (Princeton, NJ: Princeton University Press, [1987] 1995), 53; Paul A. Rahe, *Soft Despotism, Democracy's Drift: Montesquieu, Rousseau, Tocqueville, and the Modern Prospect* (New Haven, CT: Yale University Press, 2009), 101; and Diana J. Schaub, *Erotic Liberalism: Women and Revolution in Montesquieu's Persian Letters* (Lanham, MD: Rowman & Littlefield, 1995), xi.

[22] Michael Zuckert writes that for Montesquieu "even a despotism, abhorrent as such a system is, may be the best option available in certain sorts of circumstances. Because of this, Montesquieu refuses to lay down a standard of legitimacy that would deny such a government some claim on the allegiance of its citizens. It is not the case ... that Montesquieu has replaced Locke's relatively stringent standard of legitimacy with some other standard that is more lenient. Rather, Montesquieu has merely set the question of legitimacy aside." Zuckert, "Natural Law, Natural Rights, and Classical Liberalism," 248. See also Shklar, *Montesquieu*, 96.

88 *The Pragmatic Enlightenment*

are so common, in what situations they might be necessary, and what can be done to improve them or to mitigate their dangers.[23] Indeed, as Vickie Sullivan points out, Montesquieu does not pronounce a single specific law to be unjust in the entirety of *The Spirit of the Laws*.[24]

None of this is to say, of course, that Montesquieu deems it impossible to make judgments between better and worse regimes, better and worse laws. On the contrary, he constantly makes such judgments. We should surely take with a grain of salt his suggestion, in the preface of *The Spirit of the Laws*, that he will strive to give "*everyone* ... new reasons for loving his duties, his prince, his country, and his laws" (SL, xliv, emphasis added); after all, it is clear that Montesquieu does not "love" despotism, however necessary it may be in certain circumstances.[25] While Montesquieu makes political judgments throughout the book, however, he does not believe that these judgments can be made a priori, or that they can apply categorically. There is, in his view, no one regime or set of laws that is uniquely in accordance with Reason or Nature; rather, "the government most in conformity with nature is the one whose particular arrangement best relates to the disposition of the people for whom it is established" (SL 1.3, 8).[26] Indeed, he claims that "laws should be so

[23] For instance, Montesquieu offers advice about whether or not despotic rule should be hereditary, what the education should be like in despotic nations, what role religion should play, how much commerce should be allowed, how the family should be structured, and so on (see, for example, SL 5.14–16, 59–66).

[24] See Vickie Sullivan, "Montesquieu's Philosophical Assault on Despotic Ideas in *The Spirit of the Laws*" (unpublished manuscript), chapter 1, ms. 14. The closest Montesquieu comes to making such a pronouncement is in book 28, chapter 17, in a passage in which he is in fact making allowances for the different mores of earlier times: "In the circumstances of the times when proof by combat and proof by hot iron and boiling water were the usages, there was such an agreement between these laws and the mores that the laws less produced injustice than they were unjust, that the effects were more innocent than the causes, that they more ran counter to fairness than they violated rights, that they were more unreasonable than tyrannical" (SL 28.17, 553).

[25] On the other hand, it is unlikely that this statement was merely a sop to the censors: this citizen of a Catholic monarchy would hardly have endeared himself to the authorities by giving his readers new reasons to love Protestant republics, for example. One of Montesquieu's *Pensées* may help to shed light on the rationale for this statement: "I do not at all think that one government ought to make other governments repulsive. The best of all is normally the one in which we live.... For since it is impossible to change it without changing manners and mores, I do not see, given the extreme brevity of life, what use it would be for men to abandon in every respect what they have gotten used to" (Pensées #934, 265). Note the "in every respect" in the last sentence.

[26] Similarly, in *The Persian Letters*, Usbek muses: "I have often asked myself what kind of government most conformed to reason. It has seemed to me that the most perfect is that which attains its goal with the least friction; thus that government is most perfect which leads men along paths most agreeable to their interests and inclinations" (PL #80, 136).

Pragmatic Liberalism 89

appropriate to the people for whom they are made that it is very unlikely that the laws of one nation can suit another" (SL 1.3, 8).[27]

Given the importance of particular circumstances in determining which regime and which laws are best suited to a given nation, Montesquieu considers it futile to theorize in abstraction from these circumstances. For him, true political philosophy rests on comparative and historical analysis – a careful examination of the many different regimes and laws that have existed around the world and throughout history, along with the effects those regimes and laws have had in different sets of circumstances. Rather than appeal to a universal foundation to offer a timeless teaching, Montesquieu shows that certain practices and institutions are preferable to others, in a particular set of circumstances, because those practices and institutions have generally proven better than the alternatives, given those circumstances.[28] But what does "better" even mean here, we might ask, without an overriding basis or benchmark by which to make such a claim? Isaiah Berlin compares Montesquieu's method to that of a physician:

A physician does not, after all, usually ask himself what precisely it is that good health consists in, and why; he takes it for granted, and calls himself a physician because he knows a healthy and normal organism from one which is sick or abnormal, and knows, moreover, that what is good for one type of organism may be fatal to another, and that what is needed in one climate is unnecessary or dangerous in another. Similarly Montesquieu assumed that the idea of political and moral health is too familiar to need analysis, that when it is present this is quite patent, and that to be rational is to recognise it for what it is, to know the symptoms, to know how to cure the relevant diseases and how to maintain the organism.[29]

---

[27] As Montesquieu scholars are fond of pointing out, this aspect of his thought was criticized by Condorcet in one of his moments of extreme political rationalism: "As truth, reason, justice, the rights of man, the interests of property, of liberty, of security are in all places the same; we cannot discover why all the provinces of a state, or even all states, should not have the same civil and criminals laws, and the same laws relative to commerce. A good law should be good for all men." Marie Jean Antoine Nicolas de Caritat, marquis de Condorcet, "Observations on the Twenty-Ninth Book of *The Spirit of Laws*," in Antoine Louis Claude, comte Destutt de Tracy, *A Commentary and Review of Montesquieu's Spirit of Laws*, trans. Thomas Jefferson (Philadelphia: William Duane, 1811), 274.

[28] Thus, Franz Neumann writes, in the introduction to his edition of *The Spirit of the Laws*, that for Montesquieu "there is ... no universally applicable solution. There are only types of solutions." See the editor's introduction in Charles de Secondat, baron de Montesquieu, *The Spirit of the Laws*, trans. Thomas Nugent (New York: Hafner, 1949), xxxii; see also xix.

[29] Isaiah Berlin, "Montesquieu," in *Against the Current: Essays in the History of Ideas*, ed. Henry Hardy (New York: Viking, [1955] 1980), 142–3.

As this analogy suggests, Montesquieu does not believe that political judgments require a vision of a perfect regime, or even a single criterion or yardstick by which to measure all regimes. On the other hand, he does not simply say, in the manner of Justice Stewart, that he knows a good political order when he sees it. As a liberal, he consistently prioritizes goods such as personal freedom, security, and prosperity. Even here, however, Montesquieu accepts not only that these goods are sometimes at odds with one another,[30] but also that what they require, what they entail, and indeed what they *mean* can vary from time to time and place to place. For instance, he defines political liberty in relation to the citizen as "the opinion one has of one's security" (SL 12.2, 188; see also 11.6, 157; 12.1, 187), but of course this kind of "opinion" depends a great deal on one's circumstances and what one has become accustomed to; hence, no one set of laws or institutions can guarantee political liberty in all cases.[31] This is why, once again, there is no substitute for careful, concrete historical and comparative analysis.

In order to get a better sense of how Montesquieu makes political judgments without relying on a universal foundation or single benchmark, let us return to his attitude toward despotism, since this is where his method or style of judgment emerges most clearly. Of the three main regime types that he discusses in *The Spirit of the Laws* – republics, monarchies, and despotisms – the latter is plainly the one he finds the most objectionable. As Sharon Krause writes, despotism "is the one phenomenon that is categorically disparaged in a work that otherwise resists categorical judgments, so that while readers may disagree about which regime Montesquieu prefers, there can be no doubt about which one he most despises."[32] This has led several commentators to suggest that Montesquieu subscribed to a kind of "negative universalism," according to which despotism serves as a *summum malum* that is always to be avoided.[33] There is a good deal

---

[30] To take only the most obvious case, personal freedom must ordinarily be restrained for the sake of security: "Liberty is the right to do everything the laws permit; and if one citizen could do what they forbid, he would no longer have liberty because the others would likewise have this same power" (SL 11.3, 155).

[31] Thus, in a later chapter Montesquieu suggests that in addition to the "real" tyranny that results from governmental violence, there is also a "tyranny ... of opinion, which is felt when those who govern establish things that run counter to a nation's way of thinking" (SL 19.3, 309).

[32] Sharon R. Krause, "Despotism in *The Spirit of Laws*," in *Montesquieu's Science of Politics: Essays on The Spirit of Laws*, ed. David W. Carrithers, Michael A. Mosher, and Paul A. Rahe (Lanham, MD: Rowman & Littlefield, 2001), 231; see also 258.

[33] See, for example, Thomas L. Pangle, *The Theological Basis of Liberal Modernity in Montesquieu's Spirit of the Laws* (Chicago: University of Chicago Press, 2010), 28; and

Pragmatic Liberalism 91

of truth to this suggestion, as Montesquieu clearly prefers "moderate" governments to despotic ones, although it must also be recalled that in his view despotic rule may be unavoidable under certain circumstances, and so cannot be considered universally illegitimate.

The question is, What drives or justifies Montesquieu's negative assessment of despotism? We have already seen that Montesquieu's "natural laws" – people's basic desires – play an important role in his political judgments, even if they do not provide universal requirements for legitimacy. Thus, he shows throughout the book that despotism "causes appalling ills to human nature" (SL 2.4, 18), heaps "insults" on human nature (SL 8.8, 118), and produces "affronts to human nature" (SL 8.21, 127).[34] On the other hand, he also suggests that despotism is in some senses the most "natural" regime type: "In order to form a moderate government, one must combine powers, regulate them, temper them, make them act.... By contrast, a despotic government leaps to view, so to speak; it is uniform throughout; as only passions are needed to establish it, everyone is good enough for that" (SL 5.14, 63). Thus, Montesquieu proclaims it "easy to understand" why "most peoples are subjected to this type of government" (SL 5.14, 63). Not only does despotism require less "art" than other forms of government, but the impulse to rule despotically is inherent in human nature: "it has eternally been observed that any man who has power is led to abuse it: he continues until he finds limits" (SL 11.4, 155). Hence, as Krause notes, human nature and its "natural laws" cannot be Montesquieu's *sole* criterion for making political judgments: "The fact that despotism is in some respects natural to human beings, that the despotic tendency is a fundamental feature of human nature, suggests that nature is not in itself a fully reliable guide for politics or an indisputable source of moral and political standards."[35]

Montesquieu argues against despotism not by proving that it runs afoul of some universal standard, but rather by displaying to his readers, in vivid historical detail, what despotic regimes look like, and what life is

---

Diana Schaub, "Of Believers and Barbarians: Montesquieu's Enlightened Toleration," in *Early Modern Skepticism and the Origins of Toleration*, ed. Alan Levine (Lanham, MD: Lexington, 1999), 242.

[34] Indeed, as Keegan Callanan points out, Montesquieu refers explicitly to human nature (*la nature humaine*) only six times in part 1 of the book – namely, the three instances cited previously, along with SL 5.14, 63; 6.9, 83; and 7.9, 104 – and all six of these references appear in the context of an attack on despotism. See Keegan Callanan, "Montesquieu, Liberalism and the Critique of Political Universalism" (Ph.D. dissertation, Duke University, 2011), 147–8.

[35] Krause, "Despotism in *The Spirit of Laws*," 258.

92   *The Pragmatic Enlightenment*

like under them. He shows that despots tend to become "lazy, ignorant, and voluptuous" (SL 2.5, 20), that their subjects are turned into "timid, ignorant, beaten-down people" (SL 5.14, 59), and that throughout despotic lands "nothing is repaired, nothing improved ... all is fallow, all is deserted" (SL 5.14, 61). He also shows that despotic regimes tend to be self-undermining for a host of reasons: despots often become hateful to their subjects, and the people have little reason not to plot against them since their subjection could hardly be any more severe; despots depend on an army to enforce their will, but they must always be wary that the army will depose them; despots tend to be aggressively expansionist, thereby opening themselves to attack from neighboring powers; the insecurity of the people prevents commerce from flourishing and thereby impoverishes the nation; and so on (see especially SL 5.14, 59–63; 8.10, 119; 8.21, 127–8). In short, as Montesquieu writes in one of the briefest of his *Pensées*, "despotism collapses of its own weight" (Pensées #671, 208; see also #885, 255).

In other words, instead of judging regimes and laws on the basis of a single principle or standard such as natural rights or utility or some human telos, Montesquieu draws on a number of partial or incomplete standards, such as how well they fulfill people's basic desires; how well they promote security, liberty, and prosperity; how stable they are; and even which character traits they encourage in people. And, to repeat, which institutions and practices will best fulfill these aims depends a great deal on a nation's particular circumstances. Given his lack of a single standard for judgment and his insistence on the importance of context, it is unsurprising that Montesquieu refuses to single out any one regime or set of institutions or practices as universally the best, and instead outlines the various benefits and drawbacks of each. Even now Montesquieu scholars have proven unable to reach a consensus on which of the two main "moderate" regime types – republics or monarchies – he ultimately preferred, if indeed he preferred one over the other at all.[36] (As

---

[36] For examples of works that depict Montesquieu as favoring republics, see Mark Hulliung, *Montesquieu and the Old Regime* (Berkeley: University of California Press, 1976); Nannerl O. Keohane, "Virtuous Republics and Glorious Monarchies: Two Models in Montesquieu's Political Thought" *Political Studies* 20.4 (December 1972): 383–96; and Eric Nelson, *The Greek Tradition in Republican Thought* (Cambridge: Cambridge University Press, 2004), chapter 5. For the argument that he was instead a proponent of monarchy, see Annelein de Dijn, *French Political Thought from Montesquieu to Tocqueville: Liberty in a Levelled Society?* (Cambridge: Cambridge University Press, 2008); Jean Ehrard, *Politique de Montesquieu* (Paris: Armand Collin, 1965); and Michael A. Mosher, "Monarchy's Paradox: Honor in the Face of Sovereign Power," in

Pragmatic Liberalism 93

will become evident in Chapter 6, my view is that he saw monarchies as far better suited to the modern world than republics, which rely on a kind of unnatural "self-renunciation" [SL 3.5, 25; see also 4.5, 35; 5.3, 43].)

Many scholars have suggested, however, that Montesquieu preferred the hybrid English government to either monarchies *or* republics, and indeed that he deemed this kind of liberal, commercial republic to be universally desirable in principle, even if not universally feasible or attainable.[37] There is no question that Montesquieu greatly admired the English regime of his time. He declares that England is the "one nation in the world whose constitution has political liberty for its direct purpose" (SL 11.5, 156), and the ensuing chapter describing this constitution – surely the most famous in the entire book – extols its separation of powers into legislative, executive, and judicial functions; its limitations on the power of judges; its popularly elected legislature; its relatively widespread franchise, and so on (see SL 11.6, 156–66).[38] In the chapter on England's mores, manners, and character, he also praises its freedom of expression; its relative (even if not complete) religious toleration; and its embrace of commerce (see SL 19.27, 325–33). Yet Montesquieu also expresses a good deal of ambivalence about this regime, particularly in the latter chapter. "As all the passions are free there," he writes, "hatred, envy, jealousy, and the ardor for enriching and distinguishing oneself … appear to their full extent" (SL 19.27, 325). So great is this "ardor" among the English, in his view, that it tends to trump other, more important qualities; as he writes elsewhere, "money is held in sovereign esteem [in England], but honor and virtue little…. The English are no longer worthy of their liberty. They sell it to the king, and if the king gave

---

    Montesquieu's Science of Politics: Essays on The Spirit of Laws, ed. David W. Carrithers, Michael A. Mosher, and Paul A. Rahe (Lanham, MD: Rowman & Littlefield, 2001). Montesquieu himself remarks in one of his *Pensées* that the question of which regime type is "best" is too vaguely formulated to answer, since "there are countless types of monarchy, aristocracy, or popular state" (Pensées #942, 267).

[37] Perhaps the fullest argument to this effect can be found in Pangle, *Montesquieu's Philosophy of Liberalism*, chapter 5. This view was also voiced by James Madison, who claimed that "the British constitution was to Montesquieu, what Homer had been to the didactic writers on epic poetry. As the latter have considered the work of the immortal bard, as the perfect model from which the principles and rules of the epic art were to be drawn, and by which all similar works were to be judged: so this great political critic appears to have viewed the constitution of England as the standard, or to use his own expression, as the mirror of political liberty." Madison, *The Federalist* #47, 250.

[38] Harvey Mansfield calls this chapter "the most famous discussion of constitutionalism in the history of political thought." Harvey C. Mansfield Jr., *Taming the Prince: The Ambivalence of Modern Executive Power* (Baltimore: Johns Hopkins University Press, 1993), 230.

94 — *The Pragmatic Enlightenment*

it back to them, they would sell it to him again."[39] Montesquieu also highlights the excessive individualism that prevails in England, writing that the people live "mostly alone with themselves" and that they are "confederates more than fellow citizens" (SL 19.27, 332). Thus, he calls England's liberty "extreme" (SL 11.6, 166) – not a term of praise from the moderate Montesquieu.[40]

Perhaps the most striking aspect of Montesquieu's sketch of the English character is that they not only lack the joie de vivre of the French (see SL 19.5, 310), but are in fact *miserable*: "The English are rich, they are free, but they are tormented by their minds.... They are really quite unhappy, with so many reasons not to be" (Pensées #26, 7; see also #310, 130; and SL 19.27, 332).[41] Montesquieu declares that the English are constantly "uneasy about their situation" and "believe themselves in danger even at the safest moments" (SL 19.27, 326). In some respects this sense of anxiety is useful, since it ensures that the people remain vigilant in defense of their liberties (see SL 19.27, 326), but in other respects it is extremely problematic. Recall that Montesquieu defines "political liberty in a citizen" as "that tranquility of spirit which comes from the opinion each one has of his security" (SL 11.6, 157). While he insists that the English do not have to fear *one another* because they are protected by the laws (see SL 19.27, 332), he admits that they do have a vague sense of uneasiness (*inquiétude*) and fearfulness *in general*. This suggests that even if England enjoys "political liberty in its relation to the constitution" (i.e., a separation of powers), it does *not* fully enjoy "political

---

[39] Charles de Secondat, baron de Montesquieu, *Notes sur l'Angleterre*, in *Oeuvres complètes de Montesquieu*, ed. Roger Callois, vol. 1 (Paris: Bibliothèque de la Pléiade, [1733] 1949), 878–80. The line about the English selling their liberty to the king is presumably a reference to the "civil list," an annual sum allocated to the king for personal expenses in the settlement of 1689, which was often used to bribe potential supporters. On the "corruption" of the English government, see also Pensées #1960, 593–5.

[40] On the danger that this "extreme" liberty among the English could undermine the very separation of powers that protects their liberty, see Sharon R. Krause, "The Spirit of Separate Powers in Montesquieu" *Review of Politics* 62.2 (spring 2000): 231–65. On Montesquieu's worries about England's highly centralized system of parliamentary sovereignty, see Lee Ward, "Montesquieu on Federalism and Anglo-Gothic Constitutionalism" *Publius* 37.4 (fall 2007): 551–77.

[41] While this misery may be in part attributable to the poor English climate (see SL 14.13, 242), Montesquieu does not see this as the sole explanation. In fact, he claims explicitly that the English character that he describes in book 19, chapter 27, follows from its constitution. At the outset of that chapter, he writes: "I have spoken in Book 11 of a free people, and I have given the principles of their constitution; let us see the effects that had to follow, the character that was formed from it, and the manners that result from it" (SL 19.27, 325).

Pragmatic Liberalism 95

liberty ... in its relation to the citizen" (i.e., tranquility of spirit and the *opinion* of security).[42]

Moreover, Montesquieu's reservations regarding England are not just the kinds of reservations that a philosopher is bound to have about any real-world model, for he claims to be examining not England's *actual* political order but the one that it *should* have: "It is not for me to examine whether the English actually enjoy this liberty or not," he asserts. "It suffices for me to say that it is established by their laws, and I seek no further" (SL 11.6, 166). This is perhaps why he speaks in the conditional voice throughout both of the main chapters on England, discussing how the English government and society "should be" (*devoir*) or "must be" (*falloir*). It is not just England itself that is lacking, for even Montesquieu's idealized rendering of its constitution and society is far from ideal in every sense. What is more, he maintains that this regime is only appropriate for England's particular circumstances, and that many elements of its constitution would be unsuitable or even harmful elsewhere. At the end of his discussion of the English constitution, he reaffirms, "I do not claim hereby to disparage other governments, or to say that this extreme political liberty should humble those who have only a moderate one. How could I say that, I who believe that the excess even of reason is not always desirable and that men almost always accommodate themselves better to middles than to extremities?" (SL 11.6, 166). This is not to say that Montesquieu did not find much to admire in the English system – plainly he did – but rather that he thought the English regime, like all regimes, had both benefits and drawbacks, and that it was suitable to some nations but not to others. Thus, I concur with those who see Montesquieu not as a champion of the English system above all others but rather as an advocate of a "liberalism of plurality,"[43] one whose key theoretical contribution to liberalism consists in his "pluralist vision of the political good."[44]

---

[42] Montesquieu stresses that these two forms of political liberty do not necessarily go hand in hand at SL 12.1, 187. Paul Rahe goes so far as to contend that the sense of uneasiness and fear among the English shows that the English regime has "an undeniable kinship with despotism" in Montesquieu's eyes. Paul A. Rahe, *Montesquieu and the Logic of Liberty: War, Religion, Commerce, Climate, Terrain, Technology, Uneasiness of Mind, the Spirit of Political Vigilance, and the Foundations of the Modern Republic* (New Haven, CT: Yale University Press, 2009), 99; see also 143; and Krause, "The Spirit of Separate Powers in Montesquieu," 248–50.

[43] Bernard Manin, "Montesquieu et la politique moderne," in *Cahiers de philosophie politique de l'Université de Reims* (Brussels: Ousia, 1985), 213; see also 192–3.

[44] Catherine Larrère, "Montesquieu and Liberalism: The Question of Pluralism," in *Montesquieu and His Legacy*, ed. Rebecca E. Kingston (Albany: SUNY Press, 2009),

96   *The Pragmatic Enlightenment*

In short, Montesquieu adopts a flexible, moderate liberalism, one that rests on concrete comparative and historical analysis rather than an abstract, universal foundation; that is attentive to the variation in the circumstances and "spirit" of different nations; and that promotes liberal principles without singling out a set of laws, institutions, or practices as universally the best or uniquely legitimate. As Pierre Manent puts it, "Montesquieu's liberalism is not aggressive like Locke's; he is liberal not only in his principles, but also in his mood or tone."[45] If Montesquieu's liberalism does not sufficiently "give diversity its due," then it is difficult to conceive of one that does.[46]

VOLTAIRE'S PRACTICAL, PRAGMATIC POLITICS

In one of the key struggles of eighteenth-century French politics, Montesquieu and Voltaire stood on opposing sides.[47] Whereas Montesquieu sought to defend and strengthen the power of the nobility, clergy, and *parlements*, Voltaire was firmly on the side of the king and his council, a stance that is evident throughout his writings on French history and politics, from his largely admiring *The Age of Louis XIV* to his not at all admiring *History of the Parlement of Paris*.[48] This point of divergence between these leading philosophes was essentially an updated version of the clash between the *thèse nobiliaire* associated with Fénelon, Boulainvilliers, and Saint-Simon and the *thèse royale* of d'Argenson,

---

283. See also Aurelian Craiutu's claim that "it was Montesquieu's endorsement of the fundamental *indeterminacy* of the political good that gave his political theory a moderate tone." Craiutu, *A Virtue for Courageous Minds*, 55; see also 63.

[45] Manent, *An Intellectual History of Liberalism*, 53.

[46] This phrase, recall, is taken from William Galston's critique of the autonomy-based form of liberalism that he associates with the Enlightenment. Galston, *Liberal Pluralism*, 23.

[47] On the relations between these two thinkers and their views of one another, see Robert Shackleton, "Allies and Enemies: Voltaire and Montesquieu," in *Essays on Montesquieu and on the Enlightenment*, ed. David Gilson and Martin Smith (Oxford: Voltaire Foundation, 1988); and the exhaustive editor's introduction in Voltaire, *Commentaire sur l'Esprit des lois*, ed. Sheila Mason, in *The Complete Works of Voltaire*, vol. 80b (Oxford: Voltaire Foundation, [1777] 2009), 209–89.

[48] See Voltaire, *The Age of Louis XIV*, trans. Martyn P. Pollack (London: J. M. Dent and Sons, [1751] 1961); and Voltaire, *Histoire du parlement de Paris*, ed. John Renwick, in *The Complete Works of Voltaire*, vol. 68 (Oxford: Voltaire Foundation, [1768] 2005). While Voltaire praises the "Sun King" for humane reforms such as lowering taxes, building hospitals, establishing a permanent police force, prohibiting dueling and repairing, cleaning, and lighting city streets, he also highlights the low points of his reign, including his ruinous imperialistic wars and especially his revocation of the Edict of Nantes, which marked the resumption of official state persecution of Protestants.

Pragmatic Liberalism

97

Dubos, and the Bourbon kings. Montesquieu, like the advocates of the *thèse nobiliaire*, saw intermediary institutions as the only effectual barriers against royal despotism, while Voltaire, with the advocates of the *thèse royale*, saw the nobility, clergy, and *parlements* as themselves the principal sources of oppression and held that a king with broad, centralized authority was the only way to curb their despotic power from being exercised on a local, immediate level.[49] Voltaire opposed the nobility because of their undeserved hereditary privileges and their history of tyrannizing the serfs who worked their lands, the clergy because of their persecution of nonconformists and their abuses of their extensive temporal powers, and the *parlements*, the chief rivals of the royal authority in the eighteenth century, because of their Jansenist leanings and their responsibility for the judicial barbarities that he so decried, such as the executions of Jean Calas and the chevalier de La Barre. (It was these judicial bodies, as much as the Church itself, that made up the *infâme* that he urged people to *écrasez*.)[50] Thus, Voltaire's royalism was based on a practical judgment about the likeliest source of compassion and reform in that period of French history – a judgment that was shared by many of the other leading thinkers of the age.[51]

Despite this conspicuous point of disagreement between Montesquieu and Voltaire, the broad contours of their political thought are actually quite similar. Like Montesquieu, Voltaire advocates liberty understood in terms of "being dependent only on the law," and not on the caprice of one's ruler(s) or fellow citizens.[52] Also like Montesquieu, he stresses the importance of humane criminal laws and rails against the horrors of the French legal system under the Criminal Ordinance of 1670.[53] Voltaire is

---

[49] On the centrality of this divide for the liberal tradition more generally, see Jacob T. Levy, "Liberalism's Divide, After Socialism and Before" *Social Philosophy & Policy* 20.1 (2003): 278–97.

[50] On Voltaire's opposition to the *parlements*, see Robert S. Tate, "Voltaire and the *Parlements*: A Reconsideration" *Studies on Voltaire and the Eighteenth Century* 241 (1986): 161–83.

[51] See Theodore Besterman, *Voltaire* (Chicago: University of Chicago Press, [1969] 1976), 314–17; and Peter Gay, *Voltaire's Politics: The Poet as Realist* (New Haven, CT: Yale University Press [1959] 1988), 87–116.

[52] Voltaire, "Thoughts on Public Administration," in *Political Writings*, trans. David Williams (Cambridge: Cambridge University Press, [1752] 1994), 216; and Voltaire, "Government," in *Questions on the Encyclopedia*, in *Political Writings*, trans. David Williams (Cambridge: Cambridge University Press, [1771] 1994), 59.

[53] See especially Voltaire, "Commentary on the Book *On Crimes and Punishments*," in *Political Writings*, trans. David Williams (Cambridge: Cambridge University Press, [1766] 1994); and Voltaire, *Prix de la justice et de l'humanité*, ed. Robert Granderoute, in *The*

best known, however, for his advocacy of freedom of expression and religious toleration. He never in fact uttered the legendary statement "I may disagree with everything you say, but I shall fight to the death for your right to say it," but the sentiment pervades his corpus.[54] And he supported religious toleration not only in word – this is arguably *the* dominant theme of his voluminous writings – but also in deed: during the last period of his life, when he lived at Ferney, Voltaire became one of the leading campaigners for the just treatment of religious minorities and dissenters in all of Europe, spending years of his rapidly advancing life defending relatively obscure victims and turning their cases into causes célèbres.[55] While Montesquieu and Voltaire were at odds regarding the best means to achieve these liberal ends in eighteenth-century France, they were largely at one regarding the ends themselves.

Voltaire also joined Montesquieu – and broke with his hero, Locke – in rejecting the social contract and natural law as political foundations. To begin with, throughout his writings Voltaire is unequivocal in affirming that human beings are inherently social, and hence that "society itself must have always existed" (EM I.intro.7, 25).[56] Further, he envisions government and political authority as arising gradually over time, rather than as the result of a formal agreement (see TM, 91–2; EM I.intro.3, 10). Not only is the idea of government based on a social contract incredibly doubtful as a matter of historical fact, in Voltaire's view; it is also invalid as a matter of right. He denies that popular consent is the only proper

---

Complete Works of Voltaire, vol. 80b (Oxford: Voltaire Foundation, [1777] 2009). For commentary, see Marcello T. Maestro, *Voltaire and Beccaria as Reformers of Criminal Law* (New York: Columbia University Press, 1942), chapters 3, 5–6.

[54] According to Roger Pearson, the source of this statement is S. G. Tallentyre's *The Friends of Voltaire* (1907); the line appears "not as a quotation but explicitly as a paraphrase of Voltaire's attitude in defence of Helvétius's *De l'esprit* (*On the Mind*) when it was banned in 1758." Roger Pearson, *Voltaire Almighty: A Life in Pursuit of Freedom* (New York: Bloomsbury, 2005), 431.

[55] Many of the works of this period of Voltaire's life are collected in Voltaire, *Treatise on Tolerance and Other Writings*, ed. Simon Harvey (Cambridge: Cambridge University Press, 2000), including not only the *Treatise on Tolerance* (1763) but also "The Story of Elisabeth Canning and the Calas Family" (1762), "An Address to the Public Concerning the Parricides Imputed to the Calas and Sirven Families" (1766), "An Account of the Death of the Chevalier de La Barre" (1766), and "The Cry of Innocent Blood" (1775). For a biography of Voltaire that concentrates on his crusades for toleration and justice in this period, see Ian Davidson, *Voltaire in Exile: The Last Years, 1753–78* (New York: Grove Press, 2004).

[56] See also EM I.intro.7, 23–4; TM, 90–1; and Voltaire, "Man," in *Questions on the Encyclopedia*, in *Political Writings*, trans. David Williams (Cambridge: Cambridge University Press, [1771] 1994), 68.

Pragmatic Liberalism

basis for political authority, or that the people have a general right to revolution whenever their government violates certain basic rights.[57] While Voltaire does utilize the concept of natural law – which, we have seen, he regards as a set of loose moral guidelines that are developed to support and protect people's basic natural desires – he refuses to use natural laws as a rigid standard by which to judge positive laws. As David Williams writes, for Voltaire "natural law belonged to the realm of speculative metaphysics, and ... was a distraction from the urgent business of securing justice in the real world."[58] Thus, we find Voltaire proclaiming that "the times are past when people like Grotius and Pufendorf ... lavished contradictions and tedium on the question of what is just and unjust. We have to get down to facts."[59]

As this call to "get down to facts" suggests, Voltaire's political thought is resolutely practical and empirical. While he was widely read in political philosophy,[60] he was intensely suspicious of abstractions and "systems," in politics no less than in other realms. Much more than Montesquieu's – or, for that matter, Hume's or Smith's – almost all of Voltaire's political writings were occasioned by a specific problem or controversy; his political ideas were deeply embedded in, and addressed to, the circumstances of eighteenth-century Europe – especially France, England, and Geneva – rather than abstract speculations meant to be applied to all possible situations.[61] As Gustave Lanson writes, Voltaire's political thought does not consist in "a fine philosophical treatise developed in the abstract to the glory of the human intellect," but rather in "a series of corrections, of repairs to the old social structure, not to be judged apart from the realities

---

[57] For an attempt, against the evidence, to portray Voltaire as a Lockean, contractarian, natural rights liberal, see Constance Rowe, *Voltaire and the State* (New York: Columbia University Press, 1955). For a corrective, see Gay, *Voltaire's Politics*.

[58] See the editor's introduction in Voltaire, *Political Writings*, ed. David Williams (Cambridge: Cambridge University Press, 1994), xxv. See also Merle L. Perkins, "Voltaire's Principles of Political Thought" *Modern Language Quarterly* 17.4 (December 1956), 300. Even Lester Crocker – no friend of Voltaire, whom he depicts as a rather careless thinker and a rigid moral universalist – maintains that "as a historian and a realist, he could not accept any theoretical intrusion of natural law theory into the realm of politics.... Voltaire never himself entertained the idea that it would be useful to object to positive laws on the basis of something so general, so nebulously connected to praxis." Lester G. Crocker, "Voltaire and the Political Philosophers" *Studies on Voltaire and the Eighteenth Century* 219 (1983), 7.

[59] Voltaire, "The Rights of Men and the Usurpation of Others," in *Political Writings*, trans. David Williams (Cambridge: Cambridge University Press, [1768] 1994), 225.

[60] See Williams, editor's introduction in Voltaire, *Political Writings*, xiii.

[61] The practical intent of Voltaire's political writings is emphasized in Gay, *Voltaire's Politics*.

100 *The Pragmatic Enlightenment*

on which they had an immediate bearing."[62] As with Montesquieu, Voltaire's political judgments rest on concrete historical and comparative analysis rather than a priori reasoning, a method that was already evident in his first major political work, the *Letters Concerning the English Nation*, which highlights the shortcomings of the government and society of eighteenth-century France through an unfavorable contrast with those of eighteenth-century England.[63] In the *Philosophical Dictionary* entry entitled "States, Governments: Which Is the Best?" Voltaire suggests that the proper grounds for evaluating the strengths and weaknesses of different regimes are travel, reading, and observation, rather than any abstract theoretical foundation (see PD, 192).

It is also noteworthy that this entry pointedly draws no conclusion about which form of government is in fact best (see PD, 194). Throughout his long career and copious writings, Voltaire never proposed a single ideal regime or a universally applicable set of laws. (Even El Dorado, the fairy-tale utopia of *Candide*, ultimately proves insufficiently enticing for the title character, and he continues on his travels after a relatively short stay there.)[64] In Voltaire's view, human nature itself presents a major obstacle to any attempt to devise an ideal form of government: human beings are sufficiently selfish and foolish that it is impossible to guarantee that *any* set of institutions or practices will ultimately prove successful. Thus he writes, in a line that encapsulates his political theory as well as any other, that "people ask every day whether a republican government is preferable to government by a king. The argument always ends up with agreement that men are very difficult to

---

[62] Gustave Lanson, *Voltaire*, trans. Robert A. Wagoner (New York: John Wiley & Sons, [1906] 1966), 157–8.

[63] For several decades it was believed that this work was written first in English by Voltaire himself and then translated into French as the *Lettres philosophiques* (1734), but it has recently been shown that the English version of 1733 was in fact anonymously translated from Voltaire's French by John Lockman. See Nicholas Cronk, "The *Letters Concerning the English Nation* as an English Work: Reconsidering the Harcourt Brown Thesis" *Studies on Voltaire and the Eighteenth Century* 2001.10 (2001): 226–39; and J. Patrick Lee, "The Unexamined Premise: Voltaire, John Lockman, and the Myth of the *English Letters*" *Studies on Voltaire and the Eighteenth Century* 2001.10 (2001): 240–70. Still, the 1733 version was approved by Voltaire and accurately captures his wit and spirit, so I have continued to use it rather than a more recent translation.

[64] See Voltaire, *Candide*, in *Candide and Related Texts*, trans. David Wootton (Indianapolis: Hackett, [1759] 2000), 41. For a helpful discussion of this episode and its political implications, see Haydn Mason, *Candide: Optimism Demolished* (New York: Twayne, 1992), 54–7. For a more detailed analysis, see William F. Bottiglia, *Voltaire's Candide: Analysis of a Classic*, second edition (Geneva: Institut et Musée Voltaire, 1964), 139–62.

Pragmatic Liberalism 101

govern."[65] An equally serious obstacle, however, is the necessity of choosing institutions and practices that suit a nation's particular circumstances. Once again like Montesquieu, Voltaire maintains that no blueprint will fit every situation and that the "best" regime for a given nation depends on that nation's history, customs, mores, and other characteristics. Hence, as Merle Perkins writes, for Voltaire "attempts to transcend the confusion of political experience in order to depict an ideal society compatible with an unchanging world of form are of little worth."[66]

As we have seen, Voltaire was a proponent of a strong monarchy in eighteenth-century France. In contrast to Montesquieu (see SL 29.18, 617), he frequently suggests that France should be ruled by a uniform civil and criminal code, largely in hopes of curbing abuses of power like those of the *parlement* of Toulouse that led to the infamous Calas affair.[67] However, he certainly never suggests that these codes – or the French system more generally – would be desirable or applicable in all times and places. On the contrary, he often presents the French regime in a rather negative light, especially in comparison with that of England. Yet Voltaire was adamant that the English regime could not be simply reproduced in France. As Peter Gay writes:

Voltaire was too good a historian to forget that institutions cannot be simply transplanted from one country to another. England had a vigorous tradition of parliamentarianism, hence the strengthening of the legislature was the road to freedom; France's legislative bodies had fallen in desuetude or had become spokesmen for class interests, hence in France the road to freedom lay in the strengthening of the king's ministers. While Voltaire held his political values from the beginning of his life to the end, he understood that the forms in which they could be realized were various. Therefore he developed a flexible, pragmatic political program.[68]

Given the history and circumstances of the France of his time – above all the enormous influence of the Church and the poverty and ignorance

---

[65] Voltaire, "Democracy," in *Questions on the Encyclopedia*, in *Political Writings*, trans. David Williams (Cambridge: Cambridge University Press, [1771] 1994), 37.

[66] Perkins, "Voltaire's Principles of Political Thought," 289–90.

[67] See, for example, PD, 289; Voltaire, "Commentary on the Book *On Crimes and Punishments*," 278; and Voltaire, *The Age of Louis XIV*, chapter 29.

[68] Peter Gay, *The Party of Humanity: Essays in the French Enlightenment* (New York: W. W. Norton, 1964), 92. Similarly, Maurice Cranston observes that "as Voltaire understood it, the history of England had for several centuries moved in a different direction from that of France.... By the end of the seventeenth century, the two kingdoms had been shaped by different histories, inherited different problems and acquired a different set of institutions; so that the same remedies could not be expected to be effective in both kingdoms." Cranston, *Philosophers and Pamphleteers*, 47.

prevalent among the common people – Voltaire was convinced that it would be better served by a strong monarchy than by a representative government.

It is also crucial to note that Voltaire saw the English regime as having important drawbacks of its own. Like Montesquieu, he frequently depicts England as a sort of ideal, lauding its mixed government, religious toleration, freedom of expression, extensive commerce, and liberal criminal laws.[69] Also like Montesquieu, however, he expresses a good deal of ambivalence about England's government and society throughout his writings. For instance, he points to the fervently partisan nature of English politics and the ubiquitous corruption of office both in his published works and in his notebooks from his stay there.[70] He also notes that the freedom of expression that he so admires was far from complete, as a man had recently been sent to the Tower for criticizing one of the king's speeches.[71] In *Candide*, he highlights the barbaric execution of Admiral John Byng for losing Minorca to the French during the Seven Years War, famously quipping that the English seemed to think it "a good idea to kill an admiral from time to time in order to encourage the others" (*pour encourager les autres*).[72] Even in the *Letters Concerning the English Nation*, in the midst of his praise for the religious toleration found in England, he underscores the fact that dissenters and Catholics were essentially second-class citizens, sardonically observing that "tho' every one is permitted to serve God in whatever mode or fashion he thinks proper ... no person can possess an employment either in *England* or *Ireland*, unless he be rank'd among the faithful, that is, professes himself a member of the Church of *England*. This reason (which carries

---

[69] For some of his best-known tributes, see LCE, 30, 34, 42; and Voltaire, "Government," 60–1.

[70] See, for instance, LCE, 33; Voltaire, *The A B C, or Dialogues between A B C*, in *Political Writings*, trans. David Williams (Cambridge: Cambridge University Press, [1768] 1994), 128; and Voltaire, *Notebooks*, vol. 2, ed. Theodore Besterman, in *The Complete Works of Voltaire*, vol. 82 (Geneva: Institut et Musée Voltaire, 1968), 529–30, 612. On Voltaire's views of English politics during his stay there – which took place from 1726 to 1728, just preceding Montesquieu's trip from 1729 to 1731 – and the background against which he wrote, see Dennis Fletcher, *Voltaire: Lettres philosophiques* (London: Grant & Cutler, 1986), 21–7.

[71] See Voltaire, *Notebooks*, vol. 1, ed. Theodore Besterman, in *The Complete Works of Voltaire*, vol. 81 (Geneva: Institut et Musée Voltaire, 1968), 66.

[72] Voltaire, *Candide*, 58–9. In a later chapter, the Manichean Martin calls attention to the freedom of speech and of the press in England, but the Venetian nobleman Pococurante replies that "partisan politics and doctrinaire thinking ... corrupt everything that this precious liberty produces which would otherwise be worth admiring." Ibid., 65–6.

Pragmatic Liberalism

mathematical evidence with it) has converted such numbers of dissenters of all persuasions, that not a twentieth part of the nation is out of the pale of the establish'd church" (LCE 26; see also 25, 33).[73] Voltaire was frequently willing to overlook such problems in his eulogies to the English regime in order to put France's shortcomings into sharper relief, but he never lost sight of them.

Moreover, in stark contrast to the ascendant Whig view of English history, according to which England had enjoyed its liberty from time immemorial – a view that Montesquieu sometimes seemed to embrace (see SL 11.6, 165–6) – Voltaire stresses that England's mixed regime with all its advantages had emerged only recently, and that it had done so only with great difficulty. He goes to great lengths to show that the English had experienced centuries upon centuries of tyranny, slavery, religious persecution, and civil war: they "waded thro' seas of blood to drown the Idol of arbitrary Power" (LCE, 34; see also 33, 37–40); their island has been "a theater of so many blood-soaked tragedies";[74] they have endured "the most frightful abuses that have ever made human nature shudder."[75] In keeping with his support for the *thèse royale* in France, Voltaire suggests that throughout most of English history the clergy and the nobility were the chief oppressors of the people. The English boast of having had a Parliament for many centuries, he notes caustically, "as tho' these assemblies ... compos'd of ecclesiastical Tyrants, and of plunderers entitled Barons, had been the guardians of the publick liberty and happiness" (LCE, 37). (Voltaire's views of feudal England are actually quite similar to Hume's and Smith's on this score.) England had resembled most other European nations until quite recently, according to Voltaire, and the present mixed regime had come about through a confluence of unique factors, ranging from the fact that Britain is an island, a characteristic that diminished the need for a large standing army, to the obstinate and freedom-loving English "spirit."[76] Voltaire dwells on the long and difficult process that brought about the English regime, and the many unique factors that sustain it, in order to highlight how unexpected and atypical it was, and how difficult it would be to emulate elsewhere. Hence, immediately after one of his more fulsome paeans to English liberty, he asks rhetorically, "Why then are these laws not followed in other countries?

---

[73] This is an allusion to the Corporation and Test Acts, which restricted public offices to members of the Anglican Church.

[74] Voltaire, "Government," 59.

[75] Ibid., 60.

[76] See ibid., 56–60.

104 *The Pragmatic Enlightenment*

Is that not the same as asking why coconuts flourish in India, but do not do very well in Rome?"[77]

Still further evidence that Voltaire believed a nation's political institutions and practices should be suited to its particular circumstances can be found in the fact that he supported a more popular government than England's – something approaching democracy – in some smaller nations such as Holland and Geneva. Voltaire lived on the doorsteps of the latter city-state for the last several decades of his life and became deeply involved in its politics. As Gay shows, over the course of the 1760s his support moved from the patricians (Négatifs) to the bourgeoisie (Représentants) and finally to the common workers (*natifs*), much to the consternation of his upper-class Genevan friends.[78] By the end of the decade, some of Voltaire's writings seem to toy with the idea that a democratic republic is the best form of government. For instance, in "Republican Ideas," a pamphlet in which he poses as "a member of a public body" writing to his fellow citizens in Geneva, Voltaire proclaims that "the most tolerable of all systems is undoubtedly the republican one, because that is the one which brings men closer to a state of natural equality."[79] Yet even in his later writings he continues to acknowledge the very real downsides of small republics – above all, their liability to descend into anarchy and thence to tyranny – and to insist that "democracy seems to suit only very small countries, and even then the country has to be favorably situated."[80]

On the opposite end of the spectrum, Voltaire believed that in other nations of his time, such as the Prussia of Frederick II and the Russia of Catherine II, an absolute monarchy was necessary. This is, of course, one of the most frequently criticized aspects of Voltaire's thought: his penchant for so-called enlightened despotism. Contrary to a common caricature of him, however, Voltaire did not advocate, as an abstract ideal, the granting of dictatorial powers to a philosopher-king in order to implement the philosophes' program against all opposition. Rather, he

---

[77] Ibid., 61.

[78] See Gay, *Voltaire's Politics*, chapter 4.

[79] Voltaire, "Republican Ideas," in *Political Writings*, trans. David Williams (Cambridge: Cambridge University Press, [1765] 1994), 207. For an essay that places this pamphlet in the context of the Genevan politics of the time, see Peter Gay, "Voltaire's *Idées républicaines*: A Study in Bibliography and Interpretation" *Studies on Voltaire and the Eighteenth Century* 6 (1958): 67–105. For other instances of Voltaire hinting at the superiority of democratic republics, see PD, 287; and Voltaire, *The A B C*, 126–7.

[80] Voltaire, "Democracy," 35. See also Voltaire, "Republican Ideas," 201–2; and Voltaire, "Politics," in *Questions on the Encyclopedia*, in *Political Writings*, trans. David Williams (Cambridge: Cambridge University Press, [1774] 1994), 83.

Pragmatic Liberalism 105

believed that absolute monarchy was well suited to nations like Prussia and Russia because of their "backward" and "uncivilized" character and because of the need to weaken traditionally privileged groups such as the nobility and clergy.[81] Moreover, he distinguishes carefully between "absolute" and "despotic" authority, favoring the former in certain situations but rejecting the latter. In Voltaire's view, even "absolute" rulers must rule through and be bound by laws; what he advocated in the case of Frederick and Catherine was more (extreme) centralization than despotism.[82] In fact, the indispensability of the rule of law is a constant theme in Voltaire's political writings, one that he returns to with almost obsessive frequency.[83] As surprising as it might seem, then, Voltaire rejects despotism – the arbitrary or lawless rule of a single individual – even more firmly than does Montesquieu, who saw it as unavoidable in certain situations.[84] In other words, the rule of law does seem to be universally desirable, in Voltaire's eyes, although this is once again a kind of "negative universalism" that is more concerned to prevent a certain

[81] Voltaire's turbulent relationship with Frederick, in particular, has received a great deal of scholarly attention, and it is unnecessary to recount its details here. Among the more useful of the accounts of this relationship and the light it sheds on Voltaire's thought are A. Owen Aldridge, *Voltaire and the Century of Light* (Princeton, NJ: Princeton University Press, 1975), chapters 9–10, 15–16; Gay, *Voltaire's Politics*, 144–71; Haydn Mason, *Voltaire: A Biography* (Baltimore: Johns Hopkins University Press, 1981), chapter 3; and Ira O. Wade, *The Intellectual Development of Voltaire* (Princeton, NJ: Princeton University Press, 1969), 292–328.

[82] In an essay published in 1752, when he was still in residence at Frederick's court in Potsdam, Voltaire writes that "despotism is the abuse of kingship, just as anarchy is the abuse of republican government. A prince who, without judicial procedure and without justice, imprisons a citizen or causes him to die, is a highwayman they call *Your Majesty*." Voltaire, "Thoughts on Public Administration," 221. See also Voltaire, *The A B C*, 98; Cranston, *Philosophers and Pamphleteers*, 42; and Gay, *The Party of Humanity*, 29.

[83] For just a few examples, see PD, 194; Voltaire, "Thoughts on Public Administration," 216–7; Voltaire, "Republican Ideas," 198; Voltaire, *The A B C*, 167; and Voltaire, "Government," 59.

[84] This is all the more surprising because, in stark contrast to Montesquieu, Voltaire was a consistent and unabashed Sinophile. See Basil Guy, *The French Image of China before and after Voltaire* (Geneva: Institut et Musée Voltaire, 1963), chapter 5. This apparent incongruity can be explained by the fact that Voltaire, unlike Montesquieu, believed that China and other nations of the East in fact enjoyed the rule of law. In his extended dialogue *The A B C*, the character B, in one of the many instances in which he seems to be speaking for Voltaire, pauses in the midst of a discussion of Montesquieu to opine: "Our authors have been pleased (I don't know why) to call the sovereigns of Asia and Africa *despots*.... I've never been to China, but ... I know from the unanimous reports from our missionaries of various sects, that China is governed by laws, and not by a single arbitrary will." Voltaire, *The A B C*, 97.

evil – arbitrary rule – in all circumstances than to demand the same type of regime, institutions, or practices in all circumstances.

Other than the rule of law – a fairly minimal requirement – Voltaire too avoids setting strict criteria that must be met in order to attain political legitimacy. On the contrary, he shows a great deal of flexibility in his political outlook, not just in terms of regime types but also in terms of even his most cherished values. As Gay notes, "he deplored poverty, hated war, campaigned against torture, but he admitted that poverty was necessary, war inevitable, and torture, in exceptional circumstances, useful."[85] While Voltaire finds laws of primogeniture "detestable," for instance, he accepts that such laws are "very good in a time of anarchy and pillage. Then the eldest son is the captain of the castle which will sooner or later be assailed by brigands. The younger sons are his chief officers, the laborers his soldiers" (PD, 288). Similarly, in "Republican Ideas" he offers a number of illustrations to show that "when times have palpably changed, there are laws that must be changed."[86] For example: "The law permitting the imprisonment of a citizen without preliminary investigation and without judicial formalities would be tolerable in times of trouble and of war; in times of peace it would be iniquitous and tyrannical."[87] "A sumptuary law, which is good in a poor republic bereft of the arts, becomes absurd when the city has become industrious and opulent."[88] Even religious toleration cannot be deemed universally desirable, in Voltaire's view: while he sees intolerance as a "ridiculous barbarity" now that "tolerance has become the dominant dogma of all respectable people in Europe," he accepts (in an apparent reference to the founding of the Genevan republic) that "if a republic was created during a time of religious war, if during these troubles it removed from its territory sects that were hostile to its own [sect], it behaved wisely, because it saw itself like a country surrounded by people stricken with the plague, and feared that someone might bring the plague in."[89] Like Montesquieu, Voltaire finds categorical political principles, made in abstraction from particular circumstances, to be ill considered and impractical.

All told, then, Voltaire's political outlook was emphatically practical and flexible, embedded in and addressed to the specific circumstances of various European nations. He supported a mixed constitutional

[85] Gay, *Voltaire's Politics*, 23.
[86] Voltaire, "Republican Ideas," 199.
[87] Ibid.
[88] Ibid.
[89] Ibid., 200–1.

Pragmatic Liberalism 107

government in England, a more popular republic in Geneva and Holland, a strong monarchy in France, and an even stronger and more centralized one in Frederick's Prussia and Catherine's Russia. While he generally had kinder things to say about England and Geneva than France, Prussia, or Russia, he did not think that any of these regimes was simply the "best" form of government. On the contrary, he insisted that such judgments cannot properly be made in the abstract, that they can only be based on contextually sensitive empirical analysis. As Lanson writes, "his program, precisely because it was a practical one, contained nothing absolute or definitive."[90]

CONVENTION AND CONTEXT IN HUME'S POLITICAL THOUGHT

While Hume has often been depicted as a conservative,[91] he was in fact, no less than Montesquieu and Voltaire, an integral member of the liberal tradition, broadly conceived.[92] To begin with, Hume shows virtually no reverence for the past, the traditional, or the ancestral; on the contrary, he often laments the "propensity almost inherent in human nature" to "declaim against present times, and magnify the virtue of remote ancestors" (EMPL, 278; see also 464), and he shows in extraordinary detail – six large volumes – that most of British history had been a story of insecurity and dependence. In the concluding paragraph of the second volume of his *History of England* – the last of the volumes in order of composition – he advises that the British "ought to be cautious in appealing to the practice of their ancestors" and suggests that the chief use of a study of British history is that it will lead people "to cherish their present

---

[90] Lanson, *Voltaire*, 159.

[91] One of the best-known statements to this effect is John Stuart Mill's contention that Hume's "absolute scepticism in speculation very naturally brought him round to Toryism in practice; for if no faith can be had in the operations of human intellect, and one side of every question is about as likely as another to be true, a man will commonly be inclined to prefer that order of things which, being no more wrong than every other, he has hitherto found compatible with his private comforts." John Stuart Mill, "Bentham," in *Essays on Ethics, Religion and Society*, ed. J. M. Robinson, in *Collected Works of John Stuart Mill*, vol. 10 (Toronto: University of Toronto Press, 1969), 80. More recently, Donald Livingston has argued that Hume was "the first conservative philosopher." Donald W. Livingston, *Hume's Philosophy of Common Life* (Chicago: University of Chicago Press, 1984), 310.

[92] Friedrich Hayek goes so far as to proclaim that "Hume gives us probably the only comprehensive statement of the legal and political philosophy which later became known as liberalism." F. A. Hayek, "The Legal and Political Philosophy of David Hume," in *Hume*, ed. V. C. Chappell (Garden City: Anchor Books, 1966), 340.

108   *The Pragmatic Enlightenment*

constitution, from a comparison or contrast with the condition of those distant times" (HE II, 525). Further, as this statement suggests, Hume found much to admire in the liberal British government and society of his time. As Frederick Whelan writes,

> he was largely satisfied with (though not dogmatically committed to) the political outcome of the seventeenth-century revolutions in Great Britain and with the modern society that was emerging in his own lifetime; for example, he endorsed the balanced constitution, representative government, the rule of law, religious toleration, liberty of philosophical speculation, private property, the pursuit of private happiness, and commercial society. Such positions constitute a readily recognizable approximation of much of the classical liberal construct.[93]

Nor did Hume simply rest content with the status quo in post-1688 Britain: he did not hesitate to push for certain reforms, above all in order to encourage commerce and free trade and to combat political factiousness and religious intolerance.[94]

Like Montesquieu and Voltaire, Hume embraced these liberal ideals without resting them on any universal foundation. He is, of course, probably history's most famous and influential critic of the notion of the social contract as the only valid basis for political legitimacy and political right. He maintains that the state of nature is "a mere philosophical fiction, which never had, and never cou'd have any reality" (THN 3.2.2.14, 317; see also EPM 3.15–16, 17) and that political authority and obligation arise not all at once, through voluntary agreement, but rather "more casually and more imperfectly" (EMPL, 39; see also 468–9). He also rejects the idea that political authority and obligation rest solely on the people's consent, holding that such a view is "repugnant to the common sentiments of mankind, and to the practice and opinion of all nations and all ages" (EMPL, 486).[95] According to Hume, the duty of allegiance

---

[93] Frederick G. Whelan, *Hume and Machiavelli: Political Realism and Liberal Thought* (Lanham, MD: Lexington, 2004), 27; see also Frederick G. Whelan, *Order and Artifice in Hume's Political Philosophy* (Princeton, NJ: Princeton University Press, 1985), 356–7.

[94] The reformist aspects of Hume's thought are emphasized – perhaps overemphasized – in John B. Stewart, *Opinion and Reform in Hume's Political Philosophy* (Princeton, NJ: Princeton University Press, 1992), especially chapters 5 and 6. See also, more recently, Neil McArthur, *David Hume's Political Theory: Law, Commerce, and the Constitution of Government* (Toronto: University of Toronto Press, 2007).

[95] Hume does not deny that popular consent may be "one just foundation of government where it has place," and he even claims that "it is surely the best and most sacred of any." He insists, however, that "it has very seldom had place in any degree, and never almost in its full extent," and thus that "some other foundation of government must also be admitted" (EMPL, 474). For an argument that Hume was, despite all of his protestations to the contrary, ultimately a contractarian at heart, see David Gauthier, "David

Pragmatic Liberalism 109

to government derives not from consent or a contract but rather from utility – the usefulness of a government that is able to preserve peace and order among people, and the necessity of obeying it if it is to prove effective – and ultimately from people's sentiments, their approval of such allegiance (see THN 3.2.8.4–9, 347–51; EPM 4.1, 28; EMPL, 480–1). In other words, a government is not legitimate because (or when) people consent to it; rather, people consent to it because (or when) it is legitimate or approval-worthy – when it has met the test of utility.[96] Hence, despite his liberal inclinations, Hume eschews the idea of natural or inalienable rights derived from the notion of the social contract – or, for that matter, from human nature, natural law, or any other source.[97]

Hume also repudiates the idea that natural law can serve as a determinate standard by which to judge positive laws. He does allow that certain rules of justice may be called "laws of nature," but he sees these rules as entirely artificial or conventional: they arise spontaneously over time as people coordinate their actions and sentiments in response to others, and come to see the utility of these rules (see THN 3.2.2.19, 311; 3.2.6.10, 342). Hume uses the term "justice" in a rather narrow sense to denote the virtue of obedience to the rules that regulate and protect property,[98] and he suggests that these rules can be considered "natural" – despite being artificial or conventional – in the sense that they develop from people's natural tendency to create social conventions, much the same way that languages develop (see THN 3.2.2.19, 311; 3.2.2.9–10, 314–15). Some scholars have interpreted Hume as believing that the rules of justice thus developed are universally the same and universally

---

Hume, Contractarian" *Philosophical Review* 88.1 (January 1979): 3–38. For rebuttals, see Stephen Buckle and Dario Castiglione, "Hume's Critique of the Contract Theory" *History of Political Thought* 12.3 (autumn 1991): 457–80; and Frederick G. Whelan, "Hume and Contractarianism" *Polity* 27.2 (winter 1994): 201–24.

[96] See Whelan, "Hume and Contractarianism," 213–14.

[97] As Whelan notes, "except for one passing reference, Hume is silent in his philosophical works with respect to the concepts of natural liberty and natural rights." Ibid., 220. (The one passing reference to "natural liberty" occurs at EPM 4.1, 28.) See also Whelan, *Order and Artifice in Hume's Political Philosophy*, 359–60; Pangle, "The Liberal Critique of Rights in Montesquieu and Hume"; and Knud Haakonssen, *Natural Law and Moral Philosophy: From Grotius to the Scottish Enlightenment* (Cambridge: Cambridge University Press, 1996), 117–19.

[98] This is largely the case in the *Treatise* and the second *Enquiry*, at least: Annette Baier shows that Hume's conception of justice grew over time, such that in the *History of England* and some of his later essays he uses the term to refer to issues concerning retributive justice and even distributive justice. See Annette C. Baier, *The Cautious Jealous Virtue: Hume on Justice* (Cambridge, MA: Harvard University Press, 2010), especially chapter 4.

valid,[99] and at times Hume himself seems to suggest as much (e.g., THN 3.3.6.5, 395; EPM App. 3.9, 99). Yet the very fact that these rules are "artificial" suggests that they are at least historically contingent: Hume holds that there is no such thing as justice "among rude and savage men" (THN 3.2.2.8, 313–14; see also 3.2.2.28, 321–2). Moreover, he maintains that even after these rules have been developed, they apply only under certain circumstances, which John Rawls famously dubs "the circumstances of justice."[100] Hume writes:

> the rules of equity or justice depend entirely on the particular state and condition, in which men are placed, and owe their origin and existence to that UTILITY, which results to the public from their strict and regular observance. Reverse, in any considerable circumstance, the condition of men: Produce extreme abundance or extreme necessity: Implant in the human breast perfect moderation and humanity or perfect rapaciousness and malice: By rendering justice totally *useless*, you thereby totally destroy its essence, and suspend its obligation upon mankind. (EPM 3.12, 16; see also THN 3.2.2.16–17, 317–18)

While the circumstances of justice – essentially, moderate scarcity and limited benevolence – are of course extraordinarily common,[101] they point to an even deeper contingency in Hume's conception of justice: the rules of justice only hold when they are useful, and they are not *always* useful. For this reason, Hume finds it obvious that justice cannot be founded on abstract reason or on any "connexions and relations of ideas, which are eternal, immutable, and universally obligatory" (THN 3.2.2.20, 318).

Still further, Hume accepts that the actual *content* of justice – the specific set of rules that are used to govern and protect property – will vary from society to society. While most societies find it necessary to regulate property by *some* "general inflexible rules" (EPM App. 3.6, 97), they each settle on their own specific rules based on what they find useful in their

---

[99] According to MacIntyre, for example, Hume treats the rules of justice "as holding for all times and places ... ever since the rules were first artificially contrived." Alasdair MacIntyre, *Whose Justice? Which Rationality?* (Notre Dame, IN: University of Notre Dame Press, 1988), 308.

[100] See John Rawls, *A Theory of Justice* (Cambridge, MA: Harvard University Press, 1971), section 22.

[101] Hume indicates, however, that the obligations of justice do not always hold even in the modern world: they do not apply to certain abundant goods, such as air and water; they are negated in times of extreme scarcity, such as among survivors of a shipwreck, inhabitants of a besieged city, or people enduring famine; they are rendered obsolete in some close personal relationships, such as among many married couples; and they cease to apply in circumstances in which no regard for others can be expected, such as in a war with "barbarians" or when a person falls "into the society of ruffians" (see EPM 3.4–11, 13–16).

Pragmatic Liberalism

particular circumstances. "In general," Hume writes, "we may observe, that all questions of property are subordinate to the authority of civil laws, which extend, refrain, modify, and alter the rules of natural justice, according to the particular *convenience* of each community" (EPM 3.34, 22, Hume's italics). As Annette Baier writes, Hume sees the rules governing property "not as universal but as varying from community to community and as changeable by human will as conditions, needs, wishes, or human fancies change."[102] Since Hume's "laws of nature," unlike Locke's, are themselves conventional, they have no prior or higher status than do civil laws (see THN 3.2.8.4, 347–8); rather, civil laws simply instantiate the rules of justice in a particular set of circumstances.[103] In short, as Krause writes, "when it comes to justice, Hume is anxious to show that there is nothing sacred (either literally or metaphorically) about this virtue":[104] it is artificial or conventional, its very existence remains contingent on certain circumstances, and its specific contents vary from society to society.

More generally, Hume is skeptical of abstract, universal standards of political right, whether derived from God, Reason, or Nature. He frequently warns that "all general maxims in politics ought to be established with great caution" (EMPL, 366; see also 87), and he stresses that "parties from *principle*, especially abstract speculative principle," tend to promote fanaticism and conflict and thereby bring about "the greatest misery and devastation" (EMPL, 60–1).[105] In his view, "a strict adherence to general rules" in politics is often the result of "bigotry and superstition" rather than reason or prudence: "In this particular, the study of history confirms the reasonings of true philosophy; which ... teaches us to regard the controversies in politics as incapable of any decision in most

---

[102] Annette C. Baier, *Moral Prejudices: Essay on Ethics* (Cambridge, MA: Harvard University Press, 1994), 55. See also Richard P. Hiskes, "Has Hume a Theory of Social Justice?" *Hume Studies* 3.2 (November 1977), 80–1; and Whelan, *Order and Artifice in Hume's Political Philosophy*, 233–4. In the *History of England* Hume concedes that even the rules governing property in feudal Europe, which included laws of primogeniture and the like, "suited the peculiar circumstances of that age" (HE I, 115).

[103] Thus, we find Hume asserting that "our property is nothing but those goods, whose constant possession is establish'd by the laws of society; that is, by the laws of justice" (THN 3.2.2.11, 315).

[104] Sharon R. Krause, "Hume and the (False) Luster of Justice" *Political Theory* 32.5 (October 2004), 638.

[105] As James King writes, "it cannot be overemphasized that Hume is fundamentally opposed to the politics of principle and thinks of it as a source of excesses and of great ills in political life." James T. King, "The Virtue of Political Skepticism" *Reason Papers* 15 (summer 1990), 26–7.

cases, and as entirely subordinate to the interest of peace and liberty" (THN 3.2.10.15, 359). In other words, Hume is wary of abstract political principles not only because they often prove dangerous, but also because he deems it impossible to escape or surmount entirely the contingency inherent in the political world and what he calls "common life." As Stuart Warner and Donald Livingston write, "his understanding of philosophy demands that in politics we begin with the provisional autonomy of the practices of our current political order. These practices can, of course, be criticized, but only in terms of other features of our practices: There is nothing else to which one can appeal."[106] Given that he saw politics as resting on convention all the way down, Hume was far from believing "That Politics May Be Reduced to a Science," despite having written an essay by that name.[107]

As the preceding statements indicate, Hume's political thought is deeply historical in character. Given the importance of custom, habit, and opinion in political life, he suggests that it is history, rather than any abstract theory, that offers the proper grounds for justification in political disputes: "Examples and precedents, uniform and ancient, can surely fix the nature of any constitution, and the limits of any form of

[106] See the editors' introduction in David Hume, *Political Writings*, ed. Stuart D. Warner and Donald W. Livingston (Indianapolis: Hackett, 1994), xviii. This is a running theme of Livingston, *Hume's Philosophy of Common Life*; and Donald W. Livingston, *Philosophical Melancholy and Delirium: Hume's Pathology of Philosophy* (Chicago: University of Chicago Press, 1998).

[107] The stated goal of this essay is to show that "so great is the force of laws, and of particular forms of government, and so little dependence have they on the humours and tempers of men, that consequences *almost* as general and certain may *sometimes* be deduced from them, as any which the mathematical sciences afford us" (EMPL, 16, emphases added). However, rather than offer a scientific basis from which to derive political principles, Hume proceeds to argue merely that each type of government has better and worse forms; for example, a representative democracy is superior to a pure democracy, a nobility that rules as a group (as in Venice) is superior to one in which each noble rules a separate fiefdom (as in Poland), and a hereditary monarchy is superior to an elective one. Moreover, James Conniff has shown that even these quite limited arguments are "disingenuous," and that Hume's true intent is "to demolish the claims made by various republican thinkers, especially Harrington, to have achieved a politics based on science," and thereby to promote political moderation. James Conniff, "Hume's Political Methodology: A Reconsideration of 'That Politics May Be Reduced to a Science'" *Review of Politics* 38.1 (January 1976), 90 and passim. See also Andrew Sabl, "When Bad Things Happen from Good People (and Vice-Versa): David Hume's Political Ethics of Revolution" *Polity* 35.1 (autumn 2002), especially 76–9. Elsewhere, Hume states explicitly that "the science of politics affords few rules, which will not admit of some exception, and which may not sometimes be controuled by fortune and accident" (EMPL, 477).

Pragmatic Liberalism

government. *There is indeed no other principle by which those landmarks or boundaries can be settled*" (HE V, 583, emphasis added; see also 545). Rather than attempt to devise timeless political ideals, Hume turns instead – in his chief political works, the *Essays* and *History of England* – to an examination of the different institutions and practices that have prevailed throughout history, how they evolved to fit different sets of circumstances, and how they compare to one another.[108] Like Montesquieu and Voltaire, then, Hume provides a nonfoundationalist case for liberalism, one that supports liberal institutions and practices not by resting them on any universal principle, but by showing that historical and comparative analyses reveal them to be relative improvements on the alternatives.[109] (In this, he follows his own dictum that "every thing in this world is judg'd of by comparison" [THN 2.1.11.18, 210; see also 2.2.8.2, 240; 3.2.10.5, 356].)

Like all liberals, Hume places a special emphasis on goods such as personal freedom, security, and prosperity, and prefers regimes that protect and promote these goods to regimes that do not. He declares that liberty constitutes "the perfection of civil society," although he is quick to note that it must be balanced with order or authority, which is "essential to [society's] very existence" (EMPL, 41; see also HE VI, 533). Hume uses the word "liberty" in a number of different senses, but the most central to his outlook is what he calls "personal" liberty (as opposed to "political" or "civil" liberty), which allows individuals to choose their own course in life – where to live, what occupation to practice, how to use their property, and so on – within the limits of, and under the protection provided by, the rule of law (HE II, 522, 524).[110] In keeping with the historical

---

[108] Knud Haakonssen rightly suggests that Hume's political theory consists above all in "an explanation of why political theorizing in abstraction from historical conditions is futile and often dangerous." Knud Haakonssen, "The Structure of Hume's Political Theory," in *The Cambridge Companion to Hume*, ed. David Fate Norton and Jacqueline Taylor, second edition (Cambridge: Cambridge University Press, 2009), 357.

[109] For an extended argument along these lines, see Don Herzog, *Without Foundations: Justification in Political Theory* (Ithaca, NY: Cornell University Press, 1985), chapter 4.

[110] Hume is always careful to differentiate liberty in this sense from license. In a letter to his publisher written shortly after the widespread rioting in London in response to the "Wilkes affair," he writes: "It pleases me to hear, that Affairs settle in London, and that the Mob are likely to be no longer predominant. I wish, that People do not take a Disgust at Liberty; a word, that has been so much profand by these polluted Mouths, that men of Sense are sick at the very mention of it. I hope a new term will be invented to express so valuable and good a thing." David Hume, letter to William Strahan, 26 October 1772, in *New Letters of David Hume*, ed. Raymond Klibansky and Ernest C. Mossner (Oxford: Clarendon Press, 1954), 196. For a discussion of the different meanings that

114   *The Pragmatic Enlightenment*

nature of his political thought, however, he does not use even this kind of liberty as a single yardstick by which to measure all regimes. As Warner and Livingston note:

> Hume does not have any grand, speculative theory of liberty to offer. For Hume, there is no timeless object called liberty that can be discovered by autonomous reason. Rather, liberty refers to a complex set of conventions or practices that have been hammered out over time. Thus, one will not find in Hume a set of necessary and sufficient conditions for applying the term 'liberty.' Instead, he presents his understanding of liberty through a narrative of the evolution of the experience of liberty.[111]

Accordingly, there is in Hume's view no one type of regime or set of institutions that uniquely affords personal liberty; it can be found under almost any form of government, monarchies as well as republics.[112]

Partly for this reason, Hume joins Montesquieu and Voltaire in denying that there is a single best regime type or a universally applicable set of laws. In fact, he voices his agreement with "a late author of genius, as well as learning" – Montesquieu – that "the laws have, or ought to have, a constant reference to the constitution of government, the manners, the climate, the religion, the commerce, the situation of each society" (EPM 3.34, 22).[113] Of course, Hume did at one point devise a sort of ideal-government-in-thought, in his "Idea of a Perfect Commonwealth." This essay outlines a plan for a federal republic that, as Hume notes, bears a certain "resemblance ... to the commonwealth of the United Provinces, a wise and renowned government" (EMPL, 526). Yet the essay itself opens and closes on a note of marked diffidence, noting the many obstacles to instituting any government formulated in the abstract, the great imprudence of doing so in the vast majority of circumstances, and the ills to which it would inevitably be subject (see EMPL, 512–14, 528–9). Moreover, as Whelan writes, "Hume offers this highly untypical essay as a speculative exercise, almost a *jeu d'esprit*."[114] More representative of Hume's outlook

---

  Hume attaches to the word "liberty," see Livingston, *Philosophical Melancholy and Delirium*, chapter 8.

[111] Warner and Livingston, editors' introduction in Hume, *Political Writings*, xxv. See also Livingston, *Philosophical Melancholy and Delirium*, 175–6, 178.

[112] For an extended argument along these lines, see Duncan Forbes, *Hume's Philosophical Politics* (Cambridge: Cambridge University Press, 1975), chapter 5.

[113] The appropriate laws and form of government are so dependent on a society's particular context, in fact, that in certain circumstances they are not necessary at all: see THN 3.2.8.1, 345.

[114] Whelan, *Order and Artifice in Hume's Political Philosophy*, 342; see also David Miller, *Philosophy and Ideology in Hume's Political Thought* (Oxford: Clarendon Press, 1981),

Pragmatic Liberalism 115

is his insistence elsewhere that it is vain to dwell on "any fine imaginary republic, of which a man may form a plan in his closet" (EMPL, 52) and that "the idea ... of a perfect and immortal commonwealth will always be found as chimerical as that of a perfect and immortal man" (HE VI, 153).[115]

As we have seen, Hume professed great admiration for the British government of his time. Indeed, he proclaims that "it may justly be affirmed, without any danger of exaggeration, that we, in this island, have ever since [the revolution of 1688] enjoyed, if not the best system of government, at least the most entire system of liberty, that ever was known amongst mankind" (HE VI, 531; see also II, 525; EMPL, 508). Yet Hume deliberately distanced himself from the self-satisfied Whig view of Britain's "matchless" constitution, a move that led to accusations, both in Hume's time and since, that he had written a "Tory" history of that nation.[116] To begin with, Hume (like Voltaire) saw Britain's "entire system of liberty" as a quite recent achievement, rather than as something that was inherent in a venerable "ancient constitution." As Knud Haakonssen puts it, in Hume's view "the freedom enjoyed by modern Britons was ... an unenvisaged outcome of the messy power politics of the Revolution and of the subsequent years," and thus "rather than the certainty of antiquity, the system of liberty had all the uncertainty of novelty."[117]

---

158. Hume characterizes the topic of the essay as one of "curiosity" and "speculation," and he accepts that the public "will be apt to regard such disquisitions both as useless and chimerical" (EMPL, 513–14). On the other hand, he also suggests, with apparent seriousness, that "if this controversy [regarding the most perfect form of government] were fixed by the universal consent of the wise and learned," then perhaps "in some future age, an opportunity might be afforded of reducing the theory to practice, either by a dissolution of some old government, or by the combination of men to form a new one, in some distant part of the world" (EMPL, 513).

[115] It is perhaps noteworthy that the latter statement occurs in the context of a discussion of James Harrington's *Oceana*, a work to which Hume's "Idea of a Perfect Commonwealth" is in part a response (see EMPL, 514–16, 523).

[116] For a classic essay on this issue, see Ernest Campbell Mossner, "Was Hume a Tory Historian? Facts and Reconsiderations" *Journal of the History of Ideas* 2.2 (April 1941): 225–36.

[117] See the editor's introduction in David Hume, *Political Essays*, ed. Knud Haakonssen (Cambridge: Cambridge University Press, 1994), xix–xx. Hume undermined Whig appeals to the "ancient constitution" not only by showing that most of English history had been a story of tyranny and dependence, but also by showing that "the English constitution, like all others, has been in a constant state of fluctuation" (HE IV, 355; see also EMPL, 498). This point is elaborated in Eugene F. Miller, "Hume on Liberty in the Successive English Constitutions," in *Liberty in Hume's History of England*, ed. Nicholas Capaldi and Donald W. Livingston (Dordrecht, Netherlands: Kluwer Academic, 1990).

In addition, Hume highlights a number of dangers and downsides inherent in the political settlement of eighteenth-century Britain.[118] First, as Smith later would, Hume laments "those numberless bars, obstructions, and imposts, which all nations of EUROPE, and none more than ENGLAND, have put upon trade" (EMPL, 324), and he paints an extremely dark picture of the predictable results of Britain's growing public debt, concluding that "either the nation must destroy public credit, or public credit will destroy the nation" (EMPL, 360–1). Moreover, in his view the mixed regime rested on a rather fragile balancing act among the different parts of the government. Thus, he largely defends the use of royal patronage to influence legislation, holding that without this "corruption" the House of Commons, with its control over the purse, would eventually become invincible (see EMPL, 44–6). Similarly, while he saw the presence of competing parties as beneficial since each helps to keep the other(s) in check, he thought that partisan zeal had started to threaten the stability of the regime (see EMPL, 55, 69, 493–4; HE V, 556). As his letters reveal, Hume's frustration with British politics increased over time. By the late 1760s, in the midst of a series of political scandals, anti-Scottish mobs in London, a financial crisis, growing public debt, and building tensions with the American colonies, Hume could go so far as to write to his publisher:

As to my Notion of public Affairs, I think there are very dangerous Tempests brewing, and the Scene thickens every moment.... Our Government has become an absolute Chimera: So much Liberty is incompatible with human Society: And it will be happy, if we can escape from it, without falling into a military Government, such as Algiers or Tunis.... You say I am of a desponding Character: On the contrary, I am of a very sanguine Disposition. Notwithstanding my Age, I hope to see a public Bankruptcy, the total Revolt of America, the Expulsion of the English from the East Indies, the Diminution of London to less than a half, and the Restoration of the Government to the King, Nobility, and Gentry of this Realm.[119]

So convinced was Hume, even early in his career, that Britain's mixed government was a precarious achievement that he felt compelled to consider which would be the better "death" for it – growing into an absolute monarchy or lapsing into a republic that tears itself apart through factiousness (see EMPL, 51–3).[120]

---

[118] For an extended discussion of some of these dangers and downsides, see Forbes, *Hume's Philosophical Politics*, chapter 5.

[119] David Hume, letter to William Strahan, 25 October 1769, in *The Letters of David Hume*, ed. J. Y. T. Greig, vol. 2 (Oxford: Clarendon Press, 1932), 209–10; see also 184, 216.

[120] In a letter Hume writes that "the English Government is ... probably not calculated for Duration, by reason of its excessive Liberty." David Hume, letter to William Strahan, 3 March 1772, in *The Letters of David Hume*, vol. 2, 261.

Pragmatic Liberalism 117

Even where Hume *does* laud British liberty, he certainly never contrasts it with French "slavery," as so many Whigs of the age did. On the contrary, he pointedly insists that "it may now be affirmed of civilized monarchies, what was formerly said in praise of republics alone, *that they are a government of Laws, not of Men*. They are found susceptible of order, method, and constancy, to a surprizing degree. Property is there secure; industry encouraged; the arts flourish" (EMPL, 94; see also 383).[121] The suggestion that monarchy is inevitably tyrannical, he says, is just so much "high political rant" (EMPL, 250). Far from seeing absolute monarchy as necessarily illegitimate, Hume accepts that it is "as *natural* and *common* a government as any" (THN 3.2.8.9, 351). Thus, in an explicit response to Locke's claim that absolute monarchy cannot properly be deemed a form of civil government at all, he deadpans: "What authority any moral reasoning can have, which leads into opinions so wide of the general practice of mankind, in every place but this single kingdom, is easy to determine" (EMPL, 487). In fact, in a letter to the Whig historian Catherine Macaulay, Hume declares openly, "I look upon all kinds of subdivision of power, from the monarchy of France to the freest democracy of some Swiss cantons, to be equally legal, if established by custom and authority."[122]

The phrase "if established by custom and authority" in this last sentence is key: Hume does not, any more than Montesquieu or Voltaire, argue that *all* governments are *always* legitimate, or that there is no such thing as tyranny or justified resistance. On the contrary, he accepts that "as government is a mere human invention for mutual advantage and security, it no longer imposes any obligation, either natural or moral, when once it ceases to have that tendency" (THN 3.2.10.16, 360; see also 3.2.9.2, 352; EMPL, 489–90). However, he too holds that what *constitutes* legitimacy (or tyranny) can vary greatly according to context. This is why he insists that it is "impossible for the laws, or even for philosophy, to establish any *particular* rules, by which we may know when

---

[121] Hume does suggest that "though monarchial governments have approached nearer to popular ones, in gentleness and stability; they are still inferior," but he goes on to argue that "time will bring these species of government still nearer an equality" as monarchies like France reform their arbitrary tax policies and popular governments become overwhelmed with debt (EMPL, 94–5). For a helpful discussion of Hume's views of monarchy and other forms of government, see Miller, *Philosophy and Ideology in Hume's Political Thought*, chapter 7.

[122] David Hume, letter to Catherine Macaulay, 29 March 1764, in *New Letters of David Hume*, 81. See also Hume's claim that "time and custom give authority to all forms of government" (THN 3.2.11.19, 362).

resistance is lawful; and decide all controversies, which may arise on that subject" (THN 3.2.10.16, 360). Thus, as Richard Dees has stressed, Hume approved of the revolution of 1688, at least in retrospect, not "because absolute monarchies are tyrannical in and of themselves, but because such a monarchy was at odds with the practice of politics in *late seventeenth-century Britain.*"[123]

The centrality of historical context in deciding all political questions is especially evident in Hume's *History of England*, which reveals that he saw even the liberal practices and values that he held most dear, such as the rule of law, personal liberty, and religious toleration, as desirable only under the proper conditions.[124] As he indicates throughout the six volumes of this work, the limited, liberal government that emerged from the settlement of 1688 – in the wake of the decline of the feudal lords, the rise of commerce and a middle class, the consequent increase in the power of the Commons, the emergence of Puritanism, and the more general growth in the belief in individual liberty – would have been utterly inappropriate before all of these developments. While Hume sees the rule of law as central to the good government of modern Britain as well as "civilized monarchies" like France – at one point he calls law "the source of all security and happiness" (EMPL, 124) – he approves of the nearly arbitrary power exercised by Henry VII, holding that the "state of the country required great discretionary power in the sovereign; nor will the same maxims of government suit such a rude people, that may be proper in a more advanced stage of society" (HE III, 469).[125] We have already seen the high value that he places on personal liberty, but he also accepts that it might need to be curtailed drastically when circumstances demand it. Thus, he applauds Alfred the Great – among the very best of England's

---

[123] Richard H. Dees, "Hume and the Contexts of Politics" *Journal of the History of Philosophy* 30.2 (April 1992), 234; see also 231–40 more generally.

[124] The importance of context for the political pronouncements of the *History* is stressed by Dees (see ibid.) as well as in Herzog, *Without Foundations*, 189–202.

[125] In particular, Hume endorses Henry's use of the star-chamber, a sort of council or court that, as he recounts in the next volume of the *History*, "possessed an unlimited discretionary authority of fining, imprisoning, and inflicting corporal punishment, and whose jurisdiction extended to all sorts of offences, contempts, and disorders, that lay not within the reach of the common law.... There needed but this one court in any government, to put an end to all regular, legal, and exact plans of liberty" (HE IV, 356). Nevertheless, Hume holds that, given the disorderly state of Britain at the turn of the sixteenth century, "the establishment of the Star-chamber or the enlargement of its power in the reign of Henry VII. might have been as wise as the abolition of it in that of Charles I" (HE III, 469).

Pragmatic Liberalism

monarchs, in his eyes – for restricting people's freedom of movement in order to administer criminal justice more efficiently: demanding "a strict confinement in [people's] habitation ... might perhaps be regarded as destructive of liberty and commerce in a polished state; but it was well calculated to reduce that fierce and licentious people under the salutary restraint of law and government" (HE I, 77). Similarly, Hume loathes religious persecution and considers toleration "the true secret for managing religious factions" (HE IV, 352) in his own time, but he accepts that before the English civil wars, such toleration would likely have produced widespread, devastating conflict. In the time of Charles I, he notes, religious toleration "was generally deemed ... incompatible with all good government. No age or nation, among the moderns, had ever set an example of such an indulgence: And it seems unreasonable to judge of the measures, embraced during one period, by the maxims, which prevail in another" (HE V, 240).[126] The liberal government that was so well suited to eighteenth-century Britain, in other words, would have led to anarchy in the early seventeenth century, much less the ninth (the time of Alfred's reign).

None of this is to suggest that Hume's embrace of liberal institutions and practices was partial or halfhearted. His political essays, in particular, reveal an overwhelmingly positive view of the kind of modern, liberal, commercial society that was emerging in eighteenth-century Britain. He famously insists, against the worries voiced by civic republicans and many religious traditions, that "ages of refinement are both the happiest and most virtuous" (EMPL, 269) and that they are marked by an "indissoluble chain" of industry, knowledge, and humanity (EMPL, 271). Yet Hume's liberalism is, like Montesquieu's and Voltaire's, highly flexible. Given the central role that custom, habit, and opinion play in the political world, he maintains that one must always begin with the prevailing conventions of a given society, rather than an abstract standard of political right, and that seeking to impose a single pattern on all societies would be reckless in the extreme. Almost all political orders can be improved, in his view – they can be made more secure, more free, more prosperous, more civil – but such reforms must rest on careful historical and comparative analysis and must take into account the possibilities and limitations inherent in a society's particular circumstances.

---

[126] See also EMPL, 605; HE III, 433–4; HE IV, 54; and HE V, 130 and 231, where Hume indicates that toleration is only wise policy when it is "consistent with order and public safety."

120   *The Pragmatic Enlightenment*

SMITH'S HISTORICAL CASE FOR COMMERCIAL LIBERALISM

Smith's credentials as an economic liberal are, of course, impeccable: he is almost certainly history's most celebrated defender of commercial society and free trade, and he famously advocates "allowing every man to pursue his own interest his own way, upon the liberal plan of equality, liberty and justice" (WN IV.ix.3, 664). What is slightly less well known, however, is that the foremost reason why he promotes commerce is that it had helped to introduce a more liberal political and social order in the Europe of his time, particularly in Britain. At a crucial juncture in *The Wealth of Nations*, Smith writes that "commerce and manufactures gradually introduced order and good government, and with them, the liberty and security of individuals, who had before lived almost in a state of continual war with their neighbours, and of servile dependency upon their superiors. This, though it has been the least observed, is *by far* the most important of *all* their effects" (WN III.iv.4, 412, emphases added).[127] Like Montesquieu, Voltaire, and Hume, Smith advocates liberal political ideals such as limited government, religious toleration, and the freedom of expression, all underpinned by the effective rule of law. Also like these other thinkers, he advocates these ideals without resting them on any abstract or universal foundation. Accordingly, he is, along with Hume, the hero of Don Herzog's *Without Foundations*.[128]

Smith's argument against the idea that a social contract is the only valid basis of political right is, although not as detailed or famous as Hume's, just as emphatic. The "lowest and rudest state of society" in Smith's four-stages schema, the hunting stage, entails a cohesive social order even if not a government (WN V.i.a.2, 689); given the inherent sociability of human beings, he sees the idea of a presocial state of nature as an absurd fiction. Moreover, he maintains that political authority arises gradually over time, "antecedent to any civil institution" (WN V.i.b.4–8, 710–13). Thus, the idea that government could spring into being all at once, through an express agreement, strikes him as empirically unwarranted. Smith also rejects the prescriptive side of social contract theory, holding that the duty of allegiance rests not on a government's having been legitimized by popular consent but rather on the dual basis of people's

---

[127] I argue for the centrality of this passage to Smith's thought as a whole in Dennis C. Rasmussen, *The Problems and Promise of Commercial Society: Adam Smith's Response to Rousseau* (University Park: Pennsylvania State University Press, 2008); see especially 136–7, but also chapter 4 more generally.

[128] See Herzog, *Without Foundations*, 202–17.

Pragmatic Liberalism 121

natural or habitual tendency to obey established authorities (the principle that predominates in monarchies and among Tories) and the utility of having a "regular government" that is able to enforce laws and provide security (the principle that predominates in republics and among Whigs) (see LJ, 318–20, 401–2). In his lectures on jurisprudence for which we have student notes, Smith repeats many of Hume's arguments against the notion of the social contract, including the fact that this idea was virtually unheard of outside Britain, and yet political obligation was not restricted to their island; that consent cannot be imposed on future generations; that tacit consent wrongly presumes that leaving one's country is a feasible option for most people; and so on (see LJ, 316–25, 402–4). As Duncan Forbes remarks, in these lectures "Smith simply took over Hume's arguments, and the young reporter wrote them down, blow by blow, when he could have saved himself trouble by making a note like 'see Hume's *Essay on the Original Contract*.'"[129]

Also like Hume, Smith adopts a historical approach to justice and political right that rules out the possibility of universal natural laws that would provide a determinate standard by which to measure positive laws. Admittedly, this reading of Smith's approach is at odds with his own claim that "every system of positive law may be regarded as a more or less imperfect attempt towards a system of natural jurisprudence, or towards an enumeration of the particular rules of justice" (TMS VII. iv.36, 340), as well as his stated (but unfulfilled) intention to write a work on natural jurisprudence that would give an account of "the general principles which ought to run through and be the foundation of the laws of all nations" (TMS VII.iv.37, 341–2; see also Advertisement, 3).[130]

---

[129] Duncan Forbes, "Sceptical Whiggism, Commerce, and Liberty," in *Essays on Adam Smith*, ed. Andrew S. Skinner and Thomas Wilson (Oxford: Clarendon Press, 1975), 181.

[130] Shortly before his death Smith arranged to have his manuscripts consigned to the flames, thereby making it exceedingly difficult for us to surmise what this projected work might have looked like. Scholars frequently claim that the student notes that we have from Smith's course on jurisprudence give us a strong indication of what it would have included, but this seems to me doubtful for the straightforward reason that the content of the notes does not match Smith's description of the projected work very well. The *Lectures on Jurisprudence* consist mainly of a dry description of various forms of law in different ages of society, particularly in modern Britain, rather than an account of the broader, normative principles that should serve as the basis for all law and government. Even when Smith discusses "what are called natural rights," or the ways in which an individual can be injured "as a man," he simply draws on Pufendorf and Hutcheson to explain the distinction between perfect and imperfect rights and then breezily dismisses the question of "the originall or foundation from whence they arise," saying that this "need not be explained" (LJ, 13). For further support for this view, see Charles

On the strength of these statements, some scholars have read Smith as a universalist natural law thinker in the tradition of Grotius and Pufendorf.[131] I would argue, however, that Smith's account of justice in fact *precludes* the possibility of rigid rules that are the same in all times and places. Whereas Hume had seen justice as an "artificial" virtue that arises as people come to recognize the utility of rules protecting property, Smith maintains that it is rooted in the natural sentiment of resentment: for Smith, acting justly entails abstaining from actions that cause "injury" or "real and positive hurt" to others, where injury and hurt are defined as what provokes resentment in an impartial spectator (TMS II.ii.1.5, 79).[132] As we saw in Chapter 1, however, the sentiments of the impartial spectator are variable across different societies and cultures. Smith himself suggests that different things will provoke resentment – and thus constitute injury or injustice – in different contexts. Most obviously, what constitutes an injury to reputation depends a great deal on one's understanding of honor, which fluctuates widely from society to society (see LJ, 122–4). Injury to property varies as well, along with the different understandings of what counts as property in the different stages of society; in fact, Smith accepts that in hunting and gathering societies there *is* "scarce any property," and that is why there is "seldom any established magistrate or any regular administration of justice" (WN V.i.b.2, 709; see also LJ, 14 ff. and 459 ff.). Remarkably, Smith indicates that not even bodily injury is universally constant in causing resentment: torture provokes no resentment among many American Indian tribes (see TMS V.2.9, 205–6), for instance, and infanticide was widely accepted, nearly unavoidable, and therefore "surely ...

L. Griswold, *Adam Smith and the Virtues of Enlightenment* (Cambridge: Cambridge University Press, 1999), 36–7, 257. For an opposing view, see Samuel Fleischacker, *On Adam Smith's Wealth of Nations: A Philosophical Companion* (Princeton, NJ: Princeton University Press, 2004), 298–9.

[131] For a recent example, see Michael Frazer, *The Enlightenment of Sympathy: Justice and the Moral Sentiments in the Eighteenth Century and Today* (Oxford: Oxford University Press, 2010), 105–6. Even Fonna Forman-Barzilai, who generally stresses the importance of cultural context for the impartial spectator's judgments, holds that when it comes to justice Smith adopts a firmly universalist stance. See Fonna Forman-Barzilai, *Adam Smith and the Circles of Sympathy: Cosmopolitanism and Moral Theory* (Cambridge: Cambridge University Press, 2010), 24–5 and chapter 7; however, see also 249–50, where Forman-Barzilai seems to leave "wide open the question of whether justice for Smith had transcultural teeth."

[132] On the differences between Hume's and Smith's understandings of justice, see Fleischacker, *On Adam Smith's Wealth of Nations*, 151–2, 154; and Spencer J. Pack and Eric Schliesser, "Smith's Humean Criticism of Hume's Account of the Origin of Justice" *Journal of the History of Philosophy* 44.1 (January 2006), especially 61–3.

Pragmatic Liberalism

123

excusable" in very primitive societies (even if not in polite and civilized Athens) (TMS V.2.15, 210).[133]

Given the crucial role that context plays in determining what provokes resentment and thus what constitutes "injury" or "hurt," Smith's understanding of justice is necessarily contingent and variable.[134] Knud Haakonssen has recently emphasized the "historical" nature of Smith's jurisprudence, writing that for him

> what *counts* as injury is not a universal matter; it varies dramatically from one type of society to another.... His many tales of different cultures indicate that not even bodily integrity or standing as a moral agent were universal concepts and, most importantly, the nexus between the individual and the environment was subject to variations. There were moral facts, such as private property in land, which guided people in their social intercourse in one type of society but which were simply unknown and hence irrelevant to behaviour in other societies. Smith's 'natural jurisprudence' was, therefore, very much an historical jurisprudence; you would have to know what society you were talking about if your detailing of rights and duties were to be of any use.[135]

Given that the content of justice, like the content of morality more generally, is subject to historical and cultural variation, according to Smith's approach, his conception of justice cannot provide a universal, determinate standard by which to judge positive laws. Thus, I concur with the thesis advanced by Charles Griswold and Samuel Fleischacker that Smith never wrote his projected work on natural jurisprudence for the simple

---

[133] Smith seems to see these three broad types of injury as exhaustive: "A man merely as a man may be injured in three respects, either 1st, in his person; or 2[dly], in his reputation; or 3[dly], in his estate" (LJ, 8; see also 399).

[134] Recall that in *The Theory of Moral Sentiments* Smith criticizes "all those who in this and in the preceding century have treated of what is called natural jurisprudence" for "endeavour[ing] to lay down exact and precise rules for the direction of every circumstance of our behaviour" (TMS VII.iv.7, 329).

[135] See the editor's introduction in Adam Smith, *The Theory of Moral Sentiments*, ed. Knud Haakonssen (Cambridge: Cambridge University Press, 2002), ix. These arguments are repeatedly essentially verbatim in Knud Haakonssen, "Introduction: The Coherence of Smith's Thought," in *The Cambridge Companion to Adam Smith*, ed. Knud Haakonssen (Cambridge: Cambridge University Press, 2006), 6; see also 18. This stance represents an apparent about-face on this issue for Haakonssen. In his earlier book on the subject, Haakonssen had underlined the "critical" potential of Smith's jurisprudence, meaning its ability to provide a universal standard by which to judge existing laws. Indeed, in this work he had claimed that for Smith "the principle of impartiality ... really amounts to a principle of universality" and that "if we do not find room for the natural and universal in Smith's theory of justice, his whole project for a natural jurisprudence becomes unintelligible." Knud Haakonssen, *The Science of a Legislator: The Natural Jurisprudence of David Hume and Adam Smith* (Cambridge: Cambridge University Press, 1981), 137, 148; see also chapter 6 more generally.

124 *The Pragmatic Enlightenment*

reason that such a work would be impossible to square with his broader philosophical outlook.[136] As Griswold writes, "Smith could not fulfill his aspiration for a final and comprehensive philosophical system articulating the 'general principles of law and government.' To pursue questions about first principles is to seek a standpoint external to the human spectacle, and he thinks that that is unavailable."[137]

While Smith *aspired* to locate a foundation for his liberal political ideals in natural law, then, ultimately he was unable to do so, given his other philosophical commitments. Importantly, however, this failure did not cause him to abandon his liberal ideals. In fact, an alternative, nonfoundationalist case for these ideals runs throughout his corpus: while Smith calls his preferred political and economic order "the obvious and simple system of natural liberty" (WN IV.ix.51, 687; see also IV.vii.c.44, 606), in the end he advocates this type of order less because it conforms to "nature" in some sense than because he considers it preferable to the alternatives, all things considered. In other words, Smith defends commercial society not because it is in accord with some natural or teleological order in the universe,[138] nor again because it alone protects people's natural and inalienable rights,[139] but rather because it had proven superior to what preceded it – namely, the hunting, shepherding, and agricultural stages of society. Smith certainly does not depict commercial society as perfect – indeed, he repeatedly and consistently stresses the many potential

---

[136] See Griswold, *Adam Smith and the Virtues of Enlightenment*, 30, 34–7, 256–8; Charles L. Griswold, "On the Incompleteness of Adam Smith's System" *Adam Smith Review* 2 (2006): 181–6; and Fleischacker, *On Adam Smith's Wealth of Nations*, 147, and chapter 8 more generally. For a dissenting view, see Ian Simpson Ross, "'Great Works upon the Anvil' in 1785: Adam Smith's Projected Corpus of Philosophy" *Adam Smith Review* 1 (2004): 40–59; and especially Ian Simpson Ross, "Reply to Charles Griswold 'On the Incompleteness of Adam Smith's System'" *Adam Smith Review* 2 (2006): 187–91.

[137] Griswold, *Adam Smith and the Virtues of Enlightenment*, 258.

[138] The question of whether Smith adopted a teleological view will be examined in greater detail in Chapter 3.

[139] Like Montesquieu, Voltaire, and Hume, Smith seldom uses the language of rights, much less natural rights, in his published works, although rights do play a prominent role in the *Lectures on Jurisprudence*. In the lectures Smith seems more or less to equate rights with justice, and to understand both as simply the flip side of injuries, or actions that an impartial spectator would resent (see LJ, 7–13, 399–401). Thus, the historical and cultural contingency inherent in Smith's conception of justice would apply to his conception of rights as well. Fleischacker speculates, I think plausibly, that Smith generally refrained from using "rights-talk" in his published works because of his "uneasiness about whether the hurts that justice protects us against could be formulated as clearly and precisely as he had originally hoped." Fleischacker, *On Adam Smith's Wealth of Nations*, 153.

Pragmatic Liberalism

dangers and drawbacks inherent in this form of society – but he sees all other forms of society as even *less* perfect.[140] Likewise, he advocates free trade because he surmises, on the basis of the available evidence, that it would prove superior to mercantilism, the reigning economic system in his time, as well as to physiocracy, the system promoted by a number of French *économistes* such as Quesnay and Turgot. As Herzog notes, this is the basic argument of book 4 of *The Wealth of Nations*: "Smith never seriously pursues his suggestion that a free market is the system of natural liberty. Despite the foundationalist echoes of the label, he defends market society by showing how it leaves people better off than mercantilism does or than the physiocratic system would."[141]

Like Montesquieu, Voltaire, and Hume, Smith draws on a number of different criteria in making these kinds of historical and comparative judgments. Needless to say, one advantage of commercial society that he emphasizes is that it generates greater prosperity – it increases the wealth of nations – compared to societies with a less extensive division of labor. Yet this is not the only, or even the most important, benefit that he identifies. Book 3 of *The Wealth of Nations* is dedicated to showing that commerce had helped to promote security and personal freedoms in modern Europe, both through the interdependence of the market and through setting in motion the decline of the feudal lords, thereby making possible a "regular government" strong enough to enforce law and order. Still another aspect of commercial society that Smith considers a relative improvement is connected with its influence on people's characters. While he accepts that an excessive preoccupation with wealth can sometimes corrupt people's moral sentiments (e.g., TMS I.iii.3.1, 61), he also holds that commercial society helps to promote traits such as reliability, decency, honesty, cooperativeness, a commitment to keeping one's promises, and a strict adherence to society's norms of justice – the so-called bourgeois virtues (e.g., TMS I.iii.3.5, 63). Smith couches all of these arguments, throughout his corpus, in explicitly comparative terms: given the enormous drawbacks of most precommercial societies – crushing poverty, nearly constant insecurity, widespread personal dependence, and so

---

[140] That Smith recognized the potential dangers and drawbacks of commercial society has been a constant theme of Smith scholarship over the past several decades. For my contribution to this theme, see Rasmussen, *The Problems and Promise of Commercial Society*, chapter 2. I pursue the idea that Smith's advocacy of commercial society rested on a historical cost-benefit analysis rather than on abstract or ideological grounds throughout chapters 3, 4, and the conclusion; see especially 92–3, 159–60.

[141] Herzog, *Without Foundations*, 224.

on – he finds it difficult to see commercial society as anything but a step forward, its very real imperfections notwithstanding.[142] This kind of historical assessment is arguably *the* central element of Smith's defense of commercial society, for, as Griswold writes, he believes that "one's affirmation of a particular theory of political economy must be informed by an appreciation of its virtues relative to the competition, and these must be understood at least in part through historical analysis."[143]

While Smith is a firm defender of commercial society, broadly speaking, he devotes far less attention to the advantages and disadvantages of specific political institutions and regime types than does Montesquieu, Voltaire, or even Hume. Although he was certainly no friend of Britain's mercantilist economic system, he had little but positive things to say about its mixed, representative government. Indeed, he insists repeatedly that the British people "are rendered as secure, as independent, and as respectable as law can make them" (WN III.iv.20, 425; see also IV.v.b.43, 540; IV.vii.c.54, 610), and he is recorded as having told his students that Britain enjoyed "a happy mixture of all the different forms of government properly restrained and a perfect security to liberty and property" (LJ, 421–2). In his lectures, he highlights a number of important "securities for liberty" in the British constitution, including the frequency of elections for the House of Commons, the power of the Commons to impeach the king's ministers, the independence of the judges, the right of habeas corpus, and the strictness with which judges are obliged to interpret the law (see LJ, 271–5; see also 422).[144] Yet Smith also stresses, as Montesquieu, Voltaire, and Hume had, that Britain was a highly atypical case: under the Tudors it had been essentially an absolute monarchy, like most of western Europe at that time (see

---

[142] I examine all of these arguments in much more detail, and emphasize their historical and comparative character, in Rasmussen, *The Problems and Promise of Commercial Society*, chapters 3–4.

[143] Griswold, *Adam Smith and the Virtues of Enlightenment*, 156. Similarly, Amartya Sen describes Smith as a "realization-focused comparativist" – that is, a thinker who adopts a comparative approach to politics and who is concerned with institutions that already exist or could feasibly emerge – rather than a "transcendental institutionalist" who insists on devising a perfectly just set of institutions in thought, without regard to their feasibility. See Amartya Sen, *The Idea of Justice* (Cambridge, MA: Belknap Press, 2009), 5–10.

[144] The only potential dangers to the liberty of the British people, he told his students, were the standing army and the civil list, i.e., the allotment that the king often used to bribe Members of Parliament (see 269, 271, 274). Donald Winch finds Smith's tone in these lectures so affirmative as to be "congratulatory." Donald Winch, *Adam Smith's Politics: An Essay in Historiographic Revision* (Cambridge: Cambridge University Press, 1978), 63.

Pragmatic Liberalism 127

LJ, 262–5), and the British government "alone" grew more limited over the course of the seventeenth and eighteenth centuries (LJ, 265). Smith points to two main causes of this divergence, both highly specific to Britain's particular circumstances. First, because it was an island and therefore relatively secure from the threat of invasion, there was no need for a large standing army and so the king's power over the people was not as great as that of the kings on the Continent (see LJ, 265–6, 270, 421).[145] The second, and even more idiosyncratic, cause of the decline of royal power in Britain was that Queen Elizabeth sold off much of the Crown's lands, partly because she had no direct heirs, and so her Stuart successors were forced to appeal to Parliament to raise revenue. Since the power of the Lords had already declined by that time, the increased importance of taxes gave much greater power to the Commons (see LJ, 266–7, 270, 420–1).

While Smith believed that Britain's mixed, representative government was generally superior to the absolute monarchies on the Continent, then, he did not suggest that the British system could or should be simply transplanted elsewhere. Nor did he, like Locke, argue that absolute monarchy is necessarily illegitimate. Duncan Forbes, drawing on a self-referential remark of Hume's,[146] famously christens Smith a "sceptical Whig," meaning (among other things) that, in contrast to the ordinary or "vulgar" Whigs of his time, Smith did not hold to "the parochial absurdity of declaring that absolute monarchy could not be a proper form of government."[147] On the contrary, he concurred with Hume that the "civilized" monarchies of Europe had "a high degree of liberty, as well as all the other marks of a civilized society: an established order of ranks, a highly developed division of labour, opulence, and so on."[148] In *The Wealth of Nations*, Smith claims that France is "certainly the great empire of Europe which, after that of Great Britain, enjoys the mildest and most indulgent government" (WN V.ii.k.78, 905; see also IV.vii.b.52, 586), and

---

[145] At least, there was no standing army until after the civil wars of 1642–51, and even then it was relatively small and was put firmly under Parliament's control after the settlement of 1689 following the "Glorious" Revolution. While Smith apparently expressed some reservations about the standing army to his students (see previous note), in his published works his views are far less worried (see WN V.i.a.39–41, 705–7).

[146] In a letter Hume characterizes himself as "a Whig, but a very sceptical one." David Hume, letter to Henry Home, 9 February 1748, in *The Letters of David Hume*, ed. J. Y. T. Greig, vol. 1 (Oxford: Clarendon Press, 1932), 111. For a development of this idea, see Forbes, *Hume's Philosophical Politics*, chapter 5.

[147] Forbes, "Sceptical Whiggism, Commerce, and Liberty," 184; see also this essay more generally, as well as Duncan Forbes, "'Scientific' Whiggism: Adam Smith and John Millar" *Cambridge Journal* 7.2 (August 1954): 643–70.

[148] Forbes, "Sceptical Whiggism, Commerce, and Liberty," 191.

he applauds the absolute monarchies that arose throughout Europe on the heels of the feudal age for establishing a "regular government" that could effectively enforce order and administer justice (WN III.iv.15, 421). Whereas "the nobility are the greatest opposers and oppressors of liberty that we can imagine," he says in this context, "in an absolute government ... the greatest part of the nation, who were in the remote parts of the kingdom, had nothing to fear, nor were in any great danger of being oppressed by the sovereign" (LJ, 264). Indeed, Smith is referring to these monarchies when he speaks of the "order and good government, and with them, the liberty and security of individuals" that were introduced by the rise of commerce (WN III.iv.4, 412).

Given that Smith sees absolute monarchy as an acceptable form of government and that he rests the duty of allegiance on habit and utility rather than on a social contract, it should come as no surprise that, like Montesquieu, Voltaire, and Hume, he eschews the idea that there is a single set of criteria that all governments must meet in order to be considered legitimate. He certainly believes that there is such a *thing* as illegitimacy and justified resistance: "Who is there that in reading the Roman history does not acknowledge that the conduct of Nero, Caligula, or Domitian was such as entirely took away all authority from them?" he rhetorically asks (LJ, 320; see also 321–3, 434). Those who plotted against these emperors were justified "in the eyes of every unprejudiced person" (LJ, 320). Yet Smith does not think that ironclad rules can be laid down to determine exactly when a government has stepped beyond its proper limits, or when resistance is justified. As the (somewhat garbled) lectures notes have it: "No laws, no judges, have or can ascertain this matter, nor formed any precedents whereby we may judge" (LJ, 325; see also 326). All of this is, of course, a far cry from Locke's insistence that any absolute monarchy, any government that violates people's natural rights, indeed any government that levies taxes without the people's consent, must be deemed illegitimate.

Perhaps the clearest indication that Smith firmly rejects the idea of a single, universally applicable set of political institutions or practices can be found in the fact that he stresses, throughout the lectures on jurisprudence and book 5 of *The Wealth of Nations*, that different stages in the development of society require radically different levels of government. He suggests that in "the lowest and rudest state of society, such as we find it among the native tribes of North America ... there is properly neither sovereign nor commonwealth" at all, and he shows

Pragmatic Liberalism 129

that government necessarily grows more extensive as a society becomes more developed (WN V.i.a.2, 689–90; see also LJ, 207). This is true for all three of the sovereign's duties under Smith's "system of natural liberty": "The first duty of the sovereign ... that of defending the society from the violence and injustice of other independent societies, grows gradually more and more expensive, as the society advances in civilization" (WN V.i.a.42, 707). "The second duty of the sovereign, that of ... establishing an exact administration of justice, requires too very different degrees of expence in the different periods of society" (WN V.i.b.1, 708–9). "The third and last duty of the sovereign ... that of erecting and maintaining ... publick works ... requires too very different degrees of expence in the different periods of society" (WN V.i.c,1, 723). Thus, different laws and institutions are appropriate in different contexts. To take just one specific example, as much scorn as Smith pours on laws of primogeniture – in the lectures, he says that they are "contrary to nature, to reason, and to justice" (LJ, 49) – he accepts that they were perfectly sensible in the feudal age:

In those disorderly times, every great landlord was a sort of petty prince.... The security of a landed estate, therefore, the protection which its owner could afford to those who dwelt on it, depended on its greatness. To divide it up was to ruin it, and to expose every part of it to be oppressed and swallowed up by the incursions of its neighbours.... Laws frequently continue in force long after the circumstances, which first gave occasion to them, and which could alone *render them reasonable*, are no more. In the present state of Europe, the proprietor of a single acre of land is as perfectly secure of his possession as the proprietor of a hundred thousand. The right of primogeniture, however, still continues to be respected. (WN III.ii.3–4, 383–4, emphasis added; see also III.ii.6, 384)

Indeed, so contextually specific are Smith's policy recommendations in *The Wealth of Nations* that in the advertisement to the third edition he felt compelled to note (rather dispiritingly, for the modern reader) that in general when he refers to "the present state of things," he means the state they were in "in the end of the year 1775, and in the beginning of the year 1776" (WN, 8).

In short, Smith's liberalism is, like Montesquieu's, Voltaire's, and Hume's, a flexible one. Because he considers a standpoint wholly outside human society to be unattainable, he presents a historical case for modern, liberal, commercial society, defending it not on the basis of any kind of abstract or universal foundation but rather because of its proven superiority to the alternatives. Further, he relies on a number of different criteria in making this judgment, including not only how prosperous the society is but also such considerations as how secure the people are, how much independence they enjoy, and the character traits that the society encourages. And, as Dugald Stewart, Smith's contemporary and first biographer, notes, Smith was well aware that the application of his "liberal principles ... must vary, in different countries, according to the different circumstances of the case."[149]

CONCLUSION

Throughout this chapter I have emphasized the historical and contingent nature of the political thought of Hume, Smith, Montesquieu, and Voltaire, but none of this is meant to obscure or diminish the fact that these thinkers were all steadfast liberals. They all favored, consistently and unambiguously, governments and societies that afford people security under the law, that ensure personal liberties such as the freedoms of expression and of religious belief, that protect private property and encourage commerce, and so on. Yet their liberalism was particularly pragmatic and flexible in terms of both its basis and its implications. Liberalism was, in many of its early formulations and even some of its more recent ones, a highly idealistic outlook, grounded in abstract first principles such as the immutable dictates of natural law, the transhistorical requirements for legitimacy derived from a social contract, the rational (and therefore categorical) requirements of human dignity, the universal imperative to maximize utility, or the choice that rational individuals would make under certain ideal conditions. These are the varieties of liberalism that many contemporary liberals, such as the later Rawls, label (and denigrate) as "Enlightenment liberalism." We have seen, however, that Hume, Smith, Montesquieu, and Voltaire all advocated liberalism on nonfoundationalist grounds. That is, they supported liberal practices and institutions not because they saw them as uniquely in accord with Reason, Nature, or God's wishes, but rather because historical and comparative analysis revealed them to be relative improvements on the alternatives. The implications that they derived from this approach too were flexible, insofar as they stressed that different laws and practices are appropriate for societies with different circumstances, histories, customs, and so

[149] Dugald Stewart, "Account of the Life and Writings of Adam Smith, LL.D.," in Adam Smith, *Essays on Philosophical Subjects*, ed. I. S. Ross (Indianapolis: Liberty Fund, [1794] 1980), 317.

Pragmatic Liberalism 131

on. In their approach to political right, these Enlightenment figures were actually closer to the outlook of the later Rawls, and indeed much of contemporary liberal theory, than they were to the more idealistic forms of liberalism in the seventeenth and eighteenth centuries. Once again, then, these thinkers provide a realistic, contextually sensitive *alternative* to the universalism that is so often associated with the Enlightenment.

BLIND FAITH IN REASON?

3

The Age of the Limits of Reason

In 1932, the year that Ernst Cassirer effectively launched modern Enlightenment studies with his sympathetic examination of the period, another book appeared that did much to revive the main Romantic criticism of the Enlightenment: Carl Becker's *The Heavenly City of the Eighteenth-Century Philosophers*.[1] Becker's thesis, in a nutshell, was that in their attempt to conquer religious fanaticism and superstition the thinkers of the Enlightenment in fact embraced a new faith, one every bit as unquestioning and absolute as the Christian faith of the medieval world: a faith in reason and science, which they thought would offer a sort of terrestrial "grace" to true believers.[2] Two years later, Preserved Smith echoed Becker's thesis, proclaiming that "the Enlightenment resembled a new religion, of which Reason was God, Newton's *Principia* the Bible, and Voltaire the prophet.... The chief article in the creed of the new religion was faith in Reason, as the omnipotent and autonomous arbiter of all things."[3] Once again, Becker and Smith were far from the first or the last to make such a claim: if the idea that the Enlightenment promoted a kind of hegemonic moral and political universalism is the dominant

---

[1] See Ernst Cassirer, *The Philosophy of the Enlightenment*, trans. Fritz C. A. Koelln and James P. Pettegrove (Princeton, NJ: Princeton University Press, [1932] 1979); and Carl Becker, *The Heavenly City of the Eighteenth-Century Philosophers*, second edition (New Haven, CT: Yale University Press, [1932] 2003).

[2] For a persuasive critique of Becker's argument, see Peter Gay, "Carl Becker's Heavenly City," in *Carl Becker's Heavenly City Revisited*, ed. Raymond O. Rockwood (Ithaca, NY: Cornell University Press, 1958).

[3] Smith goes so far as to describe the Enlightenment's proponents as "zealots" in the cause. Preserved Smith, *A History of Modern Culture*, vol. 2: *The Enlightenment, 1687–1776* (Gloucester, MA: Peter Smith, [1934] 1957), 20–1.

135

136

The Pragmatic Enlightenment

complaint among contemporary political theorists and philosophers, the idea that it had an overweening confidence in reason has probably been the most persistent complaint, from the time of Jean-Jacques Rousseau and Edmund Burke to that of Leo Strauss and Michel Foucault. Indeed, the idea that the Enlightenment had an unreasonable faith in reason has now become a well-worn cliché.

This claim takes several different forms. Those who associate the Enlightenment with Descartes tend to assume that the thinkers of this period were rationalists in the sense that they sought to deduce a system of incontrovertible knowledge through the use of abstract or a priori reason, starting from self-evident first principles. This conception of the Enlightenment has, however, been thoroughly discredited by scholars of the period: the great majority of Enlightenment thinkers were empiricists who advocated relying on experience and experiment rather than rationalists who sought to rely exclusively on deduction and a priori first principles. (To use the terms made famous by d'Alembert, they adopted the "systematic spirit" rather than the "spirit of system.")[4] Hence, Peter Gay rightly proclaims that the Enlightenment was "not an Age of Reason, but a Revolt against Rationalism."[5] What is more, we will see in this chapter that Hume, Smith, Montesquieu, and Voltaire could all be described as *skeptical* empiricists, given that they continually stressed the limits and fallibility of human understanding. Certainly they thought that *some* form of reason is useful in *some* areas – they were philosophers, after all – but their conceptions of reason were far humbler than those of the great rationalist thinkers of the seventeenth century such as Descartes, Malebranche, Spinoza, and Leibniz, and even those of some earlier empiricists such as Hobbes and Locke.

The very fact that most Enlightenment thinkers were committed empiricists, however, has given rise to an alternative form of the claim that they had an overconfidence in reason, namely, the allegation that they had a boundless, naive faith in the ability of science and the scientific method to penetrate the secrets of nature and to produce continual

---

[4] See Jean Le Rond d'Alembert, *Preliminary Discourse to the Encyclopedia of Diderot*, trans. Richard N. Schwab (Chicago: University of Chicago Press, [1751] 1955), 22–3, 94–5. The contrast between the inductive and empirical *esprit systématique* and the deductive and rationalist *esprit de système* can also found in Condillac's *Traité des systèmes* (1749), and it served as a kind of leitmotif of Cassirer's *The Philosophy of the Enlightenment*.

[5] Peter Gay, *The Party of Humanity: Essays in the French Enlightenment* (New York: W. W. Norton, 1964), 270.

The Age of the Limits of Reason

137

progress in all realms of human life.[6] This version of the claim is more credible than the first, but it too is misleading in important respects. Like almost all Enlightenment thinkers, the four figures who are the focus of this book *were* confident that the scientific or experimental method is the most reliable way to attain useful knowledge – the best way to compensate for the limitations of the human mind. They did not, however, believe that modern science or its tools were infallible; on the contrary, they explicitly denied that it could provide conclusive or complete knowledge of the natural world. Likewise, these thinkers expected that science could and would do a great deal to promote human well-being, both by producing technological advances and by providing a kind of antidote to religious fanaticism. However, they did not believe that it could solve all problems or guarantee inevitable and endless progress. There was a strong dose of skepticism or realism in almost all of their thinking, and thus they accepted that certain ills will always be with us and that almost no improvements are pure and unmixed.

The connection that many Enlightenment thinkers drew between the spread of science and the undermining of religious fanaticism points toward a third form of the claim that they had a blind faith in reason: the widespread contention that the thinkers of this period were excessively dismissive of, or hostile toward, religion.[7] Even the Enlightenment's

---

[6] This form of the critique is, of course, at least as old as Rousseau. It is also implicit in Max Horkheimer and Theodor Adorno's critique of the Enlightenment's commitment to "instrumental reason," which they blame for inculcating an overwhelming concern for efficiency while undermining any objective basis of morality, thereby leading people to view the natural world and even their fellow human beings as little more than objects to be exploited. See Max Horkheimer and Theodor W. Adorno, *Dialectic of Enlightenment: Philosophical Fragments*, trans. Edmund Jephcott (Stanford, CA: Stanford University Press, [1947] 2002), 6. Of course, Horkheimer and Adorno's indictment was not restricted to the eighteenth century; they use the term "enlightenment" to cover an astonishingly broad range of thought – ranging "from Homer to Hitler," as it is commonly described. Yet Horkheimer makes clear elsewhere that he locates the "classical formulation" of enlightenment ideals in the works of the eighteenth-century Enlightenment and that Hume, "the father of modern positivism," was one of the foremost exponents of the kind of instrumental reason that he associates with the movement. See Max Horkheimer, "Reason against Itself: Some Remarks on Enlightenment," in *What Is Enlightenment? Eighteenth-Century Answers and Twentieth-Century Questions*, ed. James Schmidt (Berkeley: University of California Press, [1946] 1996), 361; and Max Horkheimer, *Eclipse of Reason* (New York: Seabury Press, [1947] 1974), 18. A more recent commentator writes that "it is generally agreed that it is during the Enlightenment that a commitment to scientism first crystallize[d] into a dogmatic program." Nicholas Capaldi, *The Enlightenment Project in the Analytic Conversation* (Dordrecht, Netherlands: Kluwer Academic, 1998), 19.

[7] I trust that this characterization is too familiar to require much in the way of citation. Here I will only note that while the charge is leveled at certain thinkers of the period

138   *The Pragmatic Enlightenment*

friends often acknowledge (or celebrate) this aspect of the period, as when
Gay writes that "while the variations among the philosophes are far from
negligible, they only orchestrate a single passion that bound the little
flock together, the passion to cure the spiritual malady that is religion, the
germ of ignorance, barbarity, hypocrisy, filth, and the basest self-hatred."[8]
Perhaps more than any other critique of the Enlightenment covered in
this book, this claim contains a good deal of truth with respect to Hume,
Smith, Montesquieu, and Voltaire. These four thinkers all rejected the
claims of revealed religion, they all believed that it is entirely possible for
people to be moral without believing in God, and they all devoted great
amounts of intellectual energy to condemning religious fanaticism and
intolerance. On the other hand, it must be admitted that they had quite
good reasons for criticizing the forms that religion often took in their
time, such as the official state persecution of Protestants, the regime of
ecclesiastical privilege and censorship, and the seemingly ceaseless con-
fessional strife of eighteenth-century France, not to mention the cata-
strophic Wars of Religion of the previous century. Moreover, Voltaire,
Montesquieu, Smith, and perhaps even Hume believed that a properly
moderated or "liberalized" form of religion could not only avoid most
of these ills but also provide certain positive benefits. Even Hume did
not think that reason could conclusively *disprove* the claims of revealed
religion, or that reason was all-powerful or sufficient unto itself. On the
contrary, as with the other three thinkers, his skepticism regarding religion was simply a manifestation of his general skepticism regarding *any*
claims of absolute certainty.

In all of these ways, the pragmatic Enlightenment was decidedly a limits-of-reason movement – hence my reversal of the traditional moniker of
this period in the title of this chapter. Whereas the previous two chapters
proceeded thinker by thinker, the present one is instead divided into three
sections, each devoted to one of the three forms of the claim that the
Enlightenment had a blind faith in reason just mentioned.[9] The first section shows that Hume, Smith, Montesquieu, and Voltaire were skeptical

---

more often than others, two of the most frequently cited culprits are Hume and Voltaire –
the latter of whom, Eric Voegelin asserts, "has done more than anybody else to make
the darkness of enlightened reason descend on the Western world." Eric Voegelin, *From
Enlightenment to Revolution* (Durham, NC: Duke University Press, 1975), 32.

[8] Peter Gay, *The Enlightenment: An Interpretation*, vol. 1: *The Rise of Modern Paganism*
(New York: W. W. Norton, 1966), 373.

[9] A fourth form of this claim, according to which the thinkers of the Enlightenment
embraced a kind of *political* rationalism, will be the main focus of Chapter 4.

The Age of the Limits of Reason

empiricists rather than dogmatic rationalists; the second section argues that their embrace of natural science did not blind them to its theoretical and practical limits; and the final section explores their ambivalent, but basically moderate, attitudes toward religion.

DARING NOT TO KNOW

As we saw in Chapter 1, Hume, Smith, Montesquieu, and Voltaire all held that it is the sentiments or passions, rather than reason, that serve as both the chief motivating force of human action and the ultimate basis from which moral standards are derived. This demotion of the place of reason in human life was no accident: we will see in this section that these thinkers all emphasized the limits of human understanding, particularly with regard to our ability to develop systematic or certain knowledge of either the human or natural world. This stress on the fallibility of reason marked a divergence not only from Descartes and the rationalist tradition, but also from many earlier thinkers who fell on the empiricist side of the (far too simple) rationalist-empiricist divide, such as Hobbes and Locke. While Hobbes rejected the notion of innate ideas, in some ways he went even further than Descartes in his belief in the possibility of incontrovertible knowledge, not only in the realm of, say, mathematics, but also those of morality and politics – hence his avowed aspiration to create a science of politics modeled on geometry. Indeed, he states explicitly that "politics and ethics (that is, the sciences of *just* and *unjust*, of *equity* and *inequity*) can be demonstrated *a priori*."[10] Even Locke, who was widely known for his philosophical "modesty" – and praised by Voltaire, among others, for that reason – posits that "*moral Knowledge* is as *capable of real Certainty*, as Mathematicks" and that "Reason … teaches all Mankind, who will but consult it" what the law of nature entails.[11] In this respect,

---

[10] Thomas Hobbes, *De Homine*, in *Man and Citizen*, ed. Bernard Gert (Indianapolis: Hackett, [1658] 1991), X.5, 42. Hence, Hume writes of Hobbes: "Though an enemy to religion, he partakes nothing of the spirit of scepticism; but is as positive and dogmatical as if human reason, and his reason in particular, could attain a thorough conviction in these subjects [politics and ethics]" (HE VI, 153).

[11] John Locke, *An Essay Concerning Human Understanding*, ed. Peter H. Nidditch (Oxford: Oxford University Press, [1689] 1975), IV.iv.7, 565; John Locke, *Two Treatises of Government*, ed. Peter Laslett (Cambridge: Cambridge University Press, [1689] 1988), II.2.6, 271. See also Locke, *An Essay Concerning Human Understanding*, I.3.1, 66; III.11.16, 516; IV.iii.18, 549; IV.xii.8, 643–4. Despite Hume's general sympathy with Locke's empiricism, he seems to suggest that Locke's outlook is excessively abstract and rationalistic at EHU 1.4, 6.

the outlooks of Hume, Smith, Montesquieu, and Voltaire were even more modest than that of the great exponent of philosophical modesty.

That Hume was a skeptic with regard to the power and scope of reason is, of course, well known. At the outset of *A Treatise of Human Nature*, he announces his intention to expound a "science of man" based on the "only solid foundation" that is to be had, namely, "experience and observation" (THN intro.7, 4). Hume's commitment to what he calls the "experimental method" – that is, to relying on experience and observation rather than abstract or a priori reasoning – is in many ways the unifying feature of his exceptionally wide-ranging corpus; he adopts this general approach in his writings on epistemology, psychology, ethics, politics, aesthetics, history, and religion alike.[12] Yet he also stresses the insurmountable limits of experience, and hence of the "science of man" that it affords. The central tenet of his epistemology, after all, is that absolute certainty is possible only in the realm of "relations of ideas," such as pure logic and mathematics (see EHU 4.1, 24). All of our other knowledge concerns "matters of fact," which rely on inferences from cause to effect that cannot be rationally demonstrated or proven (see EHU 4.2–23, 24–34). We believe that the striking of one billiard ball against another causes motion, for instance, only because we have observed this connection repeatedly in the past; reason alone cannot establish the reality of this kind of relationship (see EHU 4.8–10, 26–7). Thus, to take another of Hume's examples, it is impossible to demonstrate or prove that the sun will rise tomorrow just because we have observed it doing so in the past; there is no inherent contradiction in the idea that the course of nature might change (see EHU 4.2, 24; 4.18, 30–1).[13] Almost all of our most important beliefs rest on little more than habit, according to Hume, and so it is "custom," not reason, that constitutes "the great guide of human life" (EHU 5.6, 38). Outside the realm of mathematics we can know things with probability – sometimes very high probability – but never with certainty.

Nor was this simply a perfunctory concession on Hume's part: he stresses repeatedly, throughout his epistemological writings, how frail and

---

[12] See David Fate Norton, "An Introduction to Hume's Thought," in *The Cambridge Companion to Hume*, ed. David Fate Norton and Jacqueline Taylor, second edition (Cambridge: Cambridge University Press, 2009), 4–6, 30–1.

[13] The literature on Hume and the problem of induction is vast; a helpful starting point is P. J. R. Millican, "Hume's Argument Concerning Induction: Structure and Interpretation," in *David Hume: Critical Assessments*, ed. Stanley Tweyman, vol. 2 (New York: Routledge, 1995).

The Age of the Limits of Reason 141

error-prone our powers of understanding are. "Our reason," he writes, "is slow in its operations; appears not, in any degree, during the first years of infancy; and at best is, in every age and period of human life, extremely liable to error and mistake" (EHU 5.22, 45). Again: "The observation of human blindness and weakness is the result of all philosophy, and meets us, at every turn, in spite of our endeavours to elude or avoid it" (EHU 4.12, 28). This is especially true when we address the largest philosophical questions: "The whole is a riddle, an enigma, an inexplicable mystery. Doubt, uncertainty, suspence of judgment appear the only result of our most accurate scrutiny, concerning this subject."[14] In Hume's view, reason alone cannot prove (or disprove) the existence of God, give us insight into the true nature of reality, or even validate our belief in an external world or our sense of ourselves as unique individuals who exist over time. Thus, he famously ends book 1 of the *Treatise* in a state of "philosophical melancholy and delirium" (THN 1.4.7.9, 175), having found through his inquiries that "the understanding, when it acts alone, and according to its most general principles, entirely subverts itself, and leaves not the lowest degree of evidence in any proposition, either in philosophy or common life" (THN 1.4.7.7, 174).

Of course, Hume does not deem it desirable or even possible for people to live in a continual skeptical fog, constantly doubting everything that they see and think. On the contrary, he insists that human nature itself prevents this, that unmitigated skepticism is unsustainable in "common life" (see THN 1.4.7.9–10, 175; EHU 12.23, 119). Indeed, he writes that "universal Doubt ... is impossible for any Man to support" and that "the first and most trivial Accident in Life must immediately disconcert and destroy" it.[15] Since "a true sceptic will be diffident of his philosophical doubts, as well as of his philosophical conviction" (THN 1.4.7.14, 177), in Hume's view, he defends the propriety and worth of ordinary, prephilosophical "common life," even with all of the errors and illusions that accompany it.[16] In this sense, Hume's philosophy entails not outright

---

[14] David Hume, *The Natural History of Religion*, in *A Dissertation on the Passions and The Natural History of Religion*, ed. Tom L. Beauchamp (Oxford: Clarendon Press, [1757] 2007), 87.

[15] David Hume, "A Letter from a Gentleman to His Friend in *Edinburgh*," in *A Treatise of Human Nature*, ed. David Fate Norton and Mary J. Norton (Oxford: Clarendon Press, [1745] 2007), 425–6.

[16] As Richard Popkin has noted, Hume saw the ancient Pyrrhonian skeptics as overly dogmatic in their very skepticism, insofar as they insisted that people should suspend judgment on all questions. Popkin argues that Hume held the only *consistent* skeptical view.

142   *The Pragmatic Enlightenment*

skepticism but rather a kind of "*mitigated* scepticism" (EHU 12.24, 120). "Be a philosopher," he counsels, "but, amidst all your philosophy, be still a man" (EHU 1.6, 7).

As this last statement indicates, however, Hume does not advocate the abandonment of philosophy altogether; he does not see skepticism as useless simply because it is impossible to sustain universal doubt on all matters. In fact, he stresses how beneficial it is for people to recognize the limits of reason, even if they do not live constantly in the light of that recognition. In the concluding chapter of *An Enquiry Concerning Human Understanding*, Hume points to two useful effects of the "mitigated" skepticism that he advocates. First, an awareness of "the strange infirmities of human understanding, even in its most perfect state" should "naturally inspire [people] with more modesty and reserve, and diminish their fond opinion of themselves, and their prejudice against their antagonists" (EHU 12.24, 120).[17] In other words, Humean skepticism can help to inspire humility and undermine dogmatism. Such skepticism is especially important, he suggests, insofar as it is able to subvert the kind of "abstruse philosophy and metaphysical jargon" that often serve as a mask or opening for "religious fears and prejudices" (EHU 1.11–12, 9–10; see also THN 1.4.7.13, 176–7). (This is how Hume justifies his own extensive engagement with abstract metaphysical questions: "the necessity of carrying the war into the most secret recesses of the enemy" [EHU 1.12, 9].[18]) The second, and related, advantage of mitigated skepticism is that it should encourage us to limit "our enquiries to such subjects as are best adapted to the narrow capacity of human understanding" – that is, to "common life" (EHU 12.25, 120–1). Again, much of Hume's corpus is dedicated to showing that a moderate kind of reason – one that relies on observation and experience rather than a priori ratiocination and that draws only probable conclusions rather than making claims of absolute certainty – can provide a good deal of insight into the everyday world.[19]

See Richard H. Popkin, "David Hume: His Pyrrhonism and His Critique of Pyrrhonism," in *Hume*, ed. V. C. Chappell (Garden City, NY: Anchor Books, 1966), especially 91–2.

[17] See also Hume, "A Letter from a Gentleman to His Friend in *Edinburgh*," 425–6.

[18] Paul Russell has recently argued that this is also the key to resolving the apparent (and much-discussed) tension between Hume's skepticism and his "naturalism" – that is, his commitment to the experimental method – in the *Treatise*: according to Russell, both were part of his larger "irreligious" aims. See Paul Russell, *The Riddle of Hume's Treatise: Skepticism, Naturalism, and Irreligion* (Oxford: Oxford University Press, 2008).

[19] For two excellent studies that take this as a theme, see John W. Danford, *David Hume and the Problem of Reason: Recovering the Human Sciences* (New Haven, CT: Yale University Press, 1990); and Donald W. Livingston, *Hume's Philosophy of Common Life* (Chicago: University of Chicago Press, 1984).

The Age of the Limits of Reason 143

Any philosophy that attempts to go beyond simply "methodiz[ing] and correct[ing]" the "reflections of common life," however, is just so much "sophistry and illusion" (EHU 12.25–7, 121).

While Voltaire did not, like Hume, label himself as a skeptic, he too evinced a rather acute sense of the limits of reason. Throughout his career, but especially in his early *Letters Concerning the English Nation*, Voltaire showed himself to be an admirer of Bacon, Newton, and Locke and a proponent of empiricism and the experimental method, in opposition to the rationalism of Descartes (a move that was widely condemned in France as unpatriotic).[20] Like his English predecessors, Voltaire favors observation and induction over logic and deduction. He praises Locke, in particular, for his philosophical modesty and emphasis on the limits of human knowledge.[21] By contrast, he claims that Descartes was "hurried away by that systematic Spirit which throws a Cloud over the Minds of the greatest Men" (LCE, 55) and that he "gave entirely into the Humour of forming Hypotheses," which rendered his philosophy "no more than an ingenious Romance, fit only to amuse the Ignorant" (LCE, 65). Three decades later, Voltaire was still insisting that "Descartes's system is a tissue of erroneous and ridiculous fancies" (PD, 374).[22] Indeed, he proclaims that the type of philosophy that deduces categorical truths from innate ideas is "even more dangerous than the despicable jargon of the scholastics" (TM, 76).

The supreme accolade that Voltaire bestows on Newton and Locke is that they constructed no "system." Voltaire is, along with the rest of the philosophes, often criticized for not having been a "systematic" philosopher,[23] but he would likely regard this criticism as high praise: he sees comprehensive philosophical systems as far too narrow and reductive to explain the complexity and contingency that pervade the natural world and especially human life.[24] This is one of the reasons why even his

---

[20] On Voltaire's relationship to the English empiricists, see Robert Niklaus, "Voltaire et l'empirisme anglais" *Revue internationale de philosophie* 48 (1994): 9–24.

[21] See LCE, 56–9; and Voltaire, *Le Philosophe ignorant*, ed. Roland Mortier, in *The Complete Works of Voltaire*, vol. 62 (Oxford: Voltaire Foundation, [1766] 1987), chapter 29. On Voltaire's view of Locke, see Ira O. Wade, *The Intellectual Development of Voltaire* (Princeton, NJ: Princeton University Press, 1969), 619–31; and John W. Yolton, *Locke and French Materialism* (Oxford: Clarendon, 1991), 201–5.

[22] On Voltaire and Descartes, see Wade, *The Intellectual Development of Voltaire*, 589–601.

[23] This is a big part of what Alfred North Whitehead meant when he famously quipped that "*les philosophes* were not philosophers." Alfred North Whitehead, *Science and the Modern World* (Cambridge: Cambridge University Press, [1925] 2011), 73.

[24] On Voltaire's hostility to comprehensive philosophical systems, see Patrick Henry, "Voltaire as Moralist" *Journal of the History of Ideas* 38.1 (January–March 1977): 141–6.

writings on philosophical issues frequently take the form of fictional stories (*contes*), dialogues, satires, poems, and ostensibly unmethodical dictionary entries rather than treatises. Even in the *Treatise on Metaphysics*, Voltaire constantly emphasizes the impossibility of obtaining certain answers to the questions he addresses – the nature of God, whether there is a soul, whether human beings are immortal in some sense, whether we have free will, and so on – and constantly warns against attempts to proceed beyond the narrow limits of human knowledge (e.g., TM, 66, 76–8, 84, 86). As Roger Pearson writes, "perhaps Voltaire's firmest conclusion [in the *Treatise on Metaphysics*] is that he hates metaphysics: the abstractness, the logic-chopping, the seeming lack of practical relevance to the realities of living."[25] As for Voltaire's other major work on abstract philosophical questions, the title says it all: *The Ignorant Philosopher*.[26] This work opens by raising a number of questions on which we do not and cannot have final or definite knowledge: who we are, where we come from, what our purpose is, what will become of us, how we think and attain knowledge. Voltaire's ideal philosopher, as he emerges in this work and throughout his corpus, is one who recognizes these limits to what we can know, who can live with uncertainty and accept that the world often seems contradictory, and who eschews rigid dogmatism and abstract systems in favor of more modest, concrete, and achievable knowledge.

Voltaire's fierce opposition toward system building is also apparent in his *contes*, many of which mock systems and systematizers by juxtaposing them with the messiness of real human life.[27] For instance, "Micromégas," his delightful tale of space travel, impresses upon the reader that we are tiny, insignificant beings, inhabitants of one corner of a vast universe, and that we should not expect to be able to encompass such a universe in the little systems that we devise. The story ends with the wise visitor from the planet Sirius giving the Frenchmen he encounters a book of philosophy "in which they would discover the nature of things" – and which turns out to contain nothing but blank pages.[28] In "Memnon," the protagonist conceives of "the senseless project of becoming perfectly wise," and,

[25] Roger Pearson, *Voltaire Almighty: A Life in Pursuit of Freedom* (New York: Bloomsbury, 2005), 130.

[26] For an English translation of around half of this work, see Voltaire, *The Ignorant Philosopher*, in *Voltaire: Selections*, ed. Paul Edwards (New York: Macmillan [1766] 1989), 159–80. For the entire work in the original, see the edition cited in note 21.

[27] This is a key theme of Roger Pearson, *The Fables of Reason: A Study of Voltaire's 'Contes Philosophiques'* (Oxford: Clarendon Press, 1993), especially chapter 3.

[28] Voltaire, "Micromégas," in *Micromégas and Other Short Fictions*, trans. Theo Cuffe (New York: Penguin, [1752] 2002), 35.

The Age of the Limits of Reason

unsurprisingly, the rest of the story undermines his ridiculous zeal step by step.[29] Even in *Candide*, Leibnizian optimism is rejected at least as much because it is a *system* as because it is optimistic, as evidenced by the fact that Voltaire mockingly makes Pangloss a teacher of "metaphysico-theologico-cosmolonigology."[30] The concluding charge that "we must cultivate our garden" can be understood in many different senses, of course, but surely one of them must be that while philosophers like Pangloss can quibble with one another ad nauseam about metaphysical subtleties, we should limit our reach and focus on more immediate tasks.

In his constant emphasis on the inescapable limits of human knowledge, Voltaire adds to English empiricism a dash of skepticism in the tradition of Montaigne and Bayle.[31] Just as Hume proposes that we should consign most works of metaphysics to the flames,[32] Voltaire suggests that we should "put at the end of nearly all chapters on metaphysics the two letters used by Roman judges when they could not understand a lawsuit: *N. L., non liquet*, this is not clear" (PD, 74). He too holds that "in Philosophy, a Student ought to doubt of the Things he fancies he understands too easily, as much as of those he does not understand" (LCE, 67) and that "the fragility of our reason ... [is] daily made manifest."[33] Thus, the entry in his *Philosophical Dictionary* "Limits of

---

[29] Voltaire, "Memnon," in *Micromégas and Other Short Fictions*, trans. Theo Cuffe (New York: Penguin, [1750] 2002), 52.

[30] Voltaire, *Candide*, in *Candide and Related Texts*, trans. David Wootton (Indianapolis: Hackett, [1759] 2000), 2. Pangloss's refusal ever to change his mind is comical by the end of the story. "I still think as I always did, for, after all, I'm a philosopher," he proclaims, as if that explains why one must stubbornly ignore all facts and all experience. Ibid., 75. See also Pearson, *The Fables of Reason*, 114–15; and Gustave Lanson, *Voltaire*, trans. Robert A. Wagoner (New York: John Wiley & Sons, [1906] 1966), 129.

[31] For an examination of Bayle's influence on Voltaire, see H. T. Mason, *Pierre Bayle and Voltaire* (Oxford: Oxford University Press, 1963). J. B. Shank writes that Voltaire shared with Montaigne and Bayle an "insistence upon the value of the skeptical position in its own right as a final and complete philosophical stance." J. B. Shank, "Voltaire," in *The Stanford Encyclopedia of Philosophy*, ed. Edward N. Zalta (Summer 2010 edition): <http://plato.stanford.edu/archives/sum2010/entries/voltaire/>.

[32] Hume concludes the second *Enquiry* with this rather brazen suggestion: "When we run over libraries, convinced of [Hume's skeptical] principles, what havoc must we make? If we take in our hand any volume; of divinity or school metaphysics, for instance; let us ask, *Does it contain any abstract reasoning containing quantity or number?* No. *Does it contain any experimental reasoning concerning matter of fact and existence?* No. Commit it then to the flames: For it can contain nothing but sophistry and illusion" (EHU 12.34, 123).

[33] Voltaire, *Treatise on Tolerance*, in *Treatise on Tolerance and Other Writings*, ed. Simon Harvey and trans. Brian Masters (Cambridge: Cambridge University Press, [1763] 2000), 7.

146   *The Pragmatic Enlightenment*

the Human Mind" begins with the words "they are everywhere" (PD, 74). These limits were one of the key planks in Voltaire's campaign for greater toleration: given that we cannot be certain that we are right about the major religious and philosophical questions, he reasons, we should not seek to impose our beliefs on others or persecute them for theirs (e.g., PD, 393–4). In fact, Raymond Naves claims that the "critical unity" of Voltaire's thought consists precisely in his "attack on absolutes and certainties, [his] condemnation of all extremes and all fanaticisms ... since it does not become a limited, ignorant, and mortal being to want to impose his conclusions by conferring upon them an indisputable validity."[34]

Smith devotes far less attention to epistemological questions than did Hume and Voltaire. He raises none of the doubts about the existence of an external world, causation, and personal identity that so exercised Hume, and even his unpublished essay "Of the External Senses" focuses primarily on how the five senses actually work, rather than on the reliability of the knowledge that we gain through them.[35] It is clear, however, that he too is an empiricist, insofar as his books on moral philosophy and political economy and his lectures on jurisprudence all rely on observation and experience rather than a priori reasoning. Thus, he suggests that the proper role of the philosopher is not to devise abstract theories or categorical proofs but rather simply to "observe every thing" (WN I.i.9, 21).[36] Further, as Samuel Fleischacker writes, throughout his works "Smith gives strong priority to particular facts over general theories, stressing repeatedly that human knowledge is most reliable when it is highly contextual. Smith is, for this reason, perhaps the most empirical of all the empiricists, pursuing his version of 'the science of man' in a particularly messy, fact-laden rather than theory-laden way."[37] Smith certainly

---

[34] Raymond Naves, *Voltaire: L'Homme et l'oeuvre*, fifth edition (Paris: Hatier-Boivin, [1942] 1958), 148.

[35] See Samuel Fleischacker, *On Adam Smith's Wealth of Nations: A Philosophical Companion* (Princeton, NJ: Princeton University Press, 2004), 27; and Adam Smith, "Of the External Senses," in *Essays on Philosophical Subjects*, ed. W. P. D. Wightman (Indianapolis: Liberty Fund, 1980). For a study of Smith's epistemology, such as it is, which argues that he was by and large a conventionalist rather than a realist, see Ralph Lindgren, "Adam Smith's Theory of Inquiry" *Journal of Political Economy* 77.6 (November–December 1969): 897–915. For a more recent attempt to "construct an epistemology for Adam Smith," see Eric Schliesser, "Wonder in the Face of Scientific Revolutions: Adam Smith on Newton's 'Proof' of Copernicanism" *British Journal for the History of Philosophy* 13.4 (2005): 697–732.

[36] See also Adam Smith, "The History of Astronomy," in *Essays on Philosophical Subjects*, ed. W. P. D. Wightman (Indianapolis: Liberty Fund, 1980), 45–6.

[37] Fleischacker, *On Adam Smith's Wealth of Nations*, 271.

The Age of the Limits of Reason

does not, any more than Hume or Voltaire, believe that "the slow and uncertain determinations of our reason" (TMS II.i.5.10, 77) or "the weak eye of human reason" (TMS, 128) can provide conclusive answers to the important questions of human life on its own.

In stark contrast to Voltaire, Smith is often thought to have been a lover of systems and system building.[38] It is true that "system" is one of Smith's favorite words, and we have already seen that he describes his own theory of political economy as the *system* of natural liberty (see WN IV.ix.51, 687; IV.vii.c.44, 606). Yet he also highlights the baleful effects of the "spirit of system" in politics (TMS VI.ii.2.15–18, 232–4), and his system of natural liberty is in many ways "a system that liberates politics *from* system" (particularly the mercantilist variety).[39] Moreover, part 7 of *The Theory of Moral Sentiments*, which discusses earlier "Systems of Moral Philosophy," emphasizes the distortions inherent in these philosophical systems. As Charles Griswold writes, in this discussion Smith repeatedly criticizes "the reductionistic systematizing impulses of the philosophers. Over and over again, we learn that philosophers are, in effect, lovers of system."[40] For instance, Smith remarks that Chrysippus, the third head of the Stoic school, "reduced their doctrines into a scholastic or technical system of artificial definitions, divisions, and subdivisions; one of the most effectual expedients, perhaps, for extinguishing whatever degree of good sense there may be in any moral or metaphysical doctrine" (TMS VII.ii.1.41, 291). Likewise, he reproaches Epicurus for "indulg[ing] a propensity, which is natural to all men, but which philosophers in particular are apt to cultivate with a particular fondness, as the great means of displaying their ingenuity, the propensity to account for all appearances from as few principles as possible" (TMS VII.ii.2.14, 299). More broadly, Smith proclaims in *The Wealth of Nations* that "speculative systems have in all ages of the world been adopted for reasons too frivolous to have

---

[38] The editors of *The Wealth of Nations*, for instance, write that "not only were Smith's ethics, jurisprudence, and economics, marked by a degree of systematic thought of such a kind as to reveal a great capacity for model-building, but also by an attempt to delineate the boundaries of a single system of thought, of which these separate subjects were the component parts." See the "General Introduction" in WN, 4, as well as the footnote on 768–9. See also Dugald Stewart's remark about Smith's "love of system." Dugald Stewart, "Account of the Life and Writings of Adam Smith, LL.D.," in Adam Smith, *Essays on Philosophical Subjects*, ed. I. S. Ross (Indianapolis: Liberty Fund, [1794] 1980), 306; see also 326.

[39] Charles L. Griswold, *Adam Smith and the Virtues of Enlightenment* (Cambridge: Cambridge University Press, 1999), 308.

[40] Ibid., 152. On the unsystematic – even antisystematic – nature of Smith's own moral "system," see ibid., 71–5.

148 *The Pragmatic Enlightenment*

determined the judgment of any man of common sense, in a matter of the smallest pecuniary interest. Gross sophistry has scarce ever had any influence upon the opinions of mankind, except in matters of philosophy and speculation; and in these it has frequently had the greatest" (WN V.i.f.26, 769). Thus, to say that Smith himself was a lover of philosophical systems seems a drastic overstatement. In fact, Fleischacker has persuasively argued that "the central thread running through all his work," from his early essay on the history of astronomy to *The Wealth of Nations*, is "an unusually strong commitment to the soundness of the ordinary human being's judgments, and a concern to fend off attempts, by philosophers and policy-makers, to replace those judgments with the supposedly better 'systems' invented by intellectuals."[41]

While it is clear that Smith is an empiricist and an opponent of abstract system building, the relative paucity of explicit statements on epistemological questions in his works has given rise to a debate about which school of thought, if any, he belongs to. Griswold argues that Smith represents a further development of the skeptical tradition that runs from Sextus Empiricus to Hume, given his disdain for metaphysics and simplifying systems; his constant appeals to experience and ordinary life rather than abstract reason; his emphasis on unintended consequences and unforeseen outcomes; his close friendship with and great admiration for Hume, whom he calls "by far the most illustrious philosopher and historian of the present age" (WN V.i.g.3, 790); and his view of even natural science as a historical and subjective enterprise (a view that will be discussed in the following section).[42] Fleischacker, however, suggests that Smith should instead be seen as a sort of forerunner of the "common sense" philosophy of Thomas Reid, precisely because he insists on beginning with ordinary people's judgments and largely ignores the problems raised by Hume's skepticism (causation, personal identity, and the rest).[43]

---

[41] Samuel Fleischacker, "Adam Smith," in *A Companion to Early Modern Philosophy*, ed. Steven Nadler (Oxford: Blackwell, 2002), 506. See also Fleischacker, *On Adam Smith's Wealth of Nations*, 23–4.

[42] See Griswold, *Adam Smith and the Virtues of Enlightenment*, 155–73. For an argument that Smith owes more to Hume's naturalism than his skepticism, see Ryan Patrick Hanley, "Scepticism and Naturalism in Adam Smith" *Adam Smith Review* 5 (2010): 198–212.

[43] See Fleischacker, *On Adam Smith's Wealth of Nations*, 21–6; and Samuel Fleischacker, *A Third Concept of Liberty: Judgment and Freedom in Kant and Adam Smith* (Princeton, NJ: Princeton University Press, 1999), 136. Actually, Fleischacker suggests that Smith's philosophy falls *between* those of Hume and Reid, and that he "does not make clear where he stands on the issues that divided Reid from Hume." Fleischacker, *On Adam Smith's Wealth of Nations*, 22.

The Age of the Limits of Reason 149

There is much to be said for both of these arguments, and in fact they overlap a great deal. After all, Griswold acknowledges that Smith never actually argues "in favor of the view that 'objective reality' or the essential structure of things is *unknowable*"; rather, in Griswold's view "he proceeds in the manner of a nondogmatic skeptic who avoids providing theories as to whether reality can or cannot be known."[44] Thus, Griswold interprets Smith as *enacting* Hume's "mitigated skepticism" by simply setting aside Hume's unsolvable skeptical questions and operating on the plane of ordinary life[45] – an interpretation that finds distinct echoes in Fleischacker's discussion.[46] Similarly, Griswold would surely concur with Fleischacker's claim that

perhaps taking a cue from Hume's skepticism about the capacity of philosophy to replace the judgments of "common life," Smith represents one of the first modern philosophers to be suspicious about philosophy itself – at least of philosophy as conducted from a foundationalist standpoint, a position "outside" the modes of thought and practice it examines. He brings out the rationality already inherent in common life, mapping it from within and correcting it, where necessary, with its own tools, rather than trying either to justify or to criticize it from an external standpoint.[47]

Whether we label Smith as a skeptic or as a proto–commonsense philosopher, then, it is clear that he is *skeptical* about the power and reach of reason and that he seeks to work within – and thereby to vindicate – what Hume calls "common life."

Unlike with Hume, Voltaire, and Smith, with Montesquieu there is some debate about whether he is an empiricist at all, much less a skeptical one. Few would deny that he is an empiricist in the sense that he sees all knowledge as gained through the senses,[48] but a number of scholars have suggested that he adopts a basically deductive rather than inductive approach to politics in *The Spirit of the Laws*. Montesquieu proclaims in the preface of that work that once he "set down the principles" – meaning in part, although not exclusively, his typology of regimes and the

---

[44] Griswold, *Adam Smith and the Virtues of Enlightenment*, 163.

[45] See ibid., 170–2, 356.

[46] Fleischacker writes, for instance, that "Smith neither affirms nor denies the ultimate truth of common-sense beliefs; he merely works within them." Fleischacker, *On Adam Smith's Wealth of Nations*, 22; see also 23.

[47] Fleischacker, "Adam Smith," 506. See also Fleischacker, *On Adam Smith's Wealth of Nations*, 24, 26.

[48] Montesquieu embraces this position quite explicitly in an early essay: see Charles de Secondat, baron de Montesquieu, "An Essay on the Causes that May Affect Men's Minds and Characters," trans. Melvin Richter, in *Political Theory* 4.2 (May 1976), 141–2.

"principle" or motivating force attending each of them (honor for monarchies, virtue for republics, and fear for despotisms) – he saw "particular cases conform to them as if by themselves, the histories of all nations being but their consequences" (SL, xliii). Drawing on this statement, some commentators argue that he operated in a Cartesian, rationalist manner, deducing his conclusions from these abstract first principles.[49] However, Montesquieu himself tells us that he "began by examining men" (SL, xliii) – that is, he began with empirical observation rather than a priori truths – and that when he started the work, "I followed my object without forming a design" (SL, xlv). Thus, he indicates that his "principles" are ultimately derived from, and reliant on, the empirical "details" that support them (see SL, xliv); the principles provide a framework with which to *organize* the details, but they are not themselves independent metaphysical truths.

Even more fundamentally, the entire character of the work tells against the rationalist reading. *The Spirit of the Laws* is a notoriously complicated book, one that virtually overflows with concrete particulars rather than the kind of abstract reasoning characteristic of works like Hobbes's *Leviathan* and Locke's *Second Treatise*; as David Carrithers writes, "few classics of political theory are so suffused with such a torrent of diverse facts."[50] In the course of relating all of these facts, Montesquieu introduces many exceptions, complications, and modifications to his initial typology, once again suggesting that he does not let his "principles" run roughshod over the empirical details.[51] In fact, in one of his *Pensées* Montesquieu reproaches some French historians for adopting the very method that has sometimes been attributed to him: "They don't make a system after reading history; they begin with the system and then search for proofs,"

---

[49] See, for instance, C. P. Courtney, "Montesquieu and the Problem of 'la diversité,'" in *Enlightenment Essays in Memory of Robert Shackleton*, ed. Giles Barber and C. P. Courtney (Oxford: Voltaire Foundation, 1988); Emile Durkheim, *Montesquieu and Rousseau: Forerunners of Sociology*, trans. Ralph Manheim (Ann Arbor: University of Michigan Press, 1960), 52–3; Franz Neumann's introduction in Charles de Secondat, baron de Montesquieu, *The Spirit of the Laws*, trans. Thomas Nugent (New York: Hafner, 1949), xxxiv–xxxv, liv; and Mark H. Waddicor, *Montesquieu and the Philosophy of Natural Law* (The Hague: Martinus Nijhoff, 1970), especially chapters 2–3.

[50] David W. Carrithers, "Introduction: An Appreciation of *The Spirit of Laws*," in *Montesquieu's Science of Politics: Essays on The Spirit of Laws*, ed. David W. Carrithers, Michael A. Mosher, and Paul A. Rahe (Lanham, MD: Rowman & Littlefield, 2001), 7.

[51] For a helpful discussion of this point, see Catherine Larrère, "Montesquieu and Liberalism: The Question of Pluralism," in *Montesquieu and His Legacy*, ed. Rebecca E. Kingston (Albany: SUNY Press, 2009), 285–8.

The Age of the Limits of Reason   151

he protests. "And there are so many facts over a long history, so many different ways of thinking about it, its origins are ordinarily so obscure, that one always finds materials to validate all sorts of opinions" (Pensées #190, 71). For all of these reasons, I would argue that Montesquieu too falls squarely within the empiricist camp.[52]

While Montesquieu, like Smith, offers relatively few explicit statements on epistemological questions, the statements that he does make suggest that he too holds quite moderate expectations of human reason. He writes that "reason ... never produces great effects on the minds of men [*l'esprit des hommes*]" (SL 19.27, 327) and indeed that "life is but a series of passions, sometimes stronger, sometimes weaker; now of one sort, now of another."[53] Thus, "not the mind but the heart forms our opinions."[54] Further, he too deems abstract system building a dubious enterprise: "We have scarcely ever more grossly deceived ourselves than when we have wanted to reduce men's sentiments to a system; and undoubtedly the worst copy of man is the one found in books, which are a pile of general propositions, almost always false" (Pensées #30, 9–10; see also #163, 52; SL 29.18, 617). Admittedly, Montesquieu does begin *The Spirit of the Laws* by suggesting that the universe is organized in a systematic fashion, that God created and preserved the world according to a set of invariable laws or rules (see SL 1.1, 3–4). However, he considers it unlikely that we will ever be capable of discerning these laws with any degree of certainty, writing that human beings "are limited by their nature and are consequently subject to error" (SL 1.1, 4). Again: "As an intelligent being ... [man] is a limited being; he is subject to ignorance and error, as are all finite intelligences; he loses even the imperfect knowledge he has" (SL 1.1, 5). Hence, Montesquieu indicates more than once in his *Pensées* that while there may very well be metaphysical truths, human beings cannot comprehend them: "When it is said that there are no absolute qualities, this does not mean that there are none, but that there are none for us, that our minds cannot determine them" (Pensées #1154, 309; see also #818, 238). Indeed, Judith Shklar claims that "Montesquieu had

---

[52] For further arguments along these lines, see ibid., 287; Isaiah Berlin, "Montesquieu," in *Against the Current: Essays in the History of Ideas*, ed. Henry Hardy (New York: Viking, [1955] 1980), 136–8; Simone Goyard-Fabre, *La Philosophie du droit de Montesquieu* (Paris: Klincksieck, 1973), especially chapters 1 and 3; and Werner Stark, *Montesquieu, Pioneer of the Sociology of Knowledge* (Toronto: University of Toronto Press, 1961), chapter 1.

[53] Montesquieu, "An Essay on the Causes That May Affect Men's Minds and Characters," 145.

[54] Ibid., 157.

no metaphysical aspirations whatsoever."[55] Given all of Montesquieu's reservations regarding the efficacy and reach of our rational capacities, one could say of him, as of Hume, Voltaire, and Smith, that "there is a sceptical note which runs through all his writing."[56]

Of course, Hume, Smith, Montesquieu, and Voltaire were not *simply* skeptics with regard to reason: they all preferred knowledge to ignorance and believed that reliable knowledge is more likely to emerge from rational inquiry than from revelation, authority, or unquestioned tradition. However, they were resolute in their adoption of the "systematic spirit" rather than the "spirit of system" – that is, in their advocacy of experience, experiment, and the observation of concrete particulars over and against system making, abstract theorizing, and the search for a priori first principles. Further, even compared to many of their empiricist predecessors, they evinced a rather acute sense of the limits of reason, continually stressing the weakness and fallibility of our powers of understanding and the dubiousness of most claims of absolute certitude. In their view, a degree of uncertainty is not only inevitable but also positively desirable, insofar as it helps to undermine dogmatism, fanaticism, and intolerance. Instead of Kant's famous *sapere aude* ("dare to know"), then, a more fitting motto for the pragmatic Enlightenment might in fact be "dare *not* to know," or dare to acknowledge the limits of human reason.[57]

THE USES AND LIMITS OF NATURAL SCIENCE

Given that Hume, Smith, Montesquieu, and Voltaire were skeptical empiricists, their attitude toward the natural sciences contained a touch of ambivalence. On the one hand, as empiricists they all believed wholeheartedly in the scientific or experimental method as the most reliable way to attain useful knowledge – that is, the best way to compensate

---

[55] Judith N. Shklar, *Montesquieu* (Oxford: Oxford University Press, 1987), 70. Similarly, Emile Durkheim writes that "nothing in [Montesquieu's] entire work suggests the slightest concern with metaphysical problems." Durkheim, *Montesquieu and Rousseau*, 45.

[56] Berlin, "Montesquieu," 136. For further interpretations of Montesquieu as a skeptic in some sense, see Mark Hulliung, *Montesquieu and the Old Regime* (Berkeley: University of California Press, 1976), 108–9; and Shklar, *Montesquieu*, 26–7.

[57] For a similar suggestion with respect to the French Enlightenment more generally, see Keith Baker, "Epistémologie et politique: Pourquoi l'*Encyclopédie* est-elle un dictionnaire?" in *L'Encyclopédie: Du réseau au livre et du livre au réseau*, ed. Robert Morrisey and Philippe Roger (Paris: Champion, 2001), 53. For Kant's motto, see Immanuel Kant, "An Answer to the Question: What Is Enlightenment?", in *Practical Philosophy*, trans. Mary J. Gregor (Cambridge: Cambridge University Press, [1784] 1996), 17.

The Age of the Limits of Reason 153

for the limitations of the human mind, and the surest means of achieving technological progress and thereby promoting material well-being. In this, they were at one with the founders of the modern scientific outlook such as Bacon and Newton. On the other hand, as *skeptical* empiricists they doubted that the scientific method could ever offer infallible or complete knowledge of the natural world. In their view, even something like Newton's laws of motion, which Newton himself took to be underwritten by God and therefore universal and immutable,[58] must remain permanently subject to revision. Further, while they believed that science could provide certain technological and even moral benefits, above all by providing a kind of antidote to religious fanaticism, they were far from certain that it would guarantee inevitable or endless progress, or that it would enable people (in Bacon's words) to "subdue and overcome the necessities and miseries of humanity."[59] These thinkers saw science as immensely valuable both as a method and as a resource for improving the world, but they did not, pace Becker, place an unquestioning "faith" in it.

Of the four thinkers who are the focus of this book, Montesquieu expressed the fewest reservations about the methods and achievements of the natural sciences,[60] although even his attitude toward them was not *entirely* admiring. Early in life Montesquieu was himself a sort of amateur scientist: between 1718 and 1721 he delivered reports to the Academy of Bordeaux on subjects such as the source of echoes, the function of the renal glands, and the causes of the weight and transparency of bodies, as well as a short series of observations on natural history. In *The Spirit of the Laws* he appeals occasionally to scientific investigations to support his conclusions, particularly in the chapters on the influence of climate, where he recalls his own observation of the effects of heat and cold on a sheep's tongue under a microscope (see SL 14.2, 233). As we have seen, he opens this work with a strong avowal of the regularity

---

[58] See Isaac Newton, *Philosophiae Naturalis Principia Mathematica*, in *Philosophical Writings*, ed. Andrew Janiak (Cambridge: Cambridge University Press, [1687] 2004), 52, 57, 89–92.

[59] Francis Bacon, *The Great Instauration*, in *New Atlantis and The Great Instauration*, ed. Jerry Weinberger (Wheeling, IL: Harlan Davidson, [1620] 1989), 26.

[60] Judith Shklar argues that Montesquieu's "most fundamental and enduring conviction" was that "science is our best moral medicine." Indeed, she goes so far as to claim that natural science represented the one fixed pole in his generally skeptical and relativistic outlook, writing that Montesquieu "was neither an agonized nor an insecure sceptic. Science supplied all the certainty he needed.... The truths of science were never a part of his otherwise radical relativism." Shklar, *Montesquieu*, 8, 27.

of the natural world, proclaiming that "creation, which seems to be an arbitrary act, presupposes rules as invariable as the fate [*fatalité*] claimed by atheists" (SL 1.1, 4; see also PL #97, 161–2).[61] While Montesquieu is confident that the universe is governed according to a set of invariable laws, we have also seen that he is less than certain that human beings will ever be capable of grasping these laws in their entirety, given how limited and subject to error we are (see SL 1.1, 4–5). Thus, his writings contain a few allusions to the doubts that attend even scientific inquiry, such as his remark that systems of natural philosophy are "no sooner established than they are overturned,"[62] as well as his suggestion that "one must not criticize poets because of the defects of poetry, nor metaphysicians because of the difficulties of metaphysics, nor scientists because of the uncertainties [*incertitudes*] of science, nor geometers because of the dryness of geometry" (Pensées #1542, 444). The theoretical limits of science – of our capacity to comprehend nature's laws – is certainly not, however, a subject that he dwells on.[63]

Montesquieu also frequently stresses the benefits of technological advances such as the invention of the printing press, which enabled people to preserve and spread knowledge better (see Pensées #653, 205; #791, 233; #1745, 520), and the compass, which drew people around the world closer together and thereby "opened the universe, so to speak" (SL 21.21, 390). On the other hand, he does not believe that such advances are *always* beneficial: "If science had no other inventions but gunpowder, one would do quite well to banish it like magic," he declares (Pensées #223, 93).[64] Moreover, he recognizes that even valuable innovations such as the compass sometimes entail (or at least make possible) major drawbacks, such as the spread of diseases like smallpox (see Pensées #86, 29) and above all the kinds of depredations committed by the Spanish in the New World, which "revealed the height of cruelty" (Pensées #207, 80; see also #1268,

---

[61] In a later discussion of this passage, Montesquieu declares that these rules are invariable "because God has willed that they should be so." Charles de Secondat, baron de Montesquieu, *Défense de l'Esprit des lois*, in *Oeuvres complètes*, ed. Roger Caillois, vol. 2 (Paris: Gallimard, [1750] 1951), 1124.

[62] Charles de Secondat, baron de Montesquieu, "Discours prononcé a la rentrée de l'Academie de Bordeaux," in *Oeuvres complètes*, ed. Roger Caillois, vol. 1 (Paris: Gallimard, [1717] 1949), 7.

[63] Montesquieu does lament, though, that in his age "such a degree of esteem has been bestowed upon the natural sciences that mere indifference has been preserved for the moral" (Pensées #1871, 557; see also #1940, 581).

[64] In *The Persian Letters*, Rhedi and Usbek debate this point, with Rhedi arguing that modern firearms lead to greater violence and Usbek claiming that they encourage shorter wars and greater restraint (see PL #105–6, 174–7).

The Age of the Limits of Reason

345–7; SL 10.4, 142; PL #121, 204).[65] In *The Persian Letters*, Rhedi and Usbek stage a brief debate regarding the practical benefits and drawbacks of what they regard as "Western" science, with the former arguing that technological advances are generally used for "evil purposes" such as more efficient destruction and oppression, while the latter maintains that they make life more comfortable and peaceful, and people more industrious (see PL #105–6, 174–9). Usbek gets the final word in the contest, but Rhedi's claims are presented just as vigorously.

Montesquieu's most extensive and interesting ruminations on the effects of the natural sciences, however, are found in his "Discourse on the Motives That Ought to Encourage Us to the Sciences," delivered to the Academy of Bordeaux in 1725. This essay outlines a number of incentives to engage in scientific research, including the intrinsic pleasure of learning about the world, the ability to see just how much human beings will be able to discover, and the useful things that society gains from these discoveries.[66] Most striking, however, is Montesquieu's opening claim that

> if a Descartes had come to Mexico or Peru one hundred years before Cortez and Pizarro, and if he had taught these peoples that men, composed as they are, are not able to be immortal; that the springs of their machine, as those of all machines, wear out; that the effects of nature are only a consequence of the laws and communications of movement, then Cortez, with a handful of men, would never have destroyed the empire of Mexico, nor Pizarro that of Peru.[67]

Montesquieu realizes that this is an arresting assertion: "Can it be said that this destruction, the greatest history has ever known, was only a simple effect of the ignorance of a principle of philosophy? It can, and I am going to prove it."[68] At this point, the reader might expect him to argue that greater scientific knowledge would have allowed the Aztecs and Incans to develop greater military capabilities and thereby fend off the conquistadors, but this is precisely what he does *not* argue. In fact, he stresses that these peoples *already* had relatively advanced weapons and

---

[65] In one of his *Pensées* Montesquieu also questions the permanency of such technological innovations, musing that "it would not, perhaps, be impossible to lose the compass some day" (Pensées #797, 234).

[66] See Charles de Secondat, baron de Montesquieu, "Discourse on the Motives That Ought to Encourage Us to the Sciences," trans. Diana Schaub, *New Atlantis* 20 (spring 2008), 34–5.

[67] Ibid., 33. For a similar point, using similar language, see Pensées #1265, 338–9.

[68] Montesquieu, "Discourse on the Motives That Ought to Encourage Us to the Sciences," 33.

156   *The Pragmatic Enlightenment*

tactics, as well as advantages in terms of terrain, local knowledge, and superior courage. "How, then, were they so easily destroyed?" he asks. The answer: "All that appeared new to them – a bearded man, a horse, a firearm – had upon them the effect of a power invisible, which they believed they were incapable of resisting. It wasn't courage the Americans lacked, but only the hope of success. Thus, a bad principle of philosophy – the ignorance of a physical cause – paralyzed in a moment all the forces of two great empires."[69] In other words, perhaps the *greatest* benefit of the sciences resides not in their ability to produce new technology, but rather in their tendency to undermine excessive credulity and superstition, or to "cure people of destructive prejudices."[70] In Montesquieu's view, then, science itself can and should lead to a more critical, skeptical outlook.[71]

Voltaire's engagement with the natural sciences was more extensive than Montesquieu's, but it followed a similar pattern insofar as he was deeply involved with them early in life, after which he turned conspicuously away from the natural world and toward philosophical, political, historical, and literary pursuits. Voltaire too was a kind of amateur scientist for a brief period, conducting a number of experiments with Emilie du Châtelet when they lived at Cirey in the late 1730s,[72] and he too showed great appreciation for the practical benefits that the natural sciences afford. To take just one prominent example, he devotes the

---

[69] Ibid., 34.

[70] Ibid. Recall that helping people to "cure themselves of their destructive prejudices" is one of the stated goals of *The Spirit of the Laws* (SL, xliv).

[71] As Diana Schaub notes, while Montesquieu expects great things from science, his description of what "a Descartes" would teach the Aztecs and Incans – for example, "that men, composed as they are, are not able to be immortal; that the springs of their machine, as those of all machines, wear out" – shows that he was also aware of its limits. As Schaub writes, "he does not entertain the most radical possibilities of age-retardation and the conquest of death. He does not suggest that science could fix our 'pitiable machine.' Descartes, by contrast ... looked forward to [scientific] knowledge being used not only for 'the invention of an infinity of devices that would enable one to enjoy troublefree the fruits of the earth' but also to rid us of 'the frailty of old age.'" Diana Schaub, "Montesquieu's Popular Science" *New Atlantis* 20 (spring 2008), 44. For the quotations from Descartes, see René Descartes, *Discourse on the Method*, in *The Philosophical Writings of Descartes*, trans. John Cottingham, Robert Stoothoff, and Dugald Murdoch, vol. 1 (Cambridge: Cambridge University Press, [1637] 1985), 143.

[72] See W. H. Barber, "Voltaire at Cirey: Art and Thought," in *Studies in Eighteenth-Century French Literature: Presented to Robert Niklaus*, ed. J. H. Fox, M. H. Waddicor, and D. A. Watts (Exeter: University of Exeter Press, 1975); and Margaret Sherwood Libby, *The Attitude of Voltaire to Magic and the Sciences* (New York: Columbia University Press, 1935), 139–57.

The Age of the Limits of Reason

eleventh of his *Letters Concerning the English Nation* to a defense of smallpox inoculations, which had saved thousands of lives in England, Turkey, Russia, and China, but which the French were still resisting in large part because of opposition from the Church (see LCE, 44–8). Like Montesquieu, then, Voltaire was confident that science could improve human life in meaningful ways. On the other hand, he was far too affected by events like the Lisbon earthquake of 1755 – the disaster that killed around thirty thousand people, shook the entire European intellectual world, and provoked Voltaire's writing of *Candide* – to believe that human beings would ever truly be able to conquer nature or bend it to their will. On the contrary, he often verges on cynicism in this regard, holding that, as Ira Wade writes, "the inventions of genius have aided in drenching the earth in blood rather than in cultivating it."[73] Perhaps the greatest practical benefit of science, for Voltaire as for Montesquieu, is less the technology it produces than the critical spirit it imparts; in the chapter on the sciences in *The Age of Louis XIV*, he highlights how the growth of scientific inquiry had helped to undermine beliefs in sorcery, magic, and astrology, which only a century earlier were so widespread that scholars wrote serious treatises on them and judges used them in their deliberations.[74]

Voltaire was, in addition, one of the foremost popularizers of Newton's ideas in France.[75] (He seems to have been the first to circulate the famous – and probably apocryphal – story about Newton and the apple.)[76] Particularly in his early writings, he shows great admiration for Newton's scientific discoveries and achievements, from gravity to optics to calculus. Indeed, in a letter written during his time at Cirey he proclaims that Newton was the greatest person who ever lived, a man compared to whom even the giants of the ancient world were as children at

---

[73] Ira O. Wade, "Voltaire's Quarrel with Science" *Bucknell Review* 8.4 (December 1959), 296.

[74] See Voltaire, *The Age of Louis XIV*, trans. Martyn P. Pollack (London: J. M. Dent and Sons, [1751] 1961), chapter 31.

[75] Voltaire's principal writings on Newton are LCE, 61–86; and Voltaire, *Eléments de la philosophie de Newton*, ed. Robert L. Walters and W. H. Barber, in *The Complete Works of Voltaire*, vol. 15 (Oxford: Voltaire Foundation, [1738] 1992). On Voltaire's view of Newton, see Wade, *The Intellectual Development of Voltaire*, 601–19. On Voltaire's role in the popularization of Newton's ideas and in the "Newton wars" of eighteenth-century France, see J. B. Shank, *The Newton Wars and the Beginning of the French Enlightenment* (Chicago: University of Chicago Press, 2008), part 2.

[76] The first appearance of this story in print is in Voltaire, *An Essay on Epic Poetry*, ed. David Williams, in *The Complete Works of Voltaire*, vol. 3b (Oxford: Voltaire Foundation, [1727] 1996), 372–3. It was repeated for a wider audience at LCE, 69.

play.[77] While Voltaire shows appreciation for Newton's scientific findings, he reserves his greatest praise for Newton's willingness to acknowledge his ignorance about the final causes of the physical laws that he observed, such as that of universal gravitation. Drawing on Newton's famous proclamation that he refused to "feign hypotheses,"[78] Voltaire presents him (to a greater degree than is perhaps warranted) as a man of great caution, almost a skeptic. In his *Elements of the Philosophy of Newton*, also written during the Cirey period, Voltaire returns time and again to Newton's recognition that metaphysical truths and ultimate causes are likely "secrets of the creator, which will remain forever unknown to men."[79] As he succinctly states, Newton "knew how to doubt."[80]

Beginning in the mid-1740s, however, Voltaire's own doubts began to undermine his conviction that even the Newtonian or experimental method could furnish empirical truths with much assurance. Given the countless disputes that continued to rage unabated among the leading scientists of Europe, he began to question whether they were capable of producing conclusive knowledge of the natural world after all. Voltaire's growing disenchantment with Newtonianism and the natural sciences is visible in his revisions of the *Elements* in the editions of 1748 and especially 1756, in which he made a number of quite substantive cuts, removing arguments that he was no longer sure about and attributing others to other thinkers rather than stating them in his own name.[81] While we can be sure that "all the propositions of geometry, algebra, arithmetic are true," he suggests in his later works, "we can make mistakes in every other science" (PD, 392). "We weigh matter, we measure it, we decompose it; and if we want to take a step beyond these coarse operations we find impotence within us and an abyss before us" (PD, 296). Similarly, the blank book in "Micromégas" points toward the impossibility of truly uncovering "the nature of things."[82] As Wade notes, by the end of Voltaire's life "his objections to science are ... both vocal and persistent: it fails to answer the questions about the universe.... It has a tendency to over-mechanize the universe, and it refuses steadfastly to

---

[77] See Voltaire, letter to Pierre Joseph Thoulier d'Olivet, 18 October 1736, in *The Complete Works of Voltaire*, ed. Theodore Besterman, vol. 88 (Geneva: Institut et Musée Voltaire, 1969), 89.

[78] Newton, *Philosophiae Naturalis Principia Mathematica*, 92.

[79] Voltaire, *Eléments de la philosophie de Newton*, 240.

[80] Ibid., 232.

[81] See Walters and Barber, editors' introduction in Voltaire, *Eléments de la philosophie de Newton*, 130–40.

[82] See Voltaire, "Micromégas," 35.

The Age of the Limits of Reason 159

recognize its limitations. True it can weigh, measure, calculate, but it cannot penetrate the nature of things."[83] Thus, while Voltaire was for a time more enthusiastic about the sciences than Montesquieu ever was, for the last three decades of his life he was more disillusioned with them than Montesquieu ever was. As David Beeson and Nicholas Cronk write, "if initially Voltaire's sense of the importance of observation and the philosophical value of doubt had gone hand in hand with his adoption of a scientific method based on empiricism, in his later years the scientific method is lost, leaving only the reliance on observation and, above all, doubt."[84]

Unlike Montesquieu and Voltaire, Hume is not known to have undertaken any scientific investigations of his own, although he was exposed to a number of works of "natural philosophy" (above all those of Robert Boyle) as a student at the University of Edinburgh.[85] That he welcomed the practical achievements of the sciences is patent in his *History of England* as well as essays such as "Of the Rise and Progress of the Arts and Sciences" and "Of Refinement in the Arts"; Hume's writings are utterly devoid of nostalgic longings for a simpler time. On the other hand, he accepts, in the former essay, that "no advantages in this world are pure and unmixed" (EMPL, 130) and that scientific progress is neither inevitable nor inexorable; indeed, he proclaims that "when the arts and sciences come to perfection in any state, from the moment they naturally, or rather necessarily decline, and seldom or never revive in that nation, where they formerly flourished" (EMPL, 135; see also 137).[86] Moreover, he contends elsewhere that science and technology, for all of their benefits, are ultimately less important than they might seem: "Speculative sciences do, indeed, improve the mind; but this advantage reaches only to a few persons, who have leisure to apply themselves to them. And as to practical arts, which encrease the commodities and enjoyments of life, it is well known, that men's happiness consists not so much in an abundance of these, as in the peace and security with which they possess them" (EMPL,

---

[83] Wade, "Voltaire's Quarrel with Science," 295; see also 297.

[84] David Beeson and Nicholas Cronk, "Voltaire: Philosopher or *philosophe*?" in *The Cambridge Companion to Voltaire*, ed. Nicholas Cronk (Cambridge: Cambridge University Press, 2009), 55.

[85] See Michael Barfoot, "Hume and the Culture of Science in the Early Eighteenth Century," in *Studies in the Philosophy of the Scottish Enlightenment*, ed. M. A. Stewart (Oxford: Oxford University Press, 1990).

[86] On the trajectory of scientific progress in *The History of England*, which Hume presents as far from linear, see S. K. Wertz, "Hume and the Historiography of Science" *Journal of the History of Ideas* 54.3 (July 1993): 411–36.

160   *The Pragmatic Enlightenment*

54–5).[87] Like his French counterparts, Hume reserves his most unequivocal praise for the tendency of the sciences to act as "a sovereign antidote against superstition," and thereby to serve as "the most effectual remedy against vice and disorders of every kind" (HE II, 519).

Hume too expresses great admiration for Newton, at one point calling him "the greatest and rarest genius that ever arose for the ornament and instruction of the species" (HE VI, 542). On the other hand, he also points to definite defects in Newton's outlook, including his attachment to certain "superstitious" religious beliefs.[88] Moreover, much like Voltaire, Hume frequently amends or reinterprets Newton's thought in a way that renders it closer to Hume's own skepticism.[89] For instance, in the appendix to *A Treatise of Human Nature* he contends that "nothing is more suitable to [the Newtonian] philosophy, than a modest scepticism to a certain degree, and a fair confession of ignorance in subjects, that exceed all human capacity" (THN, 47). Similarly, in his *History of England* he remarks that "while Newton seemed to draw off the veil from some of the mysteries of nature, he shewed at the same time the imperfections of the mechanical philosophy [i.e., that of Boyle]; and thereby restored her ultimate secrets to that obscurity, in which they ever did and ever will remain" (HE VI, 542). The "seemed" in this sentence is not simply casual: Hume was far more doubtful than Newton that human beings would ever truly understand nature or its causal laws.[90] As we have seen, he denies that we can rationally demonstrate the reality of a causal relationship

---

[87] On the other hand, whereas Montesquieu lamented that the prestige of the natural sciences was beginning to encourage indifference to the "moral" sciences or liberal arts (see note 63), Hume claims otherwise: "Another advantage of industry and of refinements in the mechanical arts, is, that they commonly produce some refinements in the liberal; nor can one be carried to perfection, without being accompanied, in some degree, with the other.... The spirit of the age affects all the arts; and the minds of men, put into a fermentation, turn themselves on all sides, and carry improvements into every art and science" (EMPL, 270–1).

[88] See HE V, 155; and Hume, *The Natural History of Religion*, 75.

[89] See Eric Schliesser, "Hume's Newtonianism and Anti-Newtonianism," in *The Stanford Encyclopedia of Philosophy*, ed. Edward N. Zalta (Winter 2008 edition): <http://plato.stanford.edu/archives/win2008/entries/hume-newton/>. Hume's relationship to Newton has been much debated in the scholarly literature, and Schliesser's essay provides a useful overview.

[90] Newton holds that "the main business of natural philosophy is to argue from phenomena without feigning hypotheses, and to deduce causes from effects, till we come to the very first cause." Isaac Newton, "Queries to the *Opticks*," in *Philosophical Writings*, ed. Andrew Janiak (Cambridge: Cambridge University Press, [1721] 2004), 130. On Hume's departure from Newton in this respect, see Livingston, *Hume's Philosophy of Common Life*, 162–3.

The Age of the Limits of Reason

even in a single, ostensibly straightforward instance, such as the striking of one billiard ball against another, much less the reality of causal *laws* that govern the entire universe. In his view, "to penetrate into the nature of bodies, or explain the secret causes of their operations ... is beyond the reach of human understanding" (THN 1.2.5.26, 46).

More broadly, Hume's fallibilist view of what he calls "matters of fact" – that is, of all realms outside pure logic and mathematics – is directly at odds with the kind of incontrovertible science that many earlier thinkers had sought.[91] Without definite knowledge of causation there can be no scientific laws in the traditional sense, no inviolable regularities from which to deduce particular outcomes or events. "While we cannot give a satisfactory reason, why we believe, after a thousand experiments, that a stone will fall, or fire burn," he asks, "can we ever satisfy ourselves concerning any determination, which we may form, with regard to ... the situation of nature, from, and to eternity?" (EHU 12.25, 121). Even if scientific experiments and empirical observation can "reduce the principles, productive of natural phenomena, to a greater simplicity," he insists repeatedly, the "ultimate springs and principles [of nature] are totally shut up from human curiosity and enquiry" (EHU 4.12, 27). Thus, even "the most perfect philosophy of the natural kind only staves off our ignorance a little longer" (EHU 4.12, 28). Given the impossibility of formulating apodictic knowledge of nature, Hume finds it unsurprising that scientific theories have been perpetually superseded throughout history: "theories of abstract philosophy" that purport to explain the nature of the world "have prevailed during one age: In a successive period, these have been universally exploded: Their absurdity has been detected: Other theories and systems have supplied their place, which again gave place to their successors" (EMPL, 242). Strikingly, he suggests that this is even more true in scientific and philosophical endeavors than in artistic and literary ones: while Aristotle has yielded to Descartes, and Descartes to Newton, writers such as Homer and Virgil are still widely admired. Indeed, he claims that "*nothing* has been experienced more liable to the revolutions of chance and fashion than these pretended decisions of science" (EMPL, 242, emphasis added). Hume's skepticism certainly did not end at science's door.

Smith's writings reveal a similar combination of appreciation for the practical achievements of modern science along with reservations about

---

[91] This is a theme of Danford, *David Hume and the Problem of Reason*, especially chapter 5.

162   *The Pragmatic Enlightenment*

its ability to produce conclusive or enduring knowledge about the natural world. Dugald Stewart remarks that while Smith's "favourite pursuits" as a student at the University of Glasgow "were mathematics and natural philosophy," these "were certainly not the sciences in which he was formed to excel; nor did they long divert him from pursuits more congenial to his mind."[92] Still, Smith's modern editors are right to note that he had "an extensive knowledge of literature of a broadly scientific kind."[93] Throughout his works Smith lauds the benefits that science and technology produce. In *The Theory of Moral Sentiments*, he speaks of "the sciences and arts, which ennoble and embellish human life; which have entirely changed the whole face of the globe, have turned the rude forests of nature into agreeable and fertile plains, and made the trackless and barren ocean a new fund of subsistence, and the great high road of communication to the different nations of the earth" (TMS IV.1.10, 183–4), and he says that "all the liberal arts and sciences" help to produce "real improvements of the world we live in. Mankind are benefited, human nature is ennobled by them" (TMS VI.ii.2.3, 229). In *The Wealth of Nations*, he welcomes the invention of labor-saving devices and shows (as in the famous pin-making example) how technology helps to maximize the efficiency gains of the division of labor (see WN I.i.3, 14–15; I.i.8–9, 19–21). It is true that later in the work he highlights the deleterious effects of the division of labor on the "intellectual, social, and martial virtues" of the laborers, at least "unless government takes some pains to prevent it" (WN V.i.f.50, 782), but his overall view of technological progress is overwhelmingly positive. Indeed, whereas Montesquieu cites the invention of gunpowder as a clear instance of technology's having harmful consequences, Smith insists that because modern firearms help to give "civilized" nations a military advantage over "barbarous" ones, "the invention of fire-arms, an invention which at first sight appears to be so pernicious, is certainly favourable both to the permanency and to the extension of civilization" (WN V.i.a.44, 708).[94] Further, he too sees science as "the great antidote to the poison

---

[92] Stewart, "Account of the Life and Writings of Adam Smith, LL.D.," 270–1.

[93] D. D. Raphael and A. S. Skinner, "General Introduction," in Adam Smith, *Essays on Philosophical Subjects* (Indianapolis: Liberty Fund, 1980), 11. See also Christopher J. Berry, "Smith and Science," in *The Cambridge Companion to Adam Smith*, ed. Knud Haakonssen (Cambridge: Cambridge University Press, 2006), 114–16; and Andrew S. Skinner, *A System of Social Science: Papers Relating to Adam Smith*, second edition (Oxford: Clarendon Press, 1996), 25–6.

[94] As the editors of WN note, Hume makes a similar case at HE II, 230.

The Age of the Limits of Reason

of enthusiasm and superstition," and for this reason he suggests that the state should encourage the study of it "by instituting some sort of probation, even in the higher and more difficult sciences, to be undergone by every person before he [is] permitted to exercise any liberal profession, or before he [can] be received as a candidate for any honourable office of trust or profit" (WN V.i.g.14, 796).

Smith also welcomes the *theoretical* advances of modern science, as witnessed by his comment, in an early published letter on the state of learning in mid-eighteenth-century Europe, that "natural philosophy" is "the science which in modern times has been most happily cultivated."[95] However, in a remarkable essay on the history of astronomy, written early in life but published only posthumously, he goes to great lengths to highlight what might be called the "subjective" side of the scientific enterprise. The essay traces the developments of the field from the earliest superstitious views of the heavens to the systems of thinkers such as Ptolemy, Copernicus, Galileo, Kepler, Descartes, and Newton. However, the main purpose of the essay is to examine the nature of scientific investigation itself, as evidenced by its full title: "The Principles Which Lead and Direct Philosophical Enquires; Illustrated by the History of Astronomy." Smith argues that people engage in natural philosophy or science not principally out of "any expectation of advantage from its discoveries," as Bacon had insisted, but rather in an attempt to "sooth[e] the imagination" by accounting for unusual or perplexing events or appearances.[96] As Samuel Fleischacker writes, for Smith "scientific systems consist in constructions by which the imagination soothes the discomfort it feels when it encounters disruptions in experience."[97] Indeed, Smith goes so far as to proclaim that "all philosophical [i.e., scientific] systems" are "mere inventions of the imagination, to connect together the otherwise disjointed and discordant phaenomena of nature."[98]

Smith's claim that scientific systems are "mere inventions of the imagination" has several noteworthy implications. First, it suggests that the impetus to scientific study is highly personal; as D. D. Raphael and Andrew Skinner put it, for Smith "man is impelled to seek an explanation for observed 'appearances' as a result of a *subjective* feeling of discomfort, and … the resulting explanation or theory is therefore designed to

---

[95] Adam Smith, "Letter to the *Edinburgh Review*," in *Essays on Philosophical Subjects*, ed. J. C. Bryce (Indianapolis: Liberty Fund, [1756] 1980), 244.

[96] Smith, "The History of Astronomy," 51, 46.

[97] Fleischacker, *On Adam Smith's Wealth of Nations*, 32.

[98] Smith, "The History of Astronomy," 105.

meet some psychological need."[99] In addition, Smith's view implies that scientific theories will tend to have a backward-looking character, insofar as they are designed to solve the problems left unresolved by earlier theories. Throughout the history of astronomy, he shows, each "system" of the movements of the heavens aimed to alleviate the contradictions and irregularities inherent in the prevailing system, which in turn led to new contradictions and irregularities to be alleviated by yet another system.[100] Third, Smith is, like Montesquieu, Voltaire, and Hume, doubtful that science will ever truly be able to penetrate the secrets of nature, or to comprehend the natural world in its entirety. Hence, in his view the proper standard for judging a scientific theory is less whether it objectively captures the eternal order of nature than whether it satisfies the human craving for order and explanation. As Emma Rothschild writes, for Smith "the point of scientific enterprise is ... to imagine a system (or one system after another) which makes sense of the world, and not to discover that the world in fact makes sense. Orderliness is for Smith a quality which is 'bestowed' upon phenomena."[101]

Finally, and connected with each of these points, Smith insists that all scientific theories must remain permanently subject to revision. This is true even of Newton's laws of motion and gravity, which at the time had "prevail[ed] over all opposition, and ... advanced to the acquisition of the most universal empire that was ever established in philosophy."[102] Smith has few doubts about the brilliance of Newton and his achievements: he speaks of "the superior genius and sagacity of Sir Isaac Newton" and proclaims that his theory of gravity was "the most happy, and, we may now say, the greatest and most admirable improvement that was ever made in philosophy."[103] Even "the most sceptical cannot avoid feeling," he says, that Newton's principles "have a degree of firmness and solidity that we should in vain look for in any other system."[104] His proof? "Even we, while we have been endeavouring to represent all philosophical systems as mere inventions of the imagination, to connect together the otherwise disjointed and discordant phaenomena of nature, have insensibly

---

[99] Raphael and Skinner, "General Introduction," 5.

[100] See Fleischacker, *On Adam Smith's Wealth of Nations*, 32–4.

[101] Emma Rothschild, *Economic Sentiments: Adam Smith, Condorcet, and the Enlightenment* (Cambridge, MA: Harvard University Press, 2001), 140. Smith speaks of various thinkers "bestowing" order on natural phenomena at dozens of points throughout the essay.

[102] Smith, "The History of Astronomy," 104.

[103] Ibid., 98; see also 105.

[104] Ibid., 105.

The Age of the Limits of Reason

been drawn in, to make use of language expressing the connecting principles of this one, as if they were the real chains which Nature makes use of to bind together her several operations."[105] As the "as if" in this sentence indicates, however, Smith holds that in fact Newton's system too is a "mere invention of the imagination," rather than a discovery of an objective truth, and thus that it too will likely be superseded in time.[106] As Fleischacker writes, for Smith "it is the way of scientific systems to triumph over past ones and be triumphed over in turn. The effect of this system *of* scientific systems – this system of the philosophy of science – is to put in doubt the possibility that any scientific system, on any subject, will ever provide the final word on that subject, the invincible explanation of the problems with which it is concerned."[107] Several scholars have noted that this vision of the scientific enterprise – according to which scientific systems undergo regular and presumably endless "revolutions" as a result of recurrent attempts to resolve the discrepancies of earlier systems – bears a striking resemblance to the Kuhnian notion of scientific change through paradigm shifts.[108] It is also, needless to say, a far cry from the kind of blind faith in science's methods and dictates that Becker and others have attributed to the Enlightenment.[109]

In short, Hume, Smith, Montesquieu, and Voltaire all firmly embraced the achievements of the natural sciences but also demonstrated an awareness of their practical and theoretical limits. In their view, modern science is neither the panacea that some of its most fervent advocates envisioned

---

[105] Ibid.

[106] See Raphael and Skinner, "General Introduction," 19, 21.

[107] Fleischacker, *On Adam Smith's Wealth of Nations*, 33. Thus, Smith sardonically announces near the outset of the essay that he will "endeavour to trace [natural philosophy or science] from its first origin, up to that summit of perfection to which it is at present supposed to have arrived, and to which, indeed, it has equally been supposed to have arrived in almost all former times." Smith, "The History of Astronomy," 46. See also TMS VII.ii.4.14, 313.

[108] See, for instance, Raphael and Skinner, "General Introduction," 15; Fleischacker, *On Adam Smith's Wealth of Nations*, 32; J. Ralph Lindgren, *The Social Philosophy of Adam Smith* (The Hague: Martinus Nijhoff, 1973), 18; Schliesser, "Wonder in the Face of Scientific Revolutions," 704, 706; and Skinner, *A System of Social Science*, 44. For a dissenting view, according to which it is "far-fetched" to "saddle [Smith] with the subtleties of twentieth-century philosophy," see Christopher J. Berry, *Social Theory of the Scottish Enlightenment* (Edinburgh: Edinburgh University Press, 1997), 60; and Berry, "Smith and Science," 121–4.

[109] Even Cassirer claims that the thinkers of the Enlightenment believed that "thanks to Newton, [they] stood finally on firm ground which could never again be shaken by any future revolution of natural science" – a claim that Smith's essay on astronomy, as well as the writings of Hume and the later Voltaire, call into severe doubt. Cassirer, *The Philosophy of the Enlightenment*, 44.

nor the nightmare painted by its greatest detractors. Contemporary critics of the Enlightenment frequently suggest that its embrace of science and technology paved the way for the atrocities of the modern world, from Auschwitz to Hiroshima, but it seems safe to say that advances in these fields were a necessary but very far from sufficient condition for these events. Moreover, the thinkers of the pragmatic Enlightenment were surely right to believe that scientific and technological progress would generate undeniable advances in human well-being; as Bernard Yack notes, "it is very hard indeed for someone who has just been returned to an active life by a successful quadruple bypass operation to think of himself as a victim of his own creations."[110] Besides, Hume, Smith, Montesquieu, and Voltaire never suggested that science could solve all human problems, and they explicitly denied that it could provide conclusive or complete knowledge of the natural world. Thus, their stance toward the natural sciences would be better characterized as one of cautious appreciation than as one of blind faith.

MODERATING RELIGION

While virtually all Enlightenment thinkers welcomed the advances made possible by science and technology, their attitudes toward religion varied greatly. For much of the nineteenth and twentieth centuries, the Enlightenment was all but *defined* in terms of its hostility toward religion in general, and Christianity in particular.[111] However, recent scholarship has stressed that the relationship between the Enlightenment and religion was in fact far more complex, especially when attention is shifted away from the most radical circles of eighteenth-century Paris.[112] As we will

[110] Bernard Yack, *The Fetishism of Modernities: Epochal Self-Consciousness in Contemporary Social and Political Thought* (South Bend, IN: University of Notre Dame Press, 1997), 124–5. Nor are efforts to use science and technology to "conquer nature" and thereby ease the human estate unique to the Enlightenment: the command to subdue nature for human purposes can be found in the first chapter of the book of Genesis (1:28).

[111] Thus, the first part of Paul Hazard's classic work on the period is entitled "Christianity on Trial," and the first volume of Peter Gay's equally classic work is dubbed "The Rise of Modern Paganism." See Paul Hazard, *European Thought in the Eighteenth Century: From Montesquieu to Lessing*, trans. J. Lewis May (Cleveland: Meridian Books, [1946] 1965); and Gay, *The Enlightenment: An Interpretation*, vol. 1.

[112] See, for instance, Ulrich L. Lehner and Michael Printy, eds., *A Companion to the Catholic Enlightenment in Europe* (Leiden: Brill, 2010); Helena Rosenblatt, "The Christian Enlightenment," in *The Cambridge History of Christianity*, vol. 7: *Enlightenment, Reawakening and Revolution, 1600–1815*, ed. Stewart J. Brown and Timothy Tackett

The Age of the Limits of Reason   167

see in this section, there was a good deal of variation on this score even among the four thinkers who are the focus of this book, from Voltaire's ardent deism to Hume's fundamentally skeptical and irreligious outlook. As pragmatic thinkers, however, they all adopted a basically moderate stance. On the one hand, they all rejected the claims of Biblical revelation and special providence, denied that morality has anything to do with God's will or commandments, and devoted great amounts of intellectual energy to condemning religious fanaticism and intolerance. On the other hand, none of them – not even Hume – adopted the kind of unreservedly dismissive and antagonistic view of religion espoused by some of the more radical philosophes such as La Mettrie and d'Holbach. They did not believe that the frail powers of human reason could conclusively *disprove* the claims of revealed religion, even if it could and did cast a good deal of doubt on them, and they all saw the religious impulse – the inclination to believe in a higher power – as natural in some sense. Thus, they did not believe that religion could or would ever disappear altogether. Nor did these thinkers suppose that religious beliefs and institutions had entirely pernicious consequences. For all of their condemnation of religious fanaticism and intolerance – a subject that fairly dominates the writings of Voltaire and Hume, and is conspicuous in those of Montesquieu and Smith as well – they also acknowledged that religion had produced real benefits, such as promoting adherence to society's moral standards, providing consolation and comfort to the grieving and unfortunate, restraining rulers from exercising despotic powers, advancing liberty by encouraging people to resist absolute rule, and helping to effect humane reforms such as the abolition of slavery and the elevation of the status of women in European society. To be sure, they placed more emphasis on the ills of religion than on its advantages; indeed, it is probably safe to say that they thought organized religion *had* more ills than advantages, all things considered. In keeping with their pragmatic outlook, however, they sought to moderate or "liberalize" religion, to encourage its positive aspects and mitigate its negative ones, rather than simply disdaining or combating all religious belief, as the more radical philosophes tended to do.

Before turning to their views on this topic, it will perhaps be useful to recall very briefly the status of religion in the societies in which they

(Cambridge: Cambridge University Press, 2006); and David Sorkin, *The Religious Enlightenment: Protestants, Jews, and Catholics from London to Vienna* (Princeton, NJ: Princeton University Press, 2008).

168   *The Pragmatic Enlightenment*

lived and wrote. In eighteenth-century France, the monarchy was still considered to be instituted by divine right, and the Church enjoyed enormous power over areas such as censorship, education, and criminal law. Starting in 1685, when Louis XIV revoked the Edict of Nantes, persecution of Protestants became official government policy. The campaign against heresy was reaffirmed and extended by Louis XV and his minister the duc de Bourbon in 1724, when they instituted the death penalty for Protestant ministers and other harsh penalties – life in the galleys for men, life in prison for women – for their followers who openly practiced their faith. These punishments were "only" actually meted out to a few thousand individuals, but even those Protestants not so punished faced severe discrimination, including exclusion from a number of professions such as law, medicine, and public office; restrictions on buying and selling land; a denial of inheritance rights; and a denial of official recognition of their marriages and baptisms (which meant that all children of Protestant couples were considered illegitimate). These laws were enforced less and less strictly as the century wore on, but they were not repealed until 1787, when Louis XVI restored the civil liberties of Protestants. Eighteenth-century Britain showed appreciably more tolerance toward religious minorities than did ancien régime France, but even there non-Anglicans were barred from holding public office at either the national or local levels and were subject to double taxation. In Scotland, as recently as 1696 a twenty-year-old student named Thomas Aikenhead had been put to death for blasphemy. While the eighteenth century was an age of recurrent strife between Catholic and Protestant, Jesuit and Jansenist, Anglican and Presbyterian, it is critical to remember that Hume, Smith, Montesquieu, and Voltaire were reacting not only to the religious conflict and persecution of their own time, but also to the cataclysmic Wars of Religion that had ravaged Europe in the sixteenth and seventeenth centuries.[113] Michael Gillespie notes that

---

[113] Voltaire, for instance, literally ran a fever every year on 24 August, the anniversary of the St. Bartholomew's Day Massacre of 1572. See René Pomeau, *La Religion de Voltaire* (Paris: Librarie A.-G. Nizet, 1956), 108–10. This massacre of tens of thousands of Huguenots was not simply part of a distant and much-regretted past in the eighteenth century: Voltaire cites a 1758 pamphlet entitled *A Defense of the Massacre of Saint Bartholomew*, and he repeatedly draws attention to the annual festival held in Toulouse to celebrate the massacre, which ran up to 1762. See Voltaire, "An Address to the Public Concerning the Parricides Imputed to the Calas and Sirven Families," in *Treatise on Tolerance and Other Writings*, ed. Simon Harvey (Cambridge: Cambridge University Press, [1766] 2000), 125–7; and Voltaire, *Treatise on Tolerance*, 46, 95.

The Age of the Limits of Reason

by conservative estimates, [the Wars of Religion] claimed the lives of 10 percent of the population in England, 15 percent in France, 30 percent in Germany, and more than 50 percent in Bohemia. By comparison, European dead in World War II exceeded 10 percent only in Germany and the USSR. Within our experience only the Holocaust and the killing fields of Cambodia can begin to rival the levels of destruction that characterized the Wars of Religion.[114]

Indeed, Voltaire once calculated that, up to his time, some 9,718,800 people had been "slaughtered, drowned, burned, broken on the wheel, or hanged for the sake of [the Christian] God."[115] As this small bit of context indicates, it is not for nothing that these thinkers believed that while errors in philosophy may be ridiculous, those in religion are frequently dangerous (see THN 1.4.7.13, 177).

Voltaire is widely, and with good reason, seen as one of history's greatest scourges of Christianity. He spent a long and prolific career seeking to *écrase l'infâme*, or crush the infamous, meaning religious fanaticism and intolerance, the Church, and indeed Christianity itself.[116] Yet he most certainly did *not* want to crush belief in God altogether. Some scholars have attempted to paint Voltaire as a closet agnostic or even atheist,[117] but the vast preponderance of the evidence suggests that he was in fact a sincere, resolute, and even ardent deist.[118] In literally hundreds of books, essays, pamphlets, and letters, he constantly reiterates that everything we know about the world suggests the existence of a providential order

[114] Michael Allan Gillespie, *The Theological Origins of Modernity* (Chicago: University of Chicago Press, 2008), 130.

[115] Voltaire, "Massacres," in *Questions sur l'Encyclopédie*, vol. 7, ed. Nicholas Cronk and Christiane Mervaud, in *The Complete Works of Voltaire*, vol. 42b (Oxford: Voltaire Foundation, [1771] 2012), 191.

[116] While Voltaire did not begin to use this catchphrase until around 1760, he pursued the goal it expressed all of his adult life. There has been a good deal of scholarly debate about what exactly he meant by *l'infâme*, but I concur with Peter Gay's assessment that "interpreters who restrict *l'infâme* to intolerance or fanaticism or Roman Catholicism shrink from a conclusion that Voltaire himself drew, and drew innumerable times, in these frenetic years [his later years at Ferney]: 'Every sensible man, every honorable man, must hold the Christian sect in horror.'" Gay, *The Enlightenment: An Interpretation*, vol. 1, 391.

[117] The most prominent Voltaire scholar to make this case has been Theodore Besterman, who contends that Voltaire's "deism" is indistinguishable from agnosticism or atheism. See Theodore Besterman, "Voltaire's God" *Studies on Voltaire and the Eighteenth Century* 55 (1967): 23–41; and Theodore Besterman, *Voltaire* (Chicago: University of Chicago Press, [1969] 1976), 215–32. For another example, see Roy Porter, *The Enlightenment*, second edition (New York: Palgrave, 2001), 31.

[118] This is the conclusion of the classic work on Voltaire's religious beliefs: Pomeau, *La Religion de Voltaire*. See also Rosemary Z. Lauer, *The Mind of Voltaire: A Study of His "Constructive Deism"* (Westminster, MD: Newman Press, 1961).

overseen by a Supreme Being. In a typical Enlightenment formulation, he proclaims that "a catechist announces God to children, and Newton demonstrates him to wise men" (PD, 58). This deistic God may be quite removed from human concerns, but that he exists Voltaire has little doubt: "There are problems to be found in the view that there is a God," he acknowledges, "but in the opposite view there are absurdities" (TM, 75). Voltaire's views are well encapsulated by a famous (and probably even true) story, according to which he woke one of his visitors at Ferney early one morning in the mid-1770s and requested that he join him in climbing a nearby peak to watch the sunrise. When they reached the top and saw the dawn breaking over the Jura Mountains, Voltaire took off his hat, prostrated himself on the ground, and exclaimed, "I believe! I believe in you! Almighty God, I believe!" He then rose, replaced his hat, and drily told his guest, "As for Monsieur the son and Madame his mother, that's a different story."[119] This story, of course, attests both to Voltaire's genuine belief in God and to his opposition and incredulity toward Christianity. Indeed, it was precisely for the *sake* of the true, deistic God that Voltaire sought to rid the world of the evils of Christianity.[120]

As many commentators have noted, late in life Voltaire found himself fighting battles on two fronts, not only against the old enemy of Christian intolerance but also against the new threat of materialist atheism. In fact, as Gustave Lanson suggests, "he fought d'Holbach in his final years more than he fought the Sorbonne."[121] Far from being a closet atheist himself, Voltaire consistently regarded atheism not only as untrue but also as unnatural and dangerous. In his view, people are naturally inclined toward belief in some kind of higher power, or a number of higher powers, and thus religion of some sort has existed for as long as human beings themselves have existed.[122] He suggests that the rise of atheism among the more radical philosophes was, somewhat ironically, the fault of religious fanatics: when people are told to "believe a hundred things either obviously abominable or mathematically impossible: otherwise the God of mercy will burn you in the fires of hell, not only for millions of billions of years, but for all eternity," they are apt to revolt against such

---

[119] A more detailed version of this story can be found in Pearson, *Voltaire Almighty*, 359–60. According to Pearson, this display was prompted in part by the similar performance of the Savoyard vicar in Rousseau's *Emile*, which Voltaire had recently been rereading.

[120] See Peter Gay, *Voltaire's Politics: The Poet as Realist* (New Haven, CT: Yale University Press [1959] 1988), 258.

[121] Lanson, *Voltaire*, 149.

[122] See EM I.intro.5–6, 13–22; PD, 245–6, 350–1; and Voltaire, *Treatise on Tolerance*, 83.

The Age of the Limits of Reason

commands and conclude that God is a delusion or a sham after all (PD, 58).[123] Voltaire sees atheism not just as a kind of historical anomaly but as a harmful one, both to the morals of the masses and to the cause of the philosophes. By associating their arguments for religious toleration and critical thinking with dogmatic atheism, he insists, works like d'Holbach's *System of Nature* (1770) were doing incalculable damage to the enterprise of Enlightenment.[124]

As Voltaire's opposition to atheism on moral grounds suggests, he regarded belief in God and an afterlife as eminently useful in encouraging moral behavior. Morality is not a matter of obeying God's will or commandments, in his view – as we have seen, he holds that "moral good and evil ... exist only in relation to us" (TM, 94) – but popular belief in a rewarding and punishing God helps to sustain and enforce society's moral standards. Indeed, he proclaims that "it is ... absolutely necessary for princes and peoples to have deeply engraved in their minds the notion of a Supreme Being, creator, ruler, remunerator and avenger" and that "it is infinitely more useful to have a religion (even a bad one) than none at all" (PD, 56–7). This is one reason why he notoriously declares that "if God did not exist, it would be necessary to invent him."[125] It must be admitted that this argument shows Voltaire at his least attractive, insofar as it underscores his chronic disdain for the benighted masses (and their equally benighted rulers). On the other hand, as Peter Gay reminds us, the claim that it would be necessary to invent God if he did not in fact exist "is not a cynical injunction to rulers to invent a divine policeman for their ignorant subjects. Rather, it is part of a vehement diatribe against an atheist, written in the midst of Voltaire's dialogue with Holbach."[126] Voltaire almost certainly did not himself believe in a God who acts as "remunerator and avenger" of human actions, but nor did he believe it was necessary to invent God altogether. Moreover, the religion that he envisaged for the common people was an exceptionally simple one, shorn

---

[123] See also Voltaire, *Treatise on Tolerance*, 48; and Voltaire, *The A B C, or Dialogues between A B C*, in *Political Writings*, trans. David Williams (Cambridge: Cambridge University Press, [1768] 1994), 147–8.

[124] To be sure, Voltaire insists that "fanaticism is certainly a thousand times more baleful" than atheism, since "atheism does not inspire bloody passions, but fanaticism does" (PD, 56). However, he immediately notes that "for the most part atheists are bold and misguided scholars who reason badly" (PD, 56) and that "even if not as baleful as fanaticism, [atheism] is nearly always fatal to virtue" (PD, 57).

[125] Voltaire, *Épitre à l'auteur du livre des Trois Imposteurs*, in *Oeuvres complètes de Voltaire*, ed. Louis Moland, vol. 10 (Paris: Garnier, [1769] 1877), 403.

[126] Gay, *Voltaire's Politics*, 265.

172   *The Pragmatic Enlightenment*

of most of the mysteries and dogmas of Christianity; hence, Gay suggests that it was less a "noble lie" than a "noble white lie."[127]

As much as Voltaire mocked the metaphysical and historical claims of Christianity and reviled the persecutions of the Church, he had no quarrel with Christianity's basic ethical norms: the Golden Rule, loving one's neighbor, and so on. In fact, he was surprisingly sympathetic, particularly in his later years, to what he took to be the true and original principles of Christianity, the ones espoused by Jesus himself.[128] According to Voltaire, "Jesus taught no metaphysical dogma at all, he wrote no theological exercises ... he instituted neither monks nor inquisitors; he commanded nothing of what we see today" (PD, 273; see also 118, 393). Most importantly, Jesus displayed none of the intolerance of his later followers: "he said not a single word against the cult of the Romans, who surrounded his country. Let us imitate his indulgence, and deserve to receive it from others."[129] Voltaire also devotes no less than four of his *Letters Concerning the English Nation* – and the first four, at that – to a sympathetic portrait of the simple faith and humane tolerance of the Quakers, which he contrasts with the ostentation, superstition, and persecutions of the Catholic Church (see LCE, 9–25).[130] It is perhaps worth noting, in addition, that while Voltaire constantly ridicules the internal inconsistencies and historical inaccuracies of the Bible, he does not do so out of a position of ignorance; indeed, recent scholarship has suggested that "few in the eighteenth century knew the Bible better than he."[131]

Finally, for all of the scorn that Voltaire pours on Christianity and the Church as they existed in his day, his practical recommendations

---

[127] Ibid., 267. Gay also suggests that for Voltaire "the religion of *le peuple* is an expedient which will wither away as enlightenment spreads," leaving in its wake only his true, deistic God. Ibid., 268.

[128] See Marie-Hélène Cotoni, *L'Exégèse du Nouveau Testament dans la philosophie française du dix-huitième siècle* (Oxford: Voltaire Foundation, 1984), 342–8; and Graham Gargett, "Voltaire and the Bible," in *The Cambridge Companion to Voltaire*, ed. Nicholas Cronk (Cambridge: Cambridge University Press, 2009), 202.

[129] Voltaire, *Homily on Superstition*, in *A Treatise on Toleration and Other Essays*, trans. Joseph McCabe (Amherst, NY: Prometheus Books, [1767] 1994), 122. See also Voltaire, *Treatise on Tolerance*, chapter 14.

[130] For later sympathetic portraits of the Quakers, see PD, 392–3; and Voltaire, *Treatise on Tolerance*, 22.

[131] Gargett, "Voltaire and the Bible," 193. For a detailed study that defends Voltaire against the once-common charge that his Biblical criticism was crude, willfully misrepresentative, or merely opportunistic, see Bertram Eugene Schwarzbach, *Voltaire's Old Testament Criticism* (Geneva: Droz, 1971).

The Age of the Limits of Reason

regarding them are actually quite moderate.[132] He rails against intolerance and persecution of all kinds, of course, as well as the extensive temporal powers of the Church over censorship, education, and criminal law. But he sees this standpoint as entirely in keeping with the teachings of Jesus himself: "The religion of Jesus is unquestionably that which most positively excludes priests from all civil authority. 'Render unto Caesar the things that are Caesar's.' 'Among you there is neither first nor last.' 'My kingdom is not of this world'" (PD, 346).[133] The motto *écrasez l'infâme* might appear to be an uncompromisingly radical one, but in a letter to a fellow philosophe, d'Alembert, Voltaire equates it with nothing more than advancing France to the point that England had already reached: "I would like you to crush the infamous, that is the great point. It must be reduced to the state where it is in England.... That is the greatest service one can render to mankind."[134] And England, of course, had an established church, as Voltaire was well aware. In fact, in the *Treatise on Tolerance* he states explicitly, "I do not say that all those who profess a different religion from that of the reigning prince should share in the places and honors available to those who are of the prevailing religion. In England, Catholics are considered as belonging to the party of the Pretender, and are therefore denied office; they even pay double taxes; yet they still enjoy all the other privileges of the citizen."[135] In other words, Voltaire advocates an Erastian subordination of the church to the state, but not the elimination of all government support for religion. As long as religious minorities are guaranteed their basic civil liberties, he hopes, the result will be a flowering of religious pluralism and thence relative concord among the various sects. As he famously writes in the *Letters Concerning the English Nation*, "if one religion only were allowed in *England*, the government would very possibly become arbitrary; if there were but two, the people wou'd cut one another's throats; but as there are such a multitude, they all live happy and in peace" (LCE, 30).[136]

Montesquieu's religious beliefs are somewhat harder to discern than Voltaire's. He is, of course, famous for his indirect and elliptical writing

---

[132] This point is emphasized in the editor's introduction in Voltaire, *Treatise on Tolerance and Other Writings*, ed. Simon Harvey (Cambridge: Cambridge University Press, 2000), xvii.

[133] See also Voltaire, "Republican Ideas," in *Political Writings*, trans. David Williams (Cambridge: Cambridge University Press, [1765] 1994), 196.

[134] Voltaire, letter to Jean Le Rond d'Alembert, 23 June 1760, in *The Complete Works of Voltaire*, ed. Theodore Besterman, vol. 105 (Oxford: Voltaire Foundation, 1971), 409.

[135] Voltaire, *Treatise on Tolerance*, 20; see also 24–5.

[136] For similar sentiments, see ibid., 24; and PD, 390.

174   *The Pragmatic Enlightenment*

style, and he employs this style nowhere more than in discussions of religious matters. Throughout *The Spirit of the Laws* he goes out of his way to avoid the question of the truth or falsity of the various religions he considers, and instead focuses on their usefulness. At the outset of book 24, the first of the two books devoted to the topic of religion, he states that since he is "not a theologian but a political writer," he will "examine the various religions of the world only in relation to the good to be drawn from them in the civil state" (SL 24.1, 459).[137] It seems safe to say, however, that like Voltaire he was neither an orthodox Christian nor an outright atheist, but rather a deist or an adherent of some form of natural religion (meaning the spiritual beliefs that one can reach from reflection on the natural world, as opposed to divine revelation).[138] Thus, Montesquieu suggests in one of his *Pensées* that "the least reflection is enough for a man to cure himself of atheism. He has only to consider the Heavens, and he will find an invincible proof of the existence of God." However, he goes on to acknowledge that we cannot know much about the nature of this God: "perhaps the sole thing that reason teaches us about God is that there is an intelligent being that brings forth this order that we see in the world. But if one asks what is the nature of this being, one asks something that surpasses human reason" (Pensées #1946, 589; see also #1096, 296–8; #2095, 641). Similarly, in a published letter to William Warburton, written late in life, Montesquieu proclaims: "It is not impossible to attack revealed religions, because they rest on particular facts, and facts, by their nature, are liable to dispute. But it is not the same with natural religion, which is derived from ... the inner sentiments of man, which cannot be disputed."[139]

As this reference to "the inner sentiments of man" suggests, Montesquieu believes that there is something in human nature that "impresses on us

---

[137] See also Montesquieu, *Défense de l'Esprit des lois*, 1138.

[138] That Montesquieu was not an outright atheist is fairly uncontroversial; indeed, he remarks, "I don't understand how atheists think" (Pensées #57, 21). Mark Waddicor has argued that Montesquieu was a believing Christian in some sense, but this is very much a minority view among Montesquieu scholars. See Waddicor, *Montesquieu and the Philosophy of Natural Law*, 177–81. Montesquieu himself notes that he occupies something of a middle ground in terms of his religious beliefs: "What a business it is to be moderate in one's principles! I pass in France for having little religion and in England for having too much" (Pensées #1134, 306). As we will see, Hume faced the reverse predicament, insofar as he was reviled for his "atheism" by many Britons but mocked for his *lack* of militant atheism by the radical Parisian philosophes.

[139] Charles de Secondat, baron de Montesquieu, letter to William Warburton, May 1754?, in *Oeuvres complètes de Montesquieu*, ed. André Masson, vol. 3 (Paris: Nagel, 1955), 1509.

The Age of the Limits of Reason   175

the idea of a creator and thereby leads us toward him" (SL 1.2, 6).[140] Thus, he too sees the disbelief in any higher power as a kind of moral and theoretical aberration. Like Voltaire, Montesquieu argues that while religion can be (and often is) quite harmful, atheism is still more so. In response to Bayle's claim that "it is less dangerous to have no religion at all than to have a bad one," he insists:

> It is to reason incorrectly against religion to collect ... a long enumeration of the evils it has produced, without also making one of the good things it has done. If I wanted to recount all the evils that civil laws, monarchy, and republican government have produced in the world, I would say frightful things.... It is not a question of knowing whether it would be better for a certain man or a certain people to be without religion than to abuse the one that they have, but of knowing which is the lesser evil, that one sometimes abuse religion or that there be none among men. (SL 24.2, 460)

Montesquieu finds the idea of there being no religion among men alarming, both because he sees belief in God and an afterlife as the only effectual consolation in times of adversity (see Pensées #1266, 341) and because, yet again like Voltaire, he regards religion as a crucial prop for morality. In fact, he proclaims that "religion, even a false one, is the best warrant men can have of the integrity of men" (SL 24.8, 465).[141] This is especially important, in his view, with respect to political rulers: Montesquieu returns time and again to the idea that religion is "the only bridle that can hold those who fear no human laws" (SL 24.2, 460; see also, e.g., 3.10, 29–30; 12.29, 211; 19.18, 319; 24.3, 461–2).[142]

---

[140] Montesquieu states that this impression is "the first of the natural laws in importance, though not the first in the order of these laws," since one would naturally "think of the preservation of his being before seeking the origin of his being" (1.2, 6). After this statement Montesquieu does not mention God again in his enumeration of the laws of nature. It should also be noted that however "natural" it may be to believe in God, we are warned in the previous chapter that human beings "could at any moment forget [their] creator," and thus "the laws of religion" are necessary to call them back to God (SL 1.1, 5).

[141] Similarly, Montesquieu claims in his work on the Romans that the introduction of Epicureanism tainted the hearts and minds of the people since "religion is always the best guarantee one can have of the morals of men." Charles de Secondat, baron de Montesquieu, *Considerations on the Causes of the Greatness of the Romans and Their Decline*, trans. David Lowenthal (Indianapolis: Hackett, [1734] 1999), 97–8. In the letter to Warburton, he writes that "one who attacks revealed religion, attacks but revealed religion; but one who attacks natural religion, attacks all the religions in the world. If one teaches men that they need not be curbed by one bridle, they may think there is another; but it is much more pernicious to teach them that there are none at all." Montesquieu, letter to Warburton, May 1754?, 1509.

[142] Montesquieu never suggests that religion will *always* prevent rulers (or anyone else) from taking unjust actions, but he does seem to think it is the most effective restraint

176   *The Pragmatic Enlightenment*

Although Montesquieu reserves his highest praise for the "religion" of Stoicism (see SL 24.10, 465–6), he offers a generally positive assessment of the political effects of Christianity in *The Spirit of the Laws*. For instance, he praises Christianity for helping to hasten the abolition of slavery in Europe (see SL 15.7–8, 252, but cf. also 15.4, 249) and for helping to elevate the status of women in European society (see SL 19.18, 319; 26.9, 503). He also suggests that Christianity is better than most religions at restraining despotism and rendering political rulers less cruel: if we consider the "continual massacres of the kings and leaders of the Greeks and Romans, and ... the destruction of peoples and towns by Tamerlane and Genghis Khan," he observes, we will see that "we owe to Christianity both a certain political right in government and a certain right of nations in war, for which human nature can never be sufficiently grateful" (SL 24.3, 461–2; see also Pensées #551, 185). On the other hand, as Thomas Pangle notes, in making this case "Montesquieu seems momentarily to have forgotten what he elsewhere reminds his readers of"[143] – namely, that the Church had also carried out nearly countless acts of persecution over the centuries, such as those of the Spanish and Portuguese Inquisitions, which Montesquieu depicts as having cast a permanent stain on their supposedly enlightened age (see SL 25.13, 490–2). Indeed, throughout much of his discussion of religion, Montesquieu essentially amends or "liberalizes" Christianity, above all by stressing its gentle and humane side rather than its intolerance and its persecutions, so as to make it more consistent with his political aims than the Christianity that actually existed in his time.[144] He simply assumes – perhaps even *pretends* would not be too strong here – that Christianity must endorse the laws and institutions that are most politically salutary: "The Christian religion, which orders men to love one another, *no doubt* wants the best political laws and the best civil laws for each people," he writes, "because those

---

that is to be found: "I well know that it does not always halt a man in the heat of passion. But are we always in that state? If it does not always restrain the moment, it at least restrains a life" (Pensées #1993, 611).

[143] Thomas L. Pangle, *The Theological Basis of Liberal Modernity in Montesquieu's Spirit of the Laws* (Chicago: University of Chicago Press, 2010), 104.

[144] See ibid., 106; and Diana Schaub, "Of Believers and Barbarians: Montesquieu's Enlightened Toleration," in *Early Modern Skepticism and the Origins of Toleration*, ed. Alan Levine (Lanham, MD: Lexington, 1999), 235, 238. For instance, Montesquieu has the imaginary Jewish author of the "Very humble remonstrance to the inquisitors of Spain and Portugal" entreat the inquisitors "to act with us as [Jesus] himself would if he were still on earth. You want us to be Christians, and you do not want to be Christian yourselves" (SL 25.13, 491).

The Age of the Limits of Reason

laws are, after it, the greatest good men can give and receive" (SL 24.1, 459, emphasis added; see also 24.6, 464). Montesquieu genuinely *did* believe that Christianity was becoming more tolerant and humane in his time, and he aims to encourage this tendency through subtle, unobtrusive acts of reinterpretation; as Diana Schaub puts it, "Montesquieu seeks to alter Christian sensibilities without needlessly antagonizing them."[145]

Like Voltaire, Montesquieu lauds the benefits of religious pluralism (see PL #85, 143–4; Pensées #374, 147) and insists on the indispensability of religious toleration, claiming that the laws should require of religious sects "not only that they not disturb the state, but also that they not disturb each other" (SL 25.9, 488).[146] He is especially adamant that civil and criminal laws should not be based on religious principles and that religion should give people "counsels" rather than laws, since it aims not just for the good but for the perfect, and "perfection does not concern men or things universally" (SL 24.7, 464; see also 26.2, 495; 26.9, 502).[147] Thus, presumed offenses against God, such as sacrilege and blasphemy, should never be punished by the government; such offenses are not a matter for human judgment, and God does not need the magistrate's protection (see SL 12.4, 189–90). On the other hand, Montesquieu suggests that religion does have a legitimate role to play in the political arena. As we have seen, he hopes that belief in God and an afterlife will help to restrain the actions of political rulers. He also sees the clergy as an "intermediary institution" that, like the nobility and *parlements*, can help to check the monarch's power (see SL 2.4, 18; Pensées #470, 167–8). Moreover, at one point he suggests that religion and civil law are simply complementary

---

[145] Schaub, "Of Believers and Barbarians," 238; see also Guillaume Barrera, *Les lois du monde: Enquête sur le dessein politique de Montesquieu* (Paris: Gallimard, 2009), part 3. In the letter to Warburton, Montesquieu indicates that there is no need to oppose a revealed religion that has been properly liberalized: it may be "just" to attack revealed religion in societies in which people fear torture or death for denying certain articles of faith, he says, but the same is not true in tolerant England, "where it [i.e., revealed religion] has been so well purged of all destructive prejudices, that it can do no hurt, but on the contrary produce an infinity of good." Montesquieu, letter to Warburton, May 1754?, 1509; see also SL 19.27, 328, 330.

[146] Robert Shackleton claims, in fact, that the belief in the necessity of religious toleration "is the belief to which [Montesquieu] clung more tenaciously than to any other." Robert Shackleton, *Montesquieu: A Critical Biography* (Oxford: Oxford University Press, 1961), 354.

[147] See also Vickie B. Sullivan, "Criminal Procedure as the Most Important Knowledge and the Distinction between Human and Divine Justice in Montesquieu's *Spirit of the Laws*," in *Natural Right and Political Philosophy: Essays in Honor of Catherine Zuckert and Michael Zuckert*, ed. Ann Ward and Lee Ward (Notre Dame, IN: University of Notre Dame Press, 2013).

178   *The Pragmatic Enlightenment*

means to the same end: "As religion and the civil laws should aim principally to make people into good citizens, one sees that when either of these departs from this end, the other should aim more toward it: the less repressive religion is, the more the civil laws should repress" (SL 24.14, 468; see also Pensées #591, 193).[148] Still, Montesquieu never actually praises repressive religious principles or institutions. On the contrary, he seeks to moderate religious fervor and intolerance precisely by rendering government more liberal and society more prosperous. In a passage that Schaub notes is "remarkably forthright,"[149] he argues that attempting to moderate religion through prohibitions, threats, and force is ineffectual: "a more certain way to attack religion is by favor, by the comforts of life, by the hope of fortune; not by what reminds one of it, but by what makes one forget it; not by what makes one indignant, but by what leads one to indifference [*tiédeur*]" (SL 25.12, 489). In other words, Montesquieu's aim is to render people moderate or even lukewarm regarding religion: neither religious fanatics nor fanatical atheists (see SL 25.1, 479), but genial, tolerant believers.

There is little scholarly consensus regarding Smith's religious beliefs (or lack thereof). Some interpreters, taking their cue from his invocations of a beneficent providential order, argue that he was a theist whose core arguments rely on teleological assumptions,[150] while others depict him as a thoroughly secular thinker, perhaps even an atheist.[151] On my reading, he too

[148] The complementary roles of religion and civil law are emphasized in Rebecca E. Kingston, "Montesquieu on Religion and on the Question of Toleration," in *Montesquieu's Science of Politics: Essays on The Spirit of Laws*, ed. David W. Carrithers, Michael A. Mosher, and Paul A. Rahe (Lanham, MD: Rowman & Littlefield, 2001).

[149] Schaub, "Of Believers and Barbarians," 231. Robert Bartlett goes so far as to call this passage "the audacious peak of Montesquieu's political philosophy." Robert C. Bartlett, "On the Politics of Faith and Reason: The Project of Enlightenment in Pierre Bayle and Montesquieu" *Journal of Politics* 63.1 (February 2001), 18.

[150] This view was once fairly rare but has gained a greater following of late. See, for instance, Lisa Hill, "The Hidden Theology of Adam Smith" *European Journal of the History of Economic Thought* 8.1 (spring 2001): 1–29; Richard A. Kleer, "Final Causes in Adam Smith's *Theory of Moral Sentiments*" *Journal of the History of Philosophy* 33.2 (April 1995): 275–300; Richard A. Kleer, "The Role of Teleology in Adam Smith's *Wealth of Nations*" *History of Economics Review* 31 (winter 2000): 14–29; James R. Otteson, *Adam Smith's Marketplace of Life* (Cambridge: Cambridge University Press, 2002), 239–48, 255–7; A. M. C. Waterman, "Economics as Theology: Adam Smith's *Wealth of Nations*" *Southern Economic Journal* 68.4 (April 2002): 907–21; and the essays collected in Paul Oslington, ed., *Adam Smith as Theologian* (New York: Routledge, 2011).

[151] The most detailed case along these lines can be found in Peter Minowitz, *Profits, Priests, and Princes: Adam Smith's Emancipation of Economics from Politics and Religion* (Stanford, CA: Stanford University Press, 1993), especially chapters 6–10.

The Age of the Limits of Reason   179

was probably a deist, although one with greater tendencies toward skepticism than Voltaire or Montesquieu. As Emma Rothschild notes, Smith's references to God – particularly the kind of God that could be associated with Christianity – ebbed distinctly over the course of his career:

> Of his three major undertakings in preparing work for publication, the first edition of the *Theory of Moral Sentiments* is fairly full of references to a deity of a Christian sort, although attended with circumlocutions, indirect speech, and frequent use of the verb "to seem." The *Wealth of Nations* is almost entirely free of explicitly religious thought, and is frequently critical of established Christian religion. The extensive additions and revisions which Smith incorporated in the sixth edition of the *Theory of Moral Sentiments* form a work which is strikingly less Christian than the parts of the book remaining from earlier editions.[152]

Moreover, none of Smith's arguments about morality, politics, or economics ultimately *depends* on religious premises; in every instance in which he has recourse to the Author of Nature to explain a point, he also offers a more worldly explanation as well. Thus, I concur with Knud Haakonssen's assessment that "wherever a piece of teleology turns up in Smith it is fairly clear where we have to look in order to find a 'real' explanation in terms of what we may broadly call efficient causes."[153]

On the other hand, Smith regularly describes the belief in a higher power in quite sympathetic terms. Even in *The Wealth of Nations*, he speaks of "that pure and rational religion, free from every mixture of absurdity, imposture, or fanaticism, such as wise men have in all ages of the world wished to see established" (WN V.i.g.8, 793). Further, he argues that the belief in God and "the humble hope and expectation of a life to come" are "deeply rooted in human nature" (TMS III.2.33, 132; see also III.5.3–4, 163–4).[154] Some of his early essays suggest that belief in the gods first arose in an attempt to explain the "irregularities of nature," particularly those that elicited fear or anxiety, such as thunderstorms and eclipses.[155] In contrast to Hume, however, Smith does not

---

[152] Rothschild, *Economic Sentiments*, 129; see also 129–33 more generally.

[153] Knud Haakonssen, *The Science of a Legislator: The Natural Jurisprudence of David Hume and Adam Smith* (Cambridge: Cambridge University Press, 1981), 77. For further argument along these lines, see Fleischacker, *On Adam Smith's Wealth of Nations*, 44–5.

[154] Smith lectured on "natural theology" during his time at the University of Glasgow, but we know little about these lectures beyond John Millar's description of them as focusing in part on "those principles of the human mind upon which religion is founded." See Stewart, "Account of the Life and Writings of Adam Smith, LL.D.," 274.

[155] See Smith, "The History of Astronomy," 48–50; and Adam Smith, "The History of the Ancient Physics," in *Essays on Philosophical Subjects*, ed. W. P. D. Wightman (Indianapolis: Liberty Fund, 1980), 112–14. See also WN V.i.f.24, 767.

180   *The Pragmatic Enlightenment*

argue that religion springs entirely from negative emotions such as fear and ignorance. On the contrary, he insists that "we are led to the belief of a future state, not only by the weaknesses, by the hopes and fears of human nature, but by the noblest and best principles which belong to it, by the love of virtue, and by the abhorrence of vice and injustice" (TMS III.5.10, 169; see also VII.ii.1.45, 292).[156]

Like Voltaire and Montesquieu, Smith accords religion an important role in human life, above all in providing consolation and encouraging moral behavior. Religion's consoling function is particularly vital, he says, for those who are falsely convicted of a crime or wrongly blamed for an immoral action by everyone around them; in such cases, "that humble philosophy which confines its views to this life, can afford, perhaps, but little consolation.... Religion can alone afford them any effectual comfort. She alone can tell them, that it is of little importance what man may think of their conduct, while the all-seeing Judge of the world approves of it" (TMS III.2.12, 120–1; see also III.2.33, 131–2). Similarly, Smith argues that people are more likely to respect and obey the "general rules" of morality that their society has formed – more likely to consider them sacred – if they regard these rules as "the commands and laws of the Deity, who will finally reward the obedient, and punish the transgressors of their duty" (TMS III.5.3, 163; see also VI.ii.3.2, 235).[157] Unlike Voltaire and Montesquieu, however, Smith does *not* suggest that even a bad religion is preferable to none at all in this respect. On the contrary, he maintains that "false notions of religion are almost the only causes which can occasion any very gross perversion of our [moral] sentiments" (TMS III.6.12, 176) and that "of all the corrupters of moral sentiments ... faction and fanaticism have always been by far the greatest" (TMS III.3.43, 156).[158] Thus, he claims that we can place great confidence

---

[156] Ryan Hanley goes so far as to declare that Smith here offers "an apologia for belief." Ryan Patrick Hanley, *Adam Smith and the Character of Virtue* (Cambridge: Cambridge University Press, 2009), 143.

[157] Smith also argues, in *The Wealth of Nations*, that people of "low condition," especially those who live in large cities, often have a sense of anonymity and therefore "abandon [themselves] to every sort of low profligacy and vice." The most effectual remedy for this problem, he says, is "becoming a member of a small religious sect," where the members of the sect can attend to one another's conduct and punish any misdeeds (WN V.i.g.12, 795–6). However, the remedy here is less religion itself – e.g., belief in God or an afterlife – than the bringing to bear of the sort of mutual social pressures that are found in smaller communities. See Joseph Cropsey, *Polity and Economy: With Further Thoughts on the Principles of Adam Smith* (South Bend, IN: St. Augustine's Press, [1957] 2001), 95–6.

[158] Similarly, Smith ridicules, in a tone reminiscent of Hume, "the futile mortifications of a monastery" (TMS III.2.35, 134) and the idea that "heaven [is] to be earned only by

The Age of the Limits of Reason

in the moral integrity of religious individuals only *if* their views have not been corrupted by "the factious and party zeal of some worthless cabal" (TMS III.5.13, 170). Nor does Smith insist that religion is necessary to live a worthwhile or moral life. Indeed, in a published letter he writes of his close friend Hume – who was not, of course, a believer in any sense – that "upon the whole, I have always considered him, both in his lifetime and since his death, as approaching as nearly to the idea of a perfectly wise and virtuous man, as perhaps the nature of human frailty will permit."[159] While religion *can* encourage moral behavior, then, it does not always do so, and it is not universally necessary to do so.

With regard to the social and political effects of Christianity, Smith's attitude is ambivalent. Like Voltaire and Montesquieu, he is well aware of the harm it had done over the years. In fact, he declares that for much of the Middle Ages, the Catholic Church was "the most formidable combination that ever was formed against the authority and security of civil government, as well as against the liberty, reason, and happiness of mankind, which can flourish only where civil government is able to protect them" (WN V.i.g.24, 802–3).[160] On the other hand, he too acknowledges, particularly in his lectures on jurisprudence, that Christianity and the Church had also served some useful functions and effected some beneficial reforms. While he insists that during the feudal era the power of the clergy prevented the king from establishing a "regular government" that could provide the common people with real liberty and security, he also

---

penance and mortification, by the austerities and abasement of a monk; not by the liberal, generous, and spirited conduct of a man" (WN V.i.f.30, 771).

[159] Adam Smith, letter to William Strahan, 9 November 1776, in *The Correspondence of Adam Smith*, ed. Ernest Campbell Mossner and Ian Simpson Ross (Indianapolis: Liberty Fund, 1987), 221. The echoes of the concluding lines of Plato's eulogy of Socrates in the *Phaedo* are obvious. This comment did not sit well with Smith's religious contemporaries: as he later noted, more than a little disingenuously, this "single, and as, I thought a very harmless Sheet of paper, which I happened to Write concerning the death of our late friend Mr Hume, brought upon me ten times more abuse than the very violent attack I had made upon the whole commercial system of Great Britain." Adam Smith, letter to Andreas Holt, 26 October 1780, in *The Correspondence of Adam Smith*, 251. Little did Smith's detractors know that the published letter was actually quite restrained compared to one he wrote during Hume's final illness, in which he remarked that "poor David Hume is dying very fast, but with great chearfulness and good humour and with more real resignation to the necessary course of things, than any Whining Christian ever dyed with pretended resignation to the will of God." Adam Smith, letter to Alexander Wedderburn, 14 August 1776, in *The Correspondence of Adam Smith*, 203.

[160] However, Smith's stance is not always or wholly anticlerical: a few pages later, he proclaims that "there is scarce perhaps to be found any where in Europe a more learned, decent, independent, and respectable set of men, than the greater part of the presbyterian clergy of Holland, Geneva, Switzerland, and Scotland" (WN V.i.g.37, 810).

182   *The Pragmatic Enlightenment*

concedes that they supplied at least a partial corrective in the meantime: the clergy were, he says, the "only obstacle that stood in the way of the nobles; the only thing which made them keep some tollerable decency and moderation to their inferiors" (LJ, 90). Similarly, he notes approvingly that whereas in most countries "the laws ... being made by men generally are very severe on the women," the laws that were "introduced by the clergy ... tended to render their condition much more equall" (LJ, 146; see also 441). He likewise credits Christianity or the clergy for helping to end the practice of infanticide (see LJ, 173), for obliging parents to provide for their children (see LJ, 175, 449), and perhaps for playing a role in the abolition of slavery.[161]

Smith is the only one of our four thinkers to make an explicit case for a complete separation of church and state.[162] He argues that if the state were to refrain from supporting any church or sect – that is, if it were to allow "every man to chuse his own priest and his own religion as he thought proper," thereby encouraging a kind of free marketplace of religions – the result would likely be a great flowering of religious sects, perhaps "as many as a thousand" (WN V.i.g.8, 792–3). In this case, no one of these sects would be "considerable enough to disturb the publick tranquillity," and they would be forced to compete with one another for adherents, thereby ensuring that each has an incentive to check the power of the others. In other words, ambition would be made to counteract ambition.[163] However, Smith does not suggest that disestablishment would *alone* be sufficient to prevent religious fanaticism. On the contrary, he notes that it would put religious leaders "under the necessity of

---

[161] In the lectures Smith suggests that "the influence of the clergy, but by no means the spirit of Christianity" itself, "hastened the abolition of slavery in the west of Europe" (LJ, 454–5; see also 188–9, 191). However, in *The Wealth of Nations* he casts doubt on whether the clergy actually played much of a role in this "important ... revolution" (WN III.ii.12, 389–90).

[162] I can only offer a brief sketch of Smith's argument here; for discussion of some of its nuances, see Griswold, *Adam Smith and the Virtues of Enlightenment*, 276–88.

[163] As Samuel Fleischacker has shown, James Madison drew on Smith's case for religious disestablishment in his famous discussion of majority faction in *Federalist* 10 and 51. See Samuel Fleischacker, "Adam Smith's Reception among the American Founders, 1776–1790" *William and Mary Quarterly* 59.4 (October 2002), 907–15; and Samuel Fleischacker, "The Impact on America: Scottish Philosophy and the American Founding," in *The Cambridge Companion to the Scottish Enlightenment*, ed. Alexander Broadie (Cambridge: Cambridge University Press, 2003), 325–8. Iain McLean and Scot Peterson argue that Smith also had an indirect influence on the Establishment and Free Exercise Clauses of the First Amendment. See Iain McLean and Scot M. Peterson, "Adam Smith at the Constitutional Convention" *Loyola Law Review* 56.1 (spring 2010): 95–133.

The Age of the Limits of Reason   183

making the utmost exertion, and of using every art both to preserve and to increase the number of [their] disciples" (WN V.i.g.8, 793), and that such exertion would likely produce an overly "strict or austere" morality among the common people that is often "disagreeably rigorous and unsocial" (WN V.i.g.10–12, 794–6). In response, he calls in the aid of the arts and sciences as "very easy and effectual remedies" by which the state could combat the excessive enthusiasm of the popular religious sects (WN V.i.g.13, 796). In this way, Smith too seeks to moderate religion and subvert its political power, but by no means to eliminate it altogether.

Hume is quite plainly the most skeptical of these four thinkers regarding God and religion.[164] J. C. A. Gaskin calls his outlook one of "attenuated deism," meaning "a deism in which such evidence and reasons as remain uncontroverted add up to no more than a dim possibility that some nonprovidential god exists, a possibility too ill-understood to be affirmed or denied by a 'wise man.'"[165] Going further, Paul Russell claims that Hume's outlook would be better described as one of "irreligion," a designation that "avoids on one side attributing any form of *unqualified* or *dogmatic* atheism to him, while on the other it also makes clear that his fundamental attitude toward religion is one of *systematic hostility* and *criticism*."[166] Whatever label we choose, it is clear that Hume regards "the religious principles, which have, in fact, prevailed in the world" as little more than "sick men's dreams."[167] However, given the severe limitations that he accords to human understanding, even he does not believe that reason can conclusively *disprove* the existence of God or the claims of revealed religion, any more than it can prove

---

[164] In recent years, a few scholars have suggested that Hume's outlook was friendlier toward religion and religious belief than has traditionally been recognized, but this revisionist view is far from widely accepted. See, for instance, Will R. Jordan, "Religion in the Public Square: A Reconsideration of David Hume and Religious Establishment" *Review of Politics* 64.4 (autumn 2002): 687–713; and Donald W. Livingston, *Philosophical Melancholy and Delirium: Hume's Pathology of Philosophy* (Chicago: University of Chicago Press, 1998), especially 67–79.

[165] J. C. A. Gaskin, "Hume on Religion," in *The Cambridge Companion to Hume*, ed. David Fate Norton and Jacqueline Taylor, second edition (Cambridge: Cambridge University Press, 2009), 490. As Gaskin notes elsewhere, this viewpoint "is about as damaging to Christianity as any atheism could possibly be.... assent to the existence of god in the sense allowed by Hume is valueless for any theistic religion. It carries no duties, invites no action, allows no inferences and involves no devotion." J. C. A. Gaskin, *Hume's Philosophy of Religion*, second edition (Atlantic Highlands, NJ: Humanities Press, 1988), 222; see also 219–23 more generally.

[166] Russell, *The Riddle of Hume's Treatise*, 284. See also Thomas Holden, *Spectres of False Divinity: Hume's Moral Atheism* (Oxford: Oxford University Press, 2010).

[167] Hume, *The Natural History of Religion*, 86.

184   *The Pragmatic Enlightenment*

them.[168] Rather, his skepticism regarding religion is simply a manifestation of his general skepticism regarding *any* claims of absolute certainty. The difference between Hume's brand of irreligion and that of the more radical philosophes is illustrated by a now-famous story about Hume dining at d'Holbach's house in Paris. When Hume commented that he did not believe in out-and-out atheists, having never actually met one, d'Holbach told him to count the number of people around him at the table – there were eighteen – and said, "not bad, to be able to show you fifteen at one stroke. The other three haven't yet made up their minds."[169] While Hume was a nonbeliever, he was a comparatively cautious and broad-minded one.

In fact, Hume maintains that the "propensity to believe in invisible, intelligent power" is "if not an original instinct," then "at least a general attendant of human nature."[170] In *The Natural History of Religion* he offers an extensive examination of the origins and historical development of religious belief. He declares that belief in a higher power, or a number of higher powers, "has been very generally diffused over the human race, in all places and in all ages," although he also says that "it has neither perhaps been so universal as to admit of no exception, nor has it been, in any degree, uniform in the ideas, which it has suggested."[171] Since the forms of religious belief vary widely, and some nations have no religion at all (at least "if travellers and historians may be credited"), Hume suggests that religious belief "springs not from an original instinct or primary expression of nature," but rather from certain "secondary" principles of

---

[168] Of course, Hume does believe that experiential reasoning can cast severe *doubt* on some of the claims of revealed religion, as in his famous argument against miracles in section 10 of *An Enquiry Concerning Human Understanding*. Even there, however, he argues not that miracles are *impossible* but rather that it is never reasonable to believe a report that one has occurred, and he concludes by conceding that Christianity "is founded on *Faith*, not on reason" (EHU 10.40, 98). See also his statement that "I was resolv'd not to be an Enthusiast, in philosophy, while I was blaming other Enthusiasms." David Hume, letter to Henry Home, 2 December 1737, in *New Letters of David Hume*, ed. Raymond Klibansky and Ernest C. Mossner (Oxford: Clarendon Press, 1954), 3.

[169] This story was recorded by Diderot in a letter to his mistress. See Denis Diderot, letter to Sophie Volland, 6 October 1765, in *Correspondance*, ed. Georges Roth, vol. 5 (Paris: Minuit, 1959), 134. During his visit to Paris, Edward Gibbon lamented the "intolerant zeal" of the philosophes who "laughed at the scepticism of Hume, preached the tenets of atheism with the bigotry of dogmatists, and damned all believers with ridicule and contempt." Quoted in Ernest Campbell Mossner, *The Life of David Hume*, second edition (Oxford: Clarendon Press, 1980), 485.

[170] Hume, *The Natural History of Religion*, 86.

[171] Ibid., 33. Elsewhere, he writes that "all mankind have a strong propensity to religion at certain times and in certain dispositions" (EMPL, 199).

The Age of the Limits of Reason   185

human nature that can "be perverted by various accidents and causes, and whose operation too, in some cases, may, by an extraordinary concurrence of circumstances, be altogether prevented."[172] In other words, Hume does *not* regard belief in God as a "natural belief," meaning a belief that is ultimately indispensable, even if not rationally demonstrable.[173] (Noncontroversial examples of Humean natural beliefs include the belief in causation and in a mind-independent external world.) Moreover, he depicts religion as springing almost exclusively from the negative or "darker" features of human nature, such as fear, cowardice, and ignorance. Still, in his view religious belief is rooted sufficiently deeply in human nature that it is extraordinarily unlikely that it could or would ever disappear altogether.[174]

Whereas Voltaire and Montesquieu both suggest that even a bad religion is better than none at all, and Smith holds that religion generally promotes moral behavior as long as it is not corrupted by faction or fanaticism, Hume argues that religion usually does more harm than good, morally speaking. We have already seen his claim that the "monkish virtues" of "celibacy, fasting, penance, mortification, self-denial, humility, silence, [and] solitude" could only be seen as virtues by those swayed by "the delusive glosses of superstition and false religion" (EPM 9.3, 73). More broadly, he holds that most religious people tend to "seek the divine favour, not by virtue and good morals ... but either by frivolous observances, by intemperate zeal, by rapturous extasies, or by the belief of mysterious and absurd opinions."[175] The reason for this, he speculates, is that basic moral behavior – promoting the useful and agreeable, for oneself and for others – does not seem to them sufficiently elevated or pure, sufficiently removed from this-worldly concerns. Religious individuals

---

[172] Hume, *The Natural History of Religion*, 33.

[173] See Gaskin, *Hume's Philosophy of Religion*, chapters 6–7.

[174] In a conversation with Smith just before he died, Hume diverted himself by inventing some jocular excuses that he could give to Charon, the boatman in Hades, in an attempt to delay having to get on the boat. He imagined himself saying, "Have a little patience, good Charon, I have been endeavouring to open the eyes of the Public. If I live a few years longer, I may have the satisfaction of seeing the downfal of some of the prevailing systems of superstition." At this point, however, he envisioned Charon losing all patience and exclaiming, "You loitering rogue, that will not happen these many hundred years. Do you fancy I will grant you a lease for so long a term? Get into the boat this instant, you lazy loitering rogue." Smith, letter to William Strahan, 9 November 1776, in *The Correspondence of Adam Smith*, 219. For an earlier, and slightly harsher, version of the story, see Smith, letter to Alexander Wedderburn, 14 August 1776, in *The Correspondence of Adam Smith*, 204.

[175] Hume, *The Natural History of Religion*, 81.

186   *The Pragmatic Enlightenment*

seek to go *beyond* ordinary morality, to *suppress* their inclinations, in hopes of thereby currying divine favor and protection, but this tends to hinder the normal operations of sympathy and the regular exchange of sentiments with others. "Hence," Hume writes, "the greatest crimes have been found, in many instances, compatible with a superstitious piety and devotion: Hence it is justly regarded as unsafe to draw any certain inference in favour of a man's morals from the fervour or strictness of his religious exercises.... Nay, it has been observed, that enormities of the blackest dye have been rather apt to produce superstitious terrors, and encrease the religious passion."[176] In other words, religious beliefs and observances are not merely superfluous, but often directly contrary to morality. Indeed, Hume once claimed to a friend that "the worst speculative Sceptic ever I knew, was a much better Man than the best superstitious Devotee & Bigot."[177]

Hume also sees religion as having destructive consequences for politics, at least much of the time. In the *Dialogues Concerning Natural Religion*, the skeptic Philo responds to the claim that "religion, however corrupted, is still better than no religion at all" by asking: "How happens it then ... that all history abounds so much with accounts of its pernicious consequences on public affairs? Factions, civil wars, persecutions, subversions of government, oppression, slavery; these are the dismal consequences which always attend its prevalency over the minds of men."[178] This charge finds a great deal of concrete support throughout Hume's *History of England*, particularly in his account of the seventeenth-century civil wars and the Commonwealth period.[179] On the other hand, religious superstition and enthusiasm play a surprisingly *positive* role in this work, as well. Indeed, Hume argues that at several crucial points in English history, it was these powerful religious sentiments alone that kept an ember

---

[176] Ibid., 83. See also EMPL, 74, 77; and David Hume, *Dialogues Concerning Natural Religion*, ed. J. C. A. Gaskin (Oxford: Oxford University Press, [1779] 1993), 122–5.

[177] David Hume, letter to Gilbert Elliot of Minto, 10 March 1751, in *The Letters of David Hume*, ed. J. Y. T. Greig, vol. 1 (Oxford: Clarendon Press, 1932), 154.

[178] Hume, *Dialogues Concerning Natural Religion*, 121–2.

[179] See Eugene F. Miller, "Hume on Liberty in the Successive English Constitutions," in *Liberty in Hume's History of England*, ed. Nicholas Capaldi and Donald W. Livingston (Dordrecht: Kluwer Academic, 1990), 91–2, 94–5. On the political dangers of superstition and enthusiasm, for Hume, see Knud Haakonssen, "The Structure of Hume's Political Theory," in *The Cambridge Companion to Hume*, ed. David Fate Norton and Jacqueline Taylor, second edition (Cambridge: Cambridge University Press, 2009), especially 341–3, 369–70.

The Age of the Limits of Reason

of liberty alive.[180] Like Smith, Hume holds that during the decline of the feudal system, before the imposition of royal supremacy by the Tudors, it was the "superstitious" clergy that held society together: "It must be acknowledged, that the influence of the prelates and the clergy was often of great service to the public. Though the religion of that age can merit no better name than that of superstition, it served to unite together a body of men who had great sway over the people, and who kept the community from falling to pieces, by the factions and independant power of the nobles" (HE II, 14). Later, during Elizabeth's nearly absolute rule, Puritan "enthusiasts" were the only people willing to challenge her authority: "the precious spark of liberty had been kindled, and was preserved, by the puritans alone; and it was to this sect, whose principles appear so frivolous and habits so ridiculous, that the English owe the whole freedom of their constitution" (HE IV, 145–6). Similarly, during the early Stuart period, "so extensive was royal authority, and so firmly established in all its parts, that it is probable the patriots of that age would have despaired of ever resisting it, had they not been stimulated by religious motives, which inspire a courage unsurmountable by any human obstacle" (HE V, 558; see also 10–11, 380, 572). As much tumult as religious enthusiasm caused during the civil wars, it was also partially responsible for the revolution of 1688 that resulted in the "most entire system of liberty, that ever was known amongst mankind" (HE VI, 531; see also 470, 503). In other words, the eighteenth-century British constitution that Hume so admires was not an ancient one inherited from Saxon legislators, but the product of resistance to royal absolutism inspired by religious fanaticism. Don Herzog calls this "the consummate irony of Hume's career": "Religious fanatics, whom he detests, many of them intending the wildest excesses, irresponsibly take on imposing odds (as only they would) and destroy the English constitution – and so give birth to the rule of law."[181]

---

[180] See Miller, "Hume on Liberty in the Successive English Constitutions," 80–1, 86. Elsewhere, Hume writes that religious enthusiasm, while it can produce "the most cruel orders in human society," at the same time is "the infirmity of bold and ambitious tempers" and so "is naturally accompanied with a spirit of liberty." He contrasts enthusiasm with superstition, which "renders men tame and abject, and fits them for slavery" (EMPL, 77–8). On the connection between enthusiasm and civil liberty, see also Sharon R. Krause, "Frenzy, Gloom, and the Spirit of Liberty in Hume," in *The Arts of Rule: Essays in Honor of Harvey C. Mansfield*, ed. Sharon R. Krause and Mary Ann McGrail (Lanham, MD: Lexington, 2009), especially 296–300.

[181] Don Herzog, *Without Foundations: Justification in Political Theory* (Ithaca, NY: Cornell University Press, 1985), 199.

188   *The Pragmatic Enlightenment*

Finally, Hume's practical or political recommendations regarding religion too are quite moderate. As might be expected, he supports religious toleration, at least in the Europe of his time.[182] More surprisingly, despite all of his warnings about the baleful influence of organized religion on public life, he also mounts a strong case in *favor* of an established church. Indeed, he writes that "the union of the civil and ecclesiastical power serves extremely, in every civilized government, to the maintenance of peace and order" (HE I, 311; see also 163, 208) and that "there must be an ecclesiastical order, and a public establishment of religion in every civilized community" (HE III, 134–5). In the absence of an established church, he argues, religious intolerance and fanaticism are more likely to flourish: "Each ghostly practitioner, in order to render himself more precious and sacred in the eyes of his retainers, will inspire them with the most violent abhorrence of all other sects, and continually endeavour, by some novelty, to excite the languid devotion of his audience" (HE III, 136).[183] To prevent this situation, Hume suggests that the government should support a particular church, both financially and through its official imprimatur. Such a policy would accomplish several tasks at once: it would render the clergy dependent on, and hence subservient to, the civil authorities; it would give them a vested interest in promoting social and political stability; and, just as importantly, it would dissuade them from being overly ambitious or divisive. Government support for the clergy would, Hume declares, "bribe their indolence, by assigning stated salaries to their profession, and rendering it superfluous for them to be farther active, than merely to prevent their flock from straying in quest of new pastures" (HE III, 136). Of course, as Annette Baier remarks, "a less religious justification for establishing religion could scarcely be imagined.... The best we can do, it seems, is find the least objectionable form of religion, as a sort of inoculation against its more dangerous forms, and contrive things so that it will have the least unpleasing clerics attached to it."[184] However cynical Hume's reasoning may be, he maintains that as long as membership in the established church remains voluntary, a fairly

---

[182] On Hume's complex view of religious toleration, see Richard H. Dees, "'The Paradoxical Principle and Salutary Practice': Hume on Toleration" *Hume Studies* 31.1 (April 2005): 145–64; and Andrew Sabl, "The Last Artificial Virtue: Hume on Toleration and Its Lessons" *Political Theory* 37.4 (August 2009): 511–38.

[183] Smith makes his case for a free marketplace of religions in explicit opposition to this argument of Hume's: see WN V.i.g.3–8, 790–3.

[184] Annette C. Baier, *Death and Character: Further Reflections on Hume* (Cambridge, MA: Harvard University Press, 2008), 92.

The Age of the Limits of Reason 189

broad social consensus in support of a moderate church can be useful in the promotion of stability and public order.[185]

To be sure, few religious believers will find the outlooks of Hume, Smith, Montesquieu, and Voltaire congenial, given that their views of organized religion were largely negative and, even where positive, almost entirely instrumental. Still, in many crucial respects these thinkers adopted a moderate stance toward religion, particularly in comparison with the more radical philosophes. Rather than scoffing at all religious belief and believers, they saw belief in a higher power as natural in some sense. Rather than seeking to eradicate religion from society, they aimed to pacify or "liberalize" it, to restrain its most dangerous impulses and consequences and to encourage its more beneficial ones. Rather than seeing religion as little more than a source of intolerance and conflict, they also saw it as a potential source of much good, from promoting morality to providing consolation, and from restraining rulers to encouraging humane reforms. Indeed, so adamant were Voltaire and Montesquieu about the necessity of belief in God and an afterlife for a healthy society that many of today's secular liberals – including me – will find them overly *pessimistic* about atheism and its moral and political effects. Even Hume, the "Great Infidel" who saw religious enthusiasm as a source of grave moral ills, acknowledged the crucial positive role it had played in British history. Last, and significantly for the argument of this chapter, none of these thinkers believed that the frail powers of human reason could conclusively *refute* the claims of revealed religion, or that reason could or would ultimately conquer religion over time. Rather, they adopted a standpoint that Peter Gay calls "secular fideism":[186] they emphasized the limits of human reason, but rather than translating these limits into a call for unconditional faith, unconditional obedience to revelation, or unconditional deference to the Church, as Christian fideists did, they instead translated them into a warning against excessive confidence and unwarranted certainty. Given the insuperable frailty and fallibility of the human mind, they maintained, dogmatism of any kind is absurd.

CONCLUSION

The three sections of this chapter by no means constitute a comprehensive analysis of the views of Hume, Smith, Montesquieu, and Voltaire

---

[185] Hence, there is an established church in Hume's "perfect commonwealth": see EMPL, 520, 525.
[186] Gay, *The Enlightenment: An Interpretation*, vol. 1, 145.

on the subjects of epistemology, science, and religion; a great deal more could be said about each of these thinkers on each of these topics. This broad overview has, however, been sufficient to establish that the pragmatic Enlightenment was emphatically a limits-of-reason movement. These four thinkers stressed the centrality of the passions and sentiments in motivating human action and establishing moral standards; advocated relying on observation and experience rather than a priori first principles; evinced a good deal of wariness about metaphysics and abstract system building; denied that even the scientific method could provide conclusive or complete knowledge of the natural world; showed cautious appreciation for the practical benefits of science and technology, without suggesting that they could resolve all human problems; rejected the idea that reason could refute the claims of revealed religion; deemed belief in a higher power to be natural in some sense; and recognized that religion could serve useful functions and so sought to ameliorate its harmful effects rather than eliminate it altogether. Above all, they refused to place blind faith in *anything*, much less something so fragile and error-prone as human reason. Far more than most of their philosophic predecessors and many of their contemporaries and successors, these thinkers dared *not* to know.

4

The Perils of Political Rationalism

While it is clear that few Enlightenment thinkers were rationalists in the Cartesian sense, another allegation remains to be addressed: the claim that they were rationalists in politics. A classic statement of this charge appears in the early writings of Michael Oakeshott. According to Oakeshott, the Enlightenment – or the outlook that he calls "*philosophisme*" – sought to bring all laws, institutions, and practices before the supposedly infallible tribunal of reason, and to discard those found wanting by its standards.[1] Indeed, he claims that rather than promoting prudent repairs or reforms to their society's existing institutions, the philosophes advocated the complete elimination of the old order so that society could be rebuilt anew on a more rational basis. If "the blank sheet of infinite possibility ... has been defaced by the irrational scribblings of tradition-ridden ancestors," he writes, "then the first task of the Rationalist must be to scrub it clean: as Voltaire remarked, the only way to have good laws is to burn all existing laws and to start afresh."[2] Needless to say, Oakeshott maintains

---

[1] See especially Michael Oakeshott, "The New Bentham," in *Rationalism in Politics and Other Essays* (Indianapolis: Liberty Fund, [1932] 1991), 138–40; and Michael Oakeshott, *Morality and Politics in Modern Europe: The Harvard Lectures*, ed. Shirley Robin Letwin (New Haven, CT: Yale University Press, [1958] 1993), 97–8.

[2] Michael Oakeshott, "Rationalism in Politics," in *Rationalism in Politics and Other Essays* (Indianapolis: Liberty Fund, [1947] 1991), 9. Oakeshott maintains in this essay that the key progenitors of rationalism were not the philosophes but Bacon and Descartes, both of whom attempted to formulate new, infallible techniques of inquiry that would yield certain and universally applicable knowledge. He acknowledges that both of these thinkers harbored doubts about the techniques that they developed, but claims that rationalism arose from "the exaggeration of Bacon's hopes and the neglect of the scepticism of Descartes." He speaks only vaguely of later "commonplace minds" who corrupted or simplified the ideas of these "men of discrimination and genius," but his earlier depiction

192 *The Pragmatic Enlightenment*

that this kind of political rationalism invariably leads to misguided attempts at social engineering and dangerous upheavals like the French Revolution. The idea that the thinkers of the Enlightenment – especially the French Enlightenment – were political rationalists in this sense has a long and distinguished history, running from Edmund Burke and Joseph de Maistre in the eighteenth century through G. W. F. Hegel and Alexis de Tocqueville in the nineteenth century and Jacob Talmon and Friedrich Hayek in the twentieth century to numerous scholars in our own time.[3] It has long been assumed that, as Louis Dupré contends, "the philosophes regarded it as their task to emancipate the whole political system from its past tradition and to bring it in conformity with reason."[4]

A related, and perhaps even more prevalent, criticism of the Enlightenment is that its proponents harbored a naive faith in the possibility, or even inevitability, of endless progress – not only scientific progress (an issue that was addressed in the previous chapter), but also economic, moral, and political progress. On this view, the thinkers of this period were convinced that the steady application of reason could and would lead to a kind of utopia, or at least to continual advances in human well-being. According to Isaiah Berlin, for instance, the thinkers of the Enlightenment believed that

methods similar to those of Newtonian physics, which had achieved such triumphs in the realm of inanimate nature, could be applied with equal success to the fields of ethics, politics and human relationships in general … with the corollary that once this had been effected, it would sweep away irrational and

of the philosophes in "The New Bentham" suggests that he saw them as having played a large role in this process. See ibid., 22.

[3] See Edmund Burke, *Reflections on the Revolution in France*, ed. J. C. D. Clark (Stanford, CA: Stanford University Press, [1790] 2001), 249–52, 275–7; Joseph de Maistre, *Considerations on France*, trans. Richard A. Lebrun (Cambridge: Cambridge University Press, [1797] 1994), 47–8; G. W. F. Hegel, *Phenomenology of Spirit*, trans. A. V. Miller (Oxford: Oxford University Press, [1807] 1977), 328–55; Alexis de Tocqueville, *The Old Regime and the Revolution*, trans. Alan S. Kahan (Chicago: University of Chicago Press, [1856] 1998), 195–7, 200–2; Jacob L. Talmon, *The Origins of Totalitarian Democracy* (New York: W. W. Norton, [1952] 1970), passim; and Friedrich A. Hayek, *The Constitution of Liberty* (Chicago: University of Chicago Press, 1960), 54–6. For a few more recent claims that the philosophes were political rationalists in some sense, see Norman Hampson, "The Enlightenment in France," in *The Enlightenment in National Context*, ed. Roy Porter and Mikuláš Teich (Cambridge: Cambridge University Press, 1981), 46–7; Maurice Cranston, *Philosophers and Pamphleteers: Political Theorists of the Enlightenment* (Oxford: Oxford University Press, 1986), 1, 3, 7–8; and Gertrude Himmelfarb, *The Roads to Modernity: The British, French, and American Enlightenments* (New York: Alfred A. Knopf, 2004), part 2.

[4] Louis Dupré, *The Enlightenment and the Intellectual Foundations of Modern Culture* (New Haven, CT: Yale University Press, 2004), 181; see also 334.

The Perils of Political Rationalism

oppressive legal systems and economic policies, the replacement of which by the rule of reason would rescue men from political and moral injustice and misery and set them on the path of wisdom, happiness and virtue.[5]

So entrenched is this view, among many scholars of the period, that even major exceptions do not seem to be sufficient to alter the general rule: immediately after acknowledging that "Voltaire, in his celebrated novel *Candide*, mocked optimism," Maurice Cranston goes on to insist that nevertheless "the Enlightenment itself was an age of optimism. Although the Lisbon earthquake of 1755 shattered belief in a benevolent Deity, nothing seemed able to modify the *encyclopédistes'* faith in progress."[6] In short, critics and scholars of the Enlightenment alike have often concluded, with Paul Hazard, that "the gospel of optimism was the major plank in their platform."[7]

This chapter demonstrates, however, that neither of these broad charges is applicable to Hume, Smith, Montesquieu, or Voltaire.[8] In the first half of the chapter we will see that, far from being political rationalists in the Oakeshottian sense, these four thinkers all adopted a practical, pragmatic outlook that supports the reform of existing institutions but opposes efforts to form a wholly new "rational" order from scratch. To be sure, they did not, like Edmund Burke, revere tradition as such or believe that it had a presumptive claim to wisdom; nor were they simply advocates of the status quo. They *did* want to "change men's common way of thinking," to borrow Diderot's famous line from the *Encyclopédie*, and to push their societies in a broadly liberal direction.[9] But they did not insist that these

---

[5] Isaiah Berlin, "The Counter-Enlightenment," in *The Proper Study of Mankind: An Anthology of Essays*, ed. Henry Hardy and Roger Hausheer (New York: Farrar, Straus & Giroux [1973] 1998), 243–4.

[6] Cranston, *Philosophers and Pamphleteers*, 6.

[7] Paul Hazard, *European Thought in the Eighteenth Century: From Montesquieu to Lessing*, trans. J. Lewis May (Cleveland: Meridian Books, [1946] 1965), 18. A distinct echo of this conclusion can be found in Roy Porter's recent claim that "progress proved the ultimate Enlightenment gospel." Roy Porter, *The Creation of the Modern World: The Untold Story of the British Enlightenment* (New York: W. W. Norton, 2000), 445.

[8] As always, these four thinkers are far from alone within the Enlightenment. I have argued elsewhere that these charges do not even apply to Diderot, a thinker whom Jonathan Israel regards as one of "the three principal architects of the Radical Enlightenment," along with Spinoza and Bayle. See Dennis C. Rasmussen, "Burning Laws and Strangling Kings? Voltaire and Diderot on the Perils of Rationalism in Politics" *Review of Politics* 73.1 (winter 2011): 77–104. For Israel's statement, see Jonathan I. Israel, *Enlightenment Contested: Philosophy, Modernity, and the Emancipation of Man, 1670–1752* (Oxford: Oxford University Press, 2006), 42.

[9] Denis Diderot, "Encyclopedia," in *Rameau's Nephew and Other Works*, trans. Jacques Barzun and Ralph H. Bowen (Indianapolis: Hackett, [1755] 1956), 296.

194   *The Pragmatic Enlightenment*

reforms must be made all at once, or that the political and legal slates must be wiped clean in order to make room for a more liberal order. On the contrary, they showed a strong preference for gradual reform and consistently opposed the "spirit of system" that leads people to try to impose abstract, comprehensive ideals on society from above. Thus, just as Peter Gay proclaims that the eighteenth century was "not an Age of Reason, but a Revolt against Rationalism" in terms of its epistemology,[10] this pragmatic strand of the Enlightenment constituted a revolt against rationalism in politics.

In the second half of the chapter we will see that the charge of naive faith in economic, moral, and political progress is equally erroneous as applied to these four thinkers. Indeed, these thinkers were all deeply and manifestly – one wants to say instinctually – antiutopian. None of them believed that progress toward the liberal practices and institutions they favored was in any way inevitable or could possibly be endless or uniform. Of course, they did believe in progress in the sense that they thought the Europe of their time constituted an improvement in many respects over what had preceded it, but they did not believe in any kind of supernatural agency, transcendent design, or Hegelian dialectic that meant that it *had to be* better than what came before it, or that the future would be better still. Moreover, they insisted that even the progress that had been made in eighteenth-century Europe had generally been a mixed bag, with all of the advances and improvements complemented by important drawbacks and limitations. In short, they were far too realistic, too alive to the shortcomings of even their comparatively enlightened age, to be dupes of the sort of faith in the "historical process" that would enthrall later generations of thinkers.

THE DULL RASP OF POLITICS

Oakeshott's worries about the Enlightenment, it must be admitted, were not entirely unwarranted: there is no question that political rationalism played a prominent role in the thought of this period. Jonathan Israel notes, with obvious approval, that many of the members of his Radical Enlightenment "rejected all compromise with the past and sought to sweep away existing structures entirely" so that more a rational structure could be put in place.[11] Even so moderate a thinker as John Locke used

[10] Peter Gay, *The Party of Humanity: Essays in the French Enlightenment* (New York: W. W. Norton, 1964), 270.
[11] Jonathan Israel, *Radical Enlightenment: Philosophy and the Making of Modernity, 1650–1750* (Oxford: Oxford University Press, 2001), 11.

The Perils of Political Rationalism

the notion of the social contract to mentally sweep away all existing institutions and devise a transhistorical set of criteria that all regimes must meet in order to be considered legitimate. Yet many major Enlightenment thinkers – including Hume, Smith, Montesquieu, and Voltaire – explicitly *opposed* political rationalism, arguing that reform should be carried out gradually and that it would be foolhardy and dangerous to attempt to impose an abstract or comprehensive scheme on society all at once, no matter how "rational" it may seem. This claim is by no means a novel one. Israel, for instance, places these thinkers in the "moderate mainstream" Enlightenment and depicts them as fainthearted temporizers who were far too willing to compromise with the existing order. Indeed, Oakeshott himself acknowledges, particularly in his later writings, that Hume, Montesquieu, and perhaps Smith (although not Voltaire) were exceptions to the rationalist rule.[12] Still, given the frequency with which this charge is leveled at the Enlightenment as a whole, it will be useful to survey briefly these thinkers' views of political change and revolution in order to recall just how far they departed from the rationalist mold, the broadly liberal character of their philosophies notwithstanding. We will see that all four of them – even Voltaire – were wary of abrupt, radical political change and preferred instead to conceive of politics, as Montesquieu put it, as "a dull rasp which by slowly grinding away gains its end" (SL 14.13, 243).[13]

The idea that Hume was dubious about rationalism and radicalism in politics should be utterly noncontroversial, given his reputation as a conservative – perhaps even "the first conservative philosopher," period.[14]

---

[12] Oakeshott never offers a sustained discussion of Hume, but his few passing remarks about him are mostly positive. In fact, at one point he suggests that conservatives have more to learn from a skeptic like Hume than they do from a reactionary like Burke. See Michael Oakeshott, "On Being Conservative," in *Rationalism in Politics and Other Essays* (Indianapolis: Liberty Fund, [1956] 1991), 435. Oakeshott demonstrates high regard for Montesquieu in Michael Oakeshott, *On Human Conduct* (Oxford: Oxford University Press, 1975), 246–51. Oakeshott's published Harvard lecture on Montesquieu is also sympathetic on the whole, although his lecture on Smith is slightly less so. See Oakeshott, *Morality and Politics in Modern Europe*, 36–43, 65–9.

[13] Given the centrality of prudence and gradual reform to Montesquieu's outlook, David Carrithers claims that this is "perhaps the most revelatory sentence, in the whole *The Spirit of Laws*." David W. Carrithers, "Introduction: An Appreciation of *The Spirit of Laws*," in *Montesquieu's Science of Politics: Essays on The Spirit of Laws*, ed. David W. Carrithers, Michael A. Mosher, and Paul A. Rahe (Lanham, MD: Rowman & Littlefield, 2001), 12.

[14] Donald W. Livingston, *Hume's Philosophy of Common Life* (Chicago: University of Chicago Press, 1984), 310.

I argued in Chapter 2 that he is better seen as a member of the liberal tradition, given his lack of any reverence for the past or the traditional, his admiration for the basically liberal British regime of his day, and his readiness to advocate reforms that would move the regime in a still more liberal direction. It is true, however, that Hume's liberalism has a distinctly conservative bent, insofar as he distrusts large and sudden innovations in politics, especially those undertaken on the basis of abstract principles. Interestingly, his defense of political moderation and gradualism rests on ostensibly radical grounds – namely, skepticism.[15] While skepticism has often been used to undermine the intellectual basis of the existing order, Hume employs it in the opposite way: because human reason is so fallible and the political world is so complicated and variable, he holds, we should be wary of attempts at comprehensive revolution and grand schemes for reforming society. This viewpoint is evident in both of Hume's main political works, the *Essays* and the *History of England*. Throughout the latter work, but particularly in the Stuart volumes, he highlights the "violence, tumult, and disorder" that so often attend "great revolutions of government, and new settlements of civil constitutions" (HE VI, 528). Of the civil war period, for instance, he writes: "The sacred boundaries of the laws being once violated, nothing remained to confine the wild projects of zeal and ambition. And every successive revolution became a precedent for that which followed it" (HE V, 492). Conversely, he emphasizes the greater civility and effectiveness of gradual reform. After heaping praise on the political, legal, and judicial institutions established by Alfred the Great, Hume writes that Alfred was not "the sole author of this plan of government," but rather, "like a wise man, he contented himself with reforming, extending, and executing the institutions, which he found previously established" (HE I, 79).

Similarly, in the *Essays* Hume repeatedly proclaims himself to be a "friend to moderation" (EMPL, 15; see also 27) and continually strives to "teach us a lesson of moderation in all our political controversies" (EMPL, 53; see also 494, 500).[16] He insists that "more ill than good is ever expected" from "violent innovations" (EMPL, 477) and derides "extravagant projector[s]" who would "tamper and play with a

---

[15] For discussion of this point, see Steven J. Wulf, "The Skeptical Life in Hume's Political Thought" *Polity* 33.1 (autumn 2000): 77–99.

[16] For an argument that Hume in fact sees moderation as the foremost virtue of civic and political life, see James T. King, "The Virtue of Political Skepticism" *Reason Papers* 15 (summer 1990): 24–46.

The Perils of Political Rationalism

government and national constitution, like a quack with a sickly patient" (EMPL, 509). None of this is to suggest, of course, that Hume opposes the very idea of political reform, for plainly he does not. He applauds a great many of the changes that were made to the British constitution over its history – even some of those introduced through violent means[17] – and advocates further reforms to the constitution as it stood in his time, such as in the essays on commerce and trade.[18] Rather, his argument is that reform is generally safest and most effective when introduced in a gradual, measured way, rather than in large speculative schemes. Thus, even his essay purporting to devise a "perfect commonwealth" begins with a warning:

It is not with forms of government, as with other artificial contrivances; where an old engine may be rejected, if we can discover another more accurate and commodious, or where trials may be safely made, even though the success be doubtful. An established government has an infinite advantage, by that very circumstance of its being established; the bulk of mankind being governed by authority, not reason, and never attributing authority to any thing that has not the recommendation of antiquity. To tamper, therefore, in this affair, or try experiments merely upon the credit of supposed argument and philosophy, can never be the part of a wise magistrate, who will bear a reverence to what carries the marks of age; and though he may attempt some improvements for the public good, yet will he adjust his innovations, as much as possible, to the ancient fabric, and preserve entire the chief pillars and supports of the constitution. (EMPL, 512–13).

While Hume is not simply an uncritical apologist for the status quo, then, he does exhibit "a sustained skeptical distrust of rationalistic or visionary efforts to transcend the limitations of concrete experience."[19]

Hume's stance toward political revolution is equivocal but consistent: revolution is sometimes justifiable, but very seldom desirable. While he

---

[17] In the midst of a discussion of the dangers of deviating too far from established practices and institutions, Hume admits that "many constitutions, and none more than the British, have been improved even by violent innovations," but given that improvement through violence is an exception to the rule, he insists that "the praise, bestowed on those patriots, to whom the nation has been indebted for its privileges, ought to be given with some reserve, and surely without the least rancour against those who adhered to the ancient constitution" (HE IV, 355).

[18] Indeed, at one point Hume states that "some innovations must necessarily have place in every human institution, and it is happy where the enlightened genius of the age give these a direction to the side of reason, liberty, and justice" (EMPL, 477). The most detailed examination of the reformist side of Hume's thought is in John B. Stewart, *Opinion and Reform in Hume's Political Philosophy* (Princeton, NJ: Princeton University Press, 1992), especially chapters 5 and 6.

[19] Frederick G. Whelan, *Order and Artifice in Hume's Political Philosophy* (Princeton, NJ: Princeton University Press, 1985), 323.

does not believe that political authority rests solely on popular consent, he does maintain that extreme oppression on the part of the rulers ends the duty of allegiance on the part of the people – not because the rulers have broken a contract, but rather because the utility or interest on which allegiance is based has been undermined: "As interest ... is the immediate sanction of government, the one can have no longer being than the other; and whenever the civil magistrate carries his oppression so far as to render his authority perfectly intolerable, we are no longer bound to submit to it. The cause ceases; the effect must cease also" (THN 3.2.9.2, 352; see also EMPL, 489). On the other hand, given that frequent acts of resistance threaten "the subversion of all government, and ... universal anarchy and confusion among mankind," Hume contends that "the common rule requires submission; and 'tis only in cases of grievous tyranny and oppression, that the exception can take place" (THN 3.2.10.1, 354).[20] In other words, in practice the Tory doctrine of "passive obedience" makes a far better general rule than the Whig doctrine of the right to rebellion (see EMPL, 490–1; HE V, 544–5; HE VI, 293–4). This is one of the major flaws of social contract theory, in Hume's view: by its very nature it places an undue emphasis on the right of resistance – that is, on the conditions under which the contract would be broken. As Duncan Forbes remarks, for Hume "a political theory which makes a fetish of the right of resistance is like a theory of matrimony which makes a general rule of divorce: it is necessary, perhaps, but only in exceptional circumstances."[21]

Hume's qualms about resistance and revolution have long bolstered his reputation as a conservative, even a highly complacent one, but this reading is an exaggeration. To begin with, while Hume is indeed wary of unnecessary disturbances to public order, he is also wary of rigid rules that allow for no exceptions; his warnings against resistance and revolution constitute more a rule of thumb than a categorical imperative.[22] Moreover, opposition to violent rebellion by no means entails opposition to all change: nowhere does Hume dispute the propriety of questioning, protesting, or aspiring to repeal or alter laws that one deems unjust or

---

[20] For a helpful discussion of some concrete instances of tyranny that Hume considered sufficiently "grievous" to terminate the duty of allegiance, see Andrew Sabl, *Hume's Politics: Coordination and Crisis in the History of England* (Princeton, NJ: Princeton University Press, 2012), 115–17. I would like to thank Sabl for sharing this work with me prior to publication.

[21] Duncan Forbes, *Hume's Philosophical Politics* (Cambridge: Cambridge University Press, 1975), 323.

[22] See Thomas W. Merrill, "The Rhetoric of Rebellion in Hume's Constitutional Thought" *Review of Politics* 67.2 (spring 2005): 257–82.

The Perils of Political Rationalism

foolish. Still further, as Annette Baier notes, and as Hume's contemporaries readily recognized, his support of the duty to obey the established government contains an implicit rejection of many other forms of this duty: "the duty of obedience, in Hume's hands, gets drastically pruned of the luxuriant growth that centuries of slave-owning, patriarchal and feudal forms of life had encouraged to flourish.... All those subdivisions of the duty to obey that Stair's *Institutions*, or even Hutcheson's *Institutio*, had listed and dwelt on – servants obeying their masters, wives their husbands, children their parents, lay persons their pastors – get quietly swept away."[23]

Finally, Hume's comments on the revolution of 1688 and the chief instances of rebellion in the British empire during his own lifetime – those of the Jacobites and the American colonists – confirm that he evaluates specific acts of resistance on prudential rather than ideological grounds. He concurs that the revolution of 1688 was on the whole a "glorious" one, given its beneficial outcome, but he leaves conspicuously open the question of whether the revolution was justified *at the time*. In other words, Hume doubts that the tyranny of the Stuart kings was as great as the Whigs of his time claimed, but he also insists that the Hanoverian accession had acquired legitimacy in retrospect through the passage of time, the acquiescence of the populace, and a generally benign record of governance (see EMPL, 502–11; HE VI, 531–3; THN 3.2.10.19, 362). As for the chief rebellions of eighteenth-century Britain, Hume had very little sympathy for the Jacobite uprisings of 1715 and 1745, given that they sought to undermine a basically healthy political order through violent means (see EMPL, 615–16), but he was one of the most consistent supporters of the American colonists among the leading British thinkers of the time, in large part because he saw colonial independence as consonant with historical precedent, American public opinion, and Britain's own military and commercial interests.[24] At one point he went so far as to declare, "I am an American in my Principles, and wish we woud let them alone to govern or misgovern themselves as they think

---

[23] Annette C. Baier, *A Progress of Sentiments: Reflections on Hume's Treatise* (Cambridge, MA: Harvard University Press, 1991), 256.

[24] On Hume's views of America and the crisis regarding America in England, see Donald Livingston, "Hume, English Barbarism and American Independence," in *Scotland and America in the Age of the Enlightenment*, ed. Richard B. Sher and Jeffrey Smitten (Edinburgh: Edinburgh University Press, 1990); and J. G. A. Pocock, "Hume and the American Revolution: The Dying Thoughts of a North Briton," in *McGill Hume Studies*, ed. David Fate Norton, Nicholas Capaldi, and Wade L. Robison (San Diego: Austin Hill Press, 1979).

proper."[25] In all, then, the idea that Hume was a knee-jerk reactionary or a complacent defender of the establishment is a gross caricature. Nevertheless, there is little question that he was every bit as opposed to rationalism in politics as Oakeshott would later be.

Smith too advocates political reform but unequivocally opposes efforts to impose an abstract, comprehensive ideal on society from above. This standpoint is particularly apparent in the famous passage on the "spirit of system" that was added to the final, sixth edition of *The Theory of Moral Sentiments* in 1790. The context of this passage is a discussion of patriotism or the love of one's country, which Smith claims generally involves two different principles: "first, a certain respect and reverence for that constitution or form of government which is actually established; and secondly, an earnest desire to render the condition of our fellow-citizens as safe, respectable, and happy as we can" (TMS VI.ii.2.11, 231). In ordinary, quiet times, he says, these two principles will generally coincide: we can best serve our fellow citizens by supporting the established government. In times of "public discontent, faction, and disorder," however, "it often requires … the highest effort of political wisdom to determine when a real patriot ought to support and endeavour to re-establish the authority of the old system, and when he ought to give way to the more daring, but often more dangerous spirit of innovation" (TMS VI.ii.2.12, 231–2). Smith is not, then, *always* opposed to political innovation. He warns, however, that "a certain spirit of system" often leads people irresponsibly to seek "to new-model the constitution, and to alter, in some of its most essential parts, [the] system of government" (TMS VI.ii.2.15, 232). He explains:

The man of system … is apt to be very wise in his own conceit; and is often so enamoured with the supposed beauty of his own ideal plan of government, that he cannot suffer the smallest deviation from any part of it.… He seems to imagine that he can arrange the different members of a great society with as much ease as the hand arranges the different pieces upon a chess-board. He does not consider that the pieces upon the chess-board have no other principle of motion besides that which the hand impresses upon them; but that, in the great chess-board of human society, every single piece has a principle of motion of its own, altogether different from that which the legislature might chuse to impress upon it. (TMS VI.ii.2.17, 233–4)[26]

---

[25] David Hume, letter to Baron Mure of Caldwell, 27 October 1775, in *The Letters of David Hume*, ed. J. Y. T. Greig, vol. 2 (Oxford: Clarendon Press, 1932), 303.

[26] There is no scholarly consensus regarding Smith's specific target in this passage, if indeed there was one. The editors of *The Theory of Moral Sentiments*, among many others, suggest that it was aimed at the French revolutionaries and their English champion

The Perils of Political Rationalism

In Smith's view, attempts to impose a theoretical blueprint on society almost invariably create far more problems than they solve. A truly wise and humane reformer will not strive for perfection, but rather will respect established institutions and prejudices as much as possible: "Though he should consider some of them as in some measure abusive, he will content himself with moderating, what he often cannot annihilate without great violence.... When he cannot establish the right, he will not disdain to ameliorate the wrong; but like Solon, when he cannot establish the best system of laws, he will endeavour to establish the best that the people can bear" (TMS VI.ii.2.16, 233).[27]

Smith's opposition to the idea of moving people around as if they were chess pieces is observable in his hostility to mercantilism, the economic system that sought to guide or control people's choices through legal monopolies, bounties, duties, trade prohibitions, apprenticeship laws, settlement laws, laws of primogeniture and entail, and so on. On the other hand, his aversion to precipitate reform dictated against seeking to impose even his own "system of natural liberty" unconditionally and instantaneously. Thus, throughout *The Wealth of Nations* Smith warns

---

Richard Price. See TMS, 231n. This seems unlikely, however, in light of the fact that Smith informed his publisher that the final edition of the book was "perfectly finished to the very last sentence" in a letter written only four months after the storming of the Bastille, and a mere two weeks after Price's sermon that so exercised Edmund Burke. See Adam Smith, letter to Thomas Cadell, 18 November 1789, in "Adam Smith an Thomas Cadell: Zwei neue Briefe," ed. Heiner Klemme, in *Archiv für Geschichte der Philosophie* 73.3 (1991), 279. Given Smith's extremely deliberate writing habits and his notorious perfectionism, it seems doubtful that he would have had the time or desire to formulate comments on the unfolding events across the Channel at this early stage. Dugald Stewart and, drawing on Stewart, Istvan Hont suggest that Smith's target in this passage was instead the Physiocrats who advocated imposing a regime of perfect economic liberty all at once. See Dugald Stewart, "Account of the Life and Writings of Adam Smith, LL.D.," in Adam Smith, *Essays on Philosophical Subjects*, ed. I. S. Ross (Indianapolis: Liberty Fund, [1794] 1980), 317–19, 339; and Istvan Hont, *Jealousy of Trade: International Competition and the Nation-State in Historical Perspective* (Cambridge, MA: Belknap Press, 2005), 355, 379–87. Emma Rothschild and F. P. Lock both argue that the passage was more likely directed at some combination of the radical Whiggism of Charles James Fox and the "enlightened absolutism" of Frederick II of Prussia and Joseph II, Holy Roman Emperor. See Emma Rothschild, *Economic Sentiments: Adam Smith, Condorcet, and the Enlightenment* (Cambridge, MA: Harvard University Press, 2001), 54–5, 67; and F. P. Lock, "Adam Smith and 'The Man of System': Interpreting *The Theory of Moral Sentiments* VI.ii.2.12–18" *Adam Smith Review* 3 (2007): 37–48.

[27] The line about Solon is adapted from Plutarch, *Lives of the Noble Grecians and Romans*, ed. John Dryden, vol. 1 (New York: Modern Library, 2001), 115. Smith was sufficiently fond of the line that another version of it appears at WN IV.v.b.53, 543. Montesquieu cites it as well, proclaiming that "this is a fine speech that should be heard by all legislators" (SL 19.21, 322).

202   *The Pragmatic Enlightenment*

that his economic proposals should be implemented gradually, with due attention to the disorders they might generate. For instance, in the midst of a discussion of import duties and trade prohibitions designed to protect domestic industries – in the same chapter as the only mention of the "invisible hand" in the work – he writes: "Humanity may ... require that the freedom of trade should be restored only by slow gradations, and with a good deal of reserve and circumspection. Were those high duties and prohibitions taken away all at once, cheaper foreign goods of the same kind might be poured so fast into the home market, as to deprive all at once many thousands of our people of their ordinary employment and means of subsistence" (WN IV.ii.40, 469). "Such are the unfortunate effects of all the regulations of the mercantile system!" he laments in a later chapter. "They not only introduce very dangerous disorders into the state of the body politick, but disorders which it is often difficult to remedy, without occasioning, for a time at least, still greater disorders." Thus, he maintains that "in what manner the natural system of perfect liberty and justice ought gradually to be restored, we must leave to the wisdom of future statesmen and legislators to determine" (WN IV.vii.c.44, 606). As Istvan Hont observes, it was precisely this insistence on gradual reform that separated Smith from many of the Physiocrats, who advocated instituting a system of economic liberty all at once, in spite of all obstacle or opposition.[28] In Smith's view, even the Physiocrats, his allies in the cause of free trade, had fallen prey to the rationalist fallacy according to which there is only one set of institutions that truly corresponds to the order of Reason or Nature, and that should therefore be imposed on society immediately and in its entirety. Smith rejects this rationalist view in all of its guises and instead advocates prudent, piecemeal reform of existing institutions.

Smith's stance toward revolution resembles Hume's in many respects. As we saw in Chapter 2, he holds that the duty of allegiance rests on the dual basis of authority and utility – that is, people's habitual tendency to obey established authorities and the utility of having a "regular government" that is able to enforce order – and he argues that rebellion can be justified on *either* of these grounds. Severe oppression both

---

[28] See Hont, *Jealousy of Trade*, chapter 5, especially 362. Smith faults Quesnay, a leading Physiocrat, for imagining that society can "thrive and prosper only under a certain precise regimen, the exact regimen of perfect liberty and perfect justice," and for failing to realize that "if a nation could not prosper without the enjoyment of perfect liberty and perfect justice, there is not in the world a nation which could ever have prospered" (WN IV.ix.28, 674).

The Perils of Political Rationalism

undercuts people's sympathy and deference toward their rulers *and* diminishes the usefulness of having a neutral enforcer of the laws (see LJ, 320–1, 434). Thus, Smith claims that "a gross, flagrant, and palpable abuse [of power] no doubt" entitles the people to "rise in arms" against their government (LJ, 326). His threshold for rebellion seems to be slightly lower than Hume's, given that he expresses little doubt about the propriety of the Glorious Revolution, even in 1688,[29] but like Hume he counsels restraint in the great majority of circumstances: "No government is quite perfect, but it is better to submitt to some inconveniences than make attempts against it" (LJ, 435; see also 324, 326). For Smith as for Hume, upheavals should be avoided when at all possible, and even in cases in which a tyrannical ruler (or set of rulers) must be overthrown, as much of the old order should be preserved as is consonant with public opinion and the public interest.

To repeat: Smith is by no means opposed to reform. *The Wealth of Nations* contains a great number of concrete suggestions for improvement in areas such as trade regulations, settlement and inheritance laws, apprenticeship requirements, taxation, and education policy. Nor were his proposals all minor, easily implemented ones: as Samuel Fleischacker notes, "in the context of his time, it was quite unrealistic, not to say visionary, to urge the complete disestablishment of religion, the end of the East India Company, and a legislative union between England and America."[30] In fact, at one point Smith himself referred to *The Wealth of Nations* as "the very violent attack I ... made upon the whole commercial system of Great Britain."[31] Yet however "violent" Smith's verbal attack may have been, he certainly never advocated a wholesale restructuring of society based on an abstract theory. As Dugald Stewart writes, "he was abundantly aware of the danger to be apprehended from a rash application of political theories."[32]

---

[29] Smith is recorded as having told his students that "there could be no doubt at the Revolution that the king had exceeded the limits of his power" (LJ, 325; see also 429, 436).

[30] Samuel Fleischacker, "On Adam Smith's 'Wealth of Nations': Response" *Adam Smith Review* 2 (2006), 254.

[31] Adam Smith, letter to Andreas Holt, 26 October 1780, in *The Correspondence of Adam Smith*, ed. Ernest Campbell Mossner and Ian Simpson Ross (Indianapolis: Liberty Fund, 1987), 251.

[32] Stewart, "Account of the Life and Writings of Adam Smith, LL.D.," 317. Emma Rothschild has shown that starting in the mid-1790s Smith's friends and followers – including Stewart – felt compelled to burnish his "establishment" and "conservative" credentials in the light of the fact that he was increasingly being associated with French philosophy and

204   *The Pragmatic Enlightenment*

The thinkers of the French Enlightenment are generally thought to have been far more radical and rationalist than their Scottish counterparts, but Montesquieu is a widely acknowledged exception to this rule. As David Carrithers writes, "his rejection of the geometrical spirit sets Montesquieu apart from the later, more doctrinaire, reformist *philosophes* who sought to define a perfect world and get there – whatever the cost."[33] Like Hume and Smith, Montesquieu was a cautious advocate of liberal reform.[34] Given the comparatively illiberal nature of ancien régime France, it is unsurprising that the changes he advocated making to its government and society were more extensive than the ones Hume and Smith proposed for eighteenth-century Britain; some of the items at the top of his list included the strengthening of the *parlements*, the liberalization of the criminal laws, the promotion of commerce, and the elimination of religious persecution. Indeed, all of the reforms that he advocated, taken together, would have added up to a largely new political and social order, one that would have resembled Britain almost as much as France. Even so, Montesquieu's outlook is far removed from that of the Oakeshottian rationalist. As we saw in Chapter 2, he by no means regards the British model as appropriate for all times and places, and as we will see here, he too warns against sudden, radical breaks with the existing order, especially those founded on abstract conceptions of political right.

Like Hume and Smith, Montesquieu emphasizes that sweeping changes are liable to produce unintended and unpredictable consequences. Reformers must not only worry about correcting present abuses, he declares, but also about "the abuses of the correction itself" (SL, xliv), and "the drawbacks that one foresees ... are often less dangerous than those one cannot foresee" (SL 21.23, 397). Hence, refashioning existing institutions all at once and in their entirety is both extremely difficult and extremely hazardous. This skeptical view of radical change and

---

the French Revolution. See Rothschild, *Economic Sentiments*, chapter 2. Even if Stewart had political or prudential reasons for stressing the cautious, pragmatic side of Smith's thought, however, this element of his reading seems to me perfectly accurate.

[33] Carrithers, "Introduction: An Appreciation of *The Spirit of Laws*," 15. Even Gertrude Himmelfarb, who depicts the French Enlightenment as an assemblage of misguided radicals and rationalists, makes an exception for Montesquieu, asserting that he was "more representative of the British Enlightenment than of the French." Himmelfarb, *The Roads to Modernity*, 15; see also 18, 21, 151, 160–3.

[34] For a helpful discussion of Montesquieu and the art of liberal reform through liberal means, see Keegan Callanan, "Montesquieu, Liberalism and the Critique of Political Universalism" (Ph.D. dissertation, Duke University, 2011), chapter 5.

The Perils of Political Rationalism

comprehensive solutions permeates all of Montesquieu's works. In *The Persian Letters*, Usbek argues that political and legal changes should only be made when absolutely necessary, and even then they should be made "with trembling hands" (PL #129, 217). In the *Considerations on the Causes of the Greatness of the Romans and Their Decline*, Montesquieu states that "when a government's form has been established a long time ... it is almost always prudent to leave it alone, because the reasons for such a state having endured are often complicated and unknown, and they will cause it to maintain itself further. But when one changes the whole system, one can remedy only those inconveniences that are known in theory, and one overlooks others that can be discovered only in practice."[35] In the *Pensées*, he offers a number of "general maxims of politics" that could have come from Oakeshott's pen: "there are countless cases where the lesser evil is best"; "when correction suffices, removal must be avoided"; "correction presupposes time"; and so on (*Pensées* #1007, 281).

Montesquieu's wariness of dislocating change is evident above all, however, in *The Spirit of the Laws*.[36] In fact, one of the chief reasons why he places so much emphasis on the many factors that go into forming the "spirit" of different nations is to discourage rash attempts at general reform and to encourage prudent attention to a nation's specific circumstances (see SL 19.4–5, 310; 19.21, 321–2). Given how intimately connected a nation's government is to its history, commerce, education, climate, geography, religion, and other characteristics, he suggests, it is difficult in the extreme to change laws and institutions radically or suddenly without also changing the very character of the nation, which is almost always a perilous prospect. In book 19, chapter 5, for example, Montesquieu speaks of a nation – almost certainly France – whose "natural genius" is sociable, open, lively, and cheerful, and he cautions against undermining these qualities by imposing laws that would curb the people's indiscretions and limit their luxuries; legal attempts to restrain a

[35] Charles de Secondat, baron de Montesquieu, *Considerations on the Causes of the Greatness of the Romans and Their Decline*, trans. David Lowenthal (Indianapolis: Hackett, [1734] 1999), 160.

[36] Franz Neumann claims that it is precisely Montesquieu's resistance to "accepting any radical solution, any panacea, any utopia ... which gives the *Esprit des Lois* its color." See the editor's introduction in Charles de Secondat, baron de Montesquieu, *The Spirit of the Laws*, trans. Thomas Nugent (New York: Hafner, 1949), xix. For a different view, according to which Montesquieu was not as cautious or skeptical of far-reaching reform as many commentators suggest, see Andrea Radasanu, "Montesquieu on Moderation, Monarchy and Reform" *History of Political Thought* 31.2 (summer 2010): 283–307.

society's minor vices may inadvertently erode its greatest virtues as well (see SL 19.5, 310). Thus, he insists that changes to a nation's laws should only be made "by those who are born fortunate enough to fathom by a stroke of genius the whole of a state's constitution," and who realize that one should "let an ill remain if one fears something worse" and "let a good remain if one is in doubt about a better" (SL, xliv). Indeed, at one point Montesquieu declares that the entire reason he wrote the book was to prove that "the spirit of moderation should be that of the legislator" (SL 29.1, 602).[37]

Whereas Hume and Smith sought to shift the focus away from the right to revolution that featured so prominently in Locke's thought and Whig ideology more generally, Montesquieu is almost entirely silent on this point.[38] This is not particularly surprising, given that talk of revolution was fraught with far more danger in ancien régime France than in eighteenth-century Britain, which owed its current political settlement to the revolution of 1688. Montesquieu does maintain, as Sharon Krause has stressed, that spirited resistance to encroaching power is sometimes necessary for the maintenance of liberty, particularly in monarchies.[39] However, he approvingly notes that periodic and judicious acts of resistance generally help to *prevent* real revolution. Whereas despotic states are "full of revolutions," he declares, in well-tempered monarchies "things are very rarely carried to excess," and when grave disorders do begin to occur "people of wisdom and authority intervene; temperings

[37] On the centrality of moderation in Montesquieu's thought, see Guillaume Barrera, *Les lois du monde: Enquête sur le dessein politique de Montesquieu* (Paris: Gallimard, 2009); and Aurelian Craiutu, *A Virtue for Courageous Minds: Moderation in French Political Thought, 1748–1830* (Princeton, NJ: Princeton University Press, 2012), chapter 2. Harvey Mansfield claims that Montesquieu's political philosophy rests not on a single principle but rather on "a non-principle – moderation – that cautions men against the extremism produced by simplified principles." Harvey C. Mansfield Jr., *Taming the Prince: The Ambivalence of Modern Executive Power* (Baltimore: Johns Hopkins University Press, 1993), 215.

[38] See C. P. Courtney, "Montesquieu and Revolution," in *Lectures de Montesquieu*, ed. Edgar Mass and Alberto Postigliola (Naples: Liguori Editore, 1993). Usbek does briefly summarize the Lockean/Whig position on the right to revolution in *The Persian Letters*, but he goes on subtly to mock their reasoning. See PL #104, 173–4; and, for commentary, C. P. Courtney, "Montesquieu and English Liberty," in *Montesquieu's Science of Politics: Essays on The Spirit of Laws*, ed. David W. Carrithers, Michael A. Mosher, and Paul A. Rahe (Lanham, MD: Rowman & Littlefield, 2001), 274.

[39] See Sharon R. Krause, "The Politics of Distinction and Disobedience: Honor and the Defense of Liberty in Montesquieu" *Polity* 31.2 (spring 1999): 469–99; and Sharon R. Krause, *Liberalism with Honor* (Cambridge, MA: Harvard University Press, 2002), chapter 2.

The Perils of Political Rationalism

are proposed, agreements are reached, corrections are made; the laws become vigorous again and make themselves heard" (SL 5.11, 57). Montesquieu opposes the idea of total political revolution because he holds that in the great majority of cases "the good founded on the overthrow of the laws of the state cannot be compared with the harm that follows from this overthrow itself" (Pensées #1998, 615). Indeed, at one point he defines "tyranny" not as a type of government that deserves to be overthrown, but rather as the attempt at overthrow itself, or "the design of upsetting the established power" (SL 14.13, 243). When he says in this chapter that the English character is well suited to "frustrate the projects of tyranny," then, he refers to their tendency to *prevent* their laws and rulers from being overthrown. It may be true, as Melvin Richter remarks, that "more than anyone else, it was Montesquieu who, by reclassifying political regimes, made it possible to call the French monarchy despotic and the king a despot," and that he thereby "contributed greatly to delegitimating the monarchy of France prior to and during the French Revolution."[40] Nevertheless, given the prudent, reformist character of Montesquieu's thought, it is easy to see why in the period after 1789 he was cited as much by the revolution's opponents as by the revolutionaries themselves.[41] Like Hume and Smith, he "championed important liberal causes while nonetheless displaying a profound distrust of wrenching, ill-considered change."[42]

Far more than Hume, Smith, or Montesquieu, Voltaire is often thought to have been a political radical and rationalist. Gustave Lanson famously declared more than a century ago that his early *Letters Concerning the English Nation* was "the first bomb dropped on the *ancien régime*,"[43] and in one of the few books dedicated to Voltaire's political theory, Constance Rowe asserts that he "defined for all thinking people those universal claims of reason which he believed should be enforced by the State."[44] And, of course, the French revolutionaries themselves canonized him, moving his remains to the Pantheon in 1791; indeed, Georges Pellessier concludes that no single individual did more to contribute to the

---

[40] Melvin Richter, "Montesquieu's Comparative Analysis of Europe and Asia: Intended and Unintended Consequences," in *L'Europe de Montesquieu*, ed. Alberto Postigliola and Maria Grazia Bottaro Palumbo (Naples: Liguori Editore, 1995), 331.

[41] See Courtney, "Montesquieu and Revolution," 43–50.

[42] Carrithers, "Introduction: An Appreciation of *The Spirit of Laws*," 12.

[43] Gustave Lanson, *Voltaire*, trans. Robert A. Wagoner (New York: John Wiley & Sons, [1906] 1960), 48.

[44] Constance Rowe, *Voltaire and the State* (New York: Columbia University Press, 1955), 6.

revolution than Voltaire.[45] It is not difficult to understand why Voltaire has so often been read in this way, especially since some of his bolder claims, removed from their proper context, do seem to advocate ignoring the past or wiping the political slate clean. For instance, he writes in the *Treatise on Tolerance* that "past eras must be treated as if they had never been. One must always start from the present, from the point to which nations have thus far evolved."[46] And, in the passage that Oakeshott singles out, he asserts in his *Philosophical Dictionary*, "if you want to have good laws, burn what you have, and create new ones."[47]

Yet the context of these passages belies a purely rationalist reading, and even points in the opposite direction, toward the importance of historical context and gradual reform. The line from the *Treatise on Tolerance* appears in a chapter entitled "How tolerance may be permitted," which is addressed to political and ecclesiastical legislators, urging them to see that even if religious toleration may have proven difficult to institute in the past, the obstacles to such a policy no longer remain. Contrary to what the quoted passage itself might seem to imply, then, the historical context is in fact crucial to Voltaire's argument: his claim is that France's present legislators need not be unduly influenced by past conflicts between Catholics and Protestants, given that other nations have enjoyed relative peace after introducing religious toleration and that "all educated persons nowadays" view religious enthusiasm with derision.[48] In other words, his broader point is less that we must always ignore the past than that it is no longer appropriate, in mid-eighteenth-century France, to persecute people on the basis of religion, just as it is no longer appropriate to punish people for witchcraft.[49] A change in circumstances allows or justifies, and sometimes even requires, a change in policy – a sentiment that Oakeshott himself embraces.[50]

---

[45] See Georges Pellessier, *Voltaire philosophe* (Paris: Colin, 1908), 304.

[46] Voltaire, *Treatise on Tolerance*, in *Treatise on Tolerance and Other Writings*, ed. Simon Harvey and trans. Brian Masters (Cambridge: Cambridge University Press, [1763] 2000), 25–6.

[47] Voltaire, *Pocket Philosophical Dictionary*, in *Political Writings*, trans. David Williams (Cambridge: Cambridge University Press, 1994), 20. The section in which this line appears was added in 1771 and thus is not included in the Penguin edition of the *Philosophical Dictionary* that I have normally used, which for the most part relies on the 1769 version of the text.

[48] Voltaire, *Treatise on Tolerance*, 25.

[49] See ibid., 26.

[50] Recall from Chapter 2 that this point is made even more explicitly in Voltaire's essay "Republican Ideas," in which he argues that "when times have palpably changed, there are laws that have to be changed" and then proceeds to use the historical fluctuations in

The Perils of Political Rationalism

The line from the *Philosophical Dictionary* about burning existing laws appears in the entry "Laws," which stresses the great arbitrariness and inconsistency of laws, both within and among nations, and the great cruelty that is frequently inflicted in the name of the law. The immediate context is a comparison of these irregular laws with irregular city streets, and the burning of the laws with the Great Fire of London: "London only became worth living in since it was reduced to ashes. Since that time, its streets have been widened and straightened. Being burnt down made a city out of London. If you want to have good laws, burn what you have, and create new ones."[51] This is perhaps the closest that Voltaire ever comes to a moment of political rationalism, insofar as he does seem to be suggesting that laws that are designed in a premeditated fashion tend to be superior to those that grow organically. Even here, however, he is certainly not arguing that all existing laws should be eliminated, any more than he is advocating deliberately burning down the whole of Paris. After all, the entry as a whole shows him to be quite pessimistic about the possibility of devising and implementing a good set of laws: time and again he points to the influence of particular and short-term interests, ignorance, and superstition on legal codes.[52] As we saw in Chapter 2, he makes no effort – in this entry or elsewhere – to devise a perfect set of laws, or even to appeal to a universal standard of natural law in judging existing ones. Voltaire believes that laws can be made *better* – more liberal, more humane – but certainly not perfect. The suggestion that he was actually in favor of devising a set of rational laws from scratch and imposing them on society drastically overestimates his expectations of both philosophy and politics.

Voltaire advocated many of the same reforms to ancien régime France as Montesquieu, including the promotion of commerce, religious toleration, humane criminal laws, freedom of expression, and the like. Yet he too was far too much a realist to suppose that radical or sudden changes, even if based on sound principles, would always turn out for the best. In a line that has recently become a mantra not only in politics but also in the

---

the possibility or desirability of religious toleration to illustrate the point. See Voltaire, "Republican Ideas," in *Political Writings*, trans. David Williams (Cambridge: Cambridge University Press, [1765] 1994), 199–201.

[51] Voltaire, *Pocket Philosophical Dictionary*, 20. This reflection may have been inspired by a similar one in René Descartes, *Discourse on the Method*, in *The Philosophical Writings of Descartes*, trans. John Cottingham, Robert Stoothoff, and Dugald Murdoch, vol. 1 (Cambridge: Cambridge University Press, [1637] 1985), 116–17.

[52] See especially Voltaire, *Pocket Philosophical Dictionary*, 19–20, 22.

The Pragmatic Enlightenment

business world and the self-help industry, Voltaire maintains that in many cases "the perfect is the enemy of the good."[53] Thus, throughout his career he fought for specific, limited, and potentially realizable reforms rather than seeking to devise a theoretical blueprint for a perfect society. As we saw in Chapter 3, even his famous "battle cry," *écrasez l'infâme*, meant – at least in practice and in the short term – nothing more than reducing the status and power of the Catholic Church in France to the level of the Anglican Church in Britain. "His tactics were those of attrition, not of devastation, of practical gradualism, not of doctrinaire violence," writes William Bottiglia. "It is true that he fought with a fanatical zeal, yet his ends were moderate. He believed in small steps rather than great leaps because he understood the difficulties and the risks of social change and did not want a whole way of life to be suddenly engulfed in a diluvial disaster."[54] Hence Lanson, the scholar who proclaimed that the *Letters Concerning the English Nation* was the first bomb dropped on the ancien régime, also asserts that "Voltaire was, beyond any doubt, a conservative," or rather "a conservative in the manner of any true liberal."[55] While there may be a few ostensibly rationalist moments in Voltaire's writings, then, his general approach is one of pragmatism and reform rather than ignoring the past and wiping the slate clean.

This more realistic or chastened reading of Voltaire is reinforced by his consistent opposition to political revolution, especially violent revolution. As David Williams writes, despite the fact that he was later apotheosized by the revolutionaries, "Voltaire was never an advocate of revolution. The upheavals of 1789 would have appalled him, the power of the mob terrifying him as much, if not more, than that of autocrats."[56]

---

[53] Voltaire, *La Bégueule*, ed. Nicholas Cronk and Haydn T. Mason, in *The Complete Works of Voltaire*, vol. 74a (Oxford: Voltaire Foundation, [1772] 2006), 217. A more literal translation of this ubiquitous maxim would be "the *best* is the enemy of the good" (*le mieux est l'ennemi du bien*). While this line is almost always attributed to Voltaire, he himself ascribes it to "an Italian wise man."

[54] See the editor's introduction in *Voltaire: A Collection of Critical Essays*, ed. William F. Bottiglia (Englewood Cliffs, NJ: Prentice-Hall, 1968), 7; see also 12. Lester Crocker's interpretation of Voltaire is in general far too negative and dismissive, but he is right to suggest that for Voltaire "the job to be done was one of a limited correction of abuses, not an endeavor, based on abstract truths, to change the bases of society and direct it anew toward a 'rational-natural' ideal." Lester G. Crocker, *Nature and Culture: Ethical Thought in the French Enlightenment* (Baltimore: Johns Hopkins University Press, 1963), 450.

[55] Lanson, *Voltaire*, 159.

[56] See the editor's introduction in Voltaire, *Political Writings*, ed. David Williams (Cambridge: Cambridge University Press, 1994), xiv.

The Perils of Political Rationalism

While he desired and fought for a more liberal society, he was ever wary of upheavals brought on by extremists, abrupt and large-scale changes to the complex fabric of European civilization. Voltaire's hesitations about extending political power to the masses are rightly derided today, but they do underline the fact that in French politics he was an advocate of the *thèse royale* – the idea that the nobility, clergy, and *parlements* were the true despots, and that the only effectual means of curbing their power would be a reforming king with broad, centralized authority – rather than the inventor of a new *thèse bourgeoise*, let alone a *thèse sans-culotte*. This is perhaps why Voltaire fell out of favor among the revolutionaries soon after his apotheosis in 1791, Rousseau being much more in vogue in the later, more radical stages of the revolution.[57]

It is, of course, impossible to resolve here the vexed question of the extent to which the Enlightenment "caused" the French Revolution.[58] What can be said with some certainty, however, is that Hume, Smith, Montesquieu, and Voltaire all opposed, on principle, the idea of a wholesale restructuring of society, especially one based on an abstract conception of a perfect, "rational" order. While these thinkers all advocated a variety of liberal reforms, they also worried that sudden, radical breaks with the existing order would generally be both ineffective and dangerous. Thus, they maintained that all changes – even the liberal reforms they cherished most – should be implemented in a prudent, piecemeal fashion. In short, the cautious liberalism of these thinkers would be better described as reformist or gradualist than as rationalist, radical, or revolutionary.

PROGRESS WITHOUT TELEOLOGY

Much as political rationalism can be found in the writings of some of the more radical philosophes and even Locke, the idea of inevitable

---

[57] See Renée Waldinger, *Voltaire and Reform in the Light of the French Revolution* (Geneva: Droz, 1959), 82–6, 103. Waldinger stresses the affinities between Voltaire's thought and the reforms enacted during the early revolutionary period, but even she writes that "Voltaire's whole effort was directed toward the avoidance of ... a sudden and complete revolt. It was through evolution that he hoped to alter the inequitable practices of society." Ibid., 104.

[58] Few historians nowadays look to the thinkers of the "high" Enlightenment for the "intellectual origins of the French Revolution," as Daniel Mornet once did, although the idea that the Enlightenment was the leading cause of the revolution has been revived recently by Jonathan Israel. See Daniel Mornet, *Les Origines intellectuelles de la révolution française, 1715–1787*, fourth edition (Paris: Armand Colin, [1933] 1947); and Jonathan Israel, *Democratic Enlightenment: Philosophy, Revolution, and Human Rights, 1750–1790* (Oxford: Oxford University Press, 2011), especially chapters 34–5.

progress – progress as an intrinsic law of history – is not entirely absent from Enlightenment thought. Elements of this idea can be found in Turgot's three stages, Condorcet's ten epochs, and Kant's *Idea for a Universal History*, for example, although it truly came into its own only in the nineteenth century with figures such as Comte, Hegel, Marx, and Spencer.[59] This idea is, however, utterly foreign to the thought of Hume, Smith, Montesquieu, and Voltaire.[60] These thinkers did believe in the *possibility* of economic, moral, and political progress, precisely because it had already happened: taken as a whole, eighteenth-century Europe constituted an improvement over most of human history, in their view, the common but groundless tendency to romanticize the past notwithstanding. Yet they did not believe that these advances had resulted from some unalterable design in the historical process, or that the Europe of their time was without faults; on the contrary, they persistently mocked cosmic optimism and stressed that the progress that *had* been achieved was far from uniform or all-embracing. These thinkers saw most of human history as little more than a record of folly, conflict, and oppression, and it was this pessimistic (or perhaps realistic) view of the past that constituted their belief in progress, such as it was. The empirical observation that a degree of progress had occurred in their time is, of course, not really a *theory* of progress at all,[61] and it is entirely compatible with their recognition that the advances of their comparatively enlightened age might not even endure, much less continue indefinitely. In short, these thinkers believed in progress as a recent fact and as a possibility for the future, but by no means as an inevitable result of a teleological process.

It is truly remarkable that naive optimism is so often attributed to an era whose most famous author's most famous book is *Candide*; the Enlightenment is seen as Panglossian when it was Voltaire who *invented* this term of derision. The basic facts of the story are well known: Candide is a disciple of Doctor Pangloss, who is himself a disciple of Leibniz and his philosophical optimism. From the outset, however, the protagonist endures a long series of unrelenting misfortunes that make it impossible for him to continue to believe that ours is "the best of all possible

---

[59] On the limits of progress even in the writings of Turgot, Condorcet, and Kant, see Peter Gay, *The Enlightenment: An Interpretation*, vol. 2: *The Science of Freedom* (New York: W.W. Norton, 1969), 105–23.

[60] That the philosophes as a group were far from unqualified believers in progress was demonstrated many decades ago by Henry Vyverberg, *Historical Pessimism in the French Enlightenment* (Cambridge, MA: Harvard University Press, 1958), which includes separate chapters on Montesquieu and Voltaire.

[61] For a similar point, see Gay, *The Party of Humanity*, 271.

The Perils of Political Rationalism 213

worlds"; each turn of the story further undermines Pangloss's arguments and outlook. Through this story Voltaire impresses upon the reader, as no philosophical reasoning could, that cosmic optimism is unwarranted and foolish.[62] As Roger Pearson writes: "Rape, pillage, murder, massacre, butchery, religious intolerance and abuse, torture, hanging, storm, shipwreck, earthquake, disease, cannibalism, prostitution, political oppression and instability: all is well."[63] And the story of *Candide* is no anomaly: Voltaire ridicules optimism in myriad other works as well, perhaps most famously in his poem on the Lisbon earthquake and the entry in his *Philosophical Dictionary* entitled "All is well."[64]

Of course, in the final pages of *Candide* the title character learns to ward off boredom, depravity, and poverty and to find relative contentment through the working of his land or cultivation of his garden.[65] As David Wootton notes, judging by the conclusion it seems that Voltaire advocates replacing Pangloss's optimism (the claim that this is the best of all possible worlds) not with outright pessimism (the claim that it is the

---

[62] It should be noted, however, that Voltaire had shown a degree of sympathy for Leibniz's optimism earlier in his career. It was long assumed that his optimistic worldview was shattered by the Lisbon earthquake of 1755, but in recent years several scholars have persuasively argued that his views were in fact far more consistent than this traditional explanation suggests. See the discussion contained in the translator's introduction in Voltaire, *Candide and Related Texts*, trans. David Wootton (Indianapolis: Hackett, 2000).

[63] Roger Pearson, *The Fables of Reason: A Study of Voltaire's 'Contes Philosophiques'* (Oxford: Clarendon Press, 1993), 113.

[64] See Voltaire, "Poem on the Lisbon Disaster," in *Candide and Related Texts*, trans. David Wootton (Indianapolis: Hackett, [1756] 2000); and PD, 68–74. In *Zadig*, one of Voltaire's earlier stories, the protagonist experiences a similar litany of horrific episodes, but in this case there is a more traditional happy ending, with Zadig becoming a wise and just king, married to the queen he loves – although the appendix, which was added a few years later, entirely removes the air of easy resolution. See Voltaire, *Zadig, or Destiny*, in *Candide and Other Stories*, trans. Roger Pearson (Oxford: Oxford University Press, [1748] 2006). On the other hand, *Memnon*, yet another similar tale that also dates from well before the Lisbon disaster, seems at *least* as pessimistic as *Candide*, if not more so. See Voltaire, *Memnon*, in *Micromégas and Other Short Fictions*, trans. Theo Cuffe (New York: Penguin, [1750] 2002). An excellent study of these and all of Voltaire's other *contes* can be found in Pearson, *The Fables of Reason*.

[65] See Voltaire, *Candide*, in *Candide and Related Texts*, trans. David Wootton (Indianapolis: Hackett, [1759] 2000), 79. The famous final line, "*il faut cultiver notre jardin*," can be literally translated as "it is necessary to cultivate our garden," although Wootton renders it as "we must work our land." The question of what this line is supposed to convey has provoked a great deal of scholarly discussion and debate; see especially William F. Bottiglia, *Voltaire's Candide: Analysis of a Classic*, second edition (Geneva: Institut et Musee Voltaire, 1964), 96–138; and David Langdon, "On the Meanings of the Conclusion of *Candide*" *Studies on Voltaire and the Eighteenth Century* 238 (1985): 397–432.

worst of all worlds) but rather with meliorism, or the claim that the world can be made better.[66] Yet a better world is only a possible, not a necessary outcome, and one that human beings must create for themselves, not one that is written into history or preordained by God. And even this possibility seems to be more an individual affair than a societal or global one: Voltaire gives little indication that a perfect society – perhaps even a good one – is within human reach. From his garden Candide can watch boats carting people into exile, and others carrying severed and stuffed heads to be presented to the sultan.[67] In the end, then, *Candide*'s meliorism seems to consist as much in an escape from the world's troubles as in a solution to them.[68]

This fairly bleak view of the world is consistent with Voltaire's historical works, which are filled with repeated lamentations that "history is but a tableau of every crime and catastrophe."[69] In Voltaire's view, human history is mostly a register of cruelty and misery, broken only by four periods of cultural greatness, even if not humanity or happiness: Periclean Athens, Augustan Rome, Renaissance Italy, and the France of Louis XIV.[70] Almost the entire "Recapitulation" of the *Essay on the Mores and Spirit of Nations*, for example, is dedicated to showing that "in general all of history is a collection of crimes, follies, and misfortunes, among which one sees a few virtues and a few happy times, just as one discovers a few scattered houses in a barren desert" (EM II.197, 804). Such rhetorical flourishes are slightly misleading, however, because Voltaire *did* believe that the world had improved in recent times, at least in certain respects and in certain parts of Europe. For instance, in *The Age of Louis XIV*, he shows in some detail that the conditions of mid-eighteenth-century France were unquestionably an improvement over those of the same nation little more than a century earlier, when "the streets of Paris, narrow, badly paved and covered with filth, were overrun with thieves"; when the "spirit of discord and faction ... pervaded every community in the kingdom"; when the "gothic barbarism" of dueling

---

[66] See Wooton, translator's introduction in Voltaire, *Candide and Related Texts*, xv.

[67] See Voltaire, *Candide*, 76–7.

[68] Several scholars have emphasized, however, that Candide's affirmation that we must cultivate our garden is *not* meant to rule out political engagement or a duty to do what we can to help others. See especially Langdon, "On the Meanings of the Conclusion of *Candide*"; and Lanson, *Voltaire*, 129.

[69] Voltaire, *The Ingenu*, in *Candide and Other Stories*, trans. Roger Pearson (Oxford: Oxford University Press, [1767] 2006), 221.

[70] See Voltaire, *The Age of Louis XIV*, trans. Martyn P. Pollack (London: J. M. Dent and Sons, [1751] 1961), chapter 1.

The Perils of Political Rationalism

had "contributed to the depopulation of the country as much as civil or foreign wars"; and when "the French nation was steeped in ignorance" to the point that people believed unreservedly in astrology, sorcery, and exorcism.[71] Eighteenth-century France may not have shined in the arts to the degree that it had under Louis XIV, Voltaire concedes, but the lives of most people were far more tolerable. In the *Essay*, after reflecting on the state of Europe in the thirteenth and fourteenth centuries – centuries that included the Crusades, the Black Death, numerous wars, and interminable hunger and wretchedness among the common people – he declares that "a comparison of these centuries with our own (whatever perversities and whatever misfortunes we may undergo) must give us a sense of our good fortune, despite our almost invincible proneness to praise the past at the expense of the present" (EM I.82, 767).[72]

Yet Voltaire did not believe that the progress that Europe had experienced was inevitable, or that further progress would necessarily follow. As his incessant attacks on the Church indicate, he was only too aware of the possibility that European societies could slip back into barbarism. Even where he evinces some hope that "the world marches slowly toward wisdom," he stops to note that it must be a slow march indeed, given that even as he wrote there were still slaves in some cantons of France – indeed, slaves of monks! (EM I.83, 777).[73] In the entry "Politics" in the *Questions on the Encyclopedia*, with tongue only partly in cheek, he looks forward to a day "in another ten or twelve centuries, when men are more enlightened."[74]

More broadly, Voltaire refuses to speculate about any kind of grand pattern or plan inherent in history. As J. H. Brumfitt notes, this stance fits with his general hostility to "the spirit of system" in philosophy: "He is suspicious of all generalizations from the facts, especially when he

---

[71] Ibid., 17–18.

[72] On the tendency to bestow undue praise on the past, see also EM I.intro.17, 66; PD, 224; and Voltaire, "Anciens et modernes," in *Questions sur l'Encyclopédie*, vol. 2, ed. Nicholas Cronk and Christiane Mervaud, in *The Complete Works of Voltaire*, vol. 38 (Oxford: Voltaire Foundation, [1771] 2007), 330–1.

[73] As a result of a quirk of French law and history, feudal serfdom was still practiced by the monastery at Saint-Claude, a small town not far from Voltaire's home at Ferney, well into the eighteenth century. On Voltaire's campaign on behalf of the twelve thousand or so serfs who lived and worked there, see Ian Davidson, *Voltaire in Exile: The Last Years, 1753–78* (New York: Grove Press, 2004), 267–70; and Waldinger, *Voltaire and Reform in the Light of the French Revolution*, 64–6.

[74] Voltaire, "Politics," in *Questions on the Encyclopedia*, in *Political Writings*, trans. David Williams (Cambridge: Cambridge University Press, [1774] 1994), 84.

thinks that they may in reality be generalizations imposed on the facts."[75] Indeed, one of the main aims of Voltaire's historical works is to *refute* the idea that history is teleological or heading toward some perfect end point. Many of the best-known historical works of earlier centuries – works such as Bossuet's *Discourse on Universal History*, which drew Voltaire's particular ire – envisioned history as a divinely guided or controlled process, a succession of events dictated by God either through miraculous intervention or (more often) through his power over the hearts and minds of human beings. In deliberate contrast to this view, Voltaire delights in pointing to the utter unpredictability of events and the important role often played by seemingly trivial causes. In *The Age of Louis XIV*, for example, he suggests that the course of the Glorious Revolution was determined primarily by the personalities of James II and William III, rather than by broad impersonal forces.[76] Later, he goes so far as to attribute the fall of the duke of Marlborough, the turning out of the Whig party, and the end of the War of the Spanish Succession to the personal affronts shown by the duchess of Marlborough when she refused to give Queen Anne a pair of gloves that she desired and spilled some water on the dress of one of the queen's favorites. "Such trifles changed the face of Europe," he writes.[77] Thus, even John Gray – no admirer of Voltaire – concedes that "he was too alive to the quiddities of human circumstances and too alert to the sufferings of individual human beings to subscribe unambiguously to any grand scheme of human progress."[78]

Like Voltaire, Montesquieu considered their own age to be a comparatively enlightened one, at least in parts of Western Europe, above all because of the rise of commerce and the (relative) decline of religious intolerance. Yet even more than Voltaire, Montesquieu was in many ways a "historical pessimist," as Gilbert Chinard calls him,[79] believing that "an infinity of abuses slips into whatever is touched by the hands of men" (SL 6.1, 73). Far from adopting a theory of inevitable or endless progress, Montesquieu devotes book 8 of *The Spirit of the Laws* to showing that all regimes will, sooner or later, be corrupted.[80] He maintains that

---

[75] See the translator's introduction in *Voltaire, The Age of Louis XIV and Other Selected Writings*, trans. J. H. Brumfitt (New York: Twayne, 1963), xxiv.

[76] See Voltaire, *The Age of Louis XIV*, chapter 15.

[77] Ibid., 238.

[78] John Gray, *Voltaire* (New York: Routledge, 1999), 12; see also 45.

[79] Gilbert Chinard, "Montesquieu's Historical Pessimism," in *Studies in the History of Culture* (Menasha, WI: American Council of Learned Societies, 1942).

[80] For a helpful discussion of this argument, see Sharon R. Krause, "The Uncertain Inevitability of Decline in Montesquieu" *Political Theory* 30.5 (October 2002): 702–27.

The Perils of Political Rationalism

different regimes are corrupted in different ways, because they rely on different animating principles. As he presents it, democratic republics are corrupted either by a spirit of inequality or by a spirit of extreme equality, monarchies are corrupted when the intermediary bodies between the monarch and the people are weakened or eliminated, and "the principle of despotic government is endlessly corrupted because it is corrupt by its nature" (SL 8.10, 119). To be sure, he also indicates that a regime's corruption can be slowed, and the effects of its corruption mitigated, through wise legislation, above all through a constitutional separation and balance of powers that ensure that power is made to check power "by the arrangement of things," as in England (SL 11.4, 155). Yet not even these measures can prevent decline altogether: Montesquieu mournfully writes at the end of the chapter on the English constitution that "since all human things have an end, the state of which we are speaking will lose its liberty; it will perish" (SL 11.6, 166).[81] Montesquieu's friend William Domville later asked him to elaborate on this statement, and in his reply Montesquieu speculates that "in Europe the last sigh of liberty will be heaved by an Englishman," since England had found a way to "slow the speed with which other nations collapse entirely" – statements that are, of course, somewhat encouraging with respect to England, but also quite pessimistic with respect to the idea of progress more generally.[82]

Montesquieu's "historical pessimism" is even more conspicuous in the *Considerations on the Causes of the Greatness of the Romans and Their Decline*: throughout the narrative Rome's path from a republic

---

[81] Thomas Pangle has recently argued that, despite all of his apparent pessimism regarding the persistence of despotism and religious fanaticism, "Montesquieu does intend, and implicitly claims to have achieved, the elaboration of the framework of a universal political science that shows the reasonable likelihood of the ever increasing, undeniably manifest, historical dominance of the planet by the religion of reason" – that is, by Montesquieu's own Enlightenment ideals. On Pangle's interpretation, Montesquieu sees this development as resting above all on the beneficial effects of commerce, the new thing under the sun that will allow the modern world to escape many of the ills that have afflicted humanity throughout history. Thomas L. Pangle, *The Theological Basis of Liberal Modernity in Montesquieu's Spirit of the Laws* (Chicago: University of Chicago Press, 2010), 128. While I agree that Montesquieu ascribes great benefits to commerce, as we will see in Chapter 6, given his explicit claim that even commercial England "will lose its liberty" and therefore "perish," I am less sure that Montesquieu's outlook is quite this optimistic.

[82] Charles de Secondat, baron de Montesquieu, letter to William Domville, 22 July 1749, in *Oeuvres complètes de Montesquieu*, ed. André Masson, vol. 3 (Paris: Nagel, 1955), 1245. See also Pensées #1960, 593–6, for a longer version of this letter, one that includes more detailed speculation about the end of English liberty but that was never actually sent to Domville.

218   *The Pragmatic Enlightenment*

to an empire and thence to its fall appears to be essentially inevitable. The answers to the two questions implicit in the title – what caused the Romans' greatness, and what caused their subsequent decline – are inextricably linked, in Montesquieu's view: the simple manners, patriotic dedication, and carefully crafted institutions that enabled the Romans to conquer the world could not be sustained once they had done so, and so its decline was a direct result of its greatness.[83] As he puts it at one point, it is "the fate of nearly all the states in the world" to pass "from poverty to riches, and from riches to corruption."[84] Much as the English had found a way to delay the loss of their liberty, at least for a time, Rome was able to put off this corruption longer than most through its extraordinary customs and institutions, but not to avert it entirely.

Even *The Persian Letters*, for all of its undeniable humor, is in many ways an extremely pessimistic work: almost all of the Europeans in the book are corrupt or absurd, and Usbek, the lead character, whose voice is so often one of enlightenment and humanity, despotically rules his wives and slaves back in Persia with an iron fist. Roxana, Usbek's favorite wife, who is one of the few relatively admirable characters in the book, finds her life under Persian institutions unsupportable and commits suicide at the end. The darkness of the book, and of Montesquieu's view of history, is also apparent in Rica's review of the volumes on modern European history in a scholar's library, which for the most part present a depressing spectacle of decline from former power and grandeur. Even the volumes on England, which had recently become the "mistress of the seas" as a result of its commerce, reveal "liberty endlessly issuing from the fires of discord and sedition, the prince always tottering on an immovable throne" (PL #136, 231–2).[85]

Whereas Voltaire emphasizes the role of individual personalities and accidental factors in shaping the course of events, Montesquieu's historical accounts accord a much greater role to broad "general causes." In fact, in the *Considerations* he goes so far as to proclaim: "It is not fortune that rules the world.... There are general causes, moral and physical, which act in every monarchy, elevating it, maintaining it, or hurling it to the ground. All accidents are controlled by these causes. And if the chance of one battle – that is, a particular cause – has brought a state to

---

[83] See Montesquieu, *Considerations on the Causes of the Greatness of the Romans and Their Decline*, chapter 9 and 169.

[84] Ibid., 28–9.

[85] For a discussion of this chapter, see Chinard, "Montesquieu's Historical Pessimism," 166–7.

The Perils of Political Rationalism

ruin, some general cause made it necessary for that state to perish from a single battle. In a word, the principal trend draws with it all particular accidents."[86] Yet Montesquieu's view is not in fact quite as rigidly deterministic as this statement might seem to suggest. To begin with, he maintains in *The Spirit of the Laws* that broad "general causes" can be, and often should be, deliberately checked or counteracted through legislation and education (see SL 14.5–6, 236–7). Moreover, even in the *Considerations* he accepts that individuals often play a key role in shaping the path of history: "One of the causes of [Rome's] success was that its kings were all great men. Nowhere else in history can you find an uninterrupted succession of such statesmen and captains."[87] Similarly, Caesar was such an extraordinary man that "it would have been very difficult for him not to have been victorious, whatever army he commanded, and not to have governed any republic in which he was born."[88] It may be impossible for accidents and chance events to change broad historical trends, in Montesquieu's view – such as Rome's path from a republic to an empire, which had deep structural causes – but they *can* change the timing and the particular course of these broad trends. For instance, the comet that appeared after Caesar's assassination led the people to exalt his memory and thereby helped to reinforce Rome's imperial character at a crucial early stage.[89]

Even more importantly for our purposes, Montesquieu's belief that the broad contours of history are determined by general causes did *not* go hand in hand with an assumption that there is an overarching historical plan or design, or a perfect end point toward which the world must be moving. As David Carrithers writes, "to see rhyme and reason within

---

[86] Montesquieu, *Considerations on the Causes of the Greatness of the Romans and Their Decline*, 169. For another apparent statement of stark historical determinism, see Charles de Secondat, baron de Montesquieu, *De la politique*, in *Oeuvres complètes*, ed. Roger Caillois, vol. 1 (Paris: Gallimard, [1725] 1949), 114. For an examination of Montesquieu's (ultimately ambivalent) attitude toward historical determinism in the latter work as well as his "Reflections on the Character of Some Princes and on Some Events in Their Lives" (1731–33), see David Carrithers, "Montesquieu's Philosophy of History" *Journal of the History of Ideas* 47.1 (January–March 1986), 67–77.

[87] Montesquieu, *Considerations on the Causes of the Greatness of the Romans and Their Decline*, 25.

[88] Ibid., 106, but cf. also 107–8.

[89] See ibid., 115. On the role of contingency and human agency in the historical narrative of the *Considerations*, see also David W. Carrithers, "Montesquieu and Tocqueville as Philosophical Historians: Liberty, Determinism, and the Prospects for Freedom," in *Montesquieu and His Legacy*, ed. Rebecca E. Kingston (Albany: SUNY Press, 2009), 154–6; and Judith N. Shklar, *Montesquieu* (Oxford: Oxford University Press, 1987), 56–7.

a given series of events ... was not equivalent to perceiving a transcendent meaning in history. Montesquieu could discover that a certain series of historical happenings were set in motion by general causes without jumping to the conclusion that the overall pattern of events served some teleological goal or end."[90] Insofar as Montesquieu *does* speculate about the broad course of history, he eschews the notion of inevitable or endless progress and instead leans toward the notion of cyclical rise and fall, as exemplified by Rome. "Virtually all the nations of the world go around in this circle," he writes in his *Pensées*. "At first, they are barbarous; they conquer, and they become civilized nations; this civilization makes them bigger, and they become polite nations; politeness weakens them; they are conquered and become barbarous again" (Pensées #1917, 576; see also #100, 33; #1292, 356). This is why Montesquieu doubts that even England will enjoy its liberty and enlightenment indefinitely, and why he is in many ways even more pessimistic about the future than the author of *Candide*.

Hume's argument in favor of the superiority of the present and against the idea of a fall from ancient glory is even more forceful than Voltaire's and Montesquieu's; he makes this case at length in both the *History of England* and "Of the Populousness of Ancient Nations," by far the longest of his essays (see EMPL, 377–464). In Hume's view, "ages of refinement are both the happiest and most virtuous" (EMPL, 269), and "all kinds of government, free and absolute, seem to have undergone, in modern times, a great change for the better, with regard both to foreign and domestic management" (EMPL, 93). Likewise, he deprecates the past throughout his writings, perhaps most colorfully in a personal letter that is worth quoting at some length:

My Notion is, that the uncultivated Nations are not only inferior to civiliz'd in Government, civil, military, and eclesiastical; but also in Morals; and that their whole manner of Life is disagreeable and uneligible to the last Degree. I hope it will give no Offence ... if I declare my Opinion, that the English, till near the beginning of the last Century, are very much to be regarded as an uncultivated Nation; and that even *When good Queen Elizabeth sat on the Throne*, there was very little good Roast Beef in it, and no Liberty at all. [Even] The Castle of the Earl of Northumberland ... was no better than a Dungeon: No Chimney to let out the Smoak; no Glass Windows to keep out the Air; a glimmering Candle here and there, which coud scarce keep their Ragamuffins of Servants and Retainers

---

[90] Carrithers, "Montesquieu's Philosophy of History," 79. See also Lowenthal, translator's introduction in Montesquieu, *Considerations on the Causes of the Greatness of the Romans and Their Decline*, 13.

The Perils of Political Rationalism

from breaking their Shins or running foul of each other: No Diet but salt Beef and Mutton for nine Months of the Year, without Vegetables of any kind: Few Fires and these very poor ones.... For my part, I should rather chuse, for the Gratification of every Appetite and Passion, except that of Pride, to be a Footman in the present Family of the Duke and Dutchess of Northumberland, than to be at the head of it in the Reign of Harry the VII and VIII; And even on the head of Pride, I shoud expect in that humble station, from the courtly Demeanor of these two noble Persons better treatment, than the first of their Vassals at that time thought themselves entitled to.[91]

Given the innumerable disadvantages of earlier ages, Hume finds preposterous the widespread "humour of blaming the present, and admiring the past" (EMPL, 464; see also 278; HE III, 329; V, 142). This is one reason why he derides the popular Whig notion of an ideal "ancient constitution" that Britain should try to preserve or recover: those who truly wish to embrace Britain's ancient constitution, he mischievously suggests, should set an example by enslaving themselves to their local baron, since that was the condition of most people in most eras of recorded British history (see EMPL, 497–8).

Yet Hume does not deem modern European societies to be entirely without faults. He too accepts that "no advantages in this world are pure and unmixed" (EMPL, 130; see also 507) and that "good and ill are universally intermingled and confounded; happiness and misery, wisdom and folly, virtue and vice. Nothing is pure and entirely of a piece. All advantages are attended with disadvantages."[92] In the *Dialogues Concerning Natural Religion*, the character Philo, who is often taken to be Hume's mouthpiece, rails against Leibnizian optimism and the ceaseless miseries of this world, in the context of establishing that one cannot infer a benevolent God from the available evidence.[93] Nor did Hume believe that the progress that *had* been made would continue indefinitely. On the contrary, he holds that "there is a point of ... exaltation, from which human affairs naturally return in a contrary direction" (HE II, 519; see also EMPL, 135, 377–8).[94] Hence, almost immediately after rejoicing that "there has been

---

[91] David Hume, letter to the Reverend Thomas Percy, 16 January 1773, in *New Letters of David Hume*, ed. Raymond Klibansky and Ernest C. Mossner (Oxford: Clarendon Press, 1954), 198.

[92] David Hume, *The Natural History of Religion*, in *A Dissertation on the Passions and The Natural History of Religion*, ed. Tom L. Beauchamp (Oxford: Clarendon Press, [1757] 2007), 85.

[93] See David Hume, *Dialogues Concerning Natural Religion*, ed. J. C. A. Gaskin (Oxford: Oxford University Press, [1779] 1993), 95–115.

[94] In a letter to Lord Kames, Hume writes that "the growth of all bodies, artificial as well as natural, is stopped by internal causes, derived from their enormous size and greatness.

a sudden and sensible change in the opinions of men within these last fifty years, by the progress of learning and of liberty," he reminds us "that every government must come to a period, and that death is unavoidable to the political as well as to the animal body" (EMPL, 51).[95] Even in the letter quoted previously, after recounting the manifold ills of previous eras, he remarks, "I am only sorry to see, that the great Decline, if we ought not rather to say, the total Extinction of Literature in England, prognosticates a very short Duration of all our other Improvements, and threatens a new and sudden Inroad of Ignorance, Superstition and Barbarism."[96] As Emma Rothschild observes, in Hume's "dismal prospect" the achievements of modern civilization are continually threatened by the forces of enthusiasm and superstition, faction and corruption, empire and conquest.[97] Thus, in a letter to Turgot he politely but forcefully dissents from Turgot's conviction that "human Society is capable of perpetual Progress towards Perfection."[98]

As these statements about the precariousness of modern civilization suggest, Hume too rejects the idea that history follows a teleological path. Indeed, the very notion of inevitable progress implies an insight into the causal laws of historical development that his skepticism emphatically denies. In Hume's view, "no prudent man, however sure of his principles, dares prophesy concerning any event, or foretel the remote consequences of things" (EMPL, 47; see also 87–8). Further, like Voltaire, he underscores the importance of individual agency and accidental events

Great empires, great cities, great commerce, all of them receive a check, not from accidental events, but necessary principles." David Hume, letter to Henry Home, Lord Kames, 4 March 1758, in *The Letters of David Hume*, vol. 1, 272.

[95] After outlining his "perfect commonwealth," Hume declares that "it is needless to enquire, whether such a government would be immortal." Any government, no matter how well constructed, could be brought to ruin by "consuming plagues," "enthusiasm, or other extraordinary movements of the human mind," "whimsical and unaccountable factions," "extensive conquests," or simple "rust." Thus, he insists that it is pointless to pretend "to bestow, on any work of man, that immortality, which the Almighty seems to have refused to his own productions" (EMPL, 528–9).

[96] Hume, letter to the Reverend Thomas Percy, 16 January 1773, 199.

[97] Emma Rothschild, "The Atlantic Worlds of David Hume," in *Soundings in Atlantic History: Latent Structures and Intellectual Currents, 1500–1830*, ed. Bernard Bailyn and Patricia L. Denault (Cambridge, MA: Harvard University Press, 2009), 422. Similarly, J. G. A. Pocock writes that Hume is no "mere celebrant of modernity" and "like most Enlightened historians he thinks its achievement precarious and probably impermanent." J. G. A. Pocock, *Barbarism and Religion*, vol. 2: *Narratives of Civil Government* (Cambridge: Cambridge University Press, 1999), 197.

[98] David Hume, letter to Anne-Robert-Jacques Turgot, 16 June 1768, in *The Letters of David Hume*, vol. 2, 180–1.

The Perils of Political Rationalism

in shaping the course of history.[99] In the coda to the second volume of the *History of England* – the last volume he wrote – Hume remarks that a study of English history helps to reveal "the great mixture of accident, which commonly concurs with a small ingredient of wisdom and foresight, in erecting the complicated fabric of the most perfect government" (HE II, 525).[100] As he shows throughout the six volumes of that work, Britain's "entire system of liberty" was not just a product of broad social patterns such as the growth of commerce and the consequent rise of a middle class, but also of idiosyncratic factors such as the dogged resistance of Puritan fanatics and the personalities of figures such as Oliver Cromwell and William of Orange. For instance, while the stage for the Glorious Revolution was set by broad social forces, it still may not have occurred without William's ambition and resolve: "While every motive, civil and religious, concurred to alienate from the king [James II] every rank and denomination of men, it might be expected that his throne would, without delay, fall to pieces by its own weight," Hume remarks. "But such is the influence of established government; so averse are men from beginning hazardous enterprises; that, had not an attack been made from abroad, affairs might have remained in their present delicate situation, and James might at last have prevailed in his rash, and ill concerted projects" (HE VI, 496–7). As Richard Dees writes, in Hume's view liberty "is not the product of broad causal forces that make its rise inescapable. It is a monumental historical accident.... The English, Hume says, were deeply and profoundly lucky."[101] In short, despite his generally sanguine view of the present and his deeply negative view of the past, Hume is exceedingly skeptical of the idea of inevitable or endless progress, as of so much else.

---

[99] On this point, see Livingston, *Hume's Philosophy of Common Life*, 227–30.

[100] Similarly, in the third volume Hume declares that "the greatest affairs often depend on the most frivolous incidents" (HE III, 202). In "Of the Rise and Progress of the Arts and Sciences" he posits a methodological principle according to which "what depends upon a few persons is, in a great measure, to be ascribed to chance, or secret and unknown causes: What arises from a great number, may often be accounted for by determinate and known causes" (EMPL, 112). Yet Hume does not, like Montesquieu, suggest that the "determinate and known causes" will necessarily trump the "secret and unknown causes" in shaping the broad contours of an age, much less that they will determine the entire course of history. As Donald Livingston writes, Hume's point is simply that "on the whole, it is easier to predict, and therefore to explain, the behavior of groups than of individuals." Livingston, *Hume's Philosophy of Common Life*, 229.

[101] Richard H. Dees, "'One of the Finest and Most Subtle Inventions': Hume on Government," in *A Companion to Hume*, ed. Elizabeth S. Radcliffe (Oxford: Blackwell, 2008), 400.

Of the four thinkers who are the focus of this book, Smith is probably the one who is most often associated with the idea of inevitable progress. Gunnar Myrdal writes, for instance, that "a sunny optimism radiates from Smith's writing.... The world is for him harmonious. Enlightened self-interest increases social happiness."[102] Even Peter Gay maintains that *The Theory of Moral Sentiments* reveals Smith to be "something of a cosmic optimist who trusted unintended consequences" and who believed that "all is for the best in the only possible world that God could have made," although he grants that *The Wealth of Nations* shows "far greater respect for harsh truths and for the exceptions that modify all rules."[103] This reading of Smith derives some plausibility from the fact that he routinely speaks, in an economic context, of "the natural progress of things toward improvement," and frequently claims that as long as people enjoy security under the law this progress will generally trump almost all obstacles, including "the extravagance of government" and "the greatest errors of administration" (WN II.iii.31, 343; see also IV.v.b.43, 540; IV.ix.28, 674). His famous "invisible hand" is often taken to imply that the economic world is self-regulating and that even avaricious actions will automatically redound to the public interest. Moreover, one of the chief themes of Smith's writings is humanity's development from primitive hunting and gathering tribes to the civilized, commercial societies of his day – in Walter Bagehot's mocking phrase, "how, from being a savage, man rose to be a Scotchman."[104] Smith's "four stages" theory, which traces society's progress through its hunting, shepherding, agricultural, and commercial stages, appears to imply that society is destined to advance, in a linear and orderly fashion, through an ever-widening conquest of nature.

Yet this thoroughly optimistic reading of Smith overstates the case considerably. To begin with, Smith consistently argues that economic progress depends on ensuring that "every man" has the legal security "that he shall enjoy the fruits of his own labour" (WN IV.v.b.43, 540; see also II.iii.36, 345). This may seem to be a fairly minimal requirement, but he shows that throughout human history it has been fulfilled quite rarely.[105] Moreover, contrary to popular belief, Smith does *not* argue that

---

[102] Gunnar Myrdal, *The Political Element in the Development of Economic Theory* (London: Routledge & Kegan Paul, 1953), 107.

[103] Gay, *The Enlightenment: An Interpretation*, vol. 2, 361.

[104] Walter Bagehot, "Adam Smith as a Person," in *Biographical Studies* (London: Longmans, Green, 1895), 275–6.

[105] Not only do few people enjoy this kind of legal security in hunting, shepherding, or agricultural societies, according to Smith, but many commercial societies fail to provide it

The Perils of Political Rationalism

there is an automatic harmony of interests in society or that the mere avoidance of governmental interference is sufficient for an effective market economy. On the contrary, he claims that individual interests can be (largely) harmonized only if they are adequately channeled through the market, and that this requires the proper laws, institutions, and incentives.[106] The invisible hand that reconciles private interests with the public good is not the hand of God or Nature but rather that of competition, and competition cannot be assumed but rather must be ensured through legislation, especially through protections for property and restrictions on monopolies.

Smith rarely speculates about the economic future – he is much more concerned to explain the economic past – but some of the comments that he does offer are far from optimistic. He finds it extraordinarily unlikely that the mercantilist policies that he decries will ever be wholly eliminated: "To expect, indeed, that the freedom of trade should ever be entirely restored in Great Britain, is as absurd as to expect than an Oceana or Utopia should ever be established in it. Not only the prejudices of the publick, but what is much more unconquerable, the private interests of many individuals, irresistibly oppose it" (WN IV.ii.43, 471). Elsewhere, he remarks that two hundred years is "as long as the course of human prosperity usually endures" (WN III.iv.20, 425; see also I.ix.14, 111; II.v.22, 367) and proclaims that "the enormous debts which at present oppress ... will in the long-run probably ruin, all the great nations of Europe" (WN V.iii.10, 911). His occasional political prognostications are no more sanguine: in his lectures on jurisprudence, he speaks of "that fated dissolution that awaits every state and constitution whatever" (LJ, 414) and says of the Roman empire that "this government, as all others, seems to have a certain and fixed end which concludes it" (LJ, 238).[107]

Still further, Smith did not, any more than Voltaire, Montesquieu, or Hume, believe that the progress that had been achieved in eighteenth-century Europe was all-embracing. As much recent scholarship has stressed, Smith frequently points to the potential dangers and drawbacks

consistently and universally. Indeed, in the sentence quoted previously he goes on to say that even in England this security was not "perfected" until the revolution of 1688.

[106] The classic work on this aspect of Smith's thought is Nathan Rosenberg, "Some Institutional Aspects of the Wealth of Nations" *Journal of Political Economy* 68 (1960): 557–70.

[107] See also Smith's statement that "the violence and injustice of the rulers of mankind is an ancient evil, for which, I am afraid, the nature of human affairs can scarce admit of a remedy" (WN IV.iii.c.9, 493).

inherent in commercial society.[108] For instance: it necessarily produces great inequalities (see WN V.i.b.2, 709–10; LJ, 340–1, 490, 540); wealthy merchants and manufacturers will often collude against the public interest (see WN I.x.c.27, 145; I.xi.p.10, 267; IV.iii.c.9.9–10, 493–4; IV.viii.17, 648); an extensive division of labor can exact an immense cost in human dignity by rendering people feeble and ignorant (see WN V.i.f.50, 782; V.i.f.61, 788; LJ, 539–41); an emphasis on wealth and material goods can corrupt people's moral sentiments (see TMS I.iii.3.1, 61; IV.1.8, 181); and the desire for wealth often leads people to submit to endless toil and anxiety in the pursuit of frivolous material goods that provide only fleeting satisfaction (see TMS I.iii.2.1, 50–1; III.3.30–1, 149–50; IV.1.8–9, 181–3). Given Smith's occasional cynical statements about the future and his awareness of the many potential problems associated with commercial society, Robert Heilbroner concludes that there is a "profound pessimism" concealed within Smith's thought: "the disturbing import of *The Wealth of Nations*, taken in its entirety, is that it espouses a socio-economic system ... in which both decline and decay attend – material decline awaiting the terminus of the economic journey, moral decay suffered by society in the course of its journeying."[109] Other scholars have rightly noted that Heilbroner's conclusion fails to take sufficiently into account the various solutions and countermeasures that Smith offers for the problems that he identifies, which he believes would ameliorate many of them.[110] Still, these aspects of Smith's thought do underscore that he by no means sees "the natural progress of things" as inevitable or endless, and that he is well aware that no type of society can solve all problems. As Don Herzog writes, "Smith is no Pangloss. Natural liberty will have its problems too, even with his proposed state intervention and public education. In the world of concrete political alternatives, no measures are flawless."[111]

---

[108] For an overview, see Dennis C. Rasmussen, *The Problems and Promise of Commercial Society: Adam Smith's Response to Rousseau* (University Park: Pennsylvania State University Press, 2008), chapter 2.

[109] Robert L. Heilbroner, "The Paradox of Progress: Decline and Decay in *The Wealth of Nations*," in *Essays on Adam Smith*, ed. Andrew S. Skinner and Thomas Wilson (Oxford: Clarendon Press, 1975), 524.

[110] See, for instance, Lisa Hill, "Adam Smith and the Theme of Corruption" *Review of Politics* 68.4 (fall 2006), 646–7; Jerry Z. Muller, *Adam Smith in His Time and Ours: Designing the Decent Society* (Princeton, NJ: Princeton University Press, 1993), 246–7; and Patricia H. Werhane, *Adam Smith and His Legacy for Modern Capitalism* (Oxford: Oxford University Press, 1991), 171–3.

[111] Don Herzog, *Without Foundations: Justification in Political Theory* (Ithaca, NY: Cornell University Press, 1985), 211.

The Perils of Political Rationalism

As for the "four stages" theory, Smith uses this theory more as a heuristic device to compare different forms of society than as a rigid framework for how societies necessarily develop.[112] Contrary to what the theory is sometimes assumed to imply, Smith never suggests that history must move in a linear and orderly fashion. On the contrary, he maintains that "the natural course of things" is often diverted, as in modern Europe, where the development of commerce preceded the improvement of the countryside (see WN III.iv.18–19, 422), and he accepts that societies can and do move backward, as Europe did after the fall of Rome (see WN III.ii.1, 381–2; LJ, 49). Nor does he believe that a society's mode of subsistence wholly determines the other features of that society.[113] Smith's historical accounts rely on a number of different driving forces, including not just economic factors but also political and legal institutions; religious, geographical, and military considerations; the personalities and choices of individuals; and even simple accidents.[114] As we have seen, he points to two main historical sources of Britain's limited, mixed government, both of which are highly idiosyncratic: the fact that it is an island, which diminished the need for a large standing army (see LJ, 265–6, 270, 421), and the fact that Elizabeth sold off much of the Crown's lands, forcing her Stuart successors to rely on Parliament to raise revenue (see LJ, 266–7, 270, 420–1). Elsewhere, he proclaims that "one of the most happy parts of the British Constitution," judicial independence, was "introduced merely by chance and to ease the men in power."[115] Likewise, he declares

---

[112] On Smith's use of the "four stages" theory as a heuristic device, see Christopher J. Berry, *Social Theory of the Scottish Enlightenment* (Edinburgh: Edinburgh University Press, 1997), 114; Pocock, *Barbarism and Religion*, vol. 2, 322–3; Rasmussen, *The Problems and Promise of Commercial Society*, 99–101; and Andrew S. Skinner, *A System of Social Science: Papers Relating to Adam Smith*, second edition (Oxford: Clarendon Press, 1996), 82.

[113] The view of Smith as an economic determinist has been propounded especially by Marxist and Marxist-inspired scholars, who present him as a precursor to Marx in advancing a materialist interpretation of history. The most influential presentations of this position are Roy Pascal, "Property and Society: The Scottish Contribution of the Eighteenth Century" *Modern Quarterly* 1 (1938): 167–79; and Ronald L. Meek, "The Scottish Contribution to Marxist Sociology," in *Economics and Ideology and Other Essays: Studies in the Development of Economic Thought* (London: Chapman & Hall, 1967).

[114] See H. M. Hopfl, "From Savage to Scotsman: Conjectural History in the Scottish Enlightenment" *Journal of British Studies* 17.2 (spring 1978), especially 33–7; Knud Haakonssen, *The Science of a Legislator: The Natural Jurisprudence of David Hume and Adam Smith* (Cambridge: Cambridge University Press, 1981), chapter 8; and Donald Winch, *Adam Smith's Politics: An Essay in Historiographic Revision* (Cambridge: Cambridge University Press, 1978), 56–65.

[115] Adam Smith, *Lectures on Rhetoric and Belles Lettres*, ed. J. C. Bryce (Indianapolis: Liberty Fund, [1762–3] 1985), 176.

that after the English civil wars, the monarchy was restored "by such a concurrence of accidental circumstances as may not, upon any similar occasion, ever happen again."[116]

As with Voltaire, Montesquieu, and Hume, Smith's belief in progress, such as it was, was less about a blissful future that awaits us than about the ills that have abounded throughout human history. Indeed, significant portions of *The Wealth of Nations* and even larger portions of Smith's lectures on jurisprudence read as little more than extended descriptions of the astonishing range of afflictions that dominated the precommercial stages of society.[117] According to his account, "universal poverty" is the keynote to all aspects of life in the hunting stage (see WN V.i.b.7, 712). Given the lack of law and order and the scarcity of goods in these societies, he writes, "every savage ... is in continual danger [and] is often exposed to the greatest extremities of hunger, and frequently dies of pure want" (TMS V.2.9, 205). People in these societies – or at least the adult males (see LJ, 66, 143–4, 172) – may have a considerable degree of independence, but this personal freedom is difficult to enjoy simply because life is so utterly precarious: "unprotected by the laws of society, exposed, defenceless," a person in this kind of society "feels his weakness upon all occasions; his strength upon none."[118] The defining element of both the shepherding and agricultural stages, by contrast, is direct, personal dependence. Smith's chief example of these stages is feudal Europe, where the serfs – who constituted the vast majority of the population – were constantly and utterly subject to their lord's caprices: they had no property that was free from encroachment by their lord, they were bought and sold with the land and so were unable to move freely, they typically could not choose their own occupations, and they often had to obtain their lord's consent to marry (see WN III.ii.8, 386–7). While subsistence is not as precarious in the shepherding and agricultural stages as in the hunting stage, in other words, most people still enjoy very little liberty or security. This is perhaps the main lesson to be derived from Smith's "four stages" theory: commercial society constitutes a real advance, in his view, despite all of its problems, precisely because precommercial societies entail even

---

[116] Adam Smith, "Thoughts on the State of the Contest with America, February 1778," in *The Correspondence of Adam Smith*, ed. Ernest Campbell Mossner and Ian Simpson Ross (Indianapolis: Liberty Fund, 1987), 384.

[117] I outline Smith's account of the ills of precommercial societies at greater length in Rasmussen, *The Problems and Promise of Commercial Society*, 122–4, 141–4.

[118] Adam Smith, "The History of Astronomy," in *Essays on Philosophical Subjects*, ed. W. P. D. Wightman (Indianapolis: Liberty Fund, 1980), 48.

The Perils of Political Rationalism

greater problems. However, given that the rise of commercial society is not inevitable, that this kind of society is far from perfect, and that its future remains unclear, Smith's view is hardly one of "sunny optimism" or "cosmic optimism." Even Duncan Forbes, who sees the idea of progress as the "central theme and organizing principle" of Smith's thought, accepts that "his optimism had very definite limits.... the idea of progress of the school of Adam Smith has about it a cautious soberness lacking in Priestley and Godwin."[119]

In short, Hume, Smith, Montesquieu, and Voltaire all steadfastly avoided the kind of starry-eyed optimism that is so often attributed to the Enlightenment. To the extent that they believed in progress at all, their notion of it was much more retrospective than forward-looking, given that it stemmed more from their bleak view of the past than from their hopes for the future. These thinkers were well aware that throughout history civilizations had come and gone and would likely persist in doing so; that even the progress that had been achieved in eighteenth-century Europe was generally a mixed bag, with all of the advances and improvements complemented by important drawbacks and limitations; and that there is no reason to think that progress will continue indefinitely, or that a perfect society will ever be within human reach. Above all, they emphatically rejected the idea, which grew to be so common in the nineteenth century, that history has an overarching meaning or goal.

CONCLUSION

As we have seen throughout this chapter, Hume, Smith, Montesquieu, and Voltaire were every bit as opposed to political rationalism as they were to Cartesian rationalism. These thinkers all showed a strong preference for gradual reform and rejected the idea of imposing an abstract, comprehensive ideal on society from above, no matter how "rational" it may seem. Likewise, they all held that even if humanity had made real progress in certain realms, this progress was not inevitable and could not be endless or all-embracing. Indeed, their views stand in almost diametrical opposition to Paul Hazard's summary of the Enlightenment outlook:

The light of reason, they declared, should dispel the great masses of darkness that enshrouded the earth. They would rediscover Nature's plan. Once they had done that, all they would have to do would be to conform to it, and so restore to

---

[119] Duncan Forbes, "'Scientific' Whiggism: Adam Smith and John Millar" *Cambridge Journal* 7.2 (August 1954), 643, 649–50.

230 *The Pragmatic Enlightenment*

the human race its long-lost birthright of happiness.... Then, indeed, it would be heaven upon earth. In the beautiful bright buildings they would erect, all would be well with the generations of the future.[120]

Of course, these four figures may be among the least likely candidates, among Enlightenment thinkers, for inclusion in Hazard's caricature. While Voltaire is sometimes held to be a political rationalist or pro-torevolutionary and Smith is sometimes seen as a prophet of progress, Hazard's sketch bears a much greater resemblance to the views of, say, Thomas Paine or some of the more radical philosophes. As with the other critiques discussed in this book, however, if the charge of rationalism in politics does not apply to such central figures of the period as Hume, Smith, Montesquieu, and Voltaire, then it can hardly be said to apply to the Enlightenment more broadly. Nor are the arguments of these four thinkers irrelevant even today, when so much of academic political theory and philosophy is dedicated to "ideal theory" – that is, to the search for a perfectly just or rational order, rather than for potentially practicable reforms to existing institutions – and when Whiggish claims about the inevitable march of progress and the end of history retain their Sirens' charm for many. While contemporary liberals frequently deride the Enlightenment for its blind faith in reason, many of them would in fact benefit from a dose of these thinkers' cautious pragmatism.

[120] Hazard, *European Thought in the Eighteenth Century*, xviii.

ATOMISTIC INDIVIDUALISM?

5

The Social and Encumbered Self

In addition to the idea that the Enlightenment espoused a hegemonic form of moral and political universalism and the claim that it had an unreasonable faith in reason, a third broad indictment of this period and movement remains to be considered: the allegation that it fostered atomistic individualism. The basic charge is concisely (and memorably) articulated by James Q. Wilson:

> a fatally flawed assumption of many Enlightenment thinkers [is] that autonomous individuals can freely choose, or will, their moral life. Believing that individuals are everything [and] rights are trumps ... such thinkers have been led to design laws, practices, and institutions that leave nothing between the state and the individual save choices, contracts, and entitlements. Fourth-grade children being told how to use condoms is only one of the more perverse of the results.[1]

There are two basic components of this critique. The more strictly political component concerns the tendency of Enlightenment thinkers to favor negative liberty over positive liberty and commerce over public-spiritedness – their supposed belief that "individuals are everything," that "rights are trumps," and that people should be bound together by nothing but "choices, contracts, and entitlements." This part of the critique will be the subject of Chapter 6. The other component, which will be addressed in this chapter, is related to the Enlightenment's view of human nature, which many critics contend was overly simplistic and individualistic – the alleged assumption that "autonomous individuals can freely choose, or

---

[1] James Q. Wilson, *The Moral Sense* (New York: Free Press, 1993), 250; see also 244–6; and James Q. Wilson, *On Character: Essays by James Q. Wilson* (Washington, DC: AEI Press, 1991), 37–8.

233

will, their moral life." According to this line of argument, Enlightenment thinkers went overboard in their efforts to free people from all forms of dependence and began to conceive of the individual as entirely self-determining and self-sufficient. The critics insist that this view of the self is implausible, given that human beings are fundamentally shaped by their societies, their traditions, and their attachments to others, as well as harmful, given that it leaves the individual not emancipated but rather detached, rootless, and isolated.

The idea that Enlightenment thinkers adopted this kind of reductive view of human nature found some of its earliest proponents in Edmund Burke, J. G. Herder, and Joseph de Maistre, the latter of whom famously declared that while he had met Frenchmen, Italians, Russians, and so on, he had never met the abstract "man" of Enlightenment philosophy.[2] This idea was also prominent among nineteenth-century historicists such as G. W. F. Hegel, who tended to conceive of society in organic, holistic terms.[3] The principal expression of this criticism in recent years has come from communitarians such as Michael Sandel and Charles Taylor.[4] Sandel argues that today's prevailing public philosophy, a procedural form of liberalism that attempts to remain neutral toward the moral and religious views of its citizens, rests on the Enlightenment understanding of people as "unencumbered selves" who stand apart from their experiences and attachments to choose their own values freely.[5] He insists, against this view, that our attachments and values are not merely things

---

[2] See Joseph de Maistre, *Considerations on France*, trans. Richard A. Lebrun (Cambridge: Cambridge University Press, [1797] 1994), 53.

[3] On Hegel's critique of the Enlightenment, see Lewis P. Hinchman, *Hegel's Critique of the Enlightenment* (Gainesville: University Press of Florida, 1984); and Steven B. Smith, *Hegel's Critique of Liberalism: Rights in Context* (Chicago: University of Chicago Press, 1991), chapter 3.

[4] This complaint has been voiced by others as well, including many feminists. For instance, Jane Flax claims that the Enlightenment notion of an asocial and autonomous self requires ignoring the fact that gender and family play key roles in shaping our identities, thereby devaluing these aspects of our lives. See Jane Flax, *Thinking Fragments: Psychoanalysis, Feminism, and Postmodernism in the Contemporary West* (Berkeley: University of California Press, 1990), 229.

[5] See Michael J. Sandel, *Liberalism and the Limits of Justice*, second edition (Cambridge: Cambridge University Press, [1982] 1998); and Michael J. Sandel, *Democracy's Discontent: America in Search of a Public Philosophy* (Cambridge, MA: Harvard University Press, 1996). While Sandel's critique is aimed primarily at John Rawls and his "veil of ignorance," he sees the notion of the "unencumbered self" implicit in this construct as "perhaps the fullest expression of the Enlightenment's quest for the self-defining subject." Michael J. Sandel, "The Procedural Republic and the Unencumbered Self" *Political Theory* 12.1 (February 1984), 87.

The Social and Encumbered Self

to be chosen at a distance, but rather essential parts of who we *are*: it makes no sense to theorize about individuals in the abstract, since people are always members of a particular community, a tradition, a religion, a family, and since these kinds of attachments are what give us character and moral depth. Similarly, Taylor attributes much of the shallowness and emptiness that he sees in the modern world to the Enlightenment's vision of a "disengaged" or "self-defining" subject who chooses his or her own goals and way of life, unconstrained by authority or tradition.[6] Taylor too claims that people's identities and values can only be properly understood in relation to their communities, that "one cannot be a self on one's own" and thus that the Enlightenment view of the self is narrow and unconvincing.[7]

As with a number of the other critiques discussed in this book, there is *some* validity to this charge with respect to figures such as Locke, whose *Second Treatise* envisions abstract individuals contracting to form a civil society in order to further their own self-interest, and Kant, whose moral theory accords a central role to the notion of individual autonomy.[8] Of all the charges addressed in this study, however, this is perhaps the most flatly wrong as applied to Hume, Smith, Montesquieu, and Voltaire.[9]

---

[6] See Charles Taylor, *Hegel* (Cambridge: Cambridge University Press, 1975), 3–11; and Charles Taylor, *Sources of the Self: The Making of the Modern Identity* (Cambridge, MA: Harvard University Press, 1989), 322–32, 514. It should be noted that Taylor admits that a few "high Enlightenment" thinkers – he singles out Diderot and Hume – were less confident in the efficacy of disengaged reason than the "radical Enlightenment" on which he focuses. As with most critics, however, he continues to paint the Enlightenment in fairly broad strokes. See ibid., 340–7.

[7] Ibid., 36.

[8] It is perhaps not surprising, then, that Locke serves as Taylor's archetype of an atomistic liberal and that Kant is the key historical target of Sandel's critique of the notion of an "unencumbered self." Although it is not my purpose to defend Locke or Kant in this book, Taylor's and Sandel's appraisals seem to me overstated even with respect to these thinkers. One might note, for instance, that Locke's *Some Thoughts Concerning Education* is in fact a meditation on the importance (and inevitability) of socialization, and that the chapter on paternal power in the *Second Treatise* shows Locke to be fully aware that people are born into families, at the very least. Similarly, recent scholarship has emphasized the degree to which even Kant saw people as social and cultural agents. See, for example, Sankar Muthu, *Enlightenment against Empire* (Princeton, NJ: Princeton University Press, 2003), chapters 4–5.

[9] One scholar goes so far as to claim that "man has never been conceived of less as a solitary being" than during the French Enlightenment. See Robert Mauzi, *L'idée du bonheur dans la littérature et la pensée française au XVIIIe siècle* (Paris: Armand Colin, 1960), 590. On the social nature of human beings as a core tenet of the Scottish Enlightenment, see Christopher J. Berry, *Social Theory of the Scottish Enlightenment* (Edinburgh: Edinburgh University Press, 1997), chapter 2. Finally, on the central role of society and

The Pragmatic Enlightenment

First of all, these four thinkers were unequivocal in affirming that human beings are inherently social – drawn to others not just for instrumental reasons but also out of an innate desire for companionship. The communitarian criticisms of the Enlightenment are often leveled especially at the idea of the social contract, which seems to presuppose that people are individuals first and foremost, and part of a community only conditionally and by choice.[10] However, Hume, Smith, Montesquieu, and Voltaire all *opposed* this idea, not only because they denied that this kind of thought experiment could yield a universally applicable standard of political legitimacy, as we saw in Chapter 2, but also because they did not think that individuals *choose* to be a part of a society, much less that they contract to do so at a discrete moment in time. They rejected the notion of a presocial state of nature, and they held that political institutions arise spontaneously and gradually over time, more from necessity and habit than consent or contract. Moreover, these thinkers all concurred that people's characters, beliefs, and values are deeply shaped by their circumstances and their interactions with others, rather than somehow developed in a vacuum. Far from demanding a strong form of moral autonomy or envisioning individuals as stepping back from their particular circumstances to choose their own values, they argued that it is only in and through society that people become moral beings at all. In short, these thinkers did not see human beings as abstract, self-interested atoms at their core; on the contrary, they consistently saw them as fundamentally interdependent, not only economically and politically, but also morally and psychologically.

"THE MINDS OF MEN ARE MIRRORS TO ONE ANOTHER"

Several leading modern thinkers have contended, against the ancient view that man is by nature a political animal, that human beings are in fact radically asocial by nature. The most prominent exponents of this view are probably Thomas Hobbes and Jean-Jacques Rousseau, both of whom argue that life in the state of nature must have been almost completely

---

human sociability in Enlightenment thought more generally, see David Carrithers, "The Enlightenment Science of Society," in *Inventing Human Science*, ed. Christopher Fox, Roy Porter, and Robert Wokler (Berkeley: University of California Press, 1995).

[10] Nor are the communitarian critics alone in associating the Enlightenment with the notion of the social contract: even Ernst Cassirer declares that "eighteenth century political thought is based on [the] theory of the contract." Ernst Cassirer, *The Philosophy of the Enlightenment*, trans. Fritz C. A. Koelln and James P. Pettegrove (Princeton, NJ: Princeton University Press, [1932] 1979), 19.

The Social and Encumbered Self   237

asocial, although their arguments are based on nearly opposite grounds –
the former on the assumption that without a sovereign to enforce order
people would be driven apart by competition and combat, and the latter on the supposition that without the trappings of civilization people
would be self-sufficient and therefore indifferent to others.[11] In stark contrast to both of these views, Hume maintains that human beings are naturally drawn to live and associate with others. He states, for instance,
that "men cannot live without society" (THN 2.3.1.9, 259), that "men
always seek society" (THN 2.3.1.8, 258, Hume's italics), and indeed that
"man [is] the creature of the universe, who has the most ardent desire of
society, and is fitted for it by the most advantages" (THN 2.2.5.15, 234).
Given that people are naturally inclined to unite with others, in Hume's
view, humanity's "very first state and situation may justly be esteem'd
social," and the idea of a solitary state of nature is "a mere philosophical fiction, which never had, and never cou'd have any reality" (THN
3.2.2.14, 316–17; see also EPM 3.15–16, 17). As he succinctly states,
people are "compelled to maintain society, from necessity, from natural
inclination, and from habit" – that is, because they are obliged to do so in
order to fulfill their needs, because they instinctively want to do so, and
because they grow used to it from an early age (EMPL, 37; see also THN,
3.2.2.4, 312). In fact, human beings are inherently so sociable, according
to Hume, that "we can form no wish, which has not a reference to society. A perfect solitude is, perhaps, the greatest punishment we can suffer"
(THN 2.2.5.15, 234). "Let all the powers and elements of nature con-
spire to serve and obey one man: Let the sun rise and set at his command:
The sea and rivers roll as he pleases, and the earth furnish spontaneously

---

[11] While Hobbes extrapolates from social life in establishing what the state of nature would
look like – for instance, the fact that his contemporaries felt the need to lock their doors
and to arm themselves when they went on journeys – most of his comments on the state
of nature itself suggest that he sees it as one of almost complete isolation. For instance,
he declares that the state of nature consists in a war "of every man against every man,"
that "men live without other security than what their own strength and their own invention shall furnish them," and, most famously, that life in this state is "*solitary*, poor,
nasty, brutish, and short." Thomas Hobbes, *Leviathan*, ed. Edwin Curley (Indianapolis:
Hackett, [1651] 1994), I.13.8–9, 76, emphasis added. On the other hand, he also remarks
that "the savage people in many places of *America*" live in a condition akin to the state
of nature, and he acknowledges that they lived in "small families," at least. Ibid., I.13.11,
77. Rousseau, by contrast, argues quite explicitly that even familial bonds must have
been absent in the "pure" state of nature. See Jean-Jacques Rousseau, *Discourse on the
Origin and the Foundations of Inequality among Men*, in *The Discourses and Other
Early Political Writings*, trans. Victor Gourevitch (Cambridge: Cambridge University
Press, [1755] 1997), 145.

238   *The Pragmatic Enlightenment*

whatever may be useful or agreeable to him," he proposes. "He will still be miserable, till you give him some one person at least, with whom he may share his happiness, and whose esteem and friendship he may enjoy" (THN 2.2.5.15, 235).

While Hume presumes that some form of society has existed for as long as human beings have existed, he accepts that government and law are artificial contrivances.[12] In the late essay "Of the Origin of Government," he declares that eventually people "establish political society, in order to administer justice; without which there can be no peace among them" (EMPL, 37; see also HE I, 445, 488). Like the social contract theorists, then, he holds that government and law are instituted in order to protect people and their property from encroachment by others. Hume denies, however, that these institutions arise all at once, through an express agreement. Rather, "government commences more casually and more imperfectly," with an individual (such as a chieftain) gradually gaining more and more power as people come to recognize the benefits of having a leader to make decisions and enforce order (EMPL, 39; see also 40, 468–9). In other words, political authority is more a convention that evolves over time within a group than a result of a conscious choice or contract among individuals. As Donald Livingston notes, there is a kind of consent involved in the formation of government, in Hume's view, but "it is not the consent of a self-reflective, self-assertive individual. Rather, it is ... the 'consent' of the sort, for example, without which language would be impossible. It is deeply social and not self-assertive."[13] Hume opposes social contract theory for many reasons, as we have seen throughout this study, but one of the foremost among them is its implausibly individualistic premises.[14]

It is important to stress, as well, that Hume's claim that there would be no peace among people without a government to administer justice does *not* imply that he sees people as naturally hostile to one another, or even as wholly selfish. "So far from thinking, that men have no affection for any thing beyond themselves," he declares, "I am of [the] opinion,

[12] Hume argues that "tho' government be an invention very advantageous, and even in some circumstances absolutely necessary to mankind; it is not necessary in all circumstances, nor is it impossible for men to preserve society for some time, without having recourse to such invention" (THN 3.2.8.1, 345). He goes on to give the example of American Indian tribes who live together without a formal government.

[13] Donald W. Livingston, *Philosophical Melancholy and Delirium: Hume's Pathology of Philosophy* (Chicago: University of Chicago Press, 1998), 186.

[14] See Frederick G. Whelan, "Hume and Contractarianism" *Polity* 27.2 (winter 1994), 218–19.

The Social and Encumbered Self

that tho' it be rare to meet with one, who loves any single person better than himself; yet 'tis as rare to meet with one, in whom all the kind affections, taken together, do not over-ballance all the selfish" (THN 3.2.2.5, 313; see also EMPL, 84–5). Hence, he consistently rejects psychological egoism, or the idea – which he associates especially with Hobbes and Mandeville, but also to some degree with Locke (see EPM App. 2.3, 91) – that self-interest is the only real motivating force of human action.[15] This view simply cannot do justice to the ubiquity of sentiments such as romantic and parental love, friendship, gratitude, compassion, and generosity (see EPM App. 2.6–11, 92–4). Recall also the central role that sympathy, the faculty that communicates to us the feelings and sentiments of others, plays in Hume's conception of human nature.[16] Empirically speaking, he thinks, it is obvious that we care about and sympathize with others, particularly those who are closest to us. Thus, even if the maxim that "every man ought to be supposed a *knave*, and to have no other end, in all his actions, than private interest" is "true in *politics*" – that is, even if it is prudent to suppose that everyone will act as a knave when judging a political order – this maxim is undoubtedly "false in *fact*" (EMPL, 42–3, Hume's italics).

Moreover, Hume emphasizes, every bit as heavily as Sandel and Taylor later would, that people are fundamentally shaped by their societies and their interactions with others. Given that he sees all knowledge as resting on experience and that our direct, personal experiences are necessarily limited, he holds that many – perhaps even most – of our beliefs and opinions are ultimately derived from our education and from those around us. "All those opinions and notions of things, to which we have been accustom'd from our infancy, take such deep root, that 'tis impossible for us, by all the powers of reason and experience, to eradicate them," he writes (THN 1.3.9.17, 80; see also 1.3.9.19, 80–1).[17] This is one important reason why it is habit or "custom," and not reason, that is "the great guide of human life" (EHU 5.6, 38). And, again, Hume holds

---

[15] Hume claims that "generally speaking, the representations of [selfishness] have been carry'd much too far; and … the descriptions, which certain philosophers delight so much to form of mankind in this particular, are as wide of nature as any accounts of monsters, which we meet with in fables and romances" (THN 3.2.2.5, 313). On Hume's rejection of psychological egoism, see also Frederick G. Whelan, *Order and Artifice in Hume's Political Philosophy* (Princeton, NJ: Princeton University Press, 1985), 161–7.

[16] For a study of the role of sympathy throughout Hume's writings, see Jennifer A. Herdt, *Religion and Faction in Hume's Moral Philosophy* (Cambridge: Cambridge University Press, 1997).

[17] See also Whelan, *Order and Artifice in Hume's Political Philosophy*, 117–36.

240   *The Pragmatic Enlightenment*

that we naturally sympathize with others, meaning that our emotions or sentiments are also deeply influenced by those around us; in this sense, too, "the minds of men are mirrors to one another" (THN 2.2.6.21, 236). In *A Dissertation on the Passions*, Hume argues that "our opinions of all kinds are strongly affected by society and sympathy," going so far as to assert that "it is almost impossible for us to support any principle or sentiment, against the universal consent of every one, with whom we have any friendship or correspondence."[18] Still further, one of the upshots of Hume's famously labyrinthine discussion of personal identity in *A Treatise of Human Nature* is that our very self-conception – our sense of ourselves as unique individuals who exist over time – relies in large part on others and the "mirror" that they provide. For Hume, as Annette Baier writes, "the self is ... dependent on others for its coming to be, for its emotional life, for its self-consciousness, for its self-evaluations."[19]

Hume holds, in addition, that the socially constituted nature of the self is what underpins much of the variation among societies in terms of manners and customs. As he characterizes it in the essay "Of National Characters," "the human mind is of a very imitative nature," so that it is scarcely possible "for any set of men to converse often together, without acquiring a similitude of manners." In particular, "where a number of men are united into one political body, the occasions of their intercourse must be so frequent, for defence, commerce, and government, that, together with the same speech or language, they must acquire a resemblance in their manners, and have a common or national character, as well as a personal one, peculiar to each individual" (EMPL, 202–3). Hume warns that the concept of "national character" should not be taken to an extreme: we should bear in mind, for instance, that a society's manners and customs often change over time (see EMPL, 205–6) and that broad national characteristics by no means determine the character of every individual within a nation (see EMPL, 197; and THN 1.3.13.7, 100). Still, he believes that the influence of society on people's beliefs and sentiments is such that "some particular qualities are more frequently to be met with among one people than among their neighbours" (EMPL, 197). He

---

[18] David Hume, *A Dissertation on the Passions*, in *A Dissertation on the Passions and The Natural History of Religion*, ed. Tom L. Beauchamp (Oxford: Clarendon Press, [1757] 2007), 14. Similarly, he writes in the *History of England* that "men, guided more by custom than by reason, follow, without enquiry, the manners, which are prevalent in their own time" (HE II, 86).

[19] Annette C. Baier, *A Progress of Sentiments: Reflections on Hume's Treatise* (Cambridge, MA: Harvard University Press, 1991), 130.

The Social and Encumbered Self

ascribes the variation among societies far less to "physical causes" such as climate and terrain than to "moral causes" such as a society's form of government, religion, education, and levels of commerce and wealth.[20] Thus, differences in national character offer still further confirmation of "the great force of custom and education, which mould the human mind from its infancy, and form it into a fixed and established character" (EHU 8.11, 66).

Given that Hume understands human beings to be both naturally social and deeply influenced by their societies, his empiricist "science of man" acknowledges the impossibility of comprehending them as abstract, isolated individuals. In the introduction to the *Treatise*, he points out that in the study of human nature it is impossible to run experiments with control groups composed of individuals who are free of cultural influences and connections to others. Thus, he declares, "we must ... glean up our experiments in this science from a cautious observation of human life, and take them as they appear in the common course of the world, and by men's behaviour in company, in affairs, and in their pleasures" (THN intro.10, 6).[21] As Baier shows brilliantly, the broad movement of the *Treatise* is one away from pure, abstract rationalism and toward a more social and sentimental conception of the self and philosophy.[22] Hume begins the work with a consideration of the isolated, self-sufficient Cartesian intellect, but by the end of book 1 this entire notion has been subverted through a kind of reductio ad absurdum. At the close of that book, Hume writes that his skeptical conclusions have left him "affrighted and confounded with that forlorn solitude, in which I am plac'd in my philosophy," and that he has come to see himself as "some strange uncouth monster, who not being able to mingle and unite in society, has been expell'd [from] all human commerce, and left utterly abandon'd and disconsolate" (THN 1.4.7.1, 172). Famously, it is a return to society that cures him of this "philosophical melancholy and delirium": "I dine, I play a game of back-gammon, I converse, and am

---

[20] See especially THN 2.1.11.2, 206; and EMPL, 203 ff. At one point Hume denies that physical causes have *any* influence on national character (see EMPL, 200), but in a slightly later statement he suggests that climate may play some role after all (see EMPL, 266–7). For a comparison of Hume and Montesquieu on this topic, see Paul E. Chamley, "The Conflict between Montesquieu and Hume," in *Essays on Adam Smith*, ed. Andrew S. Skinner and Thomas Wilson (Oxford: Clarendon Press, 1975).

[21] See also James Moore, "The Social Background of Hume's Science of Human Nature," in *McGill Hume Studies*, ed. David Fate Norton, Nicholas Capaldi, and Wade L. Robison (San Diego: Austin Hill Press, 1979), 24.

[22] See Baier, *A Progress of Sentiments*.

merry with my friends; and when after three or four hour's amusement, I wou'd return to these speculations, they appear so cold, and strain'd, and ridiculous, that I cannot find in my heart to enter into them any farther" (THN 1.4.7.9, 175). In the rest of the work – books 2 and 3 – Hume goes on to underscore the passionate, sympathetic nature of the human mind and the fact that morality is ineliminably social and intersubjective. Nicholas Capaldi argues that this approach constituted nothing less than a "Copernican revolution" in philosophy: rather than seeking to understand the world from "the perspective of the egocentric, outside, disengaged observer" – an approach that boasts a venerable philosophical lineage, but that is associated especially with Descartes – Hume considers human beings "fundamentally as agents, as doers, immersed in both a physical world and a social world along with other agents."[23] In this, his thought stands in direct opposition to the communitarian caricature of the Enlightenment.

"HOW SELFISH SOEVER MAN MAY BE SUPPOSED ..."

Much more than Hume, Smith is sometimes thought to have regarded human beings as basically self-interested, if not downright selfish. One of the most frequently quoted passages in his writings, after all, holds that "it is not from the benevolence of the butcher, the brewer, or the baker, that we expect our dinner, but from their regard to their own interest. We address ourselves, not to their humanity but to their self-love, and never talk to them of our own necessities but of their advantages" (WN I.ii.2, 27). Thus, George Stigler lauds *The Wealth of Nations* as "a stupendous palace erected upon the granite of self-interest,"[24] and Joseph Crospey argues that Smith stands as a "disciple" of Hobbes in placing self-love and the desire for self-preservation at the heart of his understanding of human nature.[25] The idea that Smith conceives of people as fundamentally self-interested or selfish is belied, however, by the very first

---

[23] Capaldi describes this as a shift from an *I Think* perspective to a *We Do* perspective. Nicholas Capaldi, *Hume's Place in Moral Philosophy* (New York: Peter Lang, 1989), 22–3.

[24] George J. Stigler, "Smith's Travels on the Ship of State," in *Essays on Adam Smith*, ed. Andrew S. Skinner and Thomas Wilson (Oxford: Clarendon Press, 1975), 237.

[25] See Joseph Cropsey, *Polity and Economy: With Further Thoughts on the Principles of Adam Smith* (South Bend, IN: St. Augustine's Press, [1957] 2001), 34 and passim. For a response to Cropsey on this point, see Samuel Fleischacker, *On Adam Smith's Wealth of Nations: A Philosophical Companion* (Princeton, NJ: Princeton University Press, 2004), 100–3.

The Social and Encumbered Self

sentence of his first book: "How selfish soever man may be supposed," he writes, "there are evidently some principles in his nature, which interest him in the fortune of others, and render their happiness necessary to him, though he derives nothing from it except the pleasure of seeing it" (TMS I.i.1.1, 9). Smith goes on, in *The Theory of Moral Sentiments*, to reject vehemently the idea, which he attributes to Hobbes and Mandeville, that all sentiments and actions can ultimately be reduced to self-love (see TMS VII.iii.1.1–4, 315–17).[26]

Like Hume, Smith accords sympathy an absolutely central role in his conception of human nature. He emphasizes that we do not sympathize with all people equally: we are far more likely to identify with and care about those who are close to us than perfect strangers, for instance.[27] Yet this is often enough, he suggests, to encourage a sincere attachment to society more broadly: "Not only we ourselves, but all the objects of our kindest affections, our children, our parents, our relations, our friends, our benefactors, all those whom we naturally love and revere the most, are commonly comprehended within [our society].... It is by nature, therefore, endeared to us, not only by all our selfish, but by all our private benevolent affections" (TMS VI.ii.2.2, 227).[28] Indeed, Smith sees sympathy as so vital to the human makeup that he insists that even the pursuit of wealth is generally motivated less by material needs or desires than by the desire to be sympathized with and approved of by others (see TMS I.iii.2.1, 50–1). While we are undoubtedly sensible to appeal to the self-interest of the butcher, the brewer, and the baker when procuring our dinner rather than to hope that they will offer their wares for free, then, Smith by no means sees this kind of commercial transaction as representative of all human interactions, or self-love as underpinning all sentiments and motivations.[29]

---

[26] On Smith's rejection of psychological egoism, see Patricia H. Werhane, *Adam Smith and His Legacy for Modern Capitalism* (Oxford: Oxford University Press, 1991).

[27] This is the theme of part VI, section 2, of *The Theory of Moral Sentiments*. For an extended examination of the varying levels of sympathy in Smith's thought and their implications, see Fonna Forman-Barzilai, *Adam Smith and the Circles of Sympathy: Cosmopolitanism and Moral Theory* (Cambridge: Cambridge University Press, 2010).

[28] To be sure, Smith does not suggest that our "benevolent affections" are restricted *exclusively* to our own society: in principle, at least, "our good-will is circumscribed by no boundary, but may embrace the immensity of the universe" (TMS VI.ii.3.1, 235).

[29] Moreover, as Samuel Fleischacker notes, Smith's emphasis in this famous line is less on the butcher's, brewer's, and baker's self-love than on the *customer's* ability to understand and appeal to their interests, and on the mutual benefits that accrue from their exchange. Thus, "instead of an almost Ayn Randian exaltation of self-love," this statement in fact highlights "our capacity to be *other*-directed." Fleischacker, *On Adam Smith's Wealth of Nations*, 91.

244   *The Pragmatic Enlightenment*

Given the centrality of sympathy to Smith's conception of human nature, it should come as no surprise that he too sees people as naturally social. He declares that "man, who can subsist only in society, was fitted by nature to that situation for which he was made" (TMS II.ii.3.1, 85) and that "nature, when she formed man for society, endowed him with an original desire to please, and an original aversion to offend his brethren" (TMS III.2.6, 116). Smith holds, like Hume, that people are drawn to live and associate with others not just for instrumental reasons such as the attainment of security or the augmentation of their material interests but also (and especially) because society and mutual sympathy are necessary for them to flourish psychologically.[30] Nearly all people have an instinctive "horror of solitude" (TMS II.ii.2.3, 84; see also IV.2.12, 193), according to Smith, and interacting with others helps to keep us on an even keel whether we are experiencing good fortune or adversity: "society and conversation ... are the most powerful remedies for restoring the mind to its tranquillity, if, at any time, it has unfortunately lost it; as well as the best preservatives of that equal and happy temper, which is so necessary to self-satisfaction and enjoyment" (TMS I.i.4.10, 23; see also III.3.39–40, 154). Indeed, so important is the sympathy of others to our well-being, in his view, that he proclaims that "the chief part of human happiness arises from the consciousness of being beloved" (TMS I.ii.5.1, 41; see also I.ii.4.1, 39; III.1.7, 113).

Thus, in stark contrast to thinkers such as Mandeville and Rousseau, who "suppose, that there is in man no powerful instinct which necessarily determines him to seek society for its own sake," Smith eschews the notion of a presocial state of nature.[31] Nothing he writes about human beings or their history suggests that they could have ever lived in isolation; the "lowest and rudest state of society" in his "four stages" schema, that of the hunting stage, is still a *society* (WN V.i.a.2, 689). Smith also joins Hume in positing both that the need for government emerges only with the advent of extensive private property (see WN V.i.b.2, 709–10) and that political institutions develop by degrees, *within* society, rather than through a social contract among isolated individuals (see LJ, 207). In his view, "civil government gradually grows up" over time as certain individuals acquire authority over others on the basis of characteristics

---

[30] See James R. Otteson, *Adam Smith's Marketplace of Life* (Cambridge: Cambridge University Press, 2002), 90–1.

[31] Adam Smith, "Letter to the *Edinburgh Review*," in *Essays on Philosophical Subjects*, ed. J. C. Bryce (Indianapolis: Liberty Fund, [1756] 1980), 250.

The Social and Encumbered Self 245

such as age, wealth, birth, and "personal qualifications" such as strength, wisdom, and virtue (see WN V.i.b.3–8, 710–13).

Yet again like Hume, Smith maintains that people are fundamentally shaped by their societies and their interactions with others. As he describes it, the socialization process starts early in life, as children learn to moderate their passions "to the degree to which [their] play-fellows and companions are likely to be pleased with" (TMS III.3.22, 145). More generally, Smith holds that we have a "natural disposition to accommodate and to assimilate, as much as we can, our own sentiments, principles, and feelings, to those which we see fixed and rooted in the persons whom we are obliged to live and converse a great deal with" (TMS VI.ii.1.17, 224). Thus, the sentiments, beliefs, and customs that are common in our society – especially those that are common among our family, friends, schoolmates, coworkers, neighbors, and other acquaintances – become familiar to us, and even ingrained in us, such that we come to take them more or less for granted (see TMS V.2.2, 200–1). As we have seen, Smith posits that the effects of these kinds of environmental influences are so great that "the difference between the most dissimilar characters, between a philosopher and a common street porter, for example, seems to arise not so much from nature, as from habit, custom, and education" (WN I.ii.4, 28–9). Similarly, he highlights the fact that different "stations of life" promote different character traits. In "the middling and inferior stations of life," he suggests, people depend heavily on "the favour and good opinion of their neighbours and equals," and this tends to encourage prudent, honorable conduct (TMS I.iii.3.5, 63). Those in "the superior stations of life," by contrast, often fail to exhibit such conduct because they depend more on sycophancy and submissiveness to advance their interests: "In the courts of princes, in the drawing-rooms of the great, where success and preferment depend, not upon the esteem of intelligent and well-informed equals, but upon the fanciful and foolish favour of ignorant, presumptuous, and proud superiors; flattery and falsehood too often prevail over merit and abilities" (TMS I.iii.3.6, 63).

The socially constituted nature of the self is most evident, however, not in the variation among individuals or among "stations" but rather in that among societies. For Smith as for Hume, "the different situations of different ages and countries are apt ... to give different characters to the generality of those who live in them" (TMS V.2.7, 204). As we saw in Chapter 1, Smith places a particular emphasis on the divergences between primitive and civilized peoples in terms of manners, beliefs, and sentiments. He surmises that "savages and barbarians" are more likely

246   *The Pragmatic Enlightenment*

than "polished people" to possess the "awful" virtues of self-command not only because these virtues are required by their material circumstances, but also because they are expected by others within similar circumstances:

> Every savage undergoes a sort of Spartan discipline, and by the necessity of his situation is inured to every sort of hardship.... His circumstances not only habituate him to every sort of distress, but teach him to give way to none of the passions which that distress is apt to excite. He can expect from his countrymen no sympathy or indulgence for such weakness.... A savage, therefore, whatever be the nature of his distress, expects no sympathy from those about him, and disdains, upon that account, to expose himself, by allowing the least weakness to escape him. (TMS V.2.9, 205)

Conversely, people in more civilized societies are far less likely to expect – and hence far less likely to exhibit – this kind of "heroic and unconquerable firmness," as their comparative security and comfort allows them to "more readily enter into an animated and passionate behaviour, and ... more easily pardon some little excess" (TMS V.2.10, 207). In other words, people in primitive societies are not somehow *innately* more stoic than those in more civilized societies; rather, their manners and sentiments are formed by their circumstances and their relations with those around them. Similarly, one can expect more "gentleness and moderation" from people who live under governments that provide freedom and security than from those who live under arbitrary governments (see WN IV.vii.b.52, 586) and more "probity and punctuality" from people who live in commercial societies than from those who do not (LJ, 538–9; see also 333; WN IV.ix.13, 668). Hence, Smith too rejects the idea, which many communitarians take to be implicit in social contract theory and in liberalism more generally, that an individual could have a preformed set of sentiments, beliefs, and interests, entirely independent of others or his or her society.

Far from envisioning individuals as stepping back from their societies to choose their own values, Smith in fact argues that it is only in and through society that they become moral beings at all. "Were it possible that a human creature could grow up to manhood in some solitary place, without any communication with his own species," he writes, this individual "could no more think of his own character, of the propriety or demerit of his own sentiments and conduct, of the beauty or deformity of his own mind, than of the beauty or deformity of his own face" (TMS III.1.3, 110; see also IV.2.12, 192–3).[32] Like Hume, Smith suggests

---

[32] Charles Griswold draws our attention to the fact that Smith calls this person a human *creature*; apparently, Smith cannot even bring himself to think of a completely solitary

The Social and Encumbered Self

that other people provide a kind of "mirror" in which we observe our own sentiments and actions, and a means by which we can judge them to be proper or improper, virtuous or vicious (see TMS III.1.3, 110). Without this mirror – without the operations of sympathy and interactions with others – we would have no grounds on which to make any kind of moral judgments.[33] To be sure, Smith does not presume that we simply adopt the moral views and sentiments of those with whom we interact; rather, moral judgment is a complex, dialogical process that culminates in the adoption of the view of an "impartial spectator." Once we have internalized this ideal, we can and do pass judgment on those around us. However, this process is deeply social throughout and is literally inconceivable for an entirely isolated individual.[34]

In short, Smith agrees with Hume that we naturally sympathize with and care about others; that our beliefs and sentiments are deeply influenced by our societies; and that social interaction is necessary for our psychological well-being and for the very possibility of moral agency. As Samuel Fleischacker writes, "we are not 'utility monsters,' or relentless consumers, or atomistic individuals, for Smith; we are, pretty much, the complex, primarily social, moral, and intellectual beings we always thought we were."[35]

"SOCIETY IS AS OLD AS THE WORLD"

Like his Scottish counterparts, Voltaire denies emphatically that people are naturally independent or self-sufficient. In this, he was joined by the great majority of his fellow philosophes; Rousseau was a clear outlier among the leading thinkers of eighteenth-century France in positing an

---

individual as a human being in the full sense of the term. See Charles L. Griswold, *Adam Smith and the Virtues of Enlightenment* (Cambridge: Cambridge University Press, 1999), 105–6.

[33] Jack Russell Weinstein suggests that this aspect of Smith's moral theory "is, in contemporary parlance, communitarian, not liberal, where communitarian is understood as acknowledging some priority of the community or society, and liberal is understood as commitment to the priority of the individual and his or her identity," although Weinstein's point is less to establish that Smith was a communitarian than to show that he "transcends the liberal/communitarian dichotomy." Jack Russell Weinstein, "Sympathy, Difference, and Education: Social Unity in the Work of Adam Smith" *Economics and Philosophy* 22.1 (March 2006), 82–3.

[34] For a helpful discussion of the process of moral judgment in Smith's thought, and of why he sees independent judgment and the social construction of the self as mutually compatible, see Samuel Fleischacker, *A Third Concept of Liberty: Judgment and Freedom in Kant and Adam Smith* (Princeton, NJ: Princeton University Press, 1999), 49–51.

[35] Fleischacker, *On Adam Smith's Wealth of Nations*, 69.

248   *The Pragmatic Enlightenment*

almost completely asocial state of nature. Voltaire expresses severe doubt
"that this solitary life, attributed to our fathers [by Rousseau], is really
in accord with human nature" (EM I.intro.7, 23), in large part because
there is no empirical evidence supporting such a view: "All people discovered in the most uncultivated and frightful countries live in society,
as do beavers, ants, bees, and several other animal species. The country
has never been seen where people live separately from one another."[36]
He maintains that the instinct to live and associate with others is one
aspect of human nature that "never changes from one end of the universe
to the other ... we were not made to live in the manner of bears" (EM
I.intro.7, 25). In fact, as David Beeson and Nicholas Cronk note, the
inherent sociability of human beings is in many ways the "principal concern" of Voltaire's *Treatise on Metaphysics*, "the theme toward which the
whole work builds."[37] In the penultimate chapter of that work, entitled
"Man Considered as a Social Being," Voltaire explains that we are pre-
disposed to form social groups because of the need for the cooperation of
others to ensure our own self-preservation, because of sexual attraction
and the resultant familial love, and because of our instinctive sense of pity
or benevolence toward others (see TM, 90–1). Just as God gave bees "a
powerful instinct which makes them work and feed together," he claims,
"he gave man certain sentiments which he can never shake off and which
are the permanent ties and first laws of society in which he foresaw that
man would live" (TM, 93; see also 95). Thus, as he writes elsewhere,
"society is as old as the world."[38]

Of course, Voltaire is well aware that there have not always been "fine
cities, twenty-four pound cannons, comic operas, and convents full of

[36] Voltaire's attack on Rousseau continues: "A few practical jokers have abused their minds
to the point of advancing the astonishing paradox that man was originally created to
live alone like a lynx, and that it is society that has depraved his nature. It would be just
as valid to say that in the sea herrings were created originally to swim alone, and that
it is because of an excess of corruption that they swim in shoals from the polar sea to
our coasts.... Each animal has its own instinct; and the instinct of man, strengthened by
reason, inclines him toward society, as [it does] towards eating and drinking." Voltaire,
"Man," in *Questions on the Encyclopedia*, in *Political Writings*, trans. David Williams
(Cambridge: Cambridge University Press, [1771] 1994), 68.

[37] David Beeson and Nicholas Cronk, "Voltaire: Philosopher or *philosophe*?", in *The
Cambridge Companion to Voltaire*, ed. Nicholas Cronk (Cambridge: Cambridge
University Press, 2009), 52. See also Rosemary Z. Lauer, *The Mind of Voltaire: A Study
of His "Constructive Deism"* (Westminster, MD: Newman Press, 1961), 70–1.

[38] Voltaire, "Politics," in *Questions on the Encyclopedia*, in *Political Writings*, trans. David
Williams (Cambridge: Cambridge University Press, [1774] 1994), 81. See also Voltaire,
Dialogue between a Savage and a Graduate, in *Micromégas and Other Short Fictions*,
trans. Theo Cuffe (New York: Penguin, [1761] 2002), 123.

The Social and Encumbered Self

nuns" (EM I.intro.7, 25). When he says that society is as old as the world, he means that the instincts of self-preservation, sexual attraction, and benevolence are sufficient to produce small, primitive, family-based societies; he explicitly *denies* that these instincts alone provide a sufficient foundation for the "great empires and flourishing towns" of the modern world (TM, 91). Rather, he suggests that modern societies are built in large part on people's ostensibly "negative" passions: pride leads people to sacrifice their individual self-interest for the common good in order to earn admiration from others; the love of being in authority leads some to persuade others to obey them; greed leads people to cooperate in order to increase and protect their possessions; and envy leads them to be industrious in their attempt to outstrip others (see TM, 91–2; LCE, 131). There are, of course, clear echoes here of Mandeville's argument that private vices often lead to public benefits, and that perfect virtue would lead to the collapse of civilization as we know it.[39] While Voltaire parts from Mandeville in seeing people as naturally social, he follows him in holding that government arises not through a social contract or any kind of formal agreement but rather "by degrees," as the "cleverest" individuals use people's passions to gain control over them (TM, 91–2).[40] In the *Essay on the Mores and Spirit of Nations*, Voltaire emphasizes the great span of time necessary for civilization to develop: "there must be a conjunction of favorable circumstances over many centuries in order to form a great society of men, gathered under the same laws" (EM I.intro.3, 10; see also I.intro.7, 27).[41] Like Hume and Smith, then, Voltaire rejects the idea that civil society could be, or should be, the product of individual choice.

---

[39] As we saw in Chapter 1, the concluding chapters of Voltaire's *Treatise* were heavily influenced by Mandeville's *An Enquiry into the Origin of Moral Virtue*. On this influence, see Ira O. Wade, *Studies on Voltaire* (Princeton, NJ: Princeton University Press, 1947), 43–8; and the editor's introduction in Voltaire, *Traité de métaphysique*, ed. W. H. Barber, in *The Complete Works of Voltaire*, vol. 14 (Oxford: Voltaire Foundation, 1989), 378–81. On Voltaire's departures from Mandeville, especially on the question of natural sociability, see Felicia Gottmann, "Du Châtelet, Voltaire, and the Transformation of Mandeville's *Fable*" *History of European Ideas* 38.2 (June 2012), 229–31.

[40] See also Merle L. Perkins, "Voltaire's Principles of Political Thought" *Modern Language Quarterly* 17.4 (December 1956), 294; and Merle L. Perkins, *Voltaire's Concept of International Order* (Geneva: Institut et Musée Voltaire, 1965), 170–1. Compare Voltaire's argument here with Mandeville's claim that the first lawgivers used "dextrous Management" to gain political control over people. See Bernard Mandeville, *The Fable of the Bees: or Private Vices, Publick Benefits*, vol. 1, ed. F. B. Kaye (Indianapolis: Liberty Fund, [1723] 1988), 42, 369.

[41] Voltaire's argument here is meant in part to demonstrate the utter inadequacy of a chronology taken from a literal reading of the Bible, but it also underscores the gradual way in which he envisions political and social development more generally.

250   *The Pragmatic Enlightenment*

Voltaire also dissents from the claim, which is often associated with Mandeville, that all human passions are ultimately reducible to self-interest or self-love.[42] Like most Enlightenment thinkers, he does see self-love as a crucial and extremely common motivating force (see PD, 35), but he holds that sentiments such as pity and benevolence are every bit as real, and every bit as intrinsically human. Indeed, he writes that "our benevolence toward our own species ... is born with us and is always working within us," such that "a man is always inclined to help another man when it doesn't cost him anything" (TM, 93; see also 91). (As the latter part of this statement indicates, Voltaire acknowledges that self-love generally prevails over benevolence when the two conflict, meaning that benevolence is generally more effective at restraining us from harming others than at inducing us to put their interests ahead of ours.) The reality of this sentiment is palpable from an early age: Voltaire notes in the *Essay* that "if a child sees a fellow creature being attacked, he feels a sudden anguish; he shows this with his cries and his tears; if he can, he helps the one who is suffering." It is in this context that he claims that "sympathy [*commisération*] and justice" are the sentiments that "form the foundation of society" (EM I.intro.7, 27). Hence, Voltaire denies that society is merely an arena for the clash of individual interests and that interactions with others invariably bring out the worst in people. In a passage clearly intended as a dig at Rousseau, he declares that "the need for society has far from degraded man; it is when he moves away from society that he is degraded. Whoever wants to live completely alone would ... succeed only in changing himself into an animal."[43] Like Hume and Smith, then, Voltaire sees society as an indispensable component of human life and our psychological well-being.

Further, Voltaire too maintains that people's beliefs, sentiments, and characters are deeply influenced by their societies, rather than developed in a vacuum. Admittedly, he opens the *Treatise on Metaphysics* by announcing his intention to study human beings as if he were an observer from another planet, and thereby to adopt what Thomas Nagel calls "the view from nowhere."[44] Voltaire writes: "I shall try in my study of man to stand at first outside of his sphere and his interests, and to cast off all the prejudices formed by education, country, and especially philosophers"

[42] See Maurice Cranston, *Philosophers and Pamphleteers: Political Theorists of the Enlightenment* (Oxford: Oxford University Press, 1986), 58.
[43] Voltaire, "Man," 68.
[44] Thomas Nagel, *The View from Nowhere* (Oxford: Oxford University Press, 1986).

The Social and Encumbered Self

(TM, 66). This endeavor is motivated, of course, by his awareness of how partial and uninformed most people's views of humanity are, from the king who "views almost the whole human species as beings made to obey him and his kind," to the Turk in his seraglio who "sees men as superior beings" compared to women, to the priest who "divides the whole world into ecclesiastics and laymen" and "has no difficulty regarding the ecclesiastic part as nobler and made for leading the other" (TM, 65–6). While Voltaire hopes to avoid these kinds of invidious prejudices as much as possible, he is under no illusion that anyone – including, presumably, him – really is a person "from nowhere." After all, the idea that people are shaped by their circumstances and their interactions with others surfaces repeatedly throughout his writings. In the *Letters Concerning the English Nation*, he notes that people tend to "squar[e] their conduct, their thinking and feeling, accordingly as they are influenc'd by education" (LCE, 145). In the *Essay*, he maintains that "every man is formed by his age" (EM I.82, 774) and that "the empire of custom ... extends over all mores, over all usages" (EM II.197, 810). In the *Questions on the Encyclopedia*, the entry "Man" proclaims that since human beings are "born neither good nor wicked" it is "education, example, the system of government into which [an individual] finds he has been tossed, and ultimately opportunity" that determines the course he takes.[45] The importance of one's society and upbringing in the formation of one's character is also palpable in many of Voltaire's *contes*. For instance, the story *The Ingenu* centers on a Huron who travels to France and whose wise naiveté exposes the absurdities of the civilized – especially Christian – world. This ingenuous character turns out actually to be of French descent, but his childhood and education among the Hurons have preserved him from the superstitions of European life.[46]

As the story of the Ingenu intimates, Voltaire joins Hume and Smith in holding that "moral causes" are more important than physical causes in determining the character of an individual and the general "spirit" of a society.[47] He does occasionally mention climate as a factor in conditioning people's minds and outlooks (see, e.g., EM II.143, 321; II.157, 406;

---

[45] Voltaire, "Man," 71.

[46] See Voltaire, *The Ingenu*, in *Candide and Other Stories*, trans. Roger Pearson (Oxford: Oxford University Press, [1767] 2006).

[47] See Roberto Romani, *National Character and Public Spirit in Britain and France, 1750–1914* (Cambridge: Cambridge University Press, 2002), 33–6; and Ira O. Wade, *The Intellectual Development of Voltaire* (Princeton, NJ: Princeton University Press, 1969), 742–3.

II.183, 702), but he generally places far more emphasis on government and religion in this regard. In the entry "Climate" in the *Questions on the Encyclopedia*, for example, he writes that "climate has some power, government a hundred times more, and religion joined to government still more."[48] Hence, Voltaire frequently criticizes Montesquieu for what he takes to be Montesquieu's overemphasis on the role of climate in establishing the characters of individuals and societies.[49] As Karen O'Brien succinctly puts it, for Voltaire "human variety and identities are culturally generated."[50] Thus, he too maintains that interactions with others play a crucial role in forming people's outlooks and personalities, and that there is no such thing as an entirely independent or self-determined set of beliefs, sentiments, and interests.

"THAT FLEXIBLE BEING WHO ADAPTS HIMSELF IN SOCIETY TO THE THOUGHTS AND IMPRESSIONS OF OTHERS"

While it is clear that Hume, Smith, and Voltaire all see human beings as naturally social and invariably "encumbered" by their societies and their interactions with others, it might appear that Montesquieu diverges from them in both of these respects. After all, Montesquieu gestures toward the idea of an asocial state of nature at the outset of *The Spirit of the Laws*, and he is frequently thought to have accorded the principal role in shaping people's characters to climate and other physical causes, rather than to social interactions. This surface appearance is, however, misleading on both counts. Let us begin with the first of these issues. In book 1, chapter 2, of *The Spirit of the Laws*, Montesquieu discusses the laws of nature, which he identifies as desires or sentiments, and declares that in order to determine what these "laws" entail "one must consider a man before the establishment of societies" (SL 1.2, 6). He goes on to offer, very briefly, just such a consideration. In explicit contrast to Hobbes's vision of the state of nature as a war of all against all, he suggests that an individual in the state of nature would "feel only his weakness" and that

[48] Voltaire, "Climat," in *Questions sur l'Encyclopédie*, vol. 4, ed. Nicholas Cronk and Christiane Mervaud, in *The Complete Works of Voltaire*, vol. 40 (Oxford: Voltaire Foundation, 2009), 132.

[49] See, for example, Voltaire, *Commentaire sur l'Esprit des lois*, ed. Sheila Mason, in *The Complete Works of Voltaire*, vol. 80b (Oxford: Voltaire Foundation, [1777] 2009), 405–11, 435–7.

[50] Karen O'Brien, *Narratives of Enlightenment: Cosmopolitan History from Voltaire to Gibbon* (Cambridge: Cambridge University Press, 1997), 55.

The Social and Encumbered Self 253

"his timidity would be extreme," so that people would "flee from one another" rather than "attack one another" (SL 1.2, 6). Much as Rousseau would argue in greater detail only a few years later, Montesquieu posits that the state of nature must have been generally peaceful and that the motives for attacking others would not arise until after "the establishment of societies" (SL 1.2, 6; see also 1.3, 7; Pensées #1266, 343–4).[51] While Montesquieu rejects Hobbes's claim that people would have been combative before the advent of society, then, several scholars have concluded that, like Rousseau, he in fact sides with Hobbes in positing that people are naturally asocial.[52]

Yet immediately after stating that people in the state of nature would be fearful and hence that they would "flee from one another," Montesquieu declares that "the marks of mutual fear would soon persuade them to approach one another" (SL 1.2, 6–7). In other words, the very attribute that supposedly isolated people in this state – fearfulness – in fact draws them together. This impulse would be strengthened, Montesquieu says, by a sense of kinship or companionship with other human beings in general and by sexual or romantic attraction: people are drawn to one another by "the pleasure one animal feels at the approach of an animal of its own kind" and by "the charm that the two sexes inspire in each other" (SL 1.2, 7). These sentiments are not factitious, developed only after people are forced together by some kind of necessity or accident; rather, Montesquieu declares explicitly that they "belong to men from the outset" (SL 1.2, 7). In addition to these natural feelings, he remarks, interactions among people enable them to "succeed in gaining knowledge," and this produces yet another "motive for uniting," a bond that "other animals do not have" (SL 1.2, 7). He concludes the chapter by declaring that "the desire to live in society" can therefore be considered a natural law (SL 1.2, 7). Thus, far from viewing people as naturally asocial, as Hobbes and Rousseau do, Montesquieu suggests that the impulse

---

[51] Rousseau refers to Montesquieu's state of nature in the *Second Discourse*, but only to take issue with his claim that people in this state would be fearful and timid. See Rousseau, *Discourse on the Origin and the Foundations of Inequality among Men*, 135–6. On this connection, see Robert Derathé, "Montesquieu et Jean-Jacques Rousseau" *Revue internationale de philosophie* 9 (1950): 366–86.

[52] This is the view adopted, with some qualifications, in David Lowenthal, "Book I of Montesquieu's *The Spirit of the Laws*" *American Political Science Review* 53.2 (June 1959), 494–5; Thomas L. Pangle, *Montesquieu's Philosophy of Liberalism: A Commentary on The Spirit of the Laws* (Chicago: University of Chicago Press, 1973), 30–5; and Thomas L. Pangle, *The Theological Basis of Liberal Modernity in Montesquieu's Spirit of the Laws* (Chicago: University of Chicago Press, 2010), 21–2.

254   *The Pragmatic Enlightenment*

to live and associate with others is deeply entrenched in human nature and that an asocial state, if it were possible at all, would be surmounted almost immediately.[53]

The idea that human beings are inherently social is reiterated throughout Montesquieu's writings. In *The Persian Letters*, Usbek declares that there is no need to search for the origins of society: "If men did not form societies, if they separated and fled from one another, then we would need to ask why they kept apart. But they are tied to one another from birth; a son comes into the world beside his father and stays there – hence society and its cause" (PL #94, 155). Similarly, elsewhere in *The Spirit of the Laws* Montesquieu proclaims that human beings are "made for living in society" (SL 1.1, 5), "born to live together, [and] also born to please each other" (SL 4.2, 32), and "made ... to do all the things done in society" (SL 24.11, 466). Much like Hume, Smith, and Voltaire, he argues that this desire to please others and thereby earn their sympathy or approval is one of the key foundations of society: "It is the desire to please that gives cohesion to society, and such has been the good fortune of the human species that this self-love [*amour-propre*], which should have dissolved society, instead fortifies it and renders it unshakeable" (Pensées #464, 166). It is clear, then, that Montesquieu does not view people as selfish atoms who choose to unite for purely instrumental reasons; on the contrary, he holds that they are naturally social and that interaction with

[53] This reading is reinforced by Montesquieu's attack on the Hobbesian conception of the state of nature in one of the *Pensées* that formed a part of his early *Treatise on Duties* (1725), the full text for which has now been lost. In this entry he suggests that the state of nature would be rendered social the instant the first lone man met the first lone woman: "The first and lone man fears no one. This lone man, who would also find a lone woman, would not make war against her. All the others would be born in a family, and soon in a society. There is no warfare there; on the contrary, love, education, respect, gratitude – everything exudes peace" (Pensées #1266, 343). Given that an asocial state of nature would necessarily be fleeting, if it were possible at all, it is not entirely clear why Montesquieu felt compelled to speculate about such a state in the first place. His stated reason for doing so is that "one must consider a man before the establishment of societies" in order to "know well" the laws of nature or people's core natural sentiments. Yet two of the four natural laws that he identifies – "the natural entreaty [the sexes] always make to one another" and "the desire to live in society" – indicate precisely that "a man before the establishment of societies" probably never existed. This likely does explain, however, why he speaks in hypothetical terms throughout book 1, chapter 2, informing the reader what people in the state of nature *would* be like and the sentiments that they *would* have. Indeed, the only other chapters in the entire work that rely so heavily on the conditional voice are the two main chapters on England – that is, SL 11.6 and 19.27. See Paul A. Rahe, *Montesquieu and the Logic of Liberty: War, Religion, Commerce, Climate, Terrain, Technology, Uneasiness of Mind, the Spirit of Political Vigilance, and the Foundations of the Modern Republic* (New Haven: Yale University Press, 2009), 54.

The Social and Encumbered Self

others is an essential component of any truly human life.[54] Thus, Adam Ferguson, another key figure of the Scottish Enlightenment, sums up Montesquieu's position with the declaration that "man is born in society ... and there he remains."[55]

If we accept, along with the preponderance of the evidence, that Montesquieu views human beings as inherently social, then we must also reconsider whether he in fact views them as naturally peaceful, as he initially suggests. The key piece of evidence that he offers in support of the claim that the state of nature would be a state of peace, after all, is that people would be fearful and hence that they would flee from one another; if people are in fact *drawn to* one another, as Montesquieu quickly indicates, then perhaps their peacefulness is ephemeral or illusory as well. This conjecture is confirmed in the first lines of book 1, chapter 3, where Montesquieu states that "as soon as men are in society ... the individuals within each society begin to feel their strength; they seek to turn to their favor the principal advantages of this society, which brings about a state of war among them" (SL 1.3, 7). *This* is where Montesquieu's outlook bears some resemblance to that of Hobbes: not in the supposition that human beings are naturally asocial, but rather in the conclusion that in the absence of government and positive law their interactions, however essential to their makeup, will tend to lead to conflict.[56] Indeed, he declares that "the human race is unable to survive" in an anarchic state

[54] Like Smith, Montesquieu suggests that "solitude is ... dangerous to the mind." Charles de Secondat, baron de Montesquieu, "An Essay on the Causes That May Affect Men's Minds and Characters," trans. Melvin Richter, in *Political Theory* 4.2 (May 1976), 147.

[55] Adam Ferguson, *An Essay on the History of Civil Society*, ed. Fania Oz-Salzberger (Cambridge: Cambridge University Press [1767] 1995), 21. For more recent statements to the same effect, see Isaiah Berlin, "Montesquieu," in *Against the Current: Essays in the History of Ideas*, ed. Henry Hardy (New York: Viking, [1955] 1980), 138–9; and Melvin Richter, *The Political Theory of Montesquieu* (Cambridge: Cambridge University Press, 1977), 68.

[56] Thomas Pangle draws on this element of Montesquieu's thought in contending that he views people as naturally asocial: "The laws of nature ... impel humans toward an undefined association sought for motives of pleasure and utility. These laws do not, however, define humans as naturally social animals – in the sense that the nature of humans is aimed at any stable or satisfactory social condition: quite the contrary.... It turns out that nothing is so dangerous for man by nature as the association with his fellowman." Pangle, *The Theological Basis of Liberal Modernity in Montesquieu's Spirit of the Laws*, 21–2. However, given Montesquieu's many statements (cited previously) that human beings are "made for living in society," "born to live together," "born to please each other," and so on, I would argue that he deems social interaction to be far more central to the human makeup than Pangle suggests, the tendency toward conflict in the absence of government notwithstanding.

(Pensées #883, 254; see also #174, 58) and that "a society could not continue to exist without a government" (SL 1.3, 8; see also 30.19, 647).

Montesquieu says strikingly little, however, about when and how political institutions in fact arise. In contrast to the social contract theorists, for whom the means by which governments are (or should be) formed is the central focus, the most that Montesquieu says is that fighting among individuals and societies "bring[s] about the establishment of laws among men" (SL 1.3, 7).[57] Book 18 of *The Spirit of the Laws* forms a sort of precursor to Smith's "four stages" theory of history, but whereas Smith claims that "there is seldom any established magistrate or any regular administration of justice" (WN V.i.b.2, 709) in the hunting stage and then proceeds to explain how political institutions arise as society develops, Montesquieu posits that there are already laws in hunting societies and offers no indication about how exactly these laws might have arisen in the first place.[58] Given that Montesquieu sees people as naturally drawn to one another and that he considers government to be necessary for people's very survival, however, it is clear that he does not see government and law as resting only on a contract among otherwise isolated individuals.

The idea that Montesquieu sees climate and other physical causes as the primary determinants of people's characters is, if anything, even more erroneous than the notion that he sees human beings as naturally asocial.[59] This common allegation derives from book 14 of *The Spirit of the Laws*, which is dedicated to showing that "the character of the mind [*l'esprit*] and the passions of the heart are extremely different in the various climates" (SL 14.1, 231). Montesquieu famously argues that people

[57] Montesquieu does speak of an express agreement to form a state in book 9, but this is an agreement among republics to form a confederation, not an agreement among individuals to form a government (see SL 9.1, 131).

[58] Montesquieu does join Smith, however, in positing that laws will tend to be more extensive as society develops. He writes: "The laws are very closely related to the way that various peoples procure their subsistence. There must be a more extensive code of laws for a people attached to commerce and the sea than for a people satisfied to cultivate their lands. There must be a greater one for the latter than for a people who live by their herds. There must be a greater one for these last than for a people who live by hunting" (SL 18.8, 289; see also 18.12–13, 291; 18.17, 293).

[59] The view of Montesquieu as a crude environmental determinist has long exercised Montesquieu scholars, but has by now been thoroughly refuted. For helpful discussions, see the editor's introduction in *The Spirit of the Laws: A Compendium of the First English Edition*, ed. David W. Carrithers (Berkeley: University of California Press, 1977), 44–51; and Tzvetan Todorov, *The Imperfect Garden: The Legacy of Humanism*, trans. Carol Cosman (Princeton, NJ: Princeton University Press, 2002), 61–6.

The Social and Encumbered Self

tend to be more vigorous, courageous, and frank in cold climates and more passive, timid, and sensitive in warmer ones (see SL 14.2, 231–4). At one point, he goes so far as to suggest that in many Eastern nations the effects of climate have rendered their spirit nearly immutable (see SL 14.4, 235). Yet in the very next chapter he insists that physical causes can be, and often should be, combated through education and legislation, referring explicitly to China in this connection (SL 14.5, 236; see also 16.12, 273). More broadly, it is abundantly clear that Montesquieu does not see climate as the sole determinant of people's characters. In an oft-cited formulation in book 19, he writes that "many things govern men: climate, religion, laws, the maxims of the government, examples of past things, mores, and manners" (SL 19.4, 310). While climate is the first item on the list, it is the *only* one that constitutes a "physical" rather than a "moral" cause, as those terms were used in the eighteenth century.

In fact, throughout his career Montesquieu was consistent in according a far greater role to moral than to physical causes. In an early essay, he argues that "our temperament [*génie*] is formed to a considerable extent by the persons with whom we live" and states unambiguously that "moral causes contribute more than do physical causes to the general character of a nation and to the quality of its thinking."[60] In a letter to Hume, he praises Hume for having granted "a much greater influence to moral causes than to physical causes" in his essay "Of National Characters."[61] And in a reply to the critics of *The Spirit of the Laws*, Montesquieu proclaims that his magnum opus in fact "represents a perpetual triumph of moral [causes] over the climate, or rather, in general, over physical causes," and reproaches his critics for arguing as if he had "denied the influence of moral, political, and civil causes, even though the entire work has almost nothing else as its purpose than to establish these causes."[62] While the categorical nature of these assertions may be somewhat surprising, given the frequency with which Montesquieu has been depicted as a climatic determinist, it should be less so when we recall that at the very outset of the work he describes "man" as "that flexible being who adapts himself in society to the thoughts and impressions of others"

---

[60] Montesquieu, "An Essay on the Causes That May Affect Men's Minds and Characters," 155, 153.

[61] Charles de Secondat, baron de Montesquieu, letter to David Hume, 19 May 1749, in *Oeuvres complètes de Montesquieu*, ed. André Masson, vol. 3 (Paris: Nagel, 1955), 1230.

[62] Charles de Secondat, baron de Montesquieu, *Réponses et explications données a la Faculté de Théologie*, in *Oeuvres complètes*, ed. Roger Caillois, vol. 2 (Paris: Gallimard, [1752–4] 1951), 1173.

(SL, xliv). This aspect of Montesquieu's outlook is also underlined by the importance he attaches to education, taken in a broad sense that includes not only formal schooling but also familial upbringing and the impact of society more generally.[63] Indeed, education is the first topic that he takes up after discussing "laws in general" in book 1 and the nature and principle of the three regime types in books 2 and 3. Each society imparts a certain character or mind-set to its citizens, in his view, and while climate plays a role in this regard, it is very far from the most important factor.

The emphasis that Montesquieu places on *all* of these factors, moral and physical, shows that he is abundantly aware that individuals do not and cannot step back from their societies to choose their own beliefs and values rationally. Given the many ways in which we are constrained and shaped by factors that are beyond our control, complete intellectual and moral autonomy is in his view impossible. In this respect, Montesquieu's outlook too stands wholly at odds with the communitarian depiction of the Enlightenment.

CONCLUSION

Many leading liberal thinkers, from Locke to Kant to John Rawls, *appear* to rest their moral and political theories on a conception of human beings as self-determining atoms, at least at their core.[64] We have seen in this chapter, however, that Hume, Smith, Montesquieu, and Voltaire are all resolute in conceiving of people as neither atomistic nor self-determining. Rather than supposing that people are naturally asocial individuals

[63] Montesquieu writes that we are educated by "our fathers," by "our schoolmasters," and by "the world," noting that these three forms of education often conflict with one another in the modern world, largely because of the influence of religion on the first two (SL 4.4, 35). See also Montesquieu, "An Essay on the Causes That May Affect Men's Minds and Characters," 148, 151.

[64] I emphasize "appear" here because it is at least questionable whether any of these thinkers did in fact adopt such a view. Sandel's critique of the notion of an "unencumbered self," recall, is directly primarily at Rawls and his "original position" in which each individual's particular circumstances and characteristics are hidden behind a "veil of ignorance." However, Rawls himself insists that Sandel's critique overlooks the fact that the original position is simply a "device of representation" that allows us to reflect on what people would choose under fair circumstances. Abstracting from our particular circumstances and characteristics, he says, "no more commits us to a particular metaphysical doctrine about the nature of the self than our acting a part in a play, say of Macbeth or Lady Macbeth, commits us to thinking that we are really a king or a queen engaged in a desperate struggle for political power." John Rawls, *Political Liberalism*, expanded edition (New York: Columbia University Press, [1993] 2005), 27. On Locke and Kant, see note 8.

The Social and Encumbered Self

who choose to unite for instrumental or selfish reasons, they maintain that human beings are drawn to one another out of an innate desire for companionship, and that interactions with others form an indispensible component of any truly human life. Moreover, these four thinkers all emphasize that people's beliefs, sentiments, and characters are deeply shaped by their societies and their attachments to others. As David Carrithers writes, these thinkers, along with an array of other prominent figures of the period, accept that "far from actually creating societies through formal contracts, and far from societies simply reflecting and reifying man's uniform nature, societies preexist particular individuals and function as the crucibles in which human character, beliefs, and inclinations are formed."[65] While contemporary communitarians such as Sandel and Taylor may be dissatisfied with the political ideals of Hume, Smith, Montesquieu, and Voltaire, as we will see in the next chapter, they should find the conception of the self that lies behind these ideals far more congenial: these Enlightenment thinkers concur wholeheartedly with the claim that the notion of an "unencumbered self" or a "self-defining subject" is misguided, indeed incoherent. Thus, their writings serve as a useful reminder that adopting a liberal outlook in no way requires adopting an overly narrow or individualistic view of human nature.

[65] Carrithers, "The Enlightenment Science of Society," 249.

6

Negative Liberty for a Positive Community

Although Hume, Smith, Montesquieu, and Voltaire plainly did not adopt an overly narrow or individualistic view of human nature, the other component of the communitarians' critique of the Enlightenment – the one that really drives their assessment of the movement – is not as easily dismissed. This is the claim that the Enlightenment's *politics* were overly individualistic, that the form of liberalism that emerged in the eighteenth century entails or encourages a kind of self-interested atomism that erodes the bonds that hold the community together. According to many of the Enlightenment's critics, its embrace of what we have come to call "negative liberty" – according to which liberty is simply the absence of restraints or the ability to choose one's own course in life – undermines *true* freedom, the kind that is found in and through a political community and self-government. This component of the critique too can be traced back to the eighteenth century itself, when Rousseau denounced the Enlightenment's emphasis on self-interest over public-spiritedness and Edmund Burke, from a very different perspective, condemned its emphasis on individual rights over shared traditions. Once again, Charles Taylor serves as a useful example of the more recent incarnations of this critique. Taylor argues that the Enlightenment's ideal of "disengaged reason," which was meant to free humanity from the shackles of authority and tradition, instead leads to "a one-dimensional hedonism and atomism" in which "everyone defines his or her purposes in individual terms and only cleaves to society on instrumental grounds."[1] Thus, in his view the Enlightenment's attempt

---

[1] Charles Taylor, *Sources of the Self: The Making of the Modern Identity* (Cambridge, MA: Harvard University Press, 1989), 413.

Negative Liberty for a Positive Community 261

to promote individual freedom in fact "threatens public freedom, that is, the institutions and practices of self-government," since "a society of self-fulfillers, whose affiliations are more and more seen as revocable, cannot sustain the strong identification with the political community which public freedom needs."[2]

Critics on both sides of the political spectrum, from Marxists to social conservatives, also frequently highlight the Enlightenment's welcoming attitude toward commerce and commercial society, which they blame for corroding traditional values through the spread of luxury and selfishness, for impoverishing the sense of community by leading people to see others as merely a means to their own ends, and for fostering inequality, greed, and "possessive individualism."[3] Even Enlightenment scholars frequently admit as much, as when Roy Porter writes:

> The Enlightenment piloted a transition from *homo civilis* to *homo economicus*, which involved the rationalization of selfishness and self-interest as enlightened ideology, the privatization of virtue and the de-moralization of luxury, pride, selfishness and avarice.... With *laissez-faire* in the saddle, economic activity, divorced from traditional values, assumed a morality of its own – the rectitude of making your own way in the world as *homo faber*, an independent rational actor beholden to none.[4]

Unsurprisingly, this kind of outlook is often pinned on Smith, in particular; friends and foes of commercial society alike associate Smith with the idea that the untrammeled pursuit of self-interest is desirable because it leads to a competitive and efficient market, and thus, through an invisible hand, to the economic well-being of all.[5] In short, critics frequently blame

---

[2] Ibid., 500, 508; see also chapter 25 more generally.

[3] C. B. Macpherson does not devote much attention to the eighteenth century in his celebrated book on "possessive individualism," but he expands his analysis to include Hume, Montesquieu, and especially Smith in a later book review. See C. B. Macpherson, *The Political Theory of Possessive Individualism: Hobbes to Locke* (Oxford: Oxford University Press, 1962); and C. B. Macpherson, review of Donald Winch, *Adam Smith's Politics: An Essay in Historiographic Revision*, in *History of Political Economy* 11.3 (fall 1979): 450–4.

[4] Roy Porter, *The Creation of the Modern World: The Untold Story of the British Enlightenment* (New York: W. W. Norton, 2000), 396.

[5] This interpretation of Smith has enjoyed a long and distinguished career among economists, in particular, but it is also embraced by many political theorists and philosophers. Joseph Cropsey claims, for instance, that for Smith "'freedom' is a discharge from the inhibitions that traditionally were known as virtues. For these latter are substituted the controlled passions of self-preservation through gain, the unhampered motion of which is commerce." Joseph Cropsey, *Polity and Economy: With Further Thoughts on the Principles of Adam Smith* (South Bend, IN: St. Augustine's Press, [1957] 2001), 84. Similarly, Peter Minowitz suggests that "the impetus of *The Wealth of Nations* is to abandon the 'liberal,

the Enlightenment's advocacy of commerce, like its advocacy of negative liberty, for promoting selfishness and undermining communal life.

There is more truth in these claims than in many of the others covered in this book, with respect to Hume, Smith, Montesquieu, and Voltaire. These thinkers *did* adopt a basically negative conception of liberty, holding that freedom consists less in collective self-government than in a sense of personal security and independence, protected by the rule of law. Hence, they did not, as a rule, see liberty as inextricably connected with popular or democratic government, and they tended to advocate civil liberties – the security of person and property, the freedom of expression and conscience – far more than political liberties such as the right to vote or otherwise participate in public affairs. While their views include elements of both the "liberal" and "republican" conceptions of liberty, as those terms are often used today,[6] they stand in rather stark contrast to the "civic republican" or "civic humanist" tradition that has been brought to the fore by J. G. A. Pocock and others, according to which the highest form of freedom is instantiated in a republic of virtuous citizens who dedicate themselves to the common good through political participation and military defense.[7] Further, Hume, Smith, Montesquieu, and Voltaire *did* encourage commerce and applaud the arrival of commercial society, openly contesting the moral and political strictures on commercial activity that played such a prominent role in the Christian and civic republican traditions.[8]

generous, and spirited conduct of a man,' the 'perfection' of character, for the sake of opulence and *homo economicus*." Peter Minowitz, *Profits, Priests, and Princes: Adam Smith's Emancipation of Economics from Politics and Religion* (Stanford, CA: Stanford University Press, 1993), 147.

[6] The republican understanding of liberty as nondomination, like the liberal understanding of liberty as noninterference, is a basically "negative" one. See, for example, Philip Pettit, "Negative Liberty, Liberal and Republican" *European Journal of Philosophy* 1.1 (April 1993): 15–38.

[7] See especially J. G. A. Pocock, *The Machiavellian Moment: Florentine Political Thought and the Atlantic Republican Tradition* (Princeton, NJ: Princeton University Press, 1975); and J. G. A. Pocock, *Virtue, Commerce, and History: Essays on Political Thought and History, Chiefly in the Eighteenth Century* (Cambridge: Cambridge University Press, 1985). For Pocock's view of the Scottish Enlightenment in relation to the civic republican tradition, see J. G. A. Pocock, "Cambridge Paradigms and Scotch Philosophers: A Study of the Relations between the Civic Humanist and the Civil Jurisprudence Interpretation of Eighteenth-Century Social Thought," in *Wealth and Virtue: The Shaping of Political Economy in the Scottish Enlightenment*, ed. Istvan Hont and Michael Ignatieff (Cambridge: Cambridge University Press, 1983).

[8] On the widespread hostility to commerce in the Christian and civic republican traditions, see Jerry Z. Muller, *The Mind and the Market: Capitalism in Western Thought* (Westminster, MD: Broadway Books, 2003), chapter 1.

Negative Liberty for a Positive Community 263

In this instance, however, it is crucial to examine not only what these thinkers advocated, but *why* they advocated what they did.[9] As we will see in this chapter, Hume, Smith, Montesquieu, and Voltaire did not adopt a negative conception of liberty because they held an implausibly "unencumbered" view of the self, because they dogmatically insisted on the inviolability of natural rights, or because they wanted to reduce people to self-interested atoms who have no connection to others or to the community at large. Rather, they advocated negative liberty because they saw clearly the dangers inherent in communities that are dedicated to shared ends and "higher" purposes, above all, coercion, exclusion, and intolerance. In their view, participatory republics on the model of ancient Sparta and Rome – the apogee of the civic republican ideal – tend to require a great deal of sacrifice and self-renunciation; to cultivate an excessively militaristic and xenophobic spirit; to rely on slavery in order to afford citizens the time and opportunity to devote themselves whole-heartedly to the republic; and, somewhat ironically, to produce a divided, factious citizenry. Hence, these thinkers would surely have seen the pitting of the individual *against* the community as a false dichotomy: by focusing on the protection of the individual, they were seeking to reduce the conflict produced by the pursuit of consensus and thereby *safeguard* the community. Their goal was emphatically *not* to undercut the concern for virtue. Rather, it was to challenge the persistent efforts, on the part of political and ecclesiastical authorities, to inculcate virtue through coercive means, which history had shown to be counterproductive.

Similarly, these four thinkers did not support commerce solely, or even primarily, for the sake of the material well-being it creates, much less in order to encourage unbridled greed and selfishness. Rather, they supported commerce because they believed that it would provide a healthier way to unite people than the traditional bonds of blood, religion, and nationalism. Rather than atomizing people, they held, commerce draws them together, leading not only to greater prosperity but also to greater concord and civility by making people and nations interdependent. Extensive commerce might be incompatible with strict republican virtue, they acknowledged, but they also believed that a focus on material self-interest would help to replace dangerous and divisive passions such as xenophobia, religious intolerance, and the thirst for military

---

[9] The general argumentative strategy of this chapter was inspired in part by that of Stephen Holmes, *The Anatomy of Antiliberalism* (Cambridge, MA: Harvard University Press, 1993).

glory.[10] Moreover, they argued that commercial society helps to promote the "bourgeois" virtues of reliability, decency, cooperativeness, and so on – moral and social goods that were comparatively lacking in precommercial societies. In a word, the support that these thinkers showed for negative liberty and commerce was *not* a support of atomism or selfishness; on the contrary, they supported negative liberty and commerce precisely because they saw them as prerequisites of a healthy community.

MONTESQUIEU, *DOUX COMMERCE*, AND THE RISKS OF REPUBLICAN VIRTUE

"No word," Montesquieu writes, "has received more different significations and has struck minds in so many ways as has *liberty*." This term, he notes, has been used to denote everything from the ability to elect one's leaders to the right to bear arms to the privilege of wearing a long beard (in the case of the Russians under Peter the Great) (SL 11.2, 154; see also Pensées #884, 254–5). Montesquieu himself distinguishes among three main types of liberty: "philosophical liberty," which consists in the exercise of one's will and which he mentions only briefly[11]; "political liberty in relation to the constitution," which consists in a constitutional separation of powers and which he discusses in book 11 of *The Spirit of the Laws*; and "political liberty in relation to the citizen," which consists in the feeling or opinion of one's security and which he discusses in book 12. While Montesquieu's name has long been nearly synonymous with the idea of the separation of powers, the last of these three forms of liberty is arguably even more central to his thought.[12] In his most detailed description of what this form of liberty entails, Montesquieu declares that "political liberty in a citizen is that tranquility of spirit which comes from the opinion each one has of his security, and in order for him to

[10] The classic work on this subject is Albert O. Hirschman, *The Passions and the Interests: Political Arguments for Capitalism before Its Triumph* (Princeton, NJ: Princeton University Press, [1977] 1997). For another study on the same theme, see Stephen Holmes, "The Secret History of Self-Interest," in *Passions and Constraint: On the Theory of Liberal Democracy* (Chicago: University of Chicago Press, 1995).

[11] See SL 12.2, 188. For a discussion of this type of liberty in Montesquieu's thought, see Sharon R. Krause, "Two Concepts of Liberty in Montesquieu" *Perspectives on Political Science* 34.2 (spring 2005): 88–96.

[12] The value that Montesquieu attaches to political liberty in relation to the citizen is indicated by the fact that he suggests that this form of liberty "depends principally on the goodness of the criminal laws" and then declares that knowledge regarding "the surest rules one can observe in criminal judgments, is of more concern to mankind than anything else in the world" (SL 12.2, 188).

Negative Liberty for a Positive Community   265

have this liberty the government must be such that one citizen cannot fear another citizen" (SL 11.6, 157; see also 12.1–2, 187–8).[13] It is clear, from this description, that Montesquieu's understanding of liberty is far removed from license: if people were free to act without restraint, then they would have very good grounds indeed for fearing one another (see SL 11.3, 155). Liberty requires mores, institutions, and laws – especially criminal laws – that restrain and protect people, and so "free nations are policed nations" (Pensées #784, 232; see also SL 26.20, 514). At the same time, Montesquieu maintains that free nations also allow their citizens wide latitude of choice and movement within the bounds of the law; in one of his *Pensées* he compares a "free government" to "a big net in which fish move around without thinking they are caught" (Pensées #874, 252).[14]

Throughout his analysis of the different types of liberty, Montesquieu takes special care to distinguish them all from democratic self-rule. While philosophers and ordinary citizens alike have often associated liberty with republics – especially democratic republics – and excluded it from monarchies, he says, such a view confuses "the *power* of the people ... with the *liberty* of the people" (SL 11.2, 155, emphases added). In his view, *who* governs is ultimately less important than *how* they govern.[15] While republics *can* provide their citizens with liberty, Montesquieu holds that they are not necessarily "free states by their nature" (SL 11.4, 155). Indeed, as Annelien de Dijn has recently shown, drawing on the surviving fragments

---

[13] Montesquieu's emphasis on the *opinion* that individuals have of their security distances him from Hobbes. In the Hobbesian view, the *opinion* of security may in fact undermine *actual* security by making people complacent or prideful. Whereas Hobbes aims to promote fear in order to persuade people to seek peace and obey the law, Montesquieu fears fear itself. This is why he is, along with Montaigne, one of the key inspirations or heroes of Judith Shklar's "liberalism of fear." See Judith N. Shklar, *Ordinary Vices* (Cambridge, MA: Harvard University Press, 1984), chapter 1; and Judith N. Shklar, "The Liberalism of Fear," in *Liberalism and the Moral Life*, ed. Nancy L. Rosenblum (Cambridge, MA: Harvard University Press, 1989).

[14] Montesquieu was sufficiently fond of this image that he employed it no fewer than five times in his *Pensées*. In addition to the entry quoted previously, see #434, 161, where the net is compared to "God's justice"; #597, 193, where it is attributed to "a well-ordered monarchy"; #828, 242, where it is attributed to "a prudent and moderate monarchy or aristocracy"; and #943, 267, where it is compared to "good laws."

[15] Montesquieu does find much to admire in representative government (see SL 11.6, 159), but he never suggests that representation is *necessary* for a state to be free. Moreover, even in the midst of his praise for Britain's representative system he holds that "the people should not enter the government except to choose their representatives" (SL 11.6, 160). Thus, Shklar is right to assert that Montesquieu's liberalism consists in "an effort to avoid oppression rather than directly to promote rights to political action or self-development." Judith N. Shklar, *Montesquieu* (Oxford: Oxford University Press, 1987), 89.

from the lost manuscript "On Political Liberty" that Montesquieu wrote alongside his famous analysis of the English constitution, he deliberately sought "to wrest control over the concept of liberty from the republican admirers of classical antiquity" by demonstrating that "monarchial subjects could be just as free as republican citizens."[16] In one of these fragments, Montesquieu writes that "political liberty concerns moderate monarchies just as it does republics, and is no further from a throne than from a senate. Every man is free who has good grounds to believe that the wrath of one or many will not take away his life or possession of his property" (Pensées #884, 255; see also #751, 223; SL 11.7, 166).

Montesquieu is particularly wary of participatory republics of the kind found in ancient Greece and Rome, whose "principle" or animating force is a kind of self-denying virtue. Admittedly, at times he seems to paint these ancient republics in attractive colors, highlighting the citizens' greatness of soul and their intense dedication to their common *patrie* (e.g., SL 3.5, 25; Pensées #221, 93; #1268, 347). Thus, it is not surprising that a number of scholars have interpreted Montesquieu as favoring these virtuous republics over the other regime types.[17] Yet however admirable these republics may have been from a certain point of view, he places a far greater emphasis on their dangers and downsides.[18] Montesquieu defines republican virtue as "love of the laws and the homeland" and says that it requires "a continuous preference of the public interest over one's own" (SL 4.5, 36; see also 5.3, 43). Indeed, he declares that republican citizens "should live, act, and think only for [their homeland's] sake" (SL 5.19, 68). Because this kind of "renunciation of oneself ... is always a very painful thing," he argues, "the full power of education is needed" in republics, including censors to preserve and improve the citizens' mores as well as strict limitations on luxury, privacy, and the arts and sciences (SL 4.5, 35). At one point, he goes so far as to suggest that republican virtue requires an austerity comparable to that of a monastery (see SL 5.2, 43).

---

[16] Annelien de Dijn, "*On Political Liberty*: Montesquieu's Missing Manuscript" *Political Theory* 39.2 (April 2011), 182.

[17] See note 36 in Chapter 2.

[18] For extended discussions of some of these dangers and downsides, see David W. Carrithers, "Democratic and Aristocratic Republics: Ancient and Modern," in *Montesquieu's Science of Politics: Essays on The Spirit of Laws*, ed. David W. Carrithers, Michael A. Mosher, and Paul A. Rahe (Lanham, MD: Rowman & Littlefield, 2001); Pierre Manent, *The City of Man*, trans. Marc A. LePain (Princeton, NJ: Princeton University Press, 1998), chapter 1; and Thomas L. Pangle, *Montesquieu's Philosophy of Liberalism: A Commentary on The Spirit of the Laws* (Chicago: University of Chicago Press, 1973), chapter 4.

Negative Liberty for a Positive Community

Yet it is not only the severe demands that participatory republics place on their citizens that gives Montesquieu pause. Somewhat surprisingly, we learn later in *The Spirit of the Laws* that the republics of ancient Greece, whose citizens were supposed to form such a cohesive whole, were in fact full of constant "seditions" and "tormented by civil discord" (SL 29.3, 603; see also Pensées #32, 12). As he explains in more detail in the *Considerations on the Causes of the Greatness of the Romans and Their Decline*, the citizens of the ancient republics were only truly unified while at war. In their domestic affairs, faction was both inevitable and necessary:

We hear, in the authors, only of the divisions that ruined Rome, without seeing that these divisions were necessary to it, that they had always been there and always had to be. It was only the expansion of the republic that caused all the trouble and changed popular tumults into civil wars. There had to be divisions in Rome, for warriors who were so proud, so audacious, so terrible abroad could not be very moderate at home. To ask for men in a free state who are bold in war and timid in peace is to wish the impossible.[19]

Still further, Montesquieu holds that participatory republics are all but impossible outside small, homogeneous city-states, and even under ideal conditions they are inherently fragile (see SL 8.16, 124).[20] As he expresses it in the first half of one of his best-known lines, "the political men of Greece who lived under popular government recognized *no other force to sustain it* than virtue" (SL 3.3, 22, emphasis added).[21] Given that republican virtue is difficult to sustain, participatory republics are themselves difficult to sustain; as with Rome, their very success often breeds their

---

[19] Charles de Secondat, baron de Montesquieu, *Considerations on the Causes of the Greatness of the Romans and Their Decline*, trans. David Lowenthal (Indianapolis: Hackett, [1734] 1999), 93. Later in the work, Montesquieu declares simply that "divisions ... are always necessary for maintaining republican government." Ibid., 189.

[20] Jacob Levy notes that "for Montesquieu as for other political thinkers of his era, it could not escape notice that the most important large republic in history, Rome, and the most recent, the English Commonwealth, both ended in one form or another of military dictatorship. Comparisons between Cromwell and Caesar abound in political works of the era in general and in Montesquieu's *oeuvre* in particular." Jacob T. Levy, "Beyond Publius: Montesquieu, Liberal Republicanism and the Small-Republic Thesis" *History of Political Thought* 27.1 (spring 2006), 51–2.

[21] The second half of the line continues: "Those of today speak to us only of manufacturing, commerce, finance, wealth, and even luxury" (SL 3.3, 22–3). Rousseau would later echo this statement while removing all trace of Montesquieu's uneasiness about relying so heavily on virtue. See Jean-Jacques Rousseau, *Discourse on the Sciences and Arts*, in *The Discourses and Other Early Political Writings*, trans. Victor Gourevitch (Cambridge: Cambridge University Press, [1751] 1997), 18.

downfall. This is a crucial point: Montesquieu takes a dim view of participatory republics not only because they require a kind of self-renouncing dedication on the part of their citizens, but also because they are inherently divisive and unstable. He finds them wanting *as communities*, not just for the individuals who constitute them.

While Montesquieu frowns upon participatory republics and conceives of liberty in a basically negative sense, he by no means advocates radical individualism or atomism. On the contrary, he associates a lack of attachments among a populace with despotic regimes, where "each household is a separate empire" (SL 4.3, 34). Bonds among people are necessary for them to act cohesively and preserve their liberty, in his view, and so extreme individualism opens the door to oppression even in nondespotic states: "the independence of each individual is the purpose of the laws of Poland, and what results from this is the oppression of all" (SL 11.5, 156). In fact, Montesquieu indicates that even the English regime tends to encourage an excessive degree of individualism. He writes, for instance, that in England "each individual, always independent ... largely follow[s] his own caprices" (SL 19.27, 326) and that the people live "mostly alone with themselves," a state that renders them "timid" and "withdrawn" (SL 19.27, 332). The fact that the English tend to be mere "confederates" rather than "fellow citizens" is, in his view, one of the chief drawbacks of their generally admirable regime (SL 19.27, 332).[22] Montesquieu's opposition to excessive individualism is also apparent in the first part of the story of the Troglodytes in *The Persian Letters*, in which the Troglodytes resolve "to attend only to their personal interests, without considering those of others," and the result is an unmitigated disaster (PL #11, 23).

Given that Montesquieu recognizes the need for bonds among people but deems self-renouncing virtue to be both disagreeable and unreliable, he locates an alternative source of these bonds in commerce. Like most Enlightenment thinkers, Montesquieu ascribes numerous economic and political benefits to commerce. For instance, it promotes prosperity (see SL 21.6, 357), provides a check on the sovereign's power (see SL 21.20, 389), and ensures individuals a degree of security and independence (see

---

[22] See Sharon R. Krause, "The Spirit of Separate Powers in Montesquieu," *Review of Politics* 62.2 (spring 2000), especially 248, 257–63. For an analysis that highlights the similarities between Montesquieu's description of English individualism and Tocqueville's famous account of American individualism, see Anne M. Cohler, *Montesquieu's Comparative Politics and the Spirit of American Constitutionalism* (Lawrence: University Press of Kansas, 1988), 181–2.

Negative Liberty for a Positive Community

Pensées #776, 230).[23] Further, in stark contrast to the Christian and civic republican view of commerce as inherently corrupting, Montesquieu argues that "the spirit of commerce brings with it the spirit of frugality, economy, moderation, work, wisdom, tranquility, order, and rule" (SL 5.6, 48). Perhaps the greatest benefit that he points to, however, lies in the tendency of commerce to promote peace both among nations and among individuals. As for the relations among nations, Montesquieu declares bluntly that "the natural effect of commerce is to lead to peace. Two nations that trade with each other become reciprocally dependent; if one has an interest in buying, the other has an interest in selling, and all unions are founded on mutual needs" (SL 20.2, 338).[24] In other words, extensive commerce discourages war both by raising its costs – since warring nations will lose not only their own blood and treasure but also a trading partner – and by shifting the focus, in the international sphere, from conquest and glory to trade and prosperity. Further, he maintains that an increase in exchange and communication among different peoples will tend to breed greater familiarity and thence greater tolerance among them (see SL 15.3, 248–9; 20.1, 338).

A similar process occurs, according to Montesquieu, in the domestic sphere. At the outset of book 20 of *The Spirit of the Laws*, the first of the books devoted to the subject of commerce, he announces that "commerce cures destructive prejudices, and it is an almost general rule that everywhere there are gentle mores, there is commerce and that everywhere there is commerce, there are gentle mores" (SL 20.1, 338).[25] By inducing people to interact regularly and by rendering life more comfortable, he holds, commerce softens and refines people's manners and promotes civility and toleration – including, perhaps, religious toleration.[26] With this argument, Montesquieu became one of the leading exponents of the doctrine of *doux commerce*, according to which commerce – meaning

---

[23] Like Hume and Smith, Montesquieu argues that the benefits of commerce are generally augmented by free trade and hampered by mercantilist restrictions. See SL 20.8–9, 343–4; and Catherine Larrère, "Montesquieu on Economics and Commerce," in *Montesquieu's Science of Politics: Essays on The Spirit of Laws*, ed. David W. Carrithers, Michael A. Mosher, and Paul A. Rahe (Lanham, MD: Rowman & Littlefield, 2001).

[24] See also Pensées #1694, 506; and Charles de Secondat, baron de Montesquieu, *Réflexions sur la Monarchie Universelle en Europe*, in *Oeuvres complètes de Montesquieu*, vol. 2, ed. Roger Caillois (Paris: Gallimard, [1734] 1951), 34.

[25] Recall once again that helping people to "cure themselves of their destructive prejudices" is one of the stated goals of *The Spirit of the Laws* (SL, xliv).

[26] See SL 25.12, 489; and Thomas L. Pangle, *The Theological Basis of Liberal Modernity in Montesquieu's Spirit of the Laws* (Chicago: University of Chicago Press, 2010), 99–103.

social interaction in general, but economic trade in particular – leads to *douceur*, or gentleness and mildness.[27] None of this is to suggest that Montesquieu sees commerce as a panacea or that he supposes that it will induce people to dedicate themselves wholeheartedly to the common good. On the contrary, he consistently acknowledges that there is an inherent tension between commerce and strict republican virtue,[28] and he admits that "in countries where one is affected *only* by the spirit of commerce," as in Holland, "the smallest things, those required by humanity, are done or given for money" (SL 20.2, 338–9, emphasis added).[29] Rather, his argument is that commerce helps to replace the xenophobia and bellicosity of most precommercial societies with a comparatively civilized and pacific ethos; while "commerce corrupts pure mores," it also "polishes and softens barbarous mores, as we see every day" (SL 20.1, 338).[30] Even if commerce does not seem particularly noble when viewed from the moral heights, then, Montesquieu finds much to appreciate in its ability to moderate the harsh and divisive passions that flourished in earlier eras.

While Montesquieu holds that commerce tends to moderate people's passions, he accepts that it does not necessarily, on its own, "unite individuals" within a society, as the examples of England and Holland attest (SL 20.2, 338). Yet he by no means sees commerce as *incompatible* with a healthy level of attachments among people. After all, he certainly considers France to be a commercial nation, and he shows warm appreciation for the "sociable humor," "openness of heart," "ease in communicating," and "generosity" of the French (SL 19.5–6, 310–11). The sociable French spirit has many sources, in Montesquieu's view, ranging from its temperate climate to the luxuries and refinements that the royal court and nobility bring into favor. Two of the chief sources of this spirit, however, involve the roles of women and honor in French society. French women enjoy a greater degree of social equality and play a greater role in public

---

[27] For a brief but prominent account of this theory, see Hirschman, *The Passions and the Interests*, 59–63.

[28] See Richard B. Sher, "From Troglodytes to Americans: Montesquieu and the Scottish Enlightenment on Liberty, Virtue, and Commerce," in *Republicanism, Liberty, and Commercial Society, 1649–1776*, ed. David Wootton (Stanford, CA: Stanford University Press, 1994), 371–83.

[29] See also Pensées #552, 185; #592, 193; and Charles de Secondat, baron de Montesquieu, *Voyage de Gratz a la Haye: Hollande*, in *Oeuvres complètes de Montesquieu*, vol. 1, ed. Roger Caillois (Paris: Gallimard, [1729] 1949), 864.

[30] Hence, book 21 of *The Spirit of the Laws*, which examines the history of commerce and its effects, contains a chapter entitled "How Commerce Penetrated through Barbarism in Europe" (see SL 21.20, 387–90).

Negative Liberty for a Positive Community

life than do women in most republics (see SL 7.9, 105) and in England (see SL 19.27, 332), according to Montesquieu, and this does a great deal to encourage the politeness and sociability that one finds there (see SL 19.5, 310; 19.8, 311–12).[31] Likewise, the sense of honor, which is inculcated in France through education in the broadest sense (see SL 4.2, 31–3), helps to connect individuals with one another and with the common good without the need for self-renouncing virtue: "honor makes all the parts of the body politic move; its very action binds them, and each person works for the common good, believing he works for his individual interests" (SL 3.7, 27).[32] In other words, while Montesquieu regards commerce as an important first step – perhaps even a *necessary* first step – in fostering a healthy community, he also points to several other avenues for reaching this goal.

While Montesquieu stands unambiguously opposed to the idea of a society of atomized individuals, it is clear that his vision of a healthy community is far removed from that of the civic republican tradition. In his most explicit consideration of what true civic spirit (*l'esprit du citoyen*) entails, he emphasizes that it does not consist in self-denying virtue or in the pursuit of military glory; rather, "civic spirit is the desire to see order in the state, to feel joy in public tranquility, in the exact administration of justice, in the security of the magistrates, in the prosperity of those who govern, in the respect paid to the laws, in the stability of the monarchy or the republic" (Pensées #1269, 347). Such spirit requires real attachments to and concern for others, but it does not necessitate a constant subordination of one's own interests, or even direct political action of any kind. After all, there are many ways to serve one's community: "Civic spirit is exercising with zeal, with pleasure, with satisfaction, that type of magistracy entrusted to everyone in the body politic; for there is no one who does not participate in government – whether in his employment, or in his family, or in the management of his property" (Pensées #1269, 347). Whereas the participatory republics of the ancient world were inherently divisive and unstable, in Montesquieu's view, the liberal, commercial societies of modern Europe are able to facilitate a healthier and sturdier sense of community precisely by demanding *less* of their citizens.

---

[31] See also Michael A. Mosher, "The Judgmental Gaze of European Women: Gender, Sexuality, and the Critique of Republican Rule" *Political Theory* 22.1 (February 1994): 25–44.

[32] See also Sharon R. Krause, *Liberalism with Honor* (Cambridge, MA: Harvard University Press, 2002), chapter 2.

272   *The Pragmatic Enlightenment*

VOLTAIRE AND THE VALUE OF THE ROYAL EXCHANGE

Like Montesquieu, Voltaire conceives of liberty in a basically negative sense. As he expresses it more than once, "freedom consists in being dependent only on the law" and not on the whims of others, including the political or ecclesiastical authorities.[33] For Voltaire, this kind of freedom is exemplified by England, where – in contrast to many other European nations of the time – you can be sure "when you go to bed that you will wake up the next day with the same wealth that you had the day before; that you will not be torn from the arms of your wife and children in the middle of the night, to be taken off to some dungeon or into some desert; that on waking up you will be able to publish what you think; that if you are put on trial ... you will be judged only in accordance with the law."[34] As this emphasis on the rule of law suggests, Voltaire too is careful to distinguish liberty from license; well-executed laws are essential, he says, "to hold back the torrents that would engulf the world" without them.[35] Hence, in the *Letters Concerning the English Nation* he praises the English for pursuing "a wise and prudent Liberty" rather than unconstrained independence for each individual (LCE, 35) and for devising a system in which "the People share in the government without confusion" (LCE, 34).

As this latter statement indicates, Voltaire is by no means opposed to some form of popular participation in political affairs, at least under certain circumstances. Of course, he frequently expresses disdain for the fickle and unthinking *canaille*, remarking several times that the reason why there are so few republics in the world is that "men are very seldom worthy to govern themselves" (e.g., EM I.67, 667; PD, 193, 329). Yet he also maintains that the people can and should have a role in government when they are sufficiently educated and tolerant, as his lifelong regard for the English regime indicates. Moreover, as we saw in Chapter 2, during the last decades of his life Voltaire was to recognize the potential advantages of an even more popular form of government in small countries

---

[33] See Voltaire, "Thoughts on Public Administration," in *Political Writings*, trans. David Williams (Cambridge: Cambridge University Press, [1752] 1994), 216; and Voltaire, "Government," in *Questions on the Encyclopedia*, in *Political Writings*, trans. David Williams (Cambridge: Cambridge University Press, [1771] 1994), 59.

[34] Voltaire, "Government," 61. See also Voltaire, *The A B C, or Dialogues between A B C*, in *Political Writings*, trans. David Williams (Cambridge: Cambridge University Press, [1768] 1994), 167.

[35] Voltaire, "Republican Ideas," in *Political Writings*, trans. David Williams (Cambridge: Cambridge University Press, [1765] 1994), 198.

Negative Liberty for a Positive Community   273

such as Geneva and Holland.[36] As early as the pamphlet "Thoughts on Public Administration," first published in 1752, he suggests that freedom is found especially in regimes that include some popular element: "Freedom consists in being dependent only on the law. On that basis, today every man is free in Sweden, England, Holland, Switzerland, Geneva, and Hamburg.... But there are still provinces and huge Christian kingdoms where most of the people are slaves."[37] While this statement might seem to cast doubt on the possibility of freedom under a monarchy, on the next page he goes on to declare that the most important point is to ensure that "all ranks of society are equally protected by the law," an objective that is attainable in monarchies as long as abuses of power are prevented.[38] Thus, even where Voltaire does praise popular forms of government, he associates the freedom of these regimes less with the collective exercise of political power than with the security and personal independence that they afford their citizens.

While Voltaire finds much to admire in the liberal, commercial republics of modern Geneva and Holland, he joins Montesquieu in finding much more fault with participatory republics of the kind found in ancient Greece and Rome. He too criticizes these republics not only for their reliance on slavery[39] and for their cultivation of an excessively militaristic spirit (see PD, 290, 329), but also for their inherent factionalism and divisiveness. "People never stop singing the praises of those fine Greek republics to us," he observes, but in fact "discord and hatred existed eternally between cities, and internally within individual cities."[40] Similarly, he notes in the *Letters* that it was precisely republican Rome's internal divisions that led to its military conquests: "the Patricians and Plebeians in *Rome* were perpetually at variance," he writes, and the former "cou'd

---

[36] This point is emphasized in Peter Gay, *Voltaire's Politics: The Poet as Realist* (New Haven, CT: Yale University Press [1959] 1988), chapter 4. See also Merle L. Perkins, "Voltaire's Principles of Political Thought" *Modern Language Quarterly* 17.4 (December 1956), 298–9. For Voltaire's belief – so common in the eighteenth century – that popular government is suitable only for small countries, see Voltaire, "Republican Ideas," 201–2; Voltaire, "Democracy," in *Questions on the Encyclopedia*, in *Political Writings*, trans. David Williams (Cambridge: Cambridge University Press, [1771] 1994), 35; and Voltaire, "Politics," in *Questions on the Encyclopedia*, in *Political Writings*, trans. David Williams (Cambridge: Cambridge University Press, [1774] 1994), 83.

[37] Voltaire, "Thoughts on Public Administration," 216; see also Voltaire, *The A B C*, 126–7. Elsewhere, Voltaire writes that both Sweden and England "can be regarded as republics under a king" (PD, 328).

[38] Voltaire, "Thoughts on Public Administration," 217; see also 219–20.

[39] See Voltaire, "Democracy," 36; and Voltaire, *The A B C*, 153.

[40] Voltaire, "Government," 51.

find no other artifice to keep the latter out of the Administration than by employing them in foreign wars." Thus, "by being unhappy at home, [the Romans] triumph'd over, and possess'd themselves of the world, till at last their divisions sunk them to Slavery" (LCE, 34). Indeed, so convinced is Voltaire that participatory republics are inherently divisive that he rejects Montesquieu's claim that their "principle" or motivating force could possibly be self-renouncing virtue. If history is any indication, he suggests, "a republic is not founded on virtue at all; it is founded on the ambition of each citizen, which keeps in check the ambition of all the others; on pride which curbs pride; on the wish to dominate which does not allow anyone else to dominate. From all that laws are formed which preserve equality as much as possible."[41] While Montesquieu considers participatory republics to be fragile because of their reliance on self-renouncing virtue, Voltaire deems them fragile even absent this kind of reliance. Immediately after the sentence just quoted, he goes on to compare these republics to a dinner "in which the guests, having an equal appetite, eat at the same table, until a powerful, greedy man comes on the scene who helps himself to everything, leaving them the crumbs."[42]

Given Voltaire's suspicion regarding the very possibility of self-renouncing virtue[43] and his agreement with Mandeville that modern commercial societies are sustained by passions such as pride, greed, and envy,[44] he might seem to bear out the critics' depiction of Enlightenment thinkers as advocating a society of atomized individuals who have little concern for others or for society at large. He refuses, however, to accede entirely to Mandeville's "private vices, public benefits" thesis. "It is quite true that a well-governed society takes advantage of all vices," he writes, but he insists that more is needed for a society truly to flourish: "One can make very good remedies from poisons, but it is not from poisons that we live. By reducing *The Fable of the Bees* to its just value, it could become a useful work of morality."[45] In other words, Voltaire agrees with Mandeville that moralistic (especially religious) criticisms of pride, greed, and envy

---

[41] Voltaire, "Thoughts on Public Administration," 222; see also Voltaire, *The A B C*, 96.
[42] Voltaire, "Thoughts on Public Administration," 222.
[43] In the *Philosophical Dictionary* entry "Fatherland" (*Patrie*), Voltaire writes that "he who burns with ambition to become aedile, tribune, praetor, consul, dictator, cries out that he loves his country, and he loves only himself" (PD, 327–8).
[44] This point was discussed in Chapter 5; see note 39 and the associated text.
[45] Voltaire, "Abeilles," in *Questions sur l'Encyclopédie*, vol. 2, ed. Nicholas Cronk and Christiane Mervaud, in *The Complete Works of Voltaire*, vol. 38 (Oxford: Voltaire Foundation, [1771] 2007), 46.

Negative Liberty for a Positive Community

are commonly overdrawn, but he also regards Mandeville's apparent *praise* of these passions as overdrawn. While self-regarding actions can sometimes prove useful for society more broadly, particularly in the economic sphere, a healthy society requires *some* other-regarding actions as well. Thus, in the last entry in his *Philosophical Dictionary* Voltaire proclaims that the most useful and admirable actions consist in "doing good to one's neighbor" – relieving the poor, assisting those in danger, instructing the ignorant, and so on (see PD, 398–9). This is, of course, an ideal that Voltaire sought to illustrate by example in the last decades of his life, when he used his immense fame and influence to publicize and protest against miscarriages of justice such as those associated with Jean Calas, Pierre-Paul Sirven, and the chevalier de La Barre.[46] He also sought to promote this ideal through his most famous book, with its catalog of the many evils of the world – many even if not all of them eminently preventable – and its concluding injunction that we must cultivate *our* garden.[47] Still, Voltaire regards attempts to *force* people to devote themselves to others or to the common good – particularly in the political sphere, as in Greece and Rome – to be counterproductive.

Like Montesquieu, Voltaire maintains that one of the safest and most effectual means of breaking down the barriers among people and establishing bonds among them is through commerce. Of course, he too points to numerous other advantages of extensive trade. In the *Letters*, his first major political work, he depicts England as the commercial nation par excellence and outlines the many benefits that both the people and the state derive from this commercial bent. "As Trade enrich'd the Citizens in *England*, so it contributed to their Freedom," he writes in the letter on trade, "and this Freedom on the other Side extended their Commerce, whence arose the Grandeur of the State" (LCE, 42). In France merchants

---

[46] In this, Voltaire saw himself as following in the footsteps of Cicero, whom he depicts as the ideal philosopher–cum–public servant in his play *Rome Saved*. See Voltaire, *Rome sauvée, ou Catilina, tragédie*, ed. Paul LeClerc, in *The Complete Works of Voltaire*, vol. 31a (Oxford: Voltaire Foundation, [1749] 1992). For a biography of Voltaire that concentrates on his crusades for toleration and justice while at Ferney, see Ian Davidson, *Voltaire in Exile: The Last Years, 1753–78* (New York: Grove Press, 2004).

[47] See Voltaire, *Candide*, in *Candide and Related Texts*, trans. David Wootton (Indianapolis: Hackett, [1759] 2000), 79. While this famous line has sometimes been read as an invitation to withdraw from society and its ills, David Langdon shows that it is in fact an allusion to "the practical efforts incumbent on humanity, in the person of each or any of its members, to combat evil whenever it is humanly possible to do so." David Langdon, "On the Meanings of the Conclusion of *Candide*" *Studies on Voltaire and the Eighteenth Century* 238 (1985), 407. See also Gustave Lanson, *Voltaire*, trans. Robert A. Wagoner (New York: John Wiley and Sons, [1906] 1966), 129.

are commonly looked down upon "with sovereign Contempt," he notes sarcastically; "however, I cannot say which is most useful to a Nation; a Lord, powder'd in the tip of the Mode, who knows exactly what a Clock the King rises and goes to bed ... or a Merchant, who enriches his Country ... and contributes to the Felicity of the World" (LCE, 43). A few years later, Voltaire helped to stoke the "luxury debate" of eighteenth-century France through his poem "The Man of the World" or "The Worldling" (*Le Mondain*), which favorably contrasts the abundance and refinement of modern Europe with the penury and misery of most previous ages.[48] (This poem was condemned especially for its portrayal of the primitive and ignorant lives that Adam and Eve must have led in the Garden of Eden, complete with a description of their dirty, untrimmed fingernails.) Voltaire also highlights the fact that commerce allows ordinary people to improve their own lives without relying on the whims of kings and priests; as he puts it in the *Essay on the Mores and Spirit of Nations*, the ants can continue quietly to build their homes while the eagles and vultures tear each other to pieces overhead (EM I.81, 757).

Perhaps the principal advantage of commerce that Voltaire points to, however, lies in its ability to overcome the divisions among individuals and groups.[49] During his early travels through Holland and England, Voltaire was continually struck by the fact that people of diverse faiths were able to coexist peacefully in these commercial nations, setting aside their differences to trade together with civility and respect.[50] The classic formulation of this idea, of course, appears in his description of London's Royal Exchange in the *Letters*, a passage that is worth reproducing in its entirety:

[48] For translations of this poem and Voltaire's subsequent "Defense" of it, see Voltaire, "The Worldling," in *Commerce, Culture, and Liberty: Readings on Capitalism before Adam Smith*, ed. Henry C. Clark (Indianapolis: Liberty Fund, [1736] 2003); and Voltaire, "On Commerce and Luxury," in *Commerce, Culture, and Liberty: Readings on Capitalism before Adam Smith*, ed. Henry C. Clark (Indianapolis: Liberty Fund, [1738] 2003). For a later defense of luxury, see PD, 290–2. On the eighteenth-century luxury debate, see Christopher J. Berry, *The Idea of Luxury: A Conceptual and Historical Investigation* (Cambridge: Cambridge University Press, 1994), chapter 6.

[49] For a useful elaboration on this theme in Voltaire's writings, see Muller, *The Mind and the Market*, chapter 2.

[50] See Voltaire, letter to Marguerite Madeleine Du Moutier, marquise de Bernières, 7 October 1722, in *The Complete Works of Voltaire*, ed. Theodore Besterman, vol. 85 (Geneva: Institut et Musée Voltaire, 1968), 138; and Voltaire, *Notebooks*, vol. 1, ed. Theodore Besterman, in *The Complete Works of Voltaire*, vol. 81 (Geneva: Institut et Musée Voltaire, 1968), 51, 65.

Negative Liberty for a Positive Community

Take a view of the *Royal-Exchange* in *London*, a place more venerable than many courts of justice, where the representatives of all nations meet for the benefit of mankind. There the Jew, the Mahometan, and the Christian transact together as tho' they all profess'd the same religion, and give the name of Infidel to none but bankrupts. There the Presbyterian confides in the Anabaptist, and the Churchman depends on the Quaker's word. At the breaking up of this pacific and free assembly, some withdraw to the synagogue, and others to take a glass. This man goes and is baptiz'd in a great tub, in the name of the Father, Son, and Holy Ghost: That man has his son's foreskin cut off, whilst a sett of *Hebrew* words (quite unintelligible to him) are mumbled over his child. Others retire to their churches, and there wait for the inspiration of heaven with their hats on, and all are satisfied. (LCE, 30)[51]

There is, needless to say, an implicit contrast here with the intolerance and sectarian conflict of France, but Voltaire also contrasts the conditions of eighteenth-century Britain, in which people of all religions "live very sociably together" (LCE, 30), with those of the same nation in the previous century, when the country "was torn to pieces by the intestine wars which three or four sects had rais'd in the name of God" (LCE, 17). When religious differences are the chief focus of social interactions, the results are often discord and civil war; if the focus can be shifted to commercial exchanges and the pursuit of wealth, it becomes much easier to attain social peace. It is true that commerce does not guarantee a tight-knit community of dutiful citizens; after all, according to Voltaire's description the individuals in the Royal Exchange each go their own separate way "at the breaking up of this pacific and free assembly" (LCE, 30). Nonetheless, like Montesquieu, he holds that commerce ultimately helps to *strengthen* communal ties, not by promoting selfless devotion to others – seeking selflessly to save the souls of others is, in any case, hardly a recipe for social harmony – but rather by providing an avenue

---

[51] This famous passage has a number of antecedents and successors in Voltaire's writings. For instance, in his early notebooks he reports (in somewhat broken English): "In the Commonwealths and other free contrys one may see in a see port, as many relligions as shipps. The same god is there differently whorship'd by jews, mahometans, heathens, catholiques, quackers, anabaptistes, which write strenuously against another, but deal together freely and with trust and peace; like good players who after having humour'd their parts and fought one against another upon the stage, spend the rest of their time in drinking together." Voltaire, *Notebooks*, vol. 1, 65. Similarly, in the entry "Tolerance" in the *Philosophical Dictionary* he writes: "The Parsee, the Hindu, the Jew, the Mohammedan, the Chinese deist, the Brahman, the Greek Christian, the Roman Christian, the Protestant Christian, the Quaker Christian trade with each other in the stock exchanges of Amsterdam, London, Surat or Basra: they do not raise their daggers against one another to win souls for their religions" (PD, 387–8).

278   *The Pragmatic Enlightenment*

for self-interested cooperation that prevents the hostility created by the pursuit of consensus.

HUME AND THE "INDISSOLUBLE CHAIN" OF COMMERCIAL SOCIETY

Hume too conceives of liberty primarily in terms of personal security and independence, protected by the rule of law.[52] Indeed, at several points he suggests that the first and ultimate purpose of all law and government is "the distribution of justice," meaning the protection of people's lives and property from encroachment by others (e.g., EMPL, 37; HE I, 445, 488). Hume does not, however, conceive of liberty in terms of rights that are inherent in human nature or humanity's natural state, and that constrain the reach of legitimate political power; on the contrary, he holds that liberty can be established and maintained only through stable, orderly, and effective government.[53] Throughout most of human history, he maintains, governments were too weak to provide their citizens with sufficient protection, whether from neighboring tribes and states, from disorder and crime, or from the oppression of local lords and priests.[54] For this reason, he sees liberty as a relatively recent development, remarking that "*personal* freedom" did not become "almost general in Europe" until the rise of absolute monarchy and the end of feudal serfdom in the sixteenth century (HE II, 524, Hume's italics; see also III, 80). It was only at that point, he argues, that most people could effectively choose their own course in life – where to live, what occupation to practice, how to use

---

[52] For a discussion of the different meanings that Hume attaches to the word "liberty," and an argument that the most important of these is embodied in the rule of law, see Donald W. Livingston, *Philosophical Melancholy and Delirium: Hume's Pathology of Philosophy* (Chicago: University of Chicago Press, 1998), chapter 8.

[53] See Frederick G. Whelan, *Order and Artifice in Hume's Political Philosophy* (Princeton, NJ: Princeton University Press, 1985), 360.

[54] As Hume explains in the first volume of his *History of England*, a weak state virtually guarantees a lack of liberty: "On the whole, notwithstanding the seeming liberty or rather licentiousness of the Anglo-Saxons, the great body of the people even of the free citizens, in those ages, really enjoyed much less true liberty, than where the execution of the laws is the most severe, and where subjects are reduced to the strictest subordination and dependance on the civil magistrate. The reason is derived from the excess itself of that liberty. Men must guard themselves at any price against insults and injuries; and where they receive not protection from the laws and magistrate, they will seek it by submission to superiors, and by herding in some private confederacy, which acts under the direction of a powerful leader. And thus all anarchy is the immediate cause of tyranny, if not over the state, at least over many of the individuals" (HE I, 168–9).

Negative Liberty for a Positive Community

their property, and so on – within the limits of, and under the protection provided by, the rule of law.

As this association of the emergence of liberty with the rise of absolute monarchy suggests, Hume does not see liberty as the exclusive preserve of popular or democratic forms of government.[55] On the contrary, as we saw in Chapter 2, he insists that "it may now be affirmed of civilized monarchies, what was formerly said in praise of republics alone, *that they are a government of Laws, not of Men*. They are found susceptible of order, method, and constancy, to a surprizing degree. Property is there secure; industry encouraged; the arts flourish" (EMPL, 94, Hume's italics; see also 10). On the other hand, Hume was among the first to challenge the common idea – embraced by Montesquieu and Voltaire, among others – that republican government is suited only to small countries. In a brief discussion that did much to inspire James Madison's argument in *Federalist* 10, Hume claims that in fact "the contrary seems probable" (EMPL, 527).[56] Whereas small, direct democracies are generally subject to "tumult and faction," he writes, in large representative governments "there is compass and room enough to refine the democracy, from the lower people, who may be admitted into the first elections or first concoction of the commonwealth, to the higher magistrates, who direct all the movements. At the same time, the parts are so distant and remote, that it is very difficult, either by intrigue, prejudice, or passion, to hurry them into any measures against the public interest" (EMPL, 527–8). Even in the midst of his argument in favor of the efficacy of large republics, then, Hume emphasizes the importance of maintaining a certain distance between the government and the people – not only for the sake of the government's stability, but also for the sake of the people's liberty. "The more the master is removed from us in place and rank, the greater liberty we enjoy," he holds, because "the less are our actions inspected and

[55] For a more extended discussion of this point, see Duncan Forbes, *Hume's Philosophical Politics* (Cambridge: Cambridge University Press, 1975), chapter 5.

[56] It should be noted, however, that Hume seems to contradict this argument in a letter to his nephew, in which he suggests that the republican form of government is "only fitted for a small State." David Hume, letter to David Hume the Younger, 8 December 1775, in *The Letters of David Hume*, ed. J. Y. T. Greig, vol. 2 (Oxford: Clarendon Press, 1932), 306. Hume's impact on Madison was demonstrated in a celebrated essay by Douglass Adair: see Douglass Adair, "'That Politics May Be Reduced to a Science': David Hume, James Madison, and the Tenth Federalist," in *Fame and the Founding Fathers: Essays by Douglass Adair*, ed. Trevor Colbourn (Indianapolis: Liberty Fund, [1957] 1974). For a defense of Adair's thesis against its recent critics and an argument that Hume's *History of England* was also important for Madison, see Mark G. Spencer, "Hume and Madison on Faction" *William and Mary Quarterly* 59.4 (October 2002): 869–96.

controled" (EMPL, 383).[57] Again, liberty is a matter of personal security and independence, not of civic engagement or self-government.

It comes as no surprise, then, that Hume too opposes the ideal of the participatory republic.[58] Whereas civic republicans generally associated the strength and greatness of a state with the public-spiritedness and military valor of its citizens, Hume argues in "Of Commerce" and "Of Refinement in the Arts" that in the modern world strength and greatness are far more likely to issue from commerce, luxury, and the arts and sciences, which render the people more industrious and thus the state more prosperous. Moreover, he contends that the modern approach is far more dependable because it exploits common human tendencies and inclinations, whereas the "ancient policy" of Sparta and Rome, which required people to submit to "such grievous burthens," was "violent, and contrary to the more natural and usual course of things" (EMPL, 259). Hume's most extended critique of the participatory republic, however, is found in the essay "Of the Populousness of Ancient Nations."[59] In addition to highlighting the violence and xenophobia of the ancient republics, he notes that they relied on slavery to afford citizens the time and opportunity to devote themselves wholeheartedly to political and military affairs. For this reason alone, he says, it is clear that "human nature, in general, really enjoys more liberty at present, in the most arbitrary government of EUROPE, than it ever did during the most flourishing period of ancient times" (EMPL, 383). He claims, further, that the ancient republics experienced "such inveterate rage between factions" as "are found, in modern times amongst religious parties alone." These factions produced continual disturbances and even revolutions in the political sphere, and "the disorder, diffidence, jealousy, enmity, which must prevail [in such circumstances], are not easy for us to imagine in this age of the world" (EMPL, 407; see also 410, 415–16). Like Montesquieu and Voltaire, then, Hume

[57] See also Hume's comment that "in a government altogether republican, such as that of HOLLAND," the government generally lays "a considerable restraint on men's actions, and make[s] every private citizen pay a great respect to the government" (EMPL, 10).

[58] On Hume's departures from and criticisms of the civic republican tradition, see James Moore, "Hume's Political Science and the Classical Republican Tradition" *Canadian Journal of Political Science* 10.4 (December 1977): 809–39; Christopher J. Finlay, "Hume's Theory of Civil Society" *European Journal of Political Theory* 3.4 (October 2004): 369–91; and Neil McArthur, *David Hume's Political Theory: Law, Commerce, and the Constitution of Government* (Toronto: University of Toronto Press, 2007), chapter 4.

[59] For a useful commentary on this essay, see Ernest C. Mossner, "Hume and the Ancient-Modern Controversy, 1725–1752: A Study in Creative Scepticism" *University of Texas Studies in English* 28 (1949): 139–53.

Negative Liberty for a Positive Community
281

regards participatory republics as surprisingly divisive and factious, despite (or perhaps because of) their "violent" policy of subordinating all individual interests to the common good.

To be sure, Hume by no means repudiates the very idea of promoting virtue and striving for the common good, as Mandeville seems to do. On the contrary, he insists that factions and sects should be "detested and hated" for their tendency to "beget the fiercest animosities among men of the same nation, who ought to give mutual assistance and protection to each other," and he maintains that "general virtue and good morals in a state, which are so requisite to happiness, can never arise from the most refined precepts of philosophy, or even the severest injunctions of religion; but must proceed entirely from the virtuous education of youth, the effect of wise laws and institutions" (EMPL, 55; see also HE I, 79–80).[60] Indeed, at one point Hume goes so far as to proclaim that "a man who loves only himself, without regard to friendship and desert, merits the severest blame; and a man, who is only susceptible of friendship, without public spirit, or a regard to the community, is deficient in the most material part of virtue" (EMPL, 26–7).[61] However, he goes on to caution that false or wrongly directed "public spirit" often produces much more harm than mere selfishness does, reproaching the "zealots on both sides who kindle up the passions of their partizans, and under pretence of public good, pursue the interests and ends of their particular faction" (EMPL, 27). For this reason, he holds, the pursuit of the common good and the promotion of civic virtue should be accompanied by a spirit

---

[60] It is perhaps also worth noting, in this connection, that Hume includes a citizen militia in his "perfect commonwealth," claiming that "without a militia, it is in vain to think that any free government will ever have security or stability" (EMPL, 525; see also 520–1). However, he advocates a militia less as a means of promoting civic virtue than as a way to ensure that a large standing army will not confer excessive power on the executive or tempt him into unnecessary wars. See John Robertson, *The Scottish Enlightenment and the Militia Issue* (Edinburgh: John Donald, 1985), 60–74; and Frederick G. Whelan, *Hume and Machiavelli: Political Realism and Liberal Thought* (Lanham, MD: Lexington, 2004), 219–21.

[61] Donald Livingston remarks that "the teaching that the 'most material part of virtue' is a regard to the community places Hume in the civic humanist tradition, where man is considered as an essentially social creature and where morality has an irreducibly communitarian element. This teaching is in stark contrast to the view of Hume as a radical individualist in the liberal tradition whose highest conception of moral order is that which makes possible market exchanges for mutual profit and benefit." Livingston, *Philosophical Melancholy and Delirium*, 174. While I would not go so far as to describe Hume as a civic humanist, for all of the reasons outlined in this section, Livingston is certainly right to argue that Hume is no "radical individualist."

of moderation rather than one of zeal (see EMPL, 27–31).[62] As always, Hume aims to temper enthusiasm and the disorders it generates.

Like Montesquieu and Voltaire, Hume argues that a key means of promoting virtue, establishing bonds among people, *and* moderating zeal can be found in commerce. In stark contrast to Christian and civic republican thinkers who regarded commerce and luxury as "the source of every corruption in government, and the immediate cause of faction, sedition, civil wars, and the total loss of liberty" (EPM 2.21, 11), Hume contends that they in fact help to spread virtue and safeguard liberty.[63] In "Of Refinement of the Arts" – an essay that was, significantly, originally entitled "Of Luxury" – he argues that luxury and the arts induce people to work more diligently, to expand their minds, and to act in a more restrained and civilized manner toward others, and thus that "*industry, knowledge,* and *humanity,* are linked together by an indissoluble chain, and are found, from experience as well as reason, to be peculiar to the more polished, and, what are commonly denominated, the more luxurious ages" (EMPL, 271, Hume's italics; see also 264).[64] While people's tempers are softened and their passions moderated in commercial society, Hume nevertheless insists – in contrast to Smith, among others – that there is no need to "fear, that men, by losing their ferocity, will lose their martial spirit, or become less undaunted and vigorous in defence of their country or their liberty. The arts have no such effect in enervating either the mind or body. On the contrary, industry, their inseparable attendant, adds new force to both" (EMPL, 274).[65] Moreover, he holds that commerce and the

---

[62] Later in this essay Hume writes: "The virtue and good intentions of CATO and BRUTUS are highly laudable; but, to what purpose, did their zeal serve? Only to hasten the fatal period of the ROMAN government, and render its convulsions and dying agonies more violent and painful" (EMPL, 30).

[63] Hume concedes that luxury *can* be vicious, as when "it engrosses all a man's expence, and leaves no ability for such acts of duty and generosity as are required by his situation and fortune" – for instance, providing for the education of one's children, supporting one's friends, or helping to relieve the lot of the poor (EMPL, 279; see also 269). However, his discussion of luxury's vicious side is quite brief compared to his account of its virtues, and he insists that it is preferable to accept the potential ills of luxury than to attempt (vainly) to eradicate it, thereby creating even greater ills (see EMPL, 279–80).

[64] On the link between commerce and civility in Hume's thought, see Richard Boyd, "Manners and Morals: David Hume on Civility, Commerce, and the Social Construction of Difference," in *David Hume's Political Economy,* ed. Carl Wennerlind and Margaret Schabas (New York: Routledge, 2008).

[65] Hume continues: "And if anger, which is said to be the whetstone of courage, loses somewhat of its asperity, by politeness and refinement; a sense of honour, which is a stronger, more constant, and more governable principle, acquires fresh vigour by that elevation of genius which arises from knowledge and a good education. Add to this,

Negative Liberty for a Positive Community

arts help to undermine feudal serfdom and dependence, a development that in turn not only safeguards liberty, by creating and empowering a "middling ranking of men, who are the best and firmest basis of public liberty" (EMPL, 277; see also HE IV, 384), but also elevates people's characters, since "an industrious tradesman is both a better man and a better citizen than one of those idle retainers, who formerly depended on the great families" (HE III, 76; see also IV, 383).

Still further, Hume too maintains that commerce helps to create peaceful bonds among both nations and individuals. At least, it *can* and *should* create peaceful bonds among nations; like Montesquieu, Voltaire, and Smith, Hume argues that mercantilist policies of the sort that prevailed throughout eighteenth-century Europe harm all of the parties involved, and he admits that such policies often lead to unnecessary conflict through the misguided assumption that economics is essentially a zero-sum game.[66] He steadfastly opposes the "narrow and malignant opinion" that nations can only succeed at one another's expense, arguing that, on the contrary, "the encrease of riches and commerce in any one nation, instead of hurting, commonly promotes the riches and commerce of all its neighbours" (EMPL, 328). Whereas participatory republics generally rest on narrow loyalties and thus breed xenophobia, then, commercial societies can and should encourage the opposite tendency, at least once individuals and nations come to recognize their true interests. As Robert Manzer notes, Hume (like Smith) seeks to help this process along not only by highlighting the economic irrationality of exclusive national pride, but also by portraying it as "narrow and unenlarged, even childish and foolish."[67] "Not only as a man, but as a BRITISH subject," he pointedly announces, "I pray for the flourishing commerce of GERMANY, SPAIN, ITALY, and even FRANCE itself" (EMPL, 331).

---

that courage can neither have any duration, nor be of any use, when not accompanied with discipline and martial skill, which are seldom found among a barbarous people" (EMPL, 274).

[66] On Montesquieu and mercantilism, see the citations in note 23. On Voltaire, see Voltaire, "Dialogue between a Philosopher and a Comptroller-General of Finance," in *Political Writings*, trans. David Williams (Cambridge: Cambridge University Press, [1750] 1994). On Hume, see especially his essays "Of Money," "Of the Balance of Trade," and "Of the Jealousy of Trade." For a series of essays on this theme that concentrate especially on Hume and Smith, see Istvan Hont, *Jealousy of Trade: International Competition and the Nation-State in Historical Perspective* (Cambridge, MA: Belknap Press, 2005).

[67] Robert A. Manzer, "The Promise of Peace? Hume and Smith on the Effects of Commerce on Peace and War" *Hume Studies* 22.2 (November 1996), 371.

Just as importantly, Hume claims that commerce provides a healthy means of establishing bonds among individuals. The luxuries, arts, and sciences that are part and parcel of commercial society render people more "sociable" and offer them "a fund of conversation," he contends, thereby making it impossible that "they should be contented to remain in solitude, or live with their fellow-citizens in that distant manner, which is peculiar to ignorant and barbarous nations." Thus, in commercial societies people "flock into cities.... Particular clubs and societies are every where formed: Both sexes meet in an easy and sociable manner; and the tempers of men, as well as their behaviour, refine apace. So that ... it is impossible but they must feel an encrease of humanity, from the very habit of conversing together, and contributing to each other's pleasure and entertainment" (EMPL, 271). This sense of humanity, in turn, helps to promote a more moderate and stable political order, since "when the tempers of men are softened as well as their knowledge improved ... factions are then less inveterate, revolutions less tragical, authority less severe, and seditions less frequent" (EMPL, 274). As Richard Boyd writes, Hume's preference for modern commercial societies over participatory republics stems not only from the greater personal freedom that they afford their citizens, but also from the fact that "modern commercial republics are less contentious, stronger, and more cohesive societies, even in light of their great heterogeneity."[68]

SMITH ON COMMERCE AND COMMUNITY

Smith's conception of liberty is quite similar to those of Montesquieu, Voltaire, and Hume. Indeed, he is close to restating verbatim Montesquieu's definition of political liberty in relation to the citizen when he equates "the liberty of every individual" with "the sense which he has of his own security" (WN V.i.b.25, 722–3). Like Hume, Smith maintains that it was only after the rise of absolute monarchy in Europe, and the concomitant end of the direct, personal dependence that characterized the feudal age, that most people "became really free in our present sense of the word Freedom" (WN III.iii.5, 400; see also III.ii.8, 386–7). Thus, while he advocates leaving each individual "perfectly free to pursue his own interest his own way" in the economic sphere (WN IV.ix.51, 687; see also IV.ix.3, 664), Smith too sees liberty as far removed from license or a

---

[68] Richard Boyd, "Reappraising the Scottish Moralists and Civil Society" *Polity* 33.1 (autumn 2000), 113.

Negative Liberty for a Positive Community

mere absence of government. Like these other thinkers – but unlike, for instance, Jeremy Bentham in his extreme moments[69] – Smith recognizes that not every law undermines liberty, and in fact that liberty is *advanced* by providing predictable rules of fair play and by protecting individuals from each other and from other outside forces. As Emma Rothschild rightly notes, throughout his writings Smith is concerned that the government be *strong* enough to defend individuals against the sometimes oppressive measures of "churches, parish overseers, corporations ... masters, proprietors," and the like. This is an important and underappreciated point: "The criticism of local institutions, with their hidden, not quite public, not quite private powers, is at the heart of Smith's politics."[70]

While Smith does not dwell on the benefits and drawbacks of different regime types, he does indicate that representation can be useful in maintaining a free, effective political order. In *The Wealth of Nations*, he notes that the liberty of both the British people and the American colonists "is secured ... by an assembly of the representatives of the people" (WN IV.vii.b.51, 585), and in the lectures on jurisprudence he explains to his students that "the frequency of elections is ... a great security for the liberty of the people, as the representative must be carefull to serve his country, at least his constituents, otherwise he will be in danger of losing his place at the next elections" (LJ, 273; see also 271, 422). Moreover, he applauds England for having less stringent property requirements for voting than Scotland (see LJ, 273–4, 323, 524) and comments favorably on the fact that the American colonial governments were based on a still wider franchise (see WN IV.vii.b.51, 585). However, Smith's main reason for supporting representation and a broad franchise is that elections allow the people to check abuses of power, *not* that they enable them to attain "positive liberty" through collective self-government.[71] Hence,

---

[69] Bentham goes so far as to claim at one point that "every law is an evil, for every law is an infraction of liberty." Jeremy Bentham, *The Theory of Legislation* (Oxford: Oxford University Press, [1802] 1914), 65.

[70] Emma Rothschild, *Economic Sentiments: Adam Smith, Condorcet, and the Enlightenment* (Cambridge, MA: Harvard University Press, 2001), 71, 108; see also 32.

[71] See Samuel Fleischacker, *On Adam Smith's Wealth of Nations: A Philosophical Companion* (Princeton, NJ: Princeton University Press, 2004), 246–9. Elsewhere, Fleischacker argues that Smith upholds a "third concept of liberty" that focuses neither on a simple lack of interference nor on collective self-government, but rather on the individual exercise of judgment. See Samuel Fleischacker, *A Third Concept of Liberty: Judgment and Freedom in Kant and Adam Smith* (Princeton, NJ: Princeton University Press, 1999). For further discussion of the notions of negative, positive, and republican liberty in Smith's works, see Edward J. Harpham, "The Problem of Liberty in the Thought of Adam Smith" *Journal of the History of Economic Thought* 22.2 (June 2000): 217–37.

he too denies that liberty is restricted to democratic or representative governments – recall once more his claim that the absolute monarchies that arose in Western Europe on the heels of the feudal age provided, for essentially the first time in history, "order and good government, and with them, the liberty and security of individuals" (WN III.iv.4, 412).[72] Indeed, like Hume before him and Madison after him, Smith expresses deep concern about the "rancorous and virulent factions which are inseparable from small democracies" (WN V.iii.90, 945).

Although Smith is, like Montesquieu, occasionally thought to have had civic republican leanings,[73] he too depicts participatory republics of the kind found in ancient Greece and Rome as significant *threats* to freedom. This is true, in the first place, because the collective self-government of the citizens would have been impossible without widespread slavery: the only reason the citizens "had it in their power to attend on publick deliberations" was that they "had all their work done by slaves" (LJ, 410; see also 226, 242–3). Smith repeatedly highlights the harshness of the form of slavery practiced among the Greeks and Romans, going so far as to argue that "the freedom of the free was the cause of the great oppression of the slaves" (LJ, 182; see also 181–3, 185, 255; WN III.ii.8, 386; IV.vii.b.55). He also laments the tendency of participatory republics to subordinate the interests of individuals to the state's glory and military success. As Samuel Fleischacker writes, Smith holds that individuals "should not identify their worth with their nation's glory, both because that has nothing to do with their individual worth and because such identification is the source of one of the greatest of human evils: war."[74] Still further, Smith joins Montesquieu, Voltaire, and Hume in regarding participatory republics as markedly divisive and factious. He writes, for instance, that "all the different republics of Greece were, at home, almost always distracted by the most furious factions; and abroad, involved in the most sanguinary wars, in which each sought, not merely superiority or dominion, but either completely to extirpate all its enemies, or, what was not less cruel, to reduce them into the vilest of all states, that of domestic slavery" (TMS VII.ii.1.28, 281–2). Elsewhere, he reiterates that

---

[72] See also Duncan Forbes, "Sceptical Whiggism, Commerce, and Liberty," in *Essays on Adam Smith*, ed. Andrew S. Skinner and Thomas Wilson (Oxford: Clarendon Press, 1975).

[73] Perhaps the fullest case along these lines in recent years can be found in Pierre Force, *Self-Interest before Adam Smith: A Genealogy of Economic Science* (Cambridge: Cambridge University Press, 2003).

[74] Fleischacker, *On Adam Smith's Wealth of Nations*, 250; see also 250–7 more generally.

Negative Liberty for a Positive Community

"the factions of the Greeks were almost always violent and sanguinary" (WN V.i.f.40, 775; see also V.i.f.44, 778).[75] Thus, not only was the "liberty" of these republics restricted to a select few, it also led to continual conflicts, both among nations and within them.

Much like Montesquieu, Smith maintains that true civic spirit consists not in the pursuit of military glory or the continual subordination of one's individual interests to the common good, but rather in maintaining "a certain respect and reverence for that constitution or form of government which is actually established" and "an earnest desire to render the condition of our fellow-citizens as safe, respectable, and happy as we can" (TMS VI.ii.2.11, 231). There is, of course, a significant other-regarding element in this understanding of the love of one's country; while Smith does not place much emphasis on active participation in the political realm, he by no means advocates a society of selfish, atomized individuals.[76] On the contrary, he maintains that even if a society can "subsist" where people merely abstain from harming one another, it will not "flourish" or be "happy" unless "all the different members of [society] are bound together by the agreeable bands of love and affection, and are, as it were, drawn to one common centre of mutual good offices" (TMS II.ii.3.1–2, 85–6).[77] Given that a degree of reciprocal concern among fellow citizens is indispensable for a society truly to thrive, Smith holds that

---

[75] It must be admitted, however, that Smith views the Roman republic as far less factious than the Greek republics, because of the Romans' superior "publick morals" (WN V.i.f.40, 775).

[76] Charles Griswold contends that "as surprising as it might seem, Smith would not agree with Kant's view ... that the problem of organizing a state can be solved by a race of rational devils, that is, by a race of intelligent, self-interested utility maximizers. Intelligent self-interest *alone* will not solve the problem of social cooperation." Charles L. Griswold, *Adam Smith and the Virtues of Enlightenment* (Cambridge: Cambridge University Press, 1999), 295. For Kant's line, see Immanuel Kant, "Toward Perpetual Peace," in *Practical Philosophy*, trans. Mary J. Gregor (Cambridge: Cambridge University Press, [1795] 1996), 335.

[77] Smith does maintain that "mere justice is, upon most occasions, but a negative virtue" and that "we may often fulfil all the rules of justice by sitting still and doing nothing" (TMS II.ii.1.9, 82). However, the import of this statement – which is often invoked to demonstrate Smith's alleged lack of concern for other-regarding actions and sentiments – is drastically weakened when we recall that he defines justice as refraining from injuring others (see TMS II.ii.1.5, 79); given this definition, the claim that justice is a negative virtue is essentially a tautology. Like Hume, Smith regards justice as just one of many moral virtues, and a rather narrow one at that (as he himself notes at TMS VII.ii.1.10, 269–70). He never suggests that a person can be altogether *virtuous* or *moral* by sitting still and doing nothing; in fact, he holds that "to feel much for others and little for ourselves ... to restrain our selfish, and to indulge our benevolent affections, constitutes the perfection of human nature" (TMS I.i.5.5, 25; see also III.3.35, 152).

it is entirely within the state's purview to promote the moral character of its citizens, writing that "the civil magistrate ... may prescribe rules ... which not only prohibit mutual injuries among fellow-citizens, but command mutual good offices to a certain degree" (TMS II.ii.1.8, 81; see also WN V.i.f.61, 788). He warns, however, that "of all the duties of a law-giver ... this, perhaps, is that which it requires the greatest delicacy and reserve to execute with propriety and judgment. To neglect it altogether exposes the commonwealth to many gross disorders and shocking enormities, and to push it too far is destructive of all liberty, security, and justice" (TMS II.ii.1.8, 81).

Smith's circumspection on this point derives not from any reservations about the goal – that of encouraging "mutual good offices" among fellow citizens – but rather from severe misgivings about the means of reaching it, namely, through coercive measures enacted by politicians. Throughout his writings, Smith evinces a rather cynical view of these "insidious and crafty animal[s]," repeatedly depicting them as corrupt, partial, and grossly overconfident in their ability to effect change without producing unintended consequences (WN IV.ii.39, 468). Thus, he is fairly skeptical about the capacity of governments to promote the moral character of their citizens directly. One of the central purposes of *The Theory of Moral Sentiments* is to locate an alternative means of reaching this goal, one that does not require heavy-handed regulations on the part of the political (or ecclesiastical) authorities. Smith seeks to show that people will *naturally* tend to identify with and care about those around them, in the absence of coercive measures, thanks to the workings of sympathy, and that internal and social motivations are often far more effective than legal ones.[78] Ironically, then, for Smith "governments foster virtue best where they refuse, directly, to foster virtue at all: just as they protect economic development best where they refuse, directly, to protect development."[79]

As might be expected, Smith joins Montesquieu, Voltaire, and Hume in holding that commerce helps to sustain a healthier sense of community than was found in most precommercial eras. As we have seen, he in no way shrinks from the potential dangers and drawbacks inherent in commercial society, but he nevertheless offers an unequivocal defense of this kind of society in view of its even greater benefits. Many of these benefits

---

[78] This point was discussed in Chapter 5; see note 27 and the associated text.
[79] Samuel Fleischacker, "Adam Smith," in *A Companion to Early Modern Philosophy*, ed. Steven Nadler (Oxford: Blackwell, 2002), 518–19.

Negative Liberty for a Positive Community 289

have already been touched upon over the course of this study: Commerce increases the wealth of nations, thereby helping to ameliorate the perennial problems of penury and starvation (see WN intro.4, 10). It promotes personal security and the rule of law, both because it diminishes the direct dependence of the feudal age (see WN III.iv.4, 412; III.iv.12. 420) and because "commerce and manufactures can seldom flourish long in any state which does not enjoy a regular administration of justice, in which the people do not feel themselves secure in the possession of their property" (WN V.iii.7, 910). It encourages the "bourgeois" virtues of reliability, decency, honesty, cooperativeness, a commitment to keeping one's promises, and a strict adherence to society's norms of justice, in at least two ways. First, it expands the proportion of people in the "middling station of life," for whom "the good old proverb ... That honesty is the best policy, holds ... almost always perfectly true" (TMS I.iii.3.5, 63; see also VI.i.3–4, 212–13). Second, the activity of commerce itself helps to promote these virtues, since "wherever dealings are frequent, a man does not expect to gain so much by any one contract as by probity and punctuality on the whole, and a prudent dealer, who is sensible of his real interest, would rather chuse to lose what he has a right to than give any ground for suspicion" (LJ, 539; see also WN I.x.c.31, 146; III.iv.3, 412).

Of course, Smith does not suggest that commerce promotes *all* possible virtues. In contrast to Hume, he accepts that in commercial societies "the great body of the people" are apt to become "altogether unwarlike" (WN V.i.a.15, 697), and he admits that an extensive division of labor can have deleterious effects on the "intellectual, social, and martial virtues" of the laborers "unless government takes some pains to prevent it" (WN V.i.f.50, 782). This last phrase, however, is key: Smith argues that government can help to prevent this problem through compulsory and state-supported education, aimed especially at the poor (see WN V.i.f.52–7, 784–6).[80] An educated citizenry makes for a healthier political order, in his view, because it renders people, first, "less liable ... to the delusions of enthusiasm and superstition, which, among ignorant nations,

---

[80] Indeed, in book 5 of *The Wealth of Nations* Smith writes at greater length on education than on any other positive role of the state. Smith seems to have a greater degree of confidence in the capacity of education to promote the "intellectual" and "social" virtues than the "martial" ones; that is why he advocates relying on a professional standing army rather than on a citizen militia for purposes of defense (see WN V.i.a.23, 699–700; Vi.a.39–41, 705–7). For a more detailed discussion, see Dennis C. Rasmussen, *The Problems and Promise of Commercial Society: Adam Smith's Response to Rousseau* (University Park: Pennsylvania State University Press, 2008), 108–13.

290   *The Pragmatic Enlightenment*

frequently occasion the most dreadful disorders"; second, "more decent and orderly"; and third, "more disposed to examine, and more capable of seeing through, the interested complaints of faction and sedition." This latter advantage is especially important, he notes, for "in free countries, where the safety of the government depends very much upon the favorable judgment which the people may form of its conduct, it must surely be of the highest importance that they should not be disposed to judge rashly or capriciously concerning it" (WN V.i.f.61, 788). While Smith is skeptical about the ability of governments to foster virtue directly, through coercive measures, education offers an important means of fostering it indirectly, in a less forceful way. Commercial society, enhanced by a Smithian educational system, may not promote the virtues that the civic republicans held in the highest esteem,[81] but Smith argues that it *does* promote a number of important individual, social, and even political virtues that were comparatively lacking in precommercial societies.[82]

In addition, Smith sees commerce as a potential means of establishing bonds among nations. He argues that "the wealth of a neighbouring nation ... though dangerous in war and politicks, is certainly advantageous in trade," since "a nation that would enrich itself by foreign trade is certainly most likely to do so when its neighbours are all rich, industrious, and commercial nations" (WN IV.iii.c.11, 494–5). Like Hume, then, Smith holds that "commerce ... ought naturally to be, among nations, as among individuals, a bond of union and friendship," even if at present it has "become the most fertile source of discord and animosity" because of the foolish mercantilist assumptions based on which "nations have been taught that their interest consisted in beggaring all their neighbours" (WN IV.iii.c.9, 493). Virtually the whole of Smith's economic teaching is directed at showing that the opposite is true, that trade can be mutually beneficial and hence a source of amity rather than conflict.[83] For France

---

[81] Even where Smith highlights the need for a dutiful and well-informed citizenry, as in the passage just quoted, his concerns are quite distinct from those of the civic republican tradition: he hopes to render the people "orderly" and to enable them to *judge* political affairs properly, but he makes no mention of their actively *participating* in politics or devoting themselves wholeheartedly to the common good.

[82] For helpful analyses of the effects of commercial society on morality in Smith's thought, including both the "asset" and "liability" sides of the ledger, see Nathan Rosenberg, "Adam Smith and the Stock of Moral Capital" *History of Political Economy* 22.1 (spring 1990): 1–17; and Jerry Z. Muller, *Adam Smith in His Time and Ours: Designing the Decent Society* (Princeton, NJ: Princeton University Press, 1993), chapter 10.

[83] As Fleischacker writes, "from the very first sentence to the very last sentence of the book, Smith is implicitly or explicitly combating economic views that set nation against nation. It is indeed not much of an exaggeration to say that puncturing the fantasies that lead

Negative Liberty for a Positive Community

and England "to envy the internal happiness and prosperity of the other ... is surely beneath the dignity of two such great nations," he admonishes. If Smith's arguments are convincing, then "each nation ought ... to promote, instead of obstructing the excellence of its neighbours" (TMS VI.ii.2.3, 229).

Interestingly, Smith does not place the same emphasis that Hume does on commerce rendering individuals more "sociable" – that is, more likely to "flock into cities," to form "clubs and societies," and the like (EMPL, 271). On the contrary, the type of "prudent man" whom Smith expects to abound in commercial society prefers to remain somewhat aloof: "though capable of friendship, he is not always much disposed to general sociality. He rarely frequents, and more rarely figures in those convivial societies which are distinguished for the jollity and gaiety of their conversation" (TMS VI.i.9, 214).[84] (One wonders whether these divergent visions are in any way related to the divergent personalities of the reserved Smith and the convivial Hume.) On the other hand, Smith's "prudent man" is far from being a *Homo economicus* who cares only about his own interests; as Charles Griswold writes, "a prudent person is not a mere monad in a society of strangers, intent just on improving his or her material lot, and a society of prudent persons is not a formula for social anomie. The prudent person has moral ties to others, including those of benevolence and justice, and exhibits other virtues as well."[85] Just as importantly, Smith maintains that the personal security and independence of commercial society help to open up space for a healthier, more admirable kind of relationship than those that tended to prevail in precommercial societies.[86] Whereas in earlier eras many of the attachments among individuals were imposed either through politics (as in the participatory republics of the ancient world) or through religion (as in feudal Europe), in commercial society more of them are freely chosen by the individuals

people to seek national glory is the primary aim" of *The Wealth of Nations*. Fleischacker, *On Adam Smith's Wealth of Nations*, 252.

[84] Smith's "prudent man" is also fairly apolitical: "When distinctly called upon, he will not decline the service of his country, but he will not cabal in order to force himself into it, and would be much better pleased that the public business were well managed by some other person, than that he himself should have the trouble, and incur the responsibility, of managing it" (TMS VI.i.13, 216).

[85] Griswold, *Adam Smith and the Virtues of Enlightenment*, 206.

[86] See Allan Silver, "'Two Different Sorts of Commerce' – Friendship and Strangership in Civil Society," in *Public and Private in Thought and Practice: Perspectives on a Grand Dichotomy*, ed. Jeff Weintraub and Krishan Kumar (Chicago: University of Chicago Press, 1997), especially 50–2.

involved.[87] In Smith's view, those attachments that arise "not from a constrained sympathy ... but from a natural sympathy, from an involuntary feeling that the persons to whom we attach ourselves are the natural and proper objects of esteem and approbation" are "by far, the most respectable" (TMS VI.ii.1.18, 224–5). Far from "contaminating" previously pure personal relationships with instrumental concerns, he suggests, commerce helps to free personal relationships from the types of coercion that have abounded throughout human history. In this, as in many other respects, Smith holds that commerce helps to foster a healthier community.

CONCLUSION

Admittedly, the type of liberal, commercial society envisioned by Hume, Smith, Montesquieu, and Voltaire is unlikely to prove appealing to contemporary communitarians, just as it did not to the civic republicans of their own time. In the eyes of the critics, these thinkers place too much emphasis on the security, independence, and interests of individuals, and too little on political participation, the cultivation of a tight-knit community, and (for the civic republicans) military defense and valor. As we have seen in this chapter, however, these four thinkers all advocated liberalism and commerce in large part *in order to foster a healthier, more cohesive community*. In their view, attempts to organize society around a set of shared ends or "higher" purposes, whether political or religious, are far more likely to produce division and conflict than consensus and community. Moreover, they saw liberal, commercial societies themselves as a source of a number of important social and political virtues, such as civility, tolerance, cooperativeness, reliability, decency, and moderation. These may not be the virtues that communitarians and civic republicans most prize, but the thinkers of the pragmatic Enlightenment saw them as far more desirable – safer, more dependable, less contentious – than the Christian ("monkish") and austere republican virtues. Indeed, it is not too much to say that they advocated liberal practices and institutions on largely communitarian grounds.

Whether these thinkers were *right* to suppose that liberal, commercial societies would encourage these virtues is, of course, debatable, although I am inclined to believe that there is more truth in their arguments than

---

[87] Smith admits that some relationships in commercial society – such as those among "colleagues in office" and "partners in trade" – are to some degree "imposed by the necessity of the situation," but he by no means sees these economic relationships as representative of all attachments in commercial society (TMS VI.ii.1.15, 224).

Negative Liberty for a Positive Community 293

is often recognized.[88] When the critics reproach Enlightenment principles and values for their atomizing consequences, they frequently fail to pose the always-relevant question "compared to what?" Liberalism and commerce may not encourage the public-spirited citizenry of the communitarians' and civic republicans' dreams, but it is difficult to lament the hierarchical, exclusive, xenophobic, and often oppressive forms of social order that in fact tended to prevail in preliberal, precommercial eras. Before we join the critics in bemoaning the "corrosive" effects of liberalism and commerce on traditional values, the way they "impoverish" the sense of community, we would do well to adopt the pragmatic Enlightenment's historical and comparative perspective.

---

[88] I address this question in the conclusion of Rasmussen, *The Problems and Promise of Commercial Society*. For recent scientific and social scientific support for the view that commerce supports and is in turn supported by morality, with frequent references to Smith's thought, see Paul J. Zak and Michael C. Jensen, eds., *Moral Markets: The Critical Role of Values in the Economy* (Princeton, NJ: Princeton University Press, 2008). See also Deirdre N. McCloskey, *The Bourgeois Virtues: Ethics for an Age of Commerce* (Chicago: University of Chicago Press, 2006).

Conclusion

For a movement that did so much to inspire so many aspects of life in the modern, liberal West, the Enlightenment has met with remarkably vigorous and enduring opposition from a remarkably broad range of perspectives. In particular, the Enlightenment is regularly associated, on both the Left and the Right, with a hegemonic form of moral and political universalism, a blind faith in the power and compass of abstract reason, and a reductive and isolating focus on the individual. We have seen throughout this study, however, that each of these charges is misleading or demonstrably erroneous in the case of Hume, Smith, Montesquieu, and Voltaire – and, I would add, many other leading thinkers of eighteenth-century Europe. These thinkers in fact emphasized the importance of context in the formulation of moral standards; adopted a flexible, nonfoundationalist form of liberalism; continually stressed the limits and fallibility of human understanding; advocated a cautious reformism in politics; conceived of human beings as inherently social and deeply shaped by their interactions with others; and supported negative liberty and commerce precisely in order to foster a healthier community. The outlook of the pragmatic Enlightenment, then, flies in the face of *all* of the main criticisms of the movement.

Nor are the claims of the Enlightenment's critics the only ones called into question by the reading of Hume, Smith, Montesquieu, and Voltaire offered here. It has been extremely common, at least since the time of Edmund Burke, to view the French and British (especially Scottish) Enlightenments as deeply dissimilar, even diametrically opposed.[1] Perhaps

---

[1] For instance, Burke proudly proclaims of his British compatriots, "We are not the converts of Rousseau; we are not the disciples of Voltaire; Helvetius has made no progress

294

Conclusion 295

the most forceful and detailed case along these lines in recent years can be found in the work of Gertrude Himmelfarb, who contends that the French and British Enlightenments constituted separate and fundamentally different "roads to modernity," the former rationalist, abstract, and radical and the latter sentimentalist, empirical, and conservative.[2] Yet we have seen that two key thinkers on each side of this supposed divide – indeed, arguably *the* two key thinkers on each side – adopted strikingly similar outlooks in many crucial respects. Contrary to what one might expect from the caricatures of the two national Enlightenments, Montesquieu and Voltaire were neither rationalists nor revolutionaries, and their Scottish counterparts were not always conservative: few tracts were more provocative, in an eighteenth-century context, than Hume's *Dialogues Concerning Natural Religion*, and we have seen that Smith himself proclaimed *The Wealth of Nations* to be a "very violent attack ... upon the whole commercial system of Great Britain."[3] It is true that the charges of rationalism and radicalism might fairly be applied to some of the lesser philosophes such as d'Holbach, Helvétius, and La Mettrie, but these figures were by and large outliers[4]; most of the leading thinkers of the French Enlightenment – not only Montesquieu and Voltaire, but also

amongst us. ... We are afraid to put men to live and trade each on his own private stock of reason; because we suspect that this stock in each man is small, and that the individuals would do better to avail themselves of the general bank and capital of nations, and of ages. Many of our men of speculation, instead of exploding general prejudices, employ their sagacity to discover the latent wisdom which prevails in them. ... Your [i.e., French] literary men ... essentially differ in these points. They have no respect for the wisdom of others; but they pay it off by a very full measure of confidence in their own. With them it is a sufficient motive to destroy an old scheme of things, because it is an old one." Edmund Burke, *Reflections on the Revolution in France*, ed. J. C. D. Clark (Stanford, CA: Stanford University Press, [1790] 2001), 249–52.

[2] See Gertrude Himmelfarb, *The Roads to Modernity: The British, French, and American Enlightenments* (New York: Alfred A. Knopf, 2004). Himmelfarb herself admits that Montesquieu is an exception to her larger thesis, asserting that he was "more representative of the British Enlightenment than of the French." Ibid., 15; see also 18, 21, 151, 160–3. Yet given Montesquieu's centrality to the period and enormous influence on the other philosophes (on which see note 27 in the Introduction), this is no small caveat: an exception of this magnitude not only does not prove the rule, it suggests that the rule must be heavily modified.

[3] Adam Smith, letter to Andreas Holt, 26 October 1780, in *The Correspondence of Adam Smith*, ed. Ernest Campbell Mossner and Ian Simpson Ross (Indianapolis: Liberty Fund, 1987), 251.

[4] In fact, these figures came in for frequent and often fierce criticism from the other philosophes themselves. Mark Hulliung dubs Helvétius and La Mettrie, in particular, "the black sheep of the French Enlightenment." Mark Hulliung, *The Autocritique of Enlightenment: Rousseau and the Philosophes* (Cambridge, MA: Harvard University Press, 1994), 199.

figures such as d'Alembert, Condillac, Condorcet, and Diderot – shared much of the pragmatism and moderation that prevailed on the other side of the Channel.[5] Thus, just as John Robertson makes a "case for the Enlightenment" against those who would pluralize it out of existence by showing that two of the extreme geographic poles of the European Enlightenment, Scotland and Naples, shared a good deal of intellectual common ground, I would argue that the two national Enlightenments that have often been seen as the extreme *ideological* poles of the period, the French and Scottish Enlightenments, had far more in common than is ordinarily supposed.[6]

This analysis of the pragmatic Enlightenment also serves to challenge Jonathan Israel's bifurcation of the Enlightenment into an atheistic, materialist, egalitarian, and revolutionary "Radical Enlightenment" and an intellectually modest and socially conservative "moderate mainstream" – a split within the Enlightenment that he claims was "much the most fundamental and important thing about it."[7] Israel's argument that these two sides of the Enlightenment were fundamentally distinct and irreconcilably opposed – and that it was the ideas of the Radical Enlightenment alone that eventually transformed the entire Western world – has been contested by many, above all for imposing an unrealistically strict dichotomy on a complex reality and for overstating the reach and influence of Spinoza and his "radical" followers.[8] Nor, certainly, do all scholars share Israel's palpable sympathy for radicalism: several recent studies have reminded us that there is much to be said in favor of moderation.[9] The pragmatic Enlightenment outlined here, however, offers a slightly different kind of challenge to Israel's thesis. Rather

---

[5] See note 34 in the Introduction and the associated text.

[6] See John Robertson, *The Case for the Enlightenment: Scotland and Naples, 1680–1760* (Cambridge: Cambridge University Press, 2005).

[7] Jonathan I. Israel, *Enlightenment Contested: Philosophy, Modernity, and the Emancipation of Man, 1670–1752* (Oxford: Oxford University Press, 2006), 10. For citations of the other works in which Israel advances this view, see note 4 in the Introduction.

[8] See, for instance, Harvey Chisick, "Interpreting the Enlightenment" *European Legacy* 13.1 (February 2008): 35–57; Anthony J. La Vopa, "A New Intellectual History? Jonathan Israel's Enlightenment" *Historical Journal* 52.3 (September 2009): 717–38; Antoine Lilti, "Comment écrit-on l'histoire intellectual des Lumières? Spinozisme, radicalisme et philosophie" *Annales* 64.1 (January–February 2009): 171–206; and Samuel Moyn, "Mind the Enlightenment" *Nation* 290.21 (31 May 2010): 25–32.

[9] See, for instance, Harry Clor, *On Moderation: Defending an Ancient Virtue in a Modern World* (Waco, TX: Baylor University Press, 2008); and Aurelian Craiutu, *A Virtue for Courageous Minds: Moderation in French Political Thought, 1748–1830* (Princeton, NJ: Princeton University Press, 2012).

Conclusion 297

than simply reversing Israel's value claim and championing the moderate Enlightenment over its radical counterpart, I would argue that, as least as far as political theory is concerned, a more fundamental division may be the one between the pragmatic Enlightenment and the more idealistic strands of Enlightenment thought. Whereas the idealistic thinkers of the period sought to ground their moral, social, and political views in natural law, a priori reason, or some other abstract foundation, the members of the pragmatic Enlightenment sought to ground theirs in empirical observation, and whereas the idealists tended to seek a universally applicable standard of judgment, the pragmatists stressed the importance of institutional flexibility and sensitivity to historical and cultural context. Such categories cut across Israel's purportedly neat dichotomy, insofar as the pragmatic Enlightenment so understood would comprise not just moderates like Hume, Smith, Montesquieu, and Voltaire but also (at least on my reading) some thinkers whom Israel deems radical, such as Diderot and Condorcet, while the idealistic strands of the Enlightenment include not only many of Israel's radicals but also some of the key figures whom he sees as moderate, such as Locke and Kant.[10]

Even more important than these kinds of historical and interpretive issues, however, are the normative lessons that can be drawn from an examination of the pragmatic Enlightenment. I have argued that all thinkers who are properly classified as members of the Enlightenment – whether radical or moderate, pragmatic or idealist – were liberals in the broadest sense of the term. That is, they all supported limited government, religious toleration, freedom of expression, commerce, and humane criminal laws. This is, in my view, what gives the Enlightenment its coherence, notwithstanding its very real internal diversity, and it is also what makes a proper understanding of the Enlightenment so important: our views of the Enlightenment necessarily shape our views of the liberalism that we have inherited from it. Like the Enlightenment, however, liberalism is not a single uniform creed: there are at least as many strands of liberalism as there are of the Enlightenment. Both the contemporary critics *and* contemporary proponents of liberalism tend to associate it especially with the more idealistic strands of Enlightenment thought, such as Lockean

---

[10] These categories are only meant to be suggestive; I do not mean to set up a new pair of neatly packaged, "irreconcilably opposed intellectual blocs" of Enlightenment thought to replace Israel's. As I stressed in the Introduction, the various strands of the Enlightenment are, like the Enlightenment itself, bound to have blurry edges. For Israel's claim that the radical and moderate Enlightenments are irreconcilably opposed blocs, see Israel, *Enlightenment Contested*, x.

contractarianism, Kantian deontology, and Benthamite utilitarianism; the intellectual heirs of the idealists – especially Kant – far outnumber those of their pragmatic counterparts such as Hume, Smith, Montesquieu, and Voltaire. (Smith has many self-proclaimed disciples, to be sure, but the vast majority of them are admirers of what they take to be his views on economic policy, rather than of his broader moral and political thought.) As I have tried to show throughout this study, however, the moderate, flexible form of liberalism embodied in these pragmatic Enlightenment thinkers is an especially attractive one in many respects.

Let us begin with the question of foundations. Many liberals, from the Enlightenment to the present, have sought to ground liberalism in abstract first principles such as natural laws or natural rights, the notion of a social contract, the rational requirements of human dignity, the imperative to maximize utility, or the choice that rational individuals would make under certain ideal conditions. The thinkers of the pragmatic Enlightenment, in contrast, advocated liberalism without relying on such abstract standards of right. Instead, they made a concrete, empirical case that historical and comparative analysis shows liberal regimes and practices to be preferable to the alternatives. In making this case, moreover, they appealed not to a single standard or benchmark but rather to a number of ends or goods that must be balanced against one another, such as security, personal independence, peace, prosperity, happiness, and the promotion of certain character traits that they took to be admirable. This kind of nonfoundationalist, pluralist approach will no doubt appear weak and deflating to those who seek a certain or indisputable basis on which to rest liberal ideals. It should be immensely appealing, however, to those who remain skeptical about the possibility of transcending the contingency of the political world altogether, as well as to those who believe, with Hume, that a politics of "*principle*, especially abstract speculative principle," is apt to promote fanaticism, faction, and conflict (EMPL, 60, Hume's italics).

Similarly, many liberals, past and present, have insisted on the universal applicability of various liberal practices and institutions. Of course, contrary to the exaggerations of some of the critics, no serious thinker – liberal or otherwise – has ever suggested that the exact same laws should be imposed on all societies in their entirety. Still, liberal thinkers from Locke to the present have often posited rather stringent requirements for political legitimacy that they take to apply in all times and places. While Hume, Smith, Montesquieu, and Voltaire were by no means outright cultural relativists, their outlooks help to temper the more strident forms of

Conclusion   299

liberal universalism by incorporating a welcome dose of philosophical humility, sensitivity to context, and institutional flexibility into the liberal worldview. (They would have never enjoined their readers, as Kant did, to "let justice prevail, though the world should perish for it.")[11] These thinkers stressed that different laws and institutions are appropriate for societies with different circumstances, histories, customs, and so on, and they essentially set aside the notion that there is a specific set of criteria that all regimes must meet in order to be deemed legitimate. Thus, the liberalism of the pragmatic Enlightenment is more tolerant and less "hegemonic" than many other strands of this tradition, insofar as it does more to acknowledge and respect the historical and cultural differences among peoples, norms, and beliefs.

On a related note, Hume, Smith, Montesquieu, and Voltaire all adopted a sensibly moderate stance toward political change. Many liberals have conceived of liberalism as an inherently radical or even revolutionary outlook, one that can and should brook no compromise with beliefs, customs, and institutions that run afoul of liberal principles, no matter how widely accepted or how long-standing (think, for instance, of Thomas Paine). The thinkers of the pragmatic Enlightenment, in contrast, showed a strong preference for prudent, piecemeal reform and consistently opposed the "spirit of system" that leads people to advocate the imposition of a comprehensive ideal on society all at once. Certainly, these thinkers were neither reactionaries nor unqualified defenders of the status quo; none of them hesitated to advocate liberal reforms to the European governments and societies of their time, some of them quite far-reaching. They rightly warned, however, that attempting to restructure a government or society in a sudden, wholesale fashion is generally both ineffective and dangerous, and thus that reforms should be implemented gradually and should take into account the possibilities and limitations inherent in a given set of circumstances. Hence, they provide a recipe for liberal reform that is duly cautious and pragmatic: we must cultivate our gardens, but cannot expect perfection.

The wariness that Hume, Smith, Montesquieu, and Voltaire showed toward abrupt, sweeping change was part and parcel of their broadly skeptical view of the power and scope of human reason. According to one prominent strand of liberal thought, which runs from Kant to Rawls and

---

[11] Immanuel Kant, "Toward Perpetual Peace," in *Practical Philosophy*, trans. Mary J. Gregor (Cambridge: Cambridge University Press, [1795] 1996), 345. Indeed, Hume declares that this maxim, "by sacrificing the end to the means, shews a preposterous idea of the subordination of duties" (EMPL, 489).

300   *The Pragmatic Enlightenment*

Habermas, politics should be guided exclusively (or almost exclusively) by reason and rational deliberation, and the passions or sentiments are conceived primarily as barriers to sound thinking and the realization of just outcomes.[12] Insofar as this rationalist paradigm seeks to transcend the sentiments altogether, it rests on an implausible vision of how moral judgment and political deliberation take place. The thinkers of the pragmatic Enlightenment offered a far more realistic account, one that accepts the limits and frailty of reason and that recognizes the central role that the sentiments invariably play – and *should* play – in morality and politics. Nor did their embrace of the sentiments entail the kind of narrow subjectivism or relativism feared by the rationalists, in which morality is reduced to individual feeling and politics is reduced to rhetoric and the advantage of the stronger. As Sharon Krause and Michael Frazer have recently shown, Enlightenment sentimentalists such as Hume and Smith espoused extraordinarily rich normative theories while remaining more faithful than the rationalists to the empirical realities of the human mind and human interactions.[13]

Likewise, many liberals appear to conceive of human beings as self-determining atoms, at least at their core – individuals who are capable of standing back from their circumstances and attachments in order to choose their own values autonomously. As I suggest in Chapter 5, it is questionable whether even the moral and political theories of Locke, Kant, and Rawls – the thinkers who are most often associated with this kind of outlook – really did rest on this absurdly reductive view of the self.[14] Even so, Hume, Smith, Montesquieu, and Voltaire were all far more forthright on this point. These thinkers were unequivocal in affirming that human beings are inherently social, drawn to others not just for instrumental reasons but also out of an innate desire for companionship. Even more importantly, they were resolute in affirming that people's characters, beliefs, and values are deeply shaped by their societies and their attachments to others, rather than somehow developed in

---

[12] While Rawls and Habermas present their respective political theories as models of rational deliberation, it has recently been shown that they both surreptitiously – perhaps even unwittingly – draw on the sentiments at times. See Michael L. Frazer, "John Rawls: Between Two Enlightenments" *Political Theory* 35.6 (December 2007): 756–80; and Sharon Krause, *Civil Passions: Moral Sentiment and Democratic Deliberation* (Princeton: Princeton University Press, 2008), chapter 1.

[13] See Krause, *Civil Passions*; and Michael Frazer, *The Enlightenment of Sympathy: Justice and the Moral Sentiments in the Eighteenth Century and Today* (Oxford: Oxford University Press, 2010).

[14] See notes 8 and 64 in Chapter 5.

Conclusion

a vacuum. Far from demanding a strong form of moral autonomy, they argued that it is only in and through society that we become moral beings at all. Thus, whatever the communitarian critics might think of the pragmatic Enlightenment's political ideals, they should find little to dispute in its depiction of human nature.

Finally, Hume, Smith, Montesquieu, and Voltaire went to much greater lengths than do most contemporary liberals to show why negative liberty and commerce, rather than promoting atomism and selfishness, in fact help to foster a healthier, more cohesive community. Many contemporary liberals, ranging from libertarians such as Robert Nozick to left-liberals such as Ronald Dworkin, regard individual rights as "trumps" and show little apparent concern for the effects that this principle might have on the character of the community. Some libertarians treat free trade in a similar fashion, while many left-liberals show wariness toward commerce and the inequalities it generates, thereby implicitly accepting that it is incompatible with a healthy social order. In part because they lived during the eighteenth century and so had a keener sense of the historical *alternatives* to negative liberty and commerce, the thinkers of the pragmatic Enlightenment offered a far more robust defense of these liberal ideals and their effects on society. They argued, first, that attempts to organize society around a set of shared ends or "higher" purposes, whether political or religious, are more likely to produce division and conflict than consensus and community – hence the importance of negative liberty not just for the individual but also for society as a whole. Moreover, they supported commerce in large part because they saw it as a more reliable means of uniting people than the traditional bonds of blood, religion, and nationalism; in their view, a focus on material self-interest serves as an alternative and antidote to divisive passions such as xenophobia, intolerance, and the thirst for military glory. Still further, they contended that liberal, commercial societies themselves help to promote a number of important virtues such as civility, tolerance, cooperativeness, reliability, decency, and moderation – social and political virtues that were comparatively lacking in preliberal, precommercial eras. Hence, their historical, comparative perspective helps to remind us, in a deeper way than do most contemporary theories of liberalism, why these basic liberal ideals were (and are) so valuable and necessary in the first place.

For all of these reasons, I would suggest, this central strand of the Enlightenment is not one that contemporary liberals need shy away from. On the contrary, it is one that we can and should embrace.

Bibliography

Abramson, Kate. "Hume on Cultural Conflicts of Values." *Philosophical Studies* 94.1/2 (May 1999): 173–87.

Adair, Douglass. *Fame and the Founding Fathers: Essays by Douglass Adair*, ed. Trevor Colbourn. Indianapolis: Liberty Fund, 1974.

Adams, John. *Diary and Autobiography of John Adams*, ed. L. H. Butterfield. Four volumes. Cambridge, MA: Harvard University Press, 1961.

Aldridge, A. Owen. *Voltaire and the Century of Light*. Princeton, NJ: Princeton University Press, 1975.

d'Alembert, Jean Le Rond. *Preliminary Discourse to the Encyclopedia of Diderot*, trans. Richard N. Schwab. Chicago: University of Chicago Press, [1751] 1955.

Aubery, Pierre. "Voltaire et les Juifs: Ironie et demystification." *Studies on Voltaire and the Eighteenth Century* 24 (1963): 67–79.

Bacon, Francis. *New Atlantis and The Great Instauration*, ed. Jerry Weinberger. Wheeling, IL: Harlan Davidson, 1989.

Bagehot, Walter. *Biographical Studies*. London: Longmans, Green, 1895.

Baier, Annette C. *The Cautious Jealous Virtue: Hume on Justice*. Cambridge, MA: Harvard University Press, 2010.

   Death and Character: Further Reflections on Hume. Cambridge, MA: Harvard University Press, 2008.

   Moral Prejudices: Essay on Ethics. Cambridge, MA: Harvard University Press, 1994.

   A Progress of Sentiments: Reflections on Hume's Treatise. Cambridge, MA: Harvard University Press, 1991.

Baker, Keith. "Epistémologie et politique: Pourquoi l'*Encyclopédie* est-elle un dictionnaire?" In *L'Encyclopédie: Du réseau au livre et du livre au réseau*, ed. Robert Morrisey and Philippe Roger. Paris: Champion, 2001.

Barber, W. H. "Voltaire at Cirey: Art and Thought." In *Studies in Eighteenth-Century French Literature: Presented to Robert Niklaus*, ed. J. H. Fox, M. H. Waddicor, and D. A. Watts. Exeter: University of Exeter Press, 1975.

303

304 *Bibliography*

Barfoot, Michael. "Hume and the Culture of Science in the Early Eighteenth Century." In *Studies in the Philosophy of the Scottish Enlightenment*, ed. M. A. Stewart. Oxford: Oxford University Press, 1990.

Barrera, Guillaume. *Les lois du monde: Enquête sur le dessein politique de Montesquieu*. Paris: Gallimard, 2009.

Bartlett, Robert C. "On the Politics of Faith and Reason: The Project of Enlightenment in Pierre Bayle and Montesquieu." *Journal of Politics* 63.1 (February 2001): 1–28.

Becker, Carl. *The Heavenly City of the Eighteenth-Century Philosophers*, second edition. New Haven, CT: Yale University Press, [1932] 2003.

Beeson, David, and Nicholas Cronk. "Voltaire: Philosopher or *Philosophe*?" In *The Cambridge Companion to Voltaire*, ed. Nicholas Cronk. Cambridge: Cambridge University Press, 2009.

Bentham, Jeremy. *The Theory of Legislation*. Oxford: Oxford University Press, [1802] 1914.

Berlin, Isaiah. *Against the Current: Essays in the History of Ideas*, ed. Henry Hardy. New York: Viking, 1980.

 The Proper Study of Mankind: An Anthology of Essays, ed. Henry Hardy and Roger Hausheer. New York: Farrar, Straus & Giroux 1998.

Berry, Christopher J. *Hume, Hegel and Human Nature*. The Hague: Martinus Nijhoff, 1982.

 "Hume's Universalism: The Science of Man and the Anthropological Point of View." *British Journal for the History of Philosophy* 15.3 (August 2007): 535–50.

 The Idea of Luxury: A Conceptual and Historical Investigation. Cambridge: Cambridge University Press, 1994.

 "Smith and Science." In *The Cambridge Companion to Adam Smith*, ed. Knud Haakonssen. Cambridge: Cambridge University Press, 2006.

 Social Theory of the Scottish Enlightenment. Edinburgh: Edinburgh University Press, 1997.

Besterman, Theodore. *Voltaire*. Chicago: University of Chicago Press, [1969] 1976.

 "Voltaire's God." *Studies on Voltaire and the Eighteenth Century* 55 (1967): 23–41.

Bird, Stephen. *Reinventing Voltaire: The Politics of Commemoration in Nineteenth-Century France*. Oxford: Voltaire Foundation, 2000.

Blackburn, Simon. *Ruling Passions: A Theory of Practical Reasoning*. Oxford: Oxford University Press, 1998.

Bongie, Laurence L. *David Hume: Prophet of the Counter-Revolution*, second edition. Indianapolis: Liberty Fund, 2000.

Bottiglia, William F. *Voltaire's Candide: Analysis of a Classic*, second edition. Geneva: Institut et Musée Voltaire, 1964.

 ed. *Voltaire: A Collection of Critical Essays*. Englewood Cliffs, NJ: Prentice-Hall, 1968.

Botwinick, Aryeh. "A Case for Hume's Nonutilitarianism." *Journal of the History of Philosophy* 15.4 (October 1977): 423–35.

Bibliography

Boyd, Richard. "Manners and Morals: David Hume on Civility, Commerce, and the Social Construction of Difference." In *David Hume's Political Economy*, ed. Carl Wennerlind and Margaret Schabas. New York: Routledge, 2008.

"Reappraising the Scottish Moralists and Civil Society." *Polity* 33.1 (autumn 2000): 101–25.

Brumfitt, J. H. *Voltaire: Historian*. Oxford: Oxford University Press, 1958.

Buckle, Stephen. *Natural Law and the Theory of Property: Grotius to Hume*. Oxford: Oxford University Press, 1991.

Buckle, Stephen, and Dario Castiglione. "Hume's Critique of the Contract Theory." *History of Political Thought* 12.3 (autumn 1991): 457–80.

Burke, Edmund. *Reflections on the Revolution in France*, ed. J. C. D. Clark. Stanford, CA: Stanford University Press, [1790] 2001.

Callanan, Keegan. Montesquieu, Liberalism and the Critique of Political Universalism. Ph.D. dissertation, Duke University, 2011.

Campbell, T. D. *Adam Smith's Science of Morals*. London: Allen & Unwin, 1971.

Capaldi, Nicholas. *The Enlightenment Project in the Analytic Conversation*. Dordrecht, Netherlands: Kluwer Academic, 1998.

Hume's Place in Moral Philosophy. New York: Peter Lang, 1989.

Carrese, Paul O. *The Cloaking of Power: Montesquieu, Blackstone, and the Rise of Judicial Activism*. Chicago: University of Chicago Press, 2003.

Carrithers, David W. "Democratic and Aristocratic Republics: Ancient and Modern." In *Montesquieu's Science of Politics: Essays on The Spirit of Laws*, ed. David W. Carrithers, Michael A. Mosher, and Paul A. Rahe. Lanham, MD: Rowman & Littlefield, 2001.

"The Enlightenment Science of Society." In *Inventing Human Science*, ed. Christopher Fox, Roy Porter, and Robert Wokler. Berkeley: University of California Press, 1995.

"Introduction: An Appreciation of *The Spirit of Laws*." In *Montesquieu's Science of Politics: Essays on The Spirit of Laws*, ed. David W. Carrithers, Michael A. Mosher, and Paul A. Rahe. Lanham, MD: Rowman & Littlefield, 2001.

"Montesquieu and the Liberal Philosophy of Jurisprudence." In *Montesquieu's Science of Politics: Essays on The Spirit of Laws*, ed. David W. Carrithers, Michael A. Mosher, and Paul A. Rahe. Lanham, MD: Rowman & Littlefield, 2001.

"Montesquieu and Tocqueville as Philosophical Historians: Liberty, Determinism, and the Prospects for Freedom." In *Montesquieu and His Legacy*, ed. Rebecca E. Kingston. Albany: SUNY Press, 2009.

"Montesquieu's Philosophy of History." *Journal of the History of Ideas* 47.1 (January–March 1986): 61–80.

"Montesquieu's Philosophy of Punishment." *History of Political Thought* 19.2 (summer 1998): 213–40.

Cassirer, Ernst. *The Philosophy of the Enlightenment*, trans. Fritz C. A. Koelln and James P. Pettegrove. Princeton, NJ: Princeton University Press, [1932] 1979.

Chamley, Paul E. "The Conflict between Montesquieu and Hume." In *Essays on Adam Smith*, ed. Andrew S. Skinner and Thomas Wilson. Oxford: Clarendon Press, 1975.

Chinard, Gilbert. "Montesquieu's Historical Pessimism." In *Studies in the History of Culture*. Menasha, WI: American Council of Learned Societies, 1942.

Chisick, Harvey. "Interpreting the Enlightenment." *European Legacy* 13.1 (February 2008): 35–57.

Clark, Henry C. "Women and Humanity in Scottish Enlightenment Social Thought: The Case of Adam Smith." *Historical Reflections/Réflexions Historiques* 19.3 (summer 1993): 335–61.

Clinton, Katherine B. "Femme et Philosophe: Enlightenment Origins of Feminism." *Eighteenth-Century Studies* 8.3 (spring 1975): 283–99.

Clor, Harry. *On Moderation: Defending an Ancient Virtue in a Modern World*. Waco, TX: Baylor University Press, 2008.

Cobban, Alfred. *In Search of Humanity: The Role of the Enlightenment in Modern History*. New York: George Braziller, 1960.

Cohler, Anne M. *Montesquieu's Comparative Politics and the Spirit of American Constitutionalism*. Lawrence: University Press of Kansas, 1988.

Cohon, Rachel. *Hume's Morality: Feeling and Fabrication*. Oxford: Oxford University Press, 2008.

Comte, Auguste. *Cours de philosophie positive*. Six volumes. Paris: Bechelier, 1852.

Condorcet, Marie Jean Antoine Nicolas de Caritat, marquis de. "Observations on the Twenty-Ninth Book of *The Spirit of Laws*." In Antoine Louis Claude, comte Destutt de Tracy, *A Commentary and Review of Montesquieu's Spirit of Laws*, trans. Thomas Jefferson. Philadelphia: William Duane, 1811.

Conniff, James. "Hume's Political Methodology: A Reconsideration of 'That Politics May Be Reduced to a Science.'" *Review of Politics* 38.1 (January 1976): 88–108.

Cotoni, Marie-Hélène. *L'Exégèse du Nouveau Testament dans la philosophie française du dix-huitième siècle*. Oxford: Voltaire Foundation, 1984.

Courtney, C. P. "Montesquieu and English Liberty." In *Montesquieu's Science of Politics: Essays on The Spirit of Laws*, ed. David W. Carrithers, Michael A. Mosher, and Paul A. Rahe. Lanham, MD: Rowman & Littlefield, 2001.

"Montesquieu and Natural Law." In *Montesquieu's Science of Politics: Essays on The Spirit of Laws*, ed. David W. Carrithers, Michael A. Mosher, and Paul A. Rahe. Lanham, MD: Rowman & Littlefield, 2001.

"Montesquieu and Revolution." In *Lectures de Montesquieu*, ed. Edgar Mass and Alberto Postigliola. Naples: Liguori Editore, 1993.

"Montesquieu and the Problem of 'la diversité.'" In *Enlightenment Essays in Memory of Robert Shackleton*, ed. Giles Barber and C. P. Courtney. Oxford: Voltaire Foundation, 1988.

Craiutu, Aurelian. *A Virtue for Courageous Minds: Moderation in French Political Thought, 1748–1830*. Princeton, NJ: Princeton University Press, 2012.

Cranston, Maurice. *Philosophers and Pamphleteers: Political Theorists of the Enlightenment*. Oxford: Oxford University Press, 1986.

Crocker, Lester G. *Nature and Culture: Ethical Thought in the French Enlightenment*. Baltimore: Johns Hopkins University Press, 1963.

"Voltaire and the Political Philosophers." *Studies on Voltaire and the Eighteenth Century* 219 (1983): 1–17.

Bibliography

Cronk, Nicholas. "The *Letters Concerning the English Nation* as an English Work: Reconsidering the Harcourt Brown Thesis." *Studies on Voltaire and the Eighteenth Century* 2001:10 (2001): 226–39.

Cropsey, Joseph. *Polity and Economy: With Further Thoughts on the Principles of Adam Smith*. South Bend, IN: St. Augustine's Press, [1957] 2001.

Danford, John W. *David Hume and the Problem of Reason: Recovering the Human Sciences*. New Haven, CT: Yale University Press, 1990.

Darnton, Robert. *George Washington's False Teeth: An Unconventional Guide to the Eighteenth Century*. New York: W. W. Norton, 2003.

Darwall, Stephen. "Sympathetic Liberalism: Recent Work on Adam Smith." *Philosophy & Public Affairs* 28.2 (April 1999): 139–64.

Davidson, Ian. *Voltaire in Exile: The Last Years, 1753–78*. New York: Grove Press, 2004.

Davie, William. "Hume on Monkish Virtue." *Hume Studies* 25.1–2 (April/November 1999): 139–54.

Davies, Simon. "Reflections on Voltaire and His Idea of Colonies." *Studies on Voltaire and the Eighteenth Century* 332 (1995): 61–9.

Dees, Richard H. "Hume and the Contexts of Politics." *Journal of the History of Philosophy* 30.2 (April 1992): 219–42.

"Hume on the Characters of Virtue." *Journal of the History of Philosophy* 35.1 (January 1997): 45–64.

"'One of the Finest and Most Subtle Inventions': Hume on Government." In *A Companion to Hume*, ed. Elizabeth S. Radcliffe. Oxford: Blackwell, 2008.

"'The Paradoxical Principle and Salutary Practice': Hume on Toleration." *Hume Studies* 31.1 (April 2005): 145–64.

Derathé, Robert. "Montesquieu et Jean-Jacques Rousseau." *Revue internationale de philosophie* 9 (1950): 366–86.

Descartes, René. *The Philosophical Writings of Descartes*, trans. John Cottingham, Robert Stoothoff, and Dugald Murdoch. Two volumes. Cambridge: Cambridge University Press, 1985.

Diderot, Denis. *Correspondance*, ed. Georges Roth. Ten volumes. Paris: Minuit, 1959.

Political Writings, trans. John Hope Mason and Robert Wokler. Cambridge: Cambridge University Press, 1992.

Rameau's Nephew and other Works, trans. Jacques Barzun and Ralph H. Bowen. Indianapolis: Hackett, 1956.

Dijn, Annelien de. *French Political Thought from Montesquieu to Tocqueville: Liberty in a Levelled Society?* Cambridge: Cambridge University Press, 2008.

"*On Political Liberty*: Montesquieu's Missing Manuscript." *Political Theory* 39.2 (April 2011): 181–204.

Dupré, Louis. *The Enlightenment and the Intellectual Foundations of Modern Culture*. New Haven, CT: Yale University Press, 2004.

Durant, Will, and Ariel Durant. *The Age of Voltaire: A History of Civilization in Western Europe from 1715 to 1756*. New York: Simon & Schuster, 1965.

Durkheim, Emile. *Montesquieu and Rousseau: Forerunners of Sociology*, trans. Ralph Manheim. Ann Arbor: University of Michigan Press, 1960.

Edelstein, Dan. *The Enlightenment: A Genealogy*. Chicago: University of Chicago Press, 2010.

Ehrard, Jean. "Idée et figures de l'empire dans *l'Esprit des lois*." In *L'Empire avant l'Empire: État d'une notion au XVIIIe siècle*, ed. Gérard Loubinoux. Clermont-Farrand, France: Presses universitaires Blaise-Pascal, 2004.

Politique de Montesquieu. Paris: Armand Collin, 1965.

Ferguson, Adam. *An Essay on the History of Civil Society*, ed. Fania Oz-Salzberger. Cambridge: Cambridge University Press, [1767] 1995.

Finlay, Christopher J. "Hume's Theory of Civil Society." *European Journal of Political Theory* 3.4 (October 2004): 369–91.

Flax, Jane. *Thinking Fragments: Psychoanalysis, Feminism, and Postmodernism in the Contemporary West*. Berkeley: University of California Press, 1990.

Fleischacker, Samuel. "Adam Smith." In *A Companion to Early Modern Philosophy*, ed. Steven Nadler. Oxford: Blackwell, 2002.

"Adam Smith and Cultural Relativism." *Erasmus Journal for Philosophy and Economics* 4.2 (autumn 2011): 20–41.

"Adam Smith's Reception among the American Founders, 1776–1790." *William and Mary Quarterly* 59.4 (October 2002): 897–924.

"The Impact on America: Scottish Philosophy and the American Founding." In *The Cambridge Companion to the Scottish Enlightenment*, ed. Alexander Broadie. Cambridge: Cambridge University Press, 2003.

On Adam Smith's Wealth of Nations: A Philosophical Companion. Princeton, NJ: Princeton University Press, 2004.

"On Adam Smith's 'Wealth of Nations': Response." *Adam Smith Review* 2 (2006): 246–55.

"Philosophy in Moral Practice: Kant and Adam Smith." *Kant-Studien* 82.3 (1991): 249–69.

"Sympathy in Hume and Smith: A Contrast, Critique, and Reconstruction." In *Intersubjectivity and Objectivity in Adam Smith and Edmund Husserl: A Collection of Essays*, ed. Christel Fricke and Dagfinn Føllesdal. Frankfurt: Ontos Verlag, 2012.

A Third Concept of Liberty: Judgment and Freedom in Kant and Adam Smith. Princeton, NJ: Princeton University Press, 1999.

Fletcher, Dennis. *Voltaire: Lettres philosophiques*. London: Grant & Cutler, 1986.

Forbes, Duncan. *Hume's Philosophical Politics*. Cambridge: Cambridge University Press, 1975.

"Sceptical Whiggism, Commerce, and Liberty." In *Essays on Adam Smith*, ed. Andrew S. Skinner and Thomas Wilson. Oxford: Clarendon Press, 1975.

"'Scientific' Whiggism: Adam Smith and John Millar." *Cambridge Journal* 7.2 (August 1954): 643–70.

Force, Pierre. *Self-Interest before Adam Smith: A Genealogy of Economic Science*. Cambridge: Cambridge University Press, 2003.

Forman-Barzilai, Fonna. *Adam Smith and the Circles of Sympathy: Cosmopolitanism and Moral Theory*. Cambridge: Cambridge University Press, 2010.

Bibliography

Frazer, Michael. *The Enlightenment of Sympathy: Justice and the Moral Sentiments in the Eighteenth Century and Today*. Oxford: Oxford University Press, 2010.

"John Rawls: Between Two Enlightenments." *Political Theory* 35.6 (December 2007): 756–80.

Gargett, Graham. "Voltaire and the Bible." In *The Cambridge Companion to Voltaire*, ed. Nicholas Cronk. Cambridge: Cambridge University Press, 2009.

Garrard, Graeme. *Counter-Enlightenments: From the Eighteenth Century to the Present*. New York: Routledge, 2006.

Garrett, Aaron. "Hume's 'Original Difference': Race, National Character and the Human Sciences." *Eighteenth-Century Thought* 2 (2004): 127–52.

Gaskin, J. C. A. "Hume on Religion." In *The Cambridge Companion to Hume*, ed. David Fate Norton and Jacqueline Taylor, second edition. Cambridge: Cambridge University Press, 2009.

Hume's Philosophy of Religion, second edition. Atlantic Highlands, NJ: Humanities Press, 1988.

Gaus, Gerald F. *Contemporary Theories of Liberalism: Public Reason as a Post-Enlightenment Project*. London: Sage Publications, 2003.

Gauthier, David. "David Hume, Contractarian." *Philosophical Review* 88.1 (January 1979): 3–38.

Gay, Peter. "Carl Becker's Heavenly City." In *Carl Becker's Heavenly City Revisited*, ed. Raymond O. Rockwood. Ithaca, NY: Cornell University Press, 1958.

The Enlightenment: An Interpretation, vol. 1: *The Rise of Modern Paganism*. New York: W. W. Norton, 1966.

The Enlightenment: An Interpretation, vol. 2: *The Science of Freedom*. New York: W.W. Norton, 1969.

The Party of Humanity: Essays in the French Enlightenment. New York: W. W. Norton, 1964.

"Voltaire's *Idées républicaines*: A Study in Bibliography and Interpretation." *Studies on Voltaire and the Eighteenth Century* 6 (1958): 67–105.

Voltaire's Politics: The Poet as Realist. New Haven, CT: Yale University Press, [1959] 1988.

Gibbard, Allan. *Wise Choices, Apt Feelings: A Theory of Normative Judgment*. Cambridge, MA: Harvard University Press, 1990.

Gill, Michael B. "Humean Moral Pluralism." *History of Philosophy Quarterly* 28.1 (January 2011): 45–64.

Gillespie, Michael Allen. *The Theological Origins of Modernity*. Chicago: University of Chicago Press, 2008.

Gordon, Daniel. "Introduction: Postmodernism and the French Enlightenment." In *Postmodernism and the Enlightenment: New Perspectives in Eighteenth-Century French Intellectual History*, ed. Daniel Gordon. New York: Routledge, 2001.

"On the Supposed Obsolescence of the French Enlightenment." In *Postmodernism and the Enlightenment: New Perspectives in Eighteenth-Century French Intellectual History*, ed. Daniel Gordon. New York: Routledge, 2001.

Bibliography

Gottmann, Felicia. "Du Châtelet, Voltaire, and the Transformation of Mandeville's *Fable*." *History of European Ideas* 38.2 (June 2012): 218–32.

Goyard-Fabre, Simone. *La Philosophie du droit de Montesquieu*. Paris: Klincksieck, 1973.

Gray, John. *Enlightenment's Wake: Politics and Culture at the Close of the Modern Age*. New York: Routledge, 1995.

Voltaire. New York: Routledge, 1999.

Greene, Donald. *The Politics of Samuel Johnson*, second edition. Athens: University of Georgia Press, [1960] 1990.

Griswold, Charles L. *Adam Smith and the Virtues of Enlightenment*. Cambridge: Cambridge University Press, 1999.

"On the Incompleteness of Adam Smith's System." *Adam Smith Review* 2 (2006): 181–6.

Grotius, Hugo. *The Rights of War and Peace*, ed. Richard Tuck. Indianapolis: Liberty Fund, [1625] 2005.

Guy, Basil. *The French Image of China before and after Voltaire*. Geneva: Institut et Musée Voltaire, 1963.

Haakonssen, Knud. "Introduction: The Coherence of Smith's Thought." In *The Cambridge Companion to Adam Smith*, ed. Knud Haakonssen. Cambridge: Cambridge University Press, 2006.

Natural Law and Moral Philosophy: From Grotius to the Scottish Enlightenment. Cambridge: Cambridge University Press, 1996.

The Science of a Legislator: The Natural Jurisprudence of David Hume and Adam Smith. Cambridge: Cambridge University Press, 1981.

"The Structure of Hume's Political Theory." In *The Cambridge Companion to Hume*, ed. David Fate Norton and Jacqueline Taylor, second edition. Cambridge: Cambridge University Press, 2009.

Haakonssen, Knud, and Donald Winch. "The Legacy of Adam Smith." In *The Cambridge Companion to Adam Smith*, ed. Knud Haakonssen. Cambridge: Cambridge University Press, 2006.

Hampson, Norman. "The Enlightenment in France." In *The Enlightenment in National Context*, ed. Roy Porter and Mikuláš Teich. Cambridge: Cambridge University Press, 1981.

Will and Circumstance: Montesquieu, Rousseau and the French Revolution. Norman: University of Oklahoma Press, 1983.

Hanley, Ryan Patrick. *Adam Smith and the Character of Virtue*. Cambridge: Cambridge University Press, 2009.

"Scepticism and Naturalism in Adam Smith." *Adam Smith Review* 5 (2010): 198–212.

Hardin, Russell. *David Hume: Moral and Political Theorist*. Oxford: Oxford University Press, 2007.

Harpham, Edward J. "The Problem of Liberty in the Thought of Adam Smith." *Journal of the History of Economic Thought* 22.2 (June 2000): 217–37.

Hayek, F. A. *The Constitution of Liberty*. Chicago: University of Chicago Press, 1960.

"The Legal and Political Philosophy of David Hume." In *Hume*, ed. V. C. Chappell. Garden City, NY: Anchor Books, 1966.

Bibliography

Hazard, Paul. *European Thought in the Eighteenth Century: From Montesquieu to Lessing*, trans. J. Lewis May. Cleveland: Meridian Books, [1946] 1965.

Hegel, G. W. F. *Phenomenology of Spirit*, trans. A. V. Miller. Oxford: Oxford University Press, [1807] 1977.

Heilbroner, Robert L. "The Paradox of Progress: Decline and Decay in *The Wealth of Nations*." In *Essays on Adam Smith*, ed. Andrew S. Skinner and Thomas Wilson. Oxford: Clarendon Press, 1975.

Henry, Patrick. "Voltaire as Moralist." *Journal of the History of Ideas* 38.1 (January–March 1977): 141–6.

Herdt, Jennifer A. *Religion and Faction in Hume's Moral Philosophy*. Cambridge: Cambridge University Press, 1997.

Herzog, Don. *Without Foundations: Justification in Political Theory*. Ithaca, NY: Cornell University Press, 1985.

Hill, Lisa. "Adam Smith and the Theme of Corruption." *Review of Politics* 68.4 (2006): 636–62.

"The Hidden Theology of Adam Smith." *European Journal of the History of Economic Thought* 8.1 (spring 2001): 1–29.

Himmelfarb, Gertrude. *The Roads to Modernity: The British, French, and American Enlightenments*. New York: Alfred A. Knopf, 2004.

Hinchman, Lewis P. *Hegel's Critique of the Enlightenment*. Gainesville: University Press of Florida, 1984.

Hirschman, Albert O. *The Passions and the Interests: Political Arguments for Capitalism before Its Triumph*. Princeton, NJ: Princeton University Press, [1977] 1997.

Hiskes, Richard P. "Has Hume a Theory of Social Justice?" *Hume Studies* 3.2 (November 1977): 72–93.

Hobbes, Thomas. *Man and Citizen*, ed. Bernard Gert. Indianapolis: Hackett, 1991.

Leviathan, ed. Edwin Curley. Indianapolis: Hackett, [1651] 1994.

Holden, Thomas. *Spectres of False Divinity: Hume's Moral Atheism*. Oxford: Oxford University Press, 2010.

Holmes, Stephen. *The Anatomy of Antiliberalism*. Cambridge, MA: Harvard University Press, 1993.

"The Secret History of Self-Interest." In *Passions and Constraint: On the Theory of Liberal Democracy*. Chicago: University of Chicago Press, 1995.

Hont, Istvan. *Jealousy of Trade: International Competition and the Nation-State in Historical Perspective*. Cambridge, MA: Belknap Press, 2005.

Hopfl, H. M. "From Savage to Scotsman: Conjectural History in the Scottish Enlightenment." *Journal of British Studies* 17.2 (spring 1978): 19–40.

Horkheimer, Max. *Eclipse of Reason*. New York: Seabury Press, [1947] 1974.

"Reason against Itself: Some Remarks on Enlightenment." In *What Is Enlightenment? Eighteenth-Century Answers and Twentieth-Century Questions*, ed. James Schmidt. Berkeley: University of California Press, [1946] 1996.

Horkheimer, Max, and Theodor W. Adorno. *Dialectic of Enlightenment: Philosophical Fragments*, trans. Edmund Jephcott. Stanford, CA: Stanford University Press, [1947] 2002.

312   *Bibliography*

Hulliung, Mark. *The Autocritique of Enlightenment: Rousseau and the Philosophes.* Cambridge, MA: Harvard University Press, 1994.

Montesquieu and the Old Regime. Berkeley: University of California Press, 1976.

Hume, David. *Dialogues Concerning Natural Religion*, ed. J. C. A. Gaskin. Oxford: Oxford University Press, [1779] 1993.

A Dissertation on the Passions and The Natural History of Religion, ed. Tom L. Beauchamp. Oxford: Clarendon Press, [1757] 2007.

An Enquiry Concerning Human Understanding, ed. Tom L. Beauchamp. Oxford: Clarendon Press, [1748] 2000.

An Enquiry Concerning the Principles of Morals, ed. Tom L. Beauchamp. Oxford: Clarendon Press, [1751] 1998.

Essays, Moral, Political, and Literary, ed. Eugene F. Miller. Indianapolis: Liberty Fund, [1741–77] 1987.

The History of England, from the Invasion of Julius Caesar to the Revolution in 1688. Six volumes. Indianapolis: Liberty Fund, [1754–62] 1983.

"A Letter from a Gentleman to His Friend in *Edinburgh*." In *A Treatise of Human Nature*, ed. David Fate Norton and Mary J. Norton. Oxford: Clarendon Press, [1745] 2007.

The Letters of David Hume, ed. J. Y. T. Greig. Two volumes. Oxford: Clarendon Press, 1932.

New Letters of David Hume, ed. Raymond Klibansky and Ernest C. Mossner. Oxford: Clarendon Press, 1954.

Political Essays, ed. Knud Haakonssen. Cambridge: Cambridge University Press, 1994.

Political Writings, ed. Stuart D. Warner and Donald W. Livingston. Indianapolis: Hackett, 1994.

A Treatise of Human Nature, ed. David Fate Norton and Mary J. Norton. Oxford: Clarendon Press, [1739–40] 2007.

Immerwahr, John. "Hume's Revised Racism." *Journal of the History of Ideas* 53.3 (July–September 1992): 481–6.

Israel, Jonathan I. *Democratic Enlightenment: Philosophy, Revolution, and Human Rights, 1750–1790.* Oxford: Oxford University Press, 2011.

Enlightenment Contested: Philosophy, Modernity, and the Emancipation of Man, 1670–1752. Oxford: Oxford University Press, 2006.

Radical Enlightenment: Philosophy and the Making of Modernity, 1650–1750. Oxford: Oxford University Press, 2001.

A Revolution of the Mind: Radical Enlightenment and the Intellectual Origins of Modern Democracy. Princeton, NJ: Princeton University Press, 2010.

Jacobson, Anne Jaap, ed. *Feminist Interpretations of David Hume.* University Park: Pennsylvania State University Press, 2000.

Johnson, Samuel. *Political Writings*, ed. Donald Greene. Indianapolis: Liberty Fund, 1977.

Jordan, Will R. "Religion in the Public Square: A Reconsideration of David Hume and Religious Establishment." *Review of Politics* 64.4 (autumn 2002): 687–713.

Kant, Immanuel. *Basic Writings of Kant*, ed. Allen W. Wood. New York: Modern Library, 2001.

Bibliography

Ethical Philosophy, ed. James W. Ellington, second edition. Indianapolis: Hackett, 1994.

Practical Philosophy, ed. Mary J. Gregor. Cambridge: Cambridge University Press, 1996.

Keohane, Nannerl O. "Virtuous Republics and Glorious Monarchies: Two Models in Montesquieu's Political Thought." *Political Studies* 20.4 (December 1972): 383–96.

King, James T. "Hume on Artificial Lives, with a Rejoinder to A. C. MacIntyre." *Hume Studies* 14.1 (April 1988): 53–92.

"The Virtue of Political Skepticism." *Reason Papers* 15 (summer 1990): 24–46.

Kingston, Rebecca E. "Montesquieu on Religion and on the Question of Toleration." In *Montesquieu's Science of Politics: Essays on The Spirit of Laws*, ed. David W. Carrithers, Michael A. Mosher, and Paul A. Rahe. Lanham, MD: Rowman & Littlefield, 2001.

Kleer, Richard A. "Final Causes in Adam Smith's *Theory of Moral Sentiments*." *Journal of the History of Philosophy* 33.2 (April 1995): 275–300.

"The Role of Teleology in Adam Smith's *Wealth of Nations*." *History of Economics Review* 31 (winter 2000): 14–29.

Kra, Pauline. "Montesquieu and Women." In *French Women and the Age of Enlightenment*, ed. Samia I. Spencer. Bloomington: Indiana University Press, 1984.

Krause, Sharon R. *Civil Passions: Moral Sentiment and Democratic Deliberation.* Princeton, NJ: Princeton University Press, 2008.

"Despotism in *The Spirit of Laws*." In *Montesquieu's Science of Politics: Essays on The Spirit of Laws*, ed. David W. Carrithers, Michael A. Mosher, and Paul A. Rahe. Lanham, MD: Rowman & Littlefield, 2001.

"Frenzy, Gloom, and the Spirit of Liberty in Hume." In *The Arts of Rule: Essays in Honor of Harvey C. Mansfield*, ed. Sharon R. Krause and Mary Ann McGrail. Lanham, MD: Lexington, 2009.

"History and the Human Soul in Montesquieu." *History of Political Thought* 24.2 (summer 2003): 235–60.

"Hume and the (False) Luster of Justice." *Political Theory* 32.5 (October 2004): 628–55.

"Laws, Passion, and the Attractions of Right Action in Montesquieu." *Philosophy and Social Criticism* 32.2 (March 2006): 211–30.

Liberalism with Honor. Cambridge, MA: Harvard University Press, 2002.

"Passion, Power, and Impartiality in Hume." In *Bringing the Passions Back In: The Emotions in Political Philosophy*, ed. Rebecca Kingston and Leonard Ferry. Vancouver: UBC Press, 2008.

"The Politics of Distinction and Disobedience: Honor and the Defense of Liberty in Montesquieu." *Polity* 31.2 (spring 1999): 469–99.

"The Spirit of Separate Powers in Montesquieu." *Review of Politics* 62.2 (spring 2000): 231–65.

"Two Concepts of Liberty in Montesquieu." *Perspectives on Political Science* 34.2 (spring 2005): 88–96.

"The Uncertain Inevitability of Decline in Montesquieu." *Political Theory* 30.5 (October 2002): 702–27.

314   *Bibliography*

Langdon, David. "On the Meanings of the Conclusion of *Candide*." *Studies on Voltaire and the Eighteenth Century* **238** (1985): 397–432.

Lanson, Gustave. *Voltaire*, trans. Robert A. Wagoner. New York: John Wiley & Sons, [1906] 1966.

Larrère, Catherine. "Montesquieu and Liberalism: The Question of Pluralism." In *Montesquieu and His Legacy*, ed. Rebecca E. Kingston. Albany: SUNY Press, 2009.

    "Montesquieu on Economics and Commerce." In *Montesquieu's Science of Politics: Essays on The Spirit of Laws*, ed. David W. Carrithers, Michael A. Mosher, and Paul A. Rahe. Lanham, MD: Rowman & Littlefield, 2001.

Lauer, Rosemary Z. *The Mind of Voltaire: A Study of His "Constructive Deism."* Westminster, MD: Newman Press, 1961.

La Vopa, Anthony J. "A New Intellectual History? Jonathan Israel's Enlightenment." *Historical Journal* **52**.3 (September 2009): 717–38.

Lee, J. Patrick. "The Unexamined Premise: Voltaire, John Lockman, and the Myth of the *English Letters*." *Studies on Voltaire and the Eighteenth Century* **2001**.10 (2001): 240–70.

Lehner, Ulrich L., and Michael Printy, eds. *A Companion to the Catholic Enlightenment in Europe*. Leiden: Brill, 2010.

Levy, Jacob T. "Beyond Publius: Montesquieu, Liberal Republicanism and the Small-Republic Thesis." *History of Political Thought* **27**.1 (spring 2006): 50–90.

    "Liberalism's Divide, After Socialism and Before." *Social Philosophy & Policy* **20**.1 (2003): 278–97.

Libby, Margaret Sherwood. *The Attitude of Voltaire to Magic and the Sciences*. New York: Columbia University Press, 1935.

Lilti, Antoine. "Comment écrit-on l'histoire intellectual des Lumières? Spinozisme, radicalisme et philosophie." *Annales* **64**.1 (January–February 2009): 171–206.

Lindgren, Ralph. "Adam Smith's Theory of Inquiry." *Journal of Political Economy* **77**.6 (November–December 1969): 897–915.

    The Social Philosophy of Adam Smith. The Hague: Martinus Nijhoff, 1973.

Livingston, Donald W. "Hume, English Barbarism and American Independence." In *Scotland and America in the Age of the Enlightenment*, ed. Richard B. Sher and Jeffrey Smitten. Edinburgh: Edinburgh University Press, 1990.

    Hume's Philosophy of Common Life. Chicago: University of Chicago Press, 1984.

    Philosophical Melancholy and Delirium: Hume's Pathology of Philosophy. Chicago: University of Chicago Press, 1998.

Lock, F. P. "Adam Smith and 'The Man of System': Interpreting *The Theory of Moral Sentiments* VI.ii.2.12–18." *Adam Smith Review* **3** (2007): 37–48.

Locke, John. *An Essay Concerning Human Understanding*, ed. Peter H. Nidditch. Oxford: Oxford University Press, [1689] 1975.

    Two Treatises of Government, ed. Peter Laslett. Cambridge: Cambridge University Press, [1689] 1988.

Lottenbach, Hans. "Monkish Virtues, Artificial Lives: On Hume's Genealogy of Morals." *Canadian Journal of Philosophy* **26**.3 (September 1996): 367–88.

Bibliography

Lough, John. "Reflections on Enlightenment and Lumières." *Journal for Eighteenth-Century Studies* 8.1 (March 1985): 1–15.

Lowenthal, David. "Book I of Montesquieu's *The Spirit of the Laws.*" *American Political Science Review* 53.2 (June 1959): 485–98.

MacIntyre, Alasdair. *After Virtue*, second edition. Notre Dame, IN: University of Notre Dame Press, [1981] 1984.

"Hume on 'Is' and 'Ought'." In *Hume*, ed. V. C. Chappell. Garden City, NY: Anchor Books, 1966.

Whose Justice? Which Rationality? Notre Dame, IN: University of Notre Dame Press, 1988.

Mackie, J. L. *Ethics: Inventing Right and Wrong*. New York: Penguin, 1977.

Macpherson, C. B. *The Political Theory of Possessive Individualism: Hobbes to Locke*. Oxford: Oxford University Press, 1962.

Review of Donald Winch, *Adam Smith's Politics: An Essay in Historiographic Revision*. In *History of Political Economy* 11.3 (fall 1979): 450–4.

Madison, James. *The Federalist*, ed. George W. Carey and James McClellan. Indianapolis: Liberty Fund [1788] 2001.

Maestro, Marcello T. *Voltaire and Beccaria as Reformers of Criminal Law*. New York: Columbia University Press, 1942.

Maistre, Joseph de. *Considerations on France*, trans. Richard A. Lebrun. Cambridge: Cambridge University Press, [1797] 1994.

Mandeville, Bernard. *The Fable of the Bees: or Private Vices, Publick Benefits*, ed. F. B. Kaye. Two volumes. Indianapolis: Liberty Fund, [1723] 1988.

Manent, Pierre. *The City of Man*, trans. Marc A. LePain. Princeton, NJ: Princeton University Press, 1998.

An Intellectual History of Liberalism, trans. Rebecca Balinski. Princeton, NJ: Princeton University Press, [1987] 1995.

Manin, Bernard. "Montesquieu et la politique moderne." In *Cahiers de philosophie politique de l'Université de Reims*. Brussels: Ousia, 1985.

Mansfield, Harvey C., Jr. *Taming the Prince: The Ambivalence of Modern Executive Power*. Baltimore: Johns Hopkins University Press, 1993.

Manzer, Robert A. "The Promise of Peace? Hume and Smith on the Effects of Commerce on Peace and War." *Hume Studies* 22.2 (November 1996): 369–82.

Mason, Haydn. *Candide: Optimism Demolished*. New York: Twayne, 1992.

Pierre Bayle and Voltaire. Oxford: Oxford University Press, 1963.

Voltaire: A Biography. Baltimore: Johns Hopkins University Press, 1981.

Mason, John Hope. *The Irresistible Diderot*. London: Quartet Books, 1982.

Mauzi, Robert. *L'idée du bonheur dans la littérature et la pensée française au XVIIIe siècle*. Paris: Armand Colin, 1960.

McArthur, Neil. *David Hume's Political Theory: Law, Commerce, and the Constitution of Government*. Toronto: University of Toronto Press, 2007.

McCloskey, Deirdre N. *The Bourgeois Virtues: Ethics for an Age of Commerce*. Chicago: University of Chicago Press, 2006.

McLean, Iain, and Scot M. Peterson. "Adam Smith at the Constitutional Convention." *Loyola Law Review* 56.1 (spring 2010): 95–133.

McMahon, Darrin. *Enemies of the Enlightenment: The French Counter-Enlightenment and the Making of Modernity.* Oxford University Press, 2001.

Meek, Ronald L. "The Scottish Contribution to Marxist Sociology." In *Economics and Ideology and Other Essays: Studies in the Development of Economic Thought.* London: Chapman & Hall, 1967.

    Social Science and the Ignoble Savage. Cambridge: Cambridge University Press, 1976.

Merrill, Thomas W. "The Rhetoric of Rebellion in Hume's Constitutional Thought." *Review of Politics* 67.2 (spring 2005): 257–82.

Mill, John Stuart. *Essays on Ethics, Religion and Society,* ed. J. M. Robinson. In *Collected Works of John Stuart Mill,* vol. 10. Toronto: University of Toronto Press, 1969.

Miller, David. *Philosophy and Ideology in Hume's Political Thought.* Oxford: Clarendon Press, 1981.

Miller, Eugene F. "Hume on Liberty in the Successive English Constitutions." In *Liberty in Hume's History of England,* ed. Nicholas Capaldi and Donald W. Livingston. Dordrecht, Netherlands: Kluwer Academic, 1990.

Millican, P. J. R. "Hume's Argument Concerning Induction: Structure and Interpretation." In *David Hume: Critical Assessments,* ed. Stanley Tweyman, vol. 2. New York: Routledge, 1995.

Minowitz, Peter. *Profits, Priests, and Princes: Adam Smith's Emancipation of Economics from Politics and Religion.* Stanford, CA: Stanford University Press, 1993.

Montes, Leonidas. *Adam Smith in Context: A Critical Reassessment of Some Central Components of His Thought.* New York: Palgrave Macmillan, 2004.

Montesquieu, Charles de Secondat, baron de. *Considerations on the Causes of the Greatness of the Romans and Their Decline,* trans. David Lowenthal. Indianapolis: Hackett, [1734] 1999.

    Correspondance. In *Oeuvres complètes de Montesquieu,* ed. André Masson, vol. 3. Paris: Nagel, 1955.

    "Discourse on the Motives That Ought to Encourage Us to the Sciences," trans. Diana Schaub. In *New Atlantis* 20 (spring 2008): 33–6.

    "An Essay on the Causes That May Affect Men's Minds and Characters," trans. Melvin Richter. In *Political Theory* 4.2 (May 1976): 139–62.

    My Thoughts, trans. Henry C. Clark. Indianapolis: Liberty Fund, [c. 1720–55] 2012.

    Oeuvres complètes, ed. Roger Caillois. Two volumes. Paris: Gallimard, 1951.

    The Persian Letters, trans. George R. Healy. Indianapolis: Hackett, [1721] 1999.

    Selected Political Writings, ed. Melvin Richter. Indianapolis: Hackett, 1990.

    The Spirit of the Laws, trans. Anne M. Cohler, Basia C. Miller, and Harold S. Stone. Cambridge: Cambridge University Press, [1748] 1989.

    The Spirit of the Laws, trans. Thomas Nugent. New York: Hafner, [1748] 1949.

    The Spirit of the Laws: A Compendium of the First English Edition, ed. David W. Carrithers. Berkeley: University of California Press, 1977.

Bibliography

Moore, James. "Hume's Political Science and the Classical Republican Tradition." *Canadian Journal of Political Science* 10.4 (December 1977): 809–39.

"The Social Background of Hume's Science of Human Nature." In *McGill Hume Studies*, ed. David Fate Norton, Nicholas Capaldi, and Wade L. Robison. San Diego: Austin Hill Press, 1979.

Mornet, Daniel. *Les Origines intellectuelles de la révolution française, 1715–1787*, fourth edition. Paris: Armand Colin, [1933] 1947.

Mosher, Michael. "The Judgmental Gaze of European Women: Gender, Sexuality, and the Critique of Republican Rule." *Political Theory* 22.1 (February 1994): 25–44.

"Monarchy's Paradox: Honor in the Face of Sovereign Power." In *Montesquieu's Science of Politics: Essays on The Spirit of Laws*, ed. David W. Carrithers, Michael A. Mosher, and Paul A. Rahe. Lanham, MD: Rowman & Littlefield, 2001.

"Montesquieu on Empire and Enlightenment." In *Empire and Modern Political Thought*, ed. Sankar Muthu. Cambridge: Cambridge University Press, 2012.

Mossner, Ernest Campbell. "Hume and the Ancient-Modern Controversy, 1725–1752: A Study in Creative Scepticism." *University of Texas Studies in English* 28 (1949): 139–53.

The Life of David Hume, second edition. Oxford: Clarendon Press, 1980.

"Was Hume a Tory Historian? Facts and Reconsiderations." *Journal of the History of Ideas* 2.2 (April 1941): 225–36.

Moyn, Samuel. "Mind the Enlightenment." *Nation* 290.21 (31 May 2010): 25–32.

Muller, Jerry Z. *Adam Smith in His Time and Ours: Designing the Decent Society*. Princeton, NJ: Princeton University Press, 1993.

The Mind and the Market: Capitalism in Western Thought. Westminster, MD: Broadway Books, 2003.

Muthu, Sankar. *Enlightenment against Empire*. Princeton, NJ: Princeton University Press, 2003.

Myrdal, Gunnar. *The Political Element in the Development of Economic Theory*. London: Routledge & Kegan Paul, 1953.

Nagel, Thomas. *The View from Nowhere*. Oxford: Oxford University Press, 1986.

Naves, Raymond. *Voltaire: L'Homme et l'oeuvre*, fifth edition. Paris: Hatier-Boivin, [1942] 1958.

Nelson, Eric. *The Greek Tradition in Republican Thought*. Cambridge: Cambridge University Press, 2004.

Newton, Isaac. *Philosophical Writings*, ed. Andrew Janiak. Cambridge: Cambridge University Press, 2004.

Nietzsche, Friedrich. *The Will to Power*, trans. Walter Kaufmann. New York: Vintage, 1968.

Niklaus, Robert. "Voltaire et l'empirisme anglais." *Revue internationale de philosophie* 48 (1994): 9–24.

Nisbet, H. B. "Lessing and Philosophy." In *A Companion to the Works of Gotthold Ephraim Lessing*, ed. Barbara Fischer and Thomas C. Fox. Rochester, NY: Camden House, 2005.

Norton, David Fate. *David Hume: Common-Sense Moralist, Sceptical Metaphysician*. Princeton, NJ: Princeton University Press, 1982.

"An Introduction to Hume's Thought." In *The Cambridge Companion to Hume*, ed. David Fate Norton and Jacqueline Taylor, second edition. Cambridge: Cambridge University Press, 2009.

Norton, David Fate, and Manfred Kuehn. "The Foundations of Morality." In *The Cambridge History of Eighteenth-Century Philosophy*, ed. Knud Haakonssen, vol. 2. Cambridge: Cambridge University Press, 2006.

Nyland, Chris. "Adam Smith, Stage Theory, and the Status of Women." *History of Political Economy* 25.4 (winter 1993): 617–36.

Oakeshott, Michael. *Morality and Politics in Modern Europe: The Harvard Lectures*, ed. Shirley Robin Letwin. New Haven, CT: Yale University Press, [1958] 1993.

On Human Conduct. Oxford: Oxford University Press, 1975.

Rationalism in Politics and Other Essays. Indianapolis: Liberty Fund, 1991.

O'Brien, Karen. *Narratives of Enlightenment: Cosmopolitan History from Voltaire to Gibbon*. Cambridge: Cambridge University Press, 1997.

Oslington, Paul, ed. *Adam Smith as Theologian*. New York: Routledge, 2011.

Otteson, James R. *Adam Smith's Marketplace of Life*. Cambridge: Cambridge University Press, 2002.

Outram, Dorinda. *The Enlightenment*, second edition. Cambridge: Cambridge University Press, 2005.

Pack, Spencer J., and Eric Schliesser. "Smith's Humean Criticism of Hume's Account of the Origin of Justice." *Journal of the History of Philosophy* 44.1 (January 2006): 47–63.

Pangle, Thomas L. "The Liberal Critique of Rights in Montesquieu and Hume." *Tocqueville Review* 13.2 (1992): 31–42.

Montesquieu's Philosophy of Liberalism: A Commentary on The Spirit of the Laws. Chicago: University of Chicago Press, 1973.

The Theological Basis of Liberal Modernity in Montesquieu's Spirit of the Laws. Chicago: University of Chicago Press, 2010.

Pascal, Roy. "Property and Society: The Scottish Contribution of the Eighteenth Century." *Modern Quarterly* 1 (1938): 167–79.

Pearson, Roger. *The Fables of Reason: A Study of Voltaire's 'Contes Philosophiques'*. Oxford: Clarendon Press, 1993.

Voltaire Almighty: A Life in Pursuit of Freedom. New York: Bloomsbury, 2005.

Pellessier, Georges. *Voltaire philosophe*. Paris: Colin, 1908.

Perkins, Merle L. *Voltaire's Concept of International Order*. Geneva: Institut et Musée Voltaire, 1965.

"Voltaire's Principles of Political Thought." *Modern Language Quarterly* 17.4 (December 1956): 289–300.

Pettit, Philip. "Negative Liberty, Liberal and Republican." *European Journal of Philosophy* 1.1 (April 1993): 15–38.

Pitts, Jennifer. *A Turn to Empire: The Rise of Imperial Liberalism in Britain and France*. Princeton, NJ: Princeton University Press, 2005.

Plato. *The Republic*, trans. Allan Bloom. New York: Basic Books, 1968.

Bibliography

Plutarch. *Lives of the Noble Grecians and Romans*, ed. John Dryden. Two volumes. New York: Modern Library, 2001.

Pocock, J. G. A. *Barbarism and Religion*, vol. 1: *The Enlightenments of Edward Gibbon, 1737–1764*. Cambridge: Cambridge University Press, 1999.

Barbarism and Religion, vol. 2: *Narratives of Civil Government*. Cambridge: Cambridge University Press, 1999.

"Cambridge Paradigms and Scotch Philosophers: A Study of the Relations between the Civic Humanist and the Civil Jurisprudence Interpretation of Eighteenth-Century Social Thought." In *Wealth and Virtue: The Shaping of Political Economy in the Scottish Enlightenment*, ed. Istvan Hont and Michael Ignatieff. Cambridge: Cambridge University Press, 1983.

"Historiography and Enlightenment: A View of Their History." *Modern Intellectual History* 5.1 (April 2008): 83–96.

"Hume and the American Revolution: The Dying Thoughts of a North Briton." In *McGill Hume Studies*, ed. David Fate Norton, Nicholas Capaldi, and Wade L. Robison. San Diego: Austin Hill Press, 1979.

The Machiavellian Moment: Florentine Political Thought and the Atlantic Republican Tradition. Princeton, NJ: Princeton University Press, 1975.

"The Re-description of Enlightenment." *Proceedings of the British Academy* 125 (2004): 101–17.

Virtue, Commerce, and History: Essays on Political Thought and History, Chiefly in the Eighteenth Century. Cambridge: Cambridge University Press, 1985.

Pomeau, René. *La Religion de Voltaire*. Paris: Librarie A.-G. Nizet, 1956.

Popkin, Richard H. "David Hume: His Pyrrhonism and His Critique of Pyrrhonism." In *Hume*, ed. V. C. Chappell. Garden City, NY: Anchor Books, 1966.

"Hume's Racism." In *The High Road to Pyrrhonism*, ed. Richard A. Watson and James E. Force. San Diego: Austin Hill Press, 1980.

"Hume's Racism Reconsidered." In *The Third Force in Seventeenth-Century Thought*. Leiden: Brill, 1992.

Porter, Roy. *The Creation of the Modern World: The Untold Story of the British Enlightenment*. New York: W. W. Norton, 2000.

The Enlightenment, second edition. New York: Palgrave, 2001.

Pufendorf, Samuel. *The Whole Duty of Man, According to the Law of Nature*, ed. Ian Hunter and David Saunders. Indianapolis: Liberty Fund, [1673] 2003.

Radasanu, Andrea. "Montesquieu on Moderation, Monarchy and Reform." *History of Political Thought* 31.2 (summer 2010): 283–307.

Rahe, Paul A. *Montesquieu and the Logic of Liberty: War, Religion, Commerce, Climate, Terrain, Technology, Uneasiness of Mind, the Spirit of Political Vigilance, and the Foundations of the Modern Republic*. New Haven, CT: Yale University Press, 2009.

Soft Despotism, Democracy's Drift: Montesquieu, Rousseau, Tocqueville, and the Modern Prospect. New Haven, CT: Yale University Press, 2009.

Raphael, D. D. *The Impartial Spectator: Adam Smith's Moral Philosophy*. Oxford: Clarendon Press, 2007.

Rasmussen, Dennis C. "Adam Smith and Rousseau: Enlightenment and Counter-Enlightenment." In *The Oxford Handbook of Adam Smith*, ed. Christopher J. Berry, Maria Pia Paganelli, and Craig Smith. Oxford: Oxford University Press, 2013.

"Burning Laws and Strangling Kings? Voltaire and Diderot on the Perils of Rationalism in Politics." *Review of Politics* 73.1 (winter 2011): 77–104.

The Problems and Promise of Commercial Society: Adam Smith's Response to Rousseau. University Park: Pennsylvania State University Press, 2008.

Rawls, John. *Political Liberalism*, expanded edition. Columbia University Press, [1993] 2005.

A Theory of Justice. Cambridge, MA: Harvard University Press, 1971.

Raynor, David R. "Hume's Abstract of Adam Smith's Theory of Moral Sentiments." *Journal of the History of Philosophy* 22.1 (January 1984): 51–80.

Richter, Melvin. "Montesquieu's Comparative Analysis of Europe and Asia: Intended and Unintended Consequences." In *L'Europe de Montesquieu*, ed. Alberto Postigliola and Maria Grazia Bottaro Palumbo. Naples: Liguori Editore, 1995.

The Political Theory of Montesquieu. Cambridge: Cambridge University Press, 1977.

Robertson, John. *The Case for the Enlightenment: Scotland and Naples, 1680–1760*. Cambridge: Cambridge University Press, 2005.

The Scottish Enlightenment and the Militia Issue. Edinburgh: John Donald, 1985.

Romani, Roberto. *National Character and Public Spirit in Britain and France, 1750–1914*. Cambridge: Cambridge University Press, 2002.

Rosenberg, Nathan. "Adam Smith and the Stock of Moral Capital." *History of Political Economy* 22.1 (spring 1990): 1–17.

"Some Institutional Aspects of the Wealth of Nations." *Journal of Political Economy* 68 (1960): 557–70.

Rosenblatt, Helena. "The Christian Enlightenment." In *The Cambridge History of Christianity*, vol. 7: *Enlightenment, Reawakening and Revolution, 1600–1815*, ed. Stewart J. Brown and Timothy Tackett. Cambridge: Cambridge University Press, 2006.

Ross, Ian Simpson. "'Great Works upon the Anvil' in 1785: Adam Smith's Projected Corpus of Philosophy." *Adam Smith Review* 1 (2004): 40–59.

"Reply to Charles Griswold 'On the Incompleteness of Adam Smith's System.'" *Adam Smith Review* 2 (2006): 187–91.

Rothschild, Emma. "Adam Smith in the British Empire." In *Empire and Modern Political Thought*, ed. Sankar Muthu. Cambridge: Cambridge University Press, 2012.

"The Atlantic Worlds of David Hume." In *Soundings in Atlantic History: Latent Structures and Intellectual Currents, 1500–1830*, ed. Bernard Bailyn and Patricia L. Denault. Cambridge, MA: Harvard University Press, 2009.

Economic Sentiments: Adam Smith, Condorcet, and the Enlightenment. Cambridge, MA: Harvard University Press, 2001.

Rousseau, Jean-Jacques. *The Discourses and Other Early Political Writings*, trans. Victor Gourevitch. Cambridge: Cambridge University Press, 1997.

Bibliography

Rowe, Constance. *Voltaire and the State*. New York: Columbia University Press, 1955.

Russell, Paul. *The Riddle of Hume's Treatise: Skepticism, Naturalism, and Irreligion*. Oxford: Oxford University Press, 2008.

Sabl, Andrew. *Hume's Politics: Coordination and Crisis in the History of England*. Princeton, NJ: Princeton University Press, 2012.

"The Last Artificial Virtue: Hume on Toleration and Its Lessons." *Political Theory* 37.4 (August 2009): 511–38.

"When Bad Things Happen from Good People (and Vice-Versa): David Hume's Political Ethics of Revolution." *Polity* 35.1 (autumn 2002): 73–92.

Salkever, Stephen G. "'Cool Reflexion' and the Criticism of Values: Is, Ought, and Objectivity in Hume's Social Science." *American Political Science Review* 74.1 (March 1980): 70–7.

Sandel, Michael. *Democracy's Discontent: America in Search of a Public Philosophy*. Cambridge, MA: Harvard University Press, 1996.

Liberalism and the Limits of Justice, second edition. Cambridge: Cambridge University Press, [1982] 1998.

"The Procedural Republic and the Unencumbered Self." *Political Theory* 12.1 (February 1984): 81–96.

Sayre-McCord, Geoffrey. "Hume and the Bauhaus Theory of Ethics." *Midwest Studies in Philosophy* 20 (1995): 280–98.

"On Why Hume's 'General Point of View' Isn't Ideal – and Shouldn't Be." *Social Philosophy and Policy* 11.1 (winter 1994): 202–28.

Schaub, Diana J. "Of Believers and Barbarians: Montesquieu's Enlightened Toleration." In *Early Modern Skepticism and the Origins of Toleration*, ed. Alan Levine. Lanham, MD: Lexington, 1999.

Erotic Liberalism: Women and Revolution in Montesquieu's Persian Letters. Lanham, MD: Rowman & Littlefield, 1995).

"Montesquieu on Slavery." *Perspectives on Political Science* 34.2 (spring 2005): 72–7.

"Montesquieu on 'The Woman Problem.'" In *Finding a New Feminism: Rethinking the Woman Question for Liberal Democracy*, ed. Pamela Jensen. Lanham, MD: Rowman & Littlefield, 1996.

"Montesquieu's Popular Science." *New Atlantis* 20 (spring 2008): 37–46.

Scherr, Arthur. "Candide's Garden Revisited: Gender Equality in a Commoner's Paradise." *Eighteenth-Century Life* 17 (November 1993): 40–59.

Schliesser, Eric. "Hume's Newtonianism and Anti-Newtonianism." In *The Stanford Encyclopedia of Philosophy*, ed. Edward N. Zalta. Winter 2008 edition. <http://plato.stanford.edu/archives/win2008/entries/hume-newton/>.

"Wonder in the Face of Scientific Revolutions: Adam Smith on Newton's 'Proof' of Copernicanism." *British Journal for the History of Philosophy* 13.4 (2005): 697–732.

Schmidt, Claudia M. *David Hume: Reason in History*. University Park: Pennsylvania State University Press, 2003.

Schmidt, James. "Inventing the Enlightenment: Anti-Jacobins, British Hegelians, and the *Oxford English Dictionary*." *Journal of the History of Ideas* 64.3 (July 2003): 421–43.

"The Legacy of the Enlightenment." *Philosophy and Literature* **26**.2 (October 2002): 432–42.

"What Enlightenment Project?" *Political Theory* **28**.6 (December 2000): 734–57.

"What the Enlightenment Was, What It Still Might Be, and Why Kant May Have Been Right After All." *American Behavioral Scientist* **49**.5 (January 2006): 647–63.

ed. *What Is Enlightenment? Eighteenth-Century Answers and Twentieth-Century Questions.* Berkeley: University of California Press, 1996.

Schneewind, J. B. *The Invention of Autonomy: A History of Modern Moral Philosophy.* Cambridge: Cambridge University Press, 1998.

Schwarzbach, Bertram Eugene. "Voltaire et les juifs: Bilan et plaidoyer." *Studies on Voltaire and the Eighteenth Century* **358** (1997): 27–91.

Voltaire's Old Testament Criticism. Geneva: Droz, 1971.

Sen, Amartya. *The Idea of Justice.* Cambridge, MA: Belknap Press, 2009.

"Introduction." In Adam Smith, *The Theory of Moral Sentiments.* New York: Penguin, 2009.

Shackleton, Robert. "Allies and Enemies: Voltaire and Montesquieu." In *Essays on Montesquieu and on the Enlightenment,* ed. David Gilson and Martin Smith. Oxford: Voltaire Foundation, 1988.

Montesquieu: A Critical Biography. Oxford: Oxford University Press, 1961.

Shank, J. B. *The Newton Wars and the Beginning of the French Enlightenment.* Chicago: University of Chicago Press, 2008.

"Voltaire." In *The Stanford Encyclopedia of Philosophy,* ed. Edward N. Zalta. Summer 2010 edition. <http://plato.stanford.edu/archives/sum2010/entries/voltaire/>.

Sher, Richard B. "From Troglodytes to Americans: Montesquieu and the Scottish Enlightenment on Liberty, Virtue, and Commerce." In *Republicanism, Liberty, and Commercial Society, 1649–1776,* ed. David Wootton. Stanford, CA: Stanford University Press, 1994.

Shklar, Judith N. "The Liberalism of Fear." In *Liberalism and the Moral Life,* ed. Nancy L. Rosenblum. Cambridge, MA: Harvard University Press, 1989.

Montesquieu. Oxford: Oxford University Press, 1987.

Ordinary Vices. Cambridge, MA: Harvard University Press, 1984.

Silver, Allan. "'Two Different Sorts of Commerce' – Friendship and Strangership in Civil Society." In *Public and Private in Thought and Practice: Perspectives on a Grand Dichotomy,* ed. Jeff Weintraub and Krishan Kumar. Chicago: University of Chicago Press, 1997.

Skinner, Andrew S. *A System of Social Science: Papers Relating to Adam Smith,* second edition. Oxford: Clarendon Press, 1996.

Smith, Adam. "Adam Smith an Thomas Cadell: Zwei neue Briefe," ed. Heiner Klemme. In *Archiv für Geschichte der Philosophie* **73**.3 (1991): 277–80.

The Correspondence of Adam Smith, ed. Ernest Campbell Mossner and Ian Simpson Ross. Indianapolis: Liberty Fund, 1987.

Essays on Philosophical Subjects, ed. W. P. D. Wightman. Indianapolis: Liberty Fund, 1980.

Bibliography

An Inquiry into the Nature and Causes of the Wealth of Nations, ed. R. H. Campbell, A. S. Skinner, and W. B. Todd. Two volumes. Indianapolis: Liberty Fund [1776], 1981.

Lectures on Jurisprudence, ed. R. L. Meek, D. D. Raphael, and P. G. Stein. Indianapolis: Liberty Fund, [1762–6] 1982.

Lectures on Rhetoric and Belles Lettres, ed. J. C. Bryce. Indianapolis: Liberty Fund, [1762–3] 1985.

The Theory of Moral Sentiments, ed. D. D. Raphael and A. L. Macfie. Indianapolis: Liberty Fund, [1759–90] 1982.

The Theory of Moral Sentiments, ed. Knud Haakonssen. Cambridge: Cambridge University Press, 2002.

Smith, Michael. *The Moral Problem*. Malden, MA: Blackwell, 1994.

Smith, Preserved. *A History of Modern Culture*, vol. 2: *The Enlightenment, 1687–1776*. Gloucester, MA: Peter Smith, [1934] 1957.

Smith, Steven B. *Hegel's Critique of Liberalism: Rights in Context*. Chicago: University of Chicago Press, 1991.

Sorkin, David. *The Religious Enlightenment: Protestants, Jews, and Catholics from London to Vienna*. Princeton, NJ: Princeton University Press, 2008.

Spector, Céline. "Was Montesquieu Liberal? *The Spirit of the Laws* in the History of Liberalism." In *French Liberalism from Montesquieu to the Present Day*, ed. Raf Geenans and Helena Rosenblatt. Cambridge: Cambridge University Press, 2012.

Spencer, Mark G. "Hume and Madison on Faction." *William and Mary Quarterly* 59.4 (October 2002): 869–96.

Stark, Werner. *Montesquieu, Pioneer of the Sociology of Knowledge*. Toronto: University of Toronto Press, 1961.

Sternhell, Zeev. *The Anti-Enlightenment Tradition*, trans. David Maisel. New Haven, CT: Yale University Press, 2010.

Stewart, Dugald. "Account of the Life and Writings of Adam Smith, LL.D." In Adam Smith, *Essays on Philosophical Subjects*, ed. I. S. Ross. Indianapolis: Liberty Fund, [1794] 1980.

Stewart, John B. *Opinion and Reform in Hume's Political Philosophy*. Princeton, NJ: Princeton University Press, 1992.

Stigler, George J. "Smith's Travels on the Ship of State." In *Essays on Adam Smith*, ed. Andrew S. Skinner and Thomas Wilson. Oxford: Clarendon Press, 1975.

Sullivan, Vickie B. "Against the Despotism of a Republic: Montesquieu's Correction of Machiavelli in the Name of the Security of the Individual." *History of Political Thought* 27.2 (summer 2006): 263–89.

"Criminal Procedure as the Most Important Knowledge and the Distinction between Human and Divine Justice in Montesquieu's *Spirit of the Laws*." In *Natural Right and Political Philosophy: Essays in Honor of Catherine Zuckert and Michael Zuckert*, ed. Ann Ward and Lee Ward. Notre Dame, IN: University of Notre Dame Press, 2013.

"Montesquieu's Philosophical Assault on Despotic Ideas in The Spirit of the Laws." Unpublished manuscript.

Swanson, Christine. "Can Hume Be Read as a Virtue Ethicist?" *Hume Studies* 33.1 (2007): 91–113.

324 *Bibliography*

Talmon, Jacob L. *The Origins of Totalitarian Democracy*. New York: W. W. Norton, [1952] 1970.

Tate, Robert S. "Voltaire and the Parlements: A Reconsideration." *Studies on Voltaire and the Eighteenth Century* **241** (1986): 161–83.

Taylor, Charles. *Hegel*. Cambridge: Cambridge University Press, 1975.

Sources of the Self: The Making of the Modern Identity. Cambridge, MA: Harvard University Press, 1989.

Taylor, Jacqueline. "Hume's Later Moral Philosophy." In *The Cambridge Companion to Hume*, ed. David Fate Norton and Jacqueline Taylor, second edition. Cambridge: Cambridge University Press, 2009.

Teichgraeber, Richard F., III. *'Free Trade' and Moral Philosophy: Rethinking the Sources of Adam Smith's Wealth of Nations*. Durham, NC: Duke University Press, 1986.

Thielemann, Leland. "Voltaire and Hobbism." *Studies on Voltaire and the Eighteenth Century* 10 (1959): 237–58.

Tocqueville, Alexis de. *The Old Regime and the Revolution*, trans. Alan S. Kahan. Chicago: University of Chicago Press, [1856] 1998.

Todorov, Tzvetan. *The Imperfect Garden: The Legacy of Humanism*, trans. Carol Cosman. Princeton, NJ: Princeton University Press, 2002.

Torrey, Norman L. *The Spirit of Voltaire*. New York: Russell and Russell, [1938] 1968.

Tuck, Richard. "The 'Modern' Theory of Natural Law." In *The Languages of Political Theory in Early-Modern Europe*, ed. Anthony Pagden. Cambridge: Cambridge University Press, 1987.

Valls, Andrew. "'A Lousy Empirical Scientist': Reconsidering Hume's Racism." In *Race and Racism in Modern Philosophy*, ed. Andrew Valls. Ithaca, NY: Cornell University Press, 2005.

Vaughan, C. E. *Studies in The History of Political Philosophy before and after Rousseau*. Two volumes. New York: Russell & Russell, [1925] 1960.

Voegelin, Eric. *From Enlightenment to Revolution*. Durham, NC: Duke University Press, 1975.

Voltaire. *The Age of Louis XIV*, trans. Martyn P. Pollack. London: J. M. Dent and Sons, [1751] 1961.

The Age of Louis XIV and Other Selected Writings, trans. J. H. Brumfitt. New York: Twayne, 1963.

La Bégueule, ed. Nicholas Cronk and Haydn T. Mason. In *The Complete Works of Voltaire*, vol. 74a. Oxford: Voltaire Foundation, [1772] 2006.

Candide and Other Stories, trans. Roger Pearson. Oxford: Oxford University Press, 2006.

Candide and Related Texts, trans. David Wootton. Indianapolis: Hackett, 2000.

Commentaire sur l'Esprit des lois, ed. Sheila Mason. In *The Complete Works of Voltaire*, vol. 80b. Oxford: Voltaire Foundation, [1777] 2009.

Correspondence, ed. Theodore Besterman. Fifty-one volumes. In *The Complete Works of Voltaire*, vols. 85–135. Geneva: Institut et Musée Voltaire, 1969–77.

Bibliography

Eléments de la philosophie de Newton, ed. Robert L. Walters and W. H. Barber. In *The Complete Works of Voltaire*, vol. 15. Oxford: Voltaire Foundation, [1738] 1992.

Épitre à l'auteur du livre des Trois Imposteurs. In *Oeuvres complètes de Voltaire*, ed. Louis Moland, vol. 10. Paris: Garnier, [1769] 1877.

Essai sur les moeurs et l'esprit des nations, ed. René Pomeau. Two volumes. Paris: Garnier, [1756–69] 1963.

An Essay on Epic Poetry, ed. David Williams. In *The Complete Works of Voltaire*, vol. 3b. Oxford: Voltaire Foundation, [1727] 1996.

Histoire du parlement de Paris, ed. John Renwick. In *The Complete Works of Voltaire*, vol. 68. Oxford: Voltaire Foundation, [1768] 2005.

Letters Concerning the English Nation, ed. Nicholas Cronk. Oxford: Oxford University Press, [1733] 1994.

Micromégas and Other Short Fictions, trans. Theo Cuffe. New York: Penguin, 2002.

Notebooks, ed. Theodore Besterman. Two volumes. In *The Complete Works of Voltaire*, vols. 81–2. Geneva: Institut et Musée Voltaire, 1968.

"On Commerce and Luxury." In *Commerce, Culture, and Liberty: Readings on Capitalism before Adam Smith*, ed. Henry C. Clark. Indianapolis: Liberty Fund, [1738] 2003.

Questions sur l'Encyclopédie, ed. Nicholas Cronk and Christiane Mervaud. Six volumes to date. In *The Complete Works of Voltaire*, vols. 38–42B. Oxford: Voltaire Foundation, [1771–4] 2007–12.

Le Philosophe ignorant, ed. Roland Mortier. In *The Complete Works of Voltaire*, vol. 62. Oxford: Voltaire Foundation, [1766] 1987.

Philosophical Dictionary, trans. Theodore Besterman. London: Penguin, [1764–9] 2004.

Poème sur la loi naturelle. In *Mélanges de Voltaire*, ed. Jacques Van Den Heuvel. Paris: Gallimard, [1756] 1961.

Political Writings, trans. David Williams. Cambridge: Cambridge University Press, 1994.

Prix de la justice et de l'humanité, ed. Robert Granderoute. In *The Complete Works of Voltaire*, vol. 80b. Oxford: Voltaire Foundation, [1777] 2009.

Rome sauvée, ou Catilina, tragédie, ed. Paul LeClerc. In *The Complete Works of Voltaire*, vol. 31a. Oxford: Voltaire Foundation, [1749] 1992.

Traité de métaphysique, ed. W. H. Barber. In *The Complete Works of Voltaire*, vol. 14. Oxford: Voltaire Foundation, [1736] 1989.

Treatise on Tolerance and Other Writings, ed. Simon Harvey and trans. Brian Masters. Cambridge: Cambridge University Press, 2000.

A Treatise on Toleration and Other Essays, trans. Joseph McCabe. Amherst, NY: Prometheus Books, [1767] 1994.

Voltaire: Selections, trans. Paul Edwards. New York: Macmillan, 1989.

"The Worldling." In *Commerce, Culture, and Liberty: Readings on Capitalism before Adam Smith*, ed. Henry C. Clark. Indianapolis: Liberty Fund, [1736] 2003.

Vyverberg, Henry. *Historical Pessimism in the French Enlightenment*. Cambridge, MA: Harvard University Press, 1958.

Human Nature, Cultural Diversity, and the French Enlightenment. Oxford: Oxford University Press, 1989.

Waddicor, Mark H. *Montesquieu and the Philosophy of Natural Law.* The Hague: Martinus Nijhoff, 1970.

Wade, Ira O. *The Intellectual Development of Voltaire.* Princeton, NJ: Princeton University Press, 1969.

  Studies on Voltaire. Princeton, NJ: Princeton University Press, 1947.

  "Voltaire's Quarrel with Science." *Bucknell Review* 8.4 (December 1959): 287–98.

Waldinger, Renée. *Voltaire and Reform in the Light of the French Revolution.* Geneva: Droz, 1959.

Ward, Lee. "Montesquieu on Federalism and Anglo-Gothic Constitutionalism." *Publius* 37.4 (fall 2007): 551–77.

Warner, Stuart D. "Montesquieu's Prelude: An Interpretation of Book I of *The Spirit of the Laws.*" In *Enlightening Revolutions: Essays in Honor of Ralph Lerner,* ed. Svetozar Minkov. Lanham, MD: Lexington, 2006.

Waterman, A. M. C. "Economics as Theology: Adam Smith's *Wealth of Nations.*" *Southern Economic Journal* 68.4 (April 2002): 907–21.

Weinstein, Jack Russell. "Sympathy, Difference, and Education: Social Unity in the Work of Adam Smith." *Economics and Philosophy* 22.1 (March 2006): 79–111.

Werhane, Patricia H. *Adam Smith and His Legacy for Modern Capitalism.* Oxford: Oxford University Press, 1991.

Wertz, S. K. "Hume and the Historiography of Science." *Journal of the History of Ideas* 54.3 (July 1993): 411–36.

  "Hume, History, and Human Nature." *Journal of the History of Ideas* 36.3 (July–Sept. 1975): 481–96.

Westerman, Pauline C. "Hume and the Natural Lawyers: A Change of Landscape." In *Hume and Hume's Connexions,* ed. M. A. Stewart and John P. Wright. University Park: Pennsylvania State University Press, 1994.

Whelan, Frederick G. "Hume and Contractarianism." *Polity* 27.2 (winter 1994): 201–24.

  Hume and Machiavelli: Political Realism and Liberal Thought. Lanham, MD: Lexington, 2004.

  Order and Artifice in Hume's Political Philosophy. Princeton, NJ: Princeton University Press, 1985.

Whitehead, Alfred North. *Science and the Modern World.* Cambridge: Cambridge University Press, [1925] 2011.

Williams, Bernard. *Ethics and the Limits of Philosophy.* Cambridge, MA: Harvard University Press, 1985.

  Moral Luck. Cambridge: Cambridge University Press, 1981.

Williams, David. *Condorcet and Modernity.* Cambridge: Cambridge University Press, 2004.

Wilson, James Q. *The Moral Sense.* New York: Free Press, 1993.

  On Character: Essays by James Q. Wilson. Washington, DC: AEI Press, 1991.

Winch, Donald. *Adam Smith's Politics: An Essay in Historiographic Revision.* Cambridge: Cambridge University Press, 1978.

Bibliography

Wokler, Robert. "The Enlightenment Project and Its Critics." In *The Postmodernist Critique of the Project of Enlightenment*, ed. Sven-Eric Liedman. Amsterdam: Rodopi, 1997.

"The Enlightenment Project as Betrayed by Modernity." *History of European Ideas* 24.4–5 (1998): 301–13.

"The Enlightenment Science of Politics." In *Inventing Human Science*, ed. Christopher Fox, Roy Porter, and Robert Wokler. Berkeley: University of California Press, 1995.

"Ernst Cassirer's Enlightenment: An Exchange with Bruce Mazlish." *Studies in Eighteenth Century Culture* 29 (2000): 335–48.

"Isaiah Berlin's Enlightenment and Counter-Enlightenment." In *Isaiah Berlin's Counter-Enlightenment*, ed. Joseph Mali and Robert Wokler. Philadelphia: American Philosophical Society, 2003.

"Projecting the Enlightenment." In *After MacIntyre: Critical Perspectives on the Work of Alasdair MacIntyre*, ed. John Horton and Susan Mendus. Notre Dame, IN: University of Notre Dame Press, 1994.

Wulf, Steven J. "The Skeptical Life in Hume's Political Thought." *Polity* 33.1 (autumn 2000): 77–99.

Yack, Bernard. *The Fetishism of Modernities: Epochal Self-Consciousness in Contemporary Social and Political Thought*. South Bend, IN: University of Notre Dame Press, 1997.

Yolton, John W. *Locke and French Materialism*. Oxford: Clarendon, 1991.

Zak, Paul J., and Michael C. Jensen, eds. *Moral Markets: The Critical Role of Values in the Economy*. Princeton, NJ: Princeton University Press, 2008.

Zuckert, Michael. "Natural Law, Natural Rights, and Classical Liberalism: On Montesquieu's Critique of Hobbes." *Social Philosophy and Policy* 18.1 (winter 2001): 227–51.

Index

Abstract principles, Hume and, 111–12, 298
Adair, Douglass, 279n56
Adams, John, 11
Adorno, Theodor, 137n6
The Age of Louis XIV (Voltaire), 96, 157, 214–15, 216
Aikenhead, Thomas, 168
Alfred the Great (England), 118–19, 196
American colonies
  Hume on, 199–200
  Native Americans in, 54–5, 122–3
  Smith on, 285–6
Anarchy
  Hume on, 119, 198, 278n54
  Voltaire on, 104, 106
Anglican Church, 103n73
Annales school, 5
Anne (England), 216
Aristotle, 57, 161
Arouet, François-Marie. *See* Voltaire
Atheism
  Hume on, 183–4
  Montesquieu on, 174–5, 174n138
  Voltaire on, 170–2, 171n124
Atomistic individualism, 4. *See also* Individualism
Autonomy of individual
  Descartes on, 242

Hobbes on, 237n11, 242, 243, 254n53, 255, 265n13
Hume on, 236–42
  climate, role of, 241n20
  egoism, rejection of, 239, 239n15
  political institutions and, 238, 238n12
  social contract, rejection of, 238
  social nature of man, focus on, 236–8, 239–42
  sympathy and, 239
Kant on, 235, 235n8, 258, 300
Locke on, 235, 235n8, 239, 258, 300
Montesquieu on, 252–8
  climate, role of, 256–7
  laws and, 256n58
  moral causes, role of, 257–8
  political institutions and, 256
  social nature of man, focus on, 252–6
overview, 21–2, 233–6, 258–9, 300–1
Rawls on, 258, 258n64, 300
Rousseau on, 237n11, 253n51
Smith on, 242–7
  egoism, rejection of, 243n26
  self-love and, 242–3
  social nature of man, focus on, 244–7
  sympathy and, 243, 247

329

Index

Autonomy of individual (*cont.*)
  Voltaire on, 247–52
    climate, role of, 251–2
    moral causes, role of, 251–2
    self-love and, 250
    social nature of man, focus on,
      247–9, 250–1

Bacon, Francis, 15–16, 16n40, 143,
  153, 163, 191–2n2
Bagehot, Walter, 224
Baier, Annette, 34, 109n98, 111, 188,
  199, 240, 241
Bartlett, Robert, 178n149
Bayle, Pierre, 3, 145, 145n31, 175
Beccaria, Cesare, 12
Becker, Carl, 135–6, 153, 165
Beeson, David, 159, 248
Bentham, Jeremy
  "idealistic" liberalism and, 23
  on morality, 33
  on political liberty, 285, 285n69
  scholarly focus on, 15–16
  utilitarianism and, 2, 9, 297–8
Berlin, Isaiah, 11, 28, 60n68, 82,
  89, 192–3
Berry, Christopher J., 36n22, 235n9
Besterman, Theodore, 169n117
Blind faith in reason, 4. *See also*
  Reason
Bossuet, Jacques-Bénigne, 70, 216
Bottiglia, William, 210, 213n65
de Boulainvilliers, Henri, 96–7
de Bourbon, Duc, 168
Boyd, Richard, 282n64, 284
Boyle, Robert, 159
British Enlightenment versus French
  Enlightenment, 294–6, 294n1
Brumfitt, J.H., 70n97, 215–16
Brutus, 282n62
Burke, Edmund, 135–6, 192, 193,
  200–1n26, 234, 260,
  294–5n1
Byng, John, 102

Caesar, Julius, 219, 267n20
Calas, Jean, 97, 101, 275

Caligula (Rome), 128
Callanan, Keegan, 91n34
Campbell, T.D., 50
Candide (Voltaire), 144, 157,
  212–14, 220
Capaldi, Nicholas, 242, 242n23
Caricature of Enlightenment
  atomistic individualism, 4
  blind faith in reason, 4
  criticism of Enlightenment based
    on, 4–5, 13–14, 15
  hegemonic universalism, 3–4
Carrithers, David, 150, 195n13, 204,
  219–20, 219n86, 219n89,
  235–6n9, 259
Cassirer, Ernst, 59n65, 135, 165n109,
  236n10
Categorical imperative, 58n63
Catherine II (Russia), 104–5,
  106–7
Catholic Church
  in France, 156–7, 168
  Montesquieu on, 17–18n43, 176
  Smith on, 181
  Voltaire on, 102, 169, 172,
    210, 215
Cato, 282n62
Charles I (England), 119
Chartier, Roger, 5
du Châtelet, Emilie, 156
China
  Montesquieu on, 256–7
  Voltaire on, 69–70, 105n84
Chinard, Gilbert, 216
Chrysippus, 147
Cicero, 275n46
Circumstances of justice, Hume
  on 110
Clark, Henry, 49n46
Clarke, Samuel, 31
Climate
  Hume on, 241n20
  Montesquieu on, 256–7
  Voltaire on, 251–2
Cobban, Alfred, 10
Cohler, Anne M., 268n22
Cohon, Rachel, 35, 35n21

Index

Commerce
doux commerce, 269–70
hostility toward, 262n8
Hume on, 282–4
Montesquieu on, 268–71, 269n23
negative liberty and, 261–2
religion and, 276–8, 277n51
Smith on
negative liberty and, 288–92,
292n87
political theory, role in, 120,
124–6, 125n140
Voltaire on, 275–8
Communitarianism
criticism of Enlightenment, 21–2,
27, 234, 242, 259
Hume and, 242
negative liberty and, 260, 292–3
Smith and, 246, 247n33
social contract and, 236, 236n10
Comparative analysis. *See* Historical
and comparative analysis
Comte, Auguste, 212
de Condillac, Étienne Bonnot,
12, 295–6
de Condorcet, Marquis, 12, 12n34,
89n27, 212, 295–6, 297
*Considerations on the Causes of the
Greatness of the Romans and
Their Decline* (Montesquieu),
205, 217–19, 267
Contractarianism. *See* Social contract
Copernicus, Nicolaus, 163
Corporation and Test Acts (England),
103n73
Cortéz, Hernán, 155
Courtney, C.P., 206n38
Craiutu, Aurelian, 86n18
Cranston, Maurice, 87, 101n68, 193
Criminal Ordinance of 1670
(France), 97
Criticism of Enlightenment
blind faith in reason, based on, 4
caricature, based on, 4–5, 13–14, 15
communitarian criticism, 21–2, 27,
234, 236n10, 242, 259
feminist criticism, 234n4

historical background, 3n7
individualism, based on, 4, 300–1
Marxist criticism, 261
overview, 1
perceived elitism, based on, 5
political rationalism, based on
(*see* Political rationalism)
radicalism, based on, 15–16
by Rawls, 9, 15, 80–1, 81n2, 82, 130
universalism, based on, 3–4,
27–8n3, 294, 298–9
Crocker, Lester G., 99n58, 210n54
Cromwell, Oliver, 223, 267n20
Cronk, Nicholas, 159, 248
Crospey, Joseph, 242, 261n5
Cudworth, Ralph, 31
Cultural diversity
Hume on, 38–40, 42–4
Montesquieu on, 59–61
Smith on, 54–6
Voltaire on, 69–70, 75–6
Custom and authority, Hume and,
117–18

d'Alembert, Jean Le Rond, 12, 136,
173, 295–6
Danford, John, 40n31
d'Argenson, Comte, 96–7
Darnton, Robert, 5, 7n17
Davidson, Ian, 215n73, 275n46
Decentralization of power, 83–4
Dees, Richard, 36n23, 118, 223
Deism
of Hume, 183
of Montesquieu, 174
of Smith, 178–9
of Voltaire, 169–70, 169n117
Democracy
Hume on, 279–81, 279n56
Montesquieu on, 265–8, 265n15,
267n20
Smith on, 285–7, 290n81
Voltaire on, 272–4, 273n36
Deontology, 2, 29–30n10, 297–8
Descartes, René
generally, 161, 163
on autonomy of individual, 242

Index

Descartes, René *(cont.)*
Montesquieu on, 155, 156n71
rationalism and, 136, 139,
191–2n2
on reason, 16n40, 20
Voltaire on, 143
Despotism. *See also* Monarchy;
Tyranny
"enlightened despotism," 104–6
Montesquieu on, 17–18n43, 87–9,
87n22, 88n23, 88n25, 90–2,
95n42, 176, 217n81
Voltaire on, 104–6, 105n82
d'Holbach, Baron, 20, 167, 170, 171,
184, 295–6
Dialogues Concerning Natural
Religion (Hume), 186,
221, 295
Diderot, Denis, 3, 12, 12n34, 21,
184n169, 193, 193n8, 235n6,
295–6, 297
de Dijn, Annelien, 265–6
Diogenes, 44–5, 45n38, 58
Discourse on Universal History
(Bossuet), 70, 216
A Dissertation on the Passions
(Hume), 240
Domitian (Rome), 128
Domville, William, 217, 217n82
Doux commerce, 269–70
Dubos, Jean-Baptiste, 96–7
Dupré, Louis, 192
Durkheim, Emile, 152n55
Dworkin, Ronald, 301

Economic determinism, 227n113
Edelstein, Dan, 8n19
Edict of Nantes, 96n48, 168
Education
Montesquieu on, 256–8
Smith on, 289–90, 289n80
Egoism, 239, 239n15, 243n26
Elements of the Philosophy of
Newton (Voltaire), 157–8
Elitism, criticism of Enlightenment
based on perception of, 5
Elizabeth I (England), 127, 187, 227

Empiricism. *See also* Skepticism
of Hume, 32n15
of Locke, 139, 139n11
of Montesquieu, 64–5
natural law, lack of empiricism
in, 298
rationalism versus, 136n4, 143, 298
of Smith, 45–6
social contract, lack of empiricism
in, 298
of Voltaire, 99–100, 143, 159
Encumbered self. *See* Autonomy of
individual
Encyclopédie (Diderot), 21, 193
England
American colonies
Hume on, 199–200
Native Americans in,
54–5, 122–3
Smith on, 285–6
British Enlightenment versus French
Enlightenment, 294–6, 294n1
Corporation and Test Acts, 103n73
Glorious Revolution of 1688
(*see* Glorious Revolution
of 1688)
Hume on, 115–17, 116n120
Jacobite uprisings, 199–200
Montesquieu on, 93–5, 94n39, 217,
218, 220, 267n20, 268, 270–1
Puritanism in, 118, 187, 223
religion in, 168
Royal Exchange, 276–8
Smith on, 126–8, 227–8, 285–6
Star Chamber, 118n125
Voltaire on, 101n68, 102–4,
102n70, 102n72, 272, 276–8
"Enlightened despotism," 104–6
Enlightenment. *See also specific topic*
denial of existence of, 7
historical context of, 9n23
self-awareness of, 7–8, 8n20
time frame of, 7n17
"Enlightenment project," 27, 79, 80
An Enquiry Concerning Human
Understanding (Hume)
autonomy of individual in, 239, 241

Index

morality in, 35–6, 37
science in, 161
skepticism in, 140–3
An Enquiry Concerning the Principles of Morals (Hume)
autonomy of individual in, 237, 239
morality in, 30, 33, 38, 40, 41–5, 47
negative liberty in, 282–4
political theory in, 108–9, 114
religion in, 185
Environmental determinism, 256n59
Epicureanism, 175n141
Epicurus, 147
Epistemology
of Hume, 140–3
of Montesquieu, 149–52
overview, 152
of Smith, 146–9, 146n35
of Voltaire, 143–6
Essay on the Mores and Spirit of Nations (Voltaire)
autonomy of individual in, 248–9, 250, 251–2
morality in, 69–70, 71–2
negative liberty in, 272, 276
political theory in, 98
progress versus teleology in, 214, 215
scope of, 70n97
Essay on the Original Contract (Hume), 121
Essays, Moral, Political, and Literary (Hume)
abstract principles, rejection of, 298
autonomy of individual in, 237, 238–9, 240
morality in, 38, 39, 40–1
negative liberty in, 278, 279–80, 281–2, 291
political theory in, 107, 108–9, 110–11, 113, 114–15, 116–18, 119
progress versus teleology in, 220, 221–2, 222n95, 223n100
reform versus revolution in, 196–7, 198, 199
science in, 159–60, 161

The Federalist Papers (Madison), 93n37, 182n163, 279
Feminist criticism of Enlightenment, 234n4
Fénelon, François, 96–7
Ferguson, Adam, 12, 54n59, 255
Firth, Roderick, 49
Flax, Jane, 234n4
Fleischacker, Samuel
on Smith
epistemology and, 146, 148, 148n43, 149, 149n46
jurisprudence and, 123–4
liberty and, 285n71
morality and, 46, 51, 56
national glory and, 286, 290–1n83
reform versus revolution in, 203
religion and, 182n163
science and, 163, 165
self-love and, 243n29
social nature of man and, 247n34
Forbes, Duncan, 37, 121, 127, 198, 229
Force, Pierre, 286n73
Forman-Barzilai, Fonna, 122n131, 243n27
Foucault, Michel, 15, 135–6
"Four stages" theory
autonomy of individual and, 244–5, 256
morality and, 54–5
in political theory, 120, 122, 124–5
progress versus teleology in, 224, 227, 227n112, 228–9
Fox, Charles James, 201n26
France
Catholic Church in, 156–7, 168
Criminal Ordinance of 1670, 97
Edict of Nantes, 96n48, 168
French Enlightenment versus British or Scottish Enlightenment, 294–6, 294n1
French Revolution (*see* French Revolution)
Montesquieu on, 270–1
Protestants in, 168

France (*cont.*)
  religion in, 168
  Smith on, 129–30
Frazer, Michael, 29n9, 53n57, 300
Frederick II (Prussia), 74, 104–5,
    105n81, 106–7, 201n26
Free trade. *See* Commerce
Free will. *See* Autonomy of individual
French Revolution, 13, 191–2, 207–8,
    210–11

Galiani, Ferdinando, 12
Galileo, 163
Galston, William A., 81n3, 96n46
Gaskin, J.C.A., 183, 183n165
Gaus, Gerald, 81
Gauthier, David, 108–9n95
Gay, Peter
  generally, 3
  on Hume, 10
  on Montesquieu, 10–11
  "politics of decency," 81–2
  on rationalism, 136, 137–8, 194
  "secular fideism," 189
  on Smith, 224
  on Voltaire, 101, 104, 106,
    169n116, 171–2, 172n127
General rules of morality, Smith
    on 51–3
Geneva, Voltaire on, 104, 272–3
Genghis Khan, 176
Genovesi, Antonio, 12
Gibbon, Edward, 12, 184n169
Gill, Michael, 45n38
Gillespie, Michael, 168–9
Glorious Revolution of 1688, 118,
    127n145, 199, 203, 206, 216,
    223, 224–5n105
Godwin, William, 229
Golden Rule, 172
Gordon, Daniel, 11n32, 27–8n3
Gray, John, 80, 80n1, 82, 216
Great Britain. *See* England
Greece (Ancient)
  Hume on, 280
  Montesquieu on, 266–8
  Smith on, 56–7, 286–7, 287n75

Voltaire on, 273–4
Greene, Donald, 12n33
Griswold, Charles
  on Smith
    autonomy of individual and,
        246–7n32
    epistemology and, 147, 148, 149
    morality and, 57, 57n62
    negative liberty and, 287n76
    political theory and, 123–4, 126
    "prudent man," 291
Grotius, Hugo, 72, 99, 122

Haakonsen, Knud, 113n108, 115,
    123, 123n135, 179
Habermas, Jürgen, 14, 299–300,
    300n12
Hanley, Ryan, 54, 180n156
Harpham, Edward J., 285n71
Harrington, James, 115n115
Hayek, Friedrich A., 107n92, 192
Hazard, Paul, 1, 193, 229–30
*The Heavenly City of the Eighteenth-
    Century Philosophers*
    (Becker), 135
Hegel, G.W.F., 192, 212, 234
Hegemonic universalism, 3–4. *See also*
    Universalism
Heilbroner, Robert, 226
Helvétius, Claude Adrien, 294–6n1,
    295n4
Henry, Patrick, 73n104
Henry VII (England), 118, 118n125
Herder, J.G., 234
Herzog, Don, 120, 125, 187, 226
"High" Enlightenment, 5–6, 211n58
Himmelfarb, Gertrude, 204n33,
    294–5, 295n2
Historical and comparative analysis
  Hume and, 112–13, 118–19
  Montesquieu and, 89–90, 92–3
  Smith and, 121–4, 125–6
  Voltaire and, 100
*The History of England, from the
    Invasion of Julius Caesar to the
    Revolution in 1688* (Hume)
  autonomy of individual in, 238

Index

335

negative liberty in, 278,
281, 282–3
political theory in, 107–8, 112–13,
114–15, 116, 118–19
progress versus teleology in, 220,
221, 223, 223n100
reform versus revolution in, 196,
198, 199
religion in, 186–7, 188
science in, 159, 160
History of the Parlement of Paris
(Voltaire), 96
Hobbes, Thomas
on autonomy of individual, 239,
242, 243, 254n53, 255,
265n13
rationalism and, 16n40, 20, 136,
139, 139n10, 150
on state of nature, 236–7,
237n11, 252–4
Holland
Hume on, 280n57
Montesquieu on, 270–1
Voltaire on, 104, 272–3
Homer, 161
Hont, Istvan, 201n26, 202
Horkheimer, Max, 137n6
Huguenots, 168n113
Hulliung, Mark, 295n4
Humane criminal law, 83–4
Human nature
autonomy of individual
(*see* Autonomy of individual)
Hume on, 37
Montesquieu on, 91n34
Smith on, 53–4
Voltaire on, 70–1
Hume, David. *See also specific work*
on American colonies, 199–200
on anarchy, 119, 198, 278n54
on atheism, 183–4
on autonomy of individual, 236–42
climate, role of, 241n20
egoism, rejection of, 239, 239n15
political institutions and, 238,
238n12
social contract, rejection of, 238

social nature of man, focus on,
236–8, 239–42
sympathy and, 239
communitarianism and, 242
conservatism of, 195, 198
deism of, 183
empiricism of, 32n15
on England, 115–17, 116n120
epistemology of, 140–3
on Greece, 280
on Hobbes, 139n10
importance of, 10
on justice, 109–11, 109n98
liberalism of, 107–8
on Locke, 139n11
Locke compared, 111, 117
on luxury, 282n63
on mercantilism, 283
on militias, 281n60
moderateness of, 196–7
on monarchy, 117, 117n121, 118,
278, 279
on morality, 30–45. (*see also*
Morality)
on natural law, 108–10, 109n97
on negative liberty, 278–84
anarchy and, 278n54
commerce and, 282–4
in Holland, 280n57
political liberty and, 278–81
republicanism and, 279–81,
279n56
rule of law and, 278n52
perceived conservatism of, 13
on political liberty, 113–14,
113n110, 278–81
political rationalism, opposition to,
195–200
political theory of, 107–19. (*see also*
Political theory)
progress versus teleology in, 220–3
on race, 17–18, 18n44
on rationalism, 195, 200, 241
reform versus revolution in,
195–200, 197n17
religion and, 183–9, 183n164,
184n168, 187n180, 188n182

Index

Hume, David (*cont.*)
  on republicanism, 279–81, 279n56
  on revolution, 196, 197–200
  on Rome, 280
  on rule of law, 118–19, 278–9
  science and, 112n107, 159–61,
    159n86
  on self-love, 37
  on sentiment, 30–45
  skepticism of, 140–3
  on social contract, 108–9, 238
  on state of nature, 108–9, 237
  on sympathy, 239
  on tyranny, 198, 198n20, 199,
    278n54
  utilitarianism and, 33,
    33n18, 108–9
  on women, 17–18, 18n44
"Hume's Law," 32–3
Hutcheson, Frances, 39, 46, 53,
  53n57, 199

Idea for a Universal History
  (Kant), 212
"Idealistic" versus "pragmatic"
  Enlightenment, 296–7, 297n10
The Ignorant Philosopher
  (Voltaire), 144
Impartial spectator, 49–51, 49n46,
  50n50, 58n63
India, Voltaire on, 69–70
Individualism
  autonomy of individual
    (*see* Autonomy of individual)
  criticism of Enlightenment based
    on, 4, 300–1
  negative liberty (*see* Negative
    liberty)
  "possessive individualism," 261n3
Induction, 140n13
Inevitability of progress. *See* Progress
  versus teleology
Infanticide, 56–8
The Ingenu (Voltaire), 251
*An Inquiry into the Nature and
  Causes of the Wealth of
  Nations* (Smith)

autonomy of individual in, 244–5,
  246, 256
importance of, 10, 242
morality in, 46, 53–5
negative liberty in, 284–90
political theory in, 120, 122, 124,
  125, 126, 127–9
progress versus teleology in, 224,
  225, 226, 227, 228
reform versus revolution in,
  201–2, 203
religion in, 179, 181, 182–3
science in, 162–3
skepticism in, 146, 147, 148
Smith on, 295
Invisible hand, 201–2, 224
Israel, Jonathan, 2–3, 2n4, 23, 28,
  193n8, 194, 195, 211n58,
  296–7, 297n10

Jacobite uprisings, 199–200
James II (England), 216, 223
Jesus, 172, 173
Johnson, Samuel, 12, 12n33
Joseph II (Holy Roman Empire),
  201n26
Judaism, Voltaire on, 17–18, 17n43,
  18n45
Jurisprudence of Smith, 118n125,
  121–2n130
Justice
  Hume on, 109–11, 109n98
  Montesquieu on, 65n82
  Smith on, 48n45, 52n55, 123–4,
    287n77
  Voltaire on, 72n101

Kames, Lord, 54n59, 221–2n94
Kant, Immanuel
  on autonomy of individual, 235,
    235n8, 258, 300
  categorical imperative, 58n63
  deontology and, 2, 297–8
  on human dignity, 9
  "idealistic" liberalism and, 23
  on morality, 14–15n39, 29, 31, 58
  perceived moderateness of, 297

Index

on rationalism, 14, 31
Rawls and, 14
on reason, 152, 299–300
reputation as chief representative of
Enlightenment, 14, 14n37
scholarly focus on, 15–16
Smith compared, 287n76
teleology of, 212
universalism of, 299
Kepler, Johannes, 163
King, James T., 111n105, 196n16
Krause, Sharon
on Hume, 30–1, 111, 300
on Montesquieu
despotism and, 90, 91
morality and, 61, 62–3, 64–5
revolution and, 206

de La Barre, Jean-François, 97, 275
de La Mettrie, Julien Offray, 20, 167,
295–6, 295n4
Langdon, David, 214n68, 275n47
Lanson, Gustave, 77n113, 99–100,
107, 170, 207, 210, 214n68
Lectures on Jurisprudence (Smith)
autonomy of individual in,
244, 246
negative liberty in, 285, 286, 289
political theory in, 120–1, 122,
126–7, 128, 129
progress versus teleology in, 225,
226, 227, 228
reform versus revolution in, 202–3
religion in, 181–2
Leibniz, Gottfried Wilhelm, 20, 136,
213n62
Lessing, Gotthold, 12, 12n34
*Letters Concerning the English
Nation* (Voltaire)
autonomy of individual in,
249, 251
negative liberty in, 272,
273–4, 275–8
overview, 100
political theory in, 102–3
reform versus revolution in,
207, 210

religion in, 172, 173
science in, 156–7
skepticism in, 143, 145
translation of, 100n63
Leviathan (Hobbes), 150
Levy, Jacob, 267n20
Liberalism
of Hume, 107–8
"liberalism of fear," 265n13
pragmatic liberalism (*see* Political
theory)
Libertarianism, 301
Liberty
Bentham on, 285, 285n69
Hume on, 113–14, 113n110,
278–81
Montesquieu on, 90n30, 95n42,
264–8, 264n12
negative liberty (*see* Negative
liberty)
Smith on, 284–8
Voltaire on, 272–4
Limits of reason
overview, 20–1, 135–9, 189–90
religion and, 166–89. (*see also*
Religion)
science and, 165n107. (*see also*
Science)
skepticism, 139–52. (*see also*
Skepticism)
Livingston, Donald W., 112, 114,
223n100, 238, 278n52,
281n61
Lock, F.P., 201n26
Locke, John
on autonomy of individual, 235,
235n8, 239, 258, 300
contractarianism and, 2, 297–8
empiricism of, 139, 139n11
Hume compared, 111, 117
Hume on, 139n11
"idealistic" liberalism and, 23
on monarchy, 128
Montesquieu compared, 83, 84–5,
86–7, 86n17
on morality, 28–9
on natural law, 9, 82

Locke, John (*cont.*)
  perceived moderateness of, 297
  political rationalism of,
    194–5, 206
  political theory of, 19
  on reason, 20, 136, 150
  on revolution, 206, 206n38
  scholarly focus on, 15–16
  on separation of powers, 83n7
  Smith compared, 127, 128
  teleology of, 211–12
  Voltaire compared, 97, 99n57
  Voltaire on, 143
Louis XIV (France), 96n48, 168,
  214, 215
Louis XV (France), 168
Louis XVI (France), 168
"Low" Enlightenment, 5–6
Luxury, Hume on, 282n63

Macaulay, Catherine, 117
MacIntyre, Alasdair, 15, 27, 36n22,
  79, 80, 110n99
Macpherson, C.B., 261n3
Madison, James, 83, 93n37, 182n163,
  279, 279n56, 286
de Maistre, Joseph, 15, 192, 234
Malebranche, Nicolas, 20, 31, 136
Mandeville, Bernard, 239, 243, 244,
  249, 249n39, 250, 274–5, 281
Manent, Pierre, 96
Mansfield, Harvey, 93n38, 206n37
Manzer, Robert, 283
Marlborough, Duchess of, 216
Marlborough, Duke of, 216
Marx, Karl, 212, 227n113
Marxist criticism of
  Enlightenment, 261
Mauzi, Robert, 235n9
McMahon, Darrin, 3, 9n24
Meek, Ronald L., 227n113
Mendelssohn, Moses, 12
Mercantilism
  Hume on, 283
  Montesquieu on, 269n23, 283n66
  Smith on, 124–5, 147, 201–2
  Voltaire on, 283n66

Metaphysics, 145–6, 145n32, 151–2,
  152n55
Militias
  Hume on, 281n60
  Smith on, 289n80
Mill, John Stuart, 107n91
Millar, John, 12, 12n34, 54n59,
  179n154
Minowitz, Peter, 261–2n5
"Moderate" versus "radical"
  Enlightenment, 296–7, 297n10
Monarchy. *See also* Despotism;
  Tyranny
  Hume on, 117, 117n121, 118,
    278, 279
  Locke on, 128
  Montesquieu on, 84–5, 84n9, 87,
    207, 265n14
  Smith on, 127, 128, 284–5
  Voltaire on, 101–2, 104–5,
    106–7, 272–3
"Monkish virtues," 41–2, 44–5
de Montaigne, Michel, 145, 145n31,
  265n13
Montesquieu. *See also specific work*
  on atheism, 174–5, 174n138
  on autonomy of individual, 252–8
    climate, role of, 256–7
    laws and, 256n58
    moral causes, role of, 257–8
    political institutions and, 256
    social nature of man, focus
      on, 252–6
  on Catholic Church, 17–18n43, 176
  on China, 256–7
  deism of, 174
  on Descartes, 155, 156n71
  on despotism, 17–18n43, 87–9,
    87n22, 88n23, 88n25, 90–2,
    95n42, 176, 217n81
  doux commerce, 269–70
  on education, 256–8
  empiricism of, 64–5
  on England, 93–5, 94n39, 217, 218,
    220, 267n20, 268, 270–1
  environmental determinism of,
    256n59

Index

339

epistemology of, 149–52
on France, 270–1
on Greece, 266–8
on Hobbes, 254n53, 265n13
on human nature, 91n34
importance of, 10–11
on justice, 65n82
Locke compared, 83, 84–5, 86–7, 86n17
on mercantilism, 269n23, 283n66
on monarchy, 84–5, 84n9, 87, 207, 265n14
on morality, 58–69. (see also Morality)
on natural law, 61–5, 62n71, 66–7, 66n85, 67n89
on negative liberty, 264–71
   commerce and, 268–71, 269n23
   in England, 268, 270–1
   in France, 270–1
   in Greece, 266–8
   in Holland, 270–1
   political liberty and, 264–8, 264n12
   republicanism and, 265–8, 265n15, 267n20
   in Rome, 266–8
on nobility, 83–4, 84n9, 177–8
on "Orientalism," 17–18, 17n43
on political liberty, 90n30, 95n42, 264–8, 264n12
political rationalism, opposition to, 204–7
political theory of, 83–96 (see also Political theory)
progress versus teleology in, 216–20
reform versus revolution in, 204–7
religion and, 173–8, 175n140, 176n144
on republicanism, 265–8, 265n15, 267n20
on revolution, 87, 206–7
on Rome, 217–18, 219, 220, 266–8, 267n20
Rousseau and, 267n21
science and, 153–6, 153n60, 154n63, 156n71

on self-love, 254
on sentiment, 58–9, 62n73, 63–4
skepticism of, 149–52
on social contract, 85
on state of nature, 85, 252–3, 253n51, 254n53
on tyranny, 90n31, 207
on women, 17–18, 18n45, 176, 270–1
Morality
Bentham on, 33
Hume on, 30–45
   cultural diversity, role of, 38–40, 42–4
   human nature in, 37
   "Hume's Law" and, 33
   "monkish virtues," 41–2, 44–5
   moral pluralism, 40–1
   moral relativism versus, 33–4
   natural law in, 31–2n14
   overview, 30–1
   positivism contrasted, 32n15
   rationalism versus, 31
   reality of morality, 30n11
   reason, role of, 34–5
   religion versus, 41–2
   sentiment, role of, 30–45
   universalism in, 35–7, 36n22, 42n34, 45
Kant on, 14–15n39, 29, 31, 58
Locke on, 28–9
Montesquieu on, 58–69
   cultural diversity, role of, 59–61
   empiricism in, 64–5
   flexibility of, 65
   moral relativism versus, 65–6
   natural law in, 61–5, 62n71, 66–7, 66n85, 67n89
   normative concerns in, 64–5, 64n80
   overview, 69
   sentiment, role of, 58–9, 62n73, 63–4
   slavery, rejection of, 67–9, 67n90, 69n93
   society, effect on, 257–8

340   *Index*

Morality (*cont.*)
  torture, rejection of, 68n92
  universalism in, 63n76, 66–9
 overview, 19, 27–30, 78–9
 Smith on, 45–58
  cultural diversity, role of, 54–6
  empiricism in, 45–6
  general rules of morality, 51–3
  human nature in, 53–4
  impartial spectator, 49–51,
    49n46, 50n50, 58n63
  infanticide, rejection of, 56–8
  "particular usages," 56–8
  sentiment, role of, 46–7, 48–9
  slavery, rejection of, 57n62
  sympathy in, 46–7
  universalism in, 49–51
  utilitarianism and, 48
 Voltaire on, 69–78
  cultural diversity, role of,
    69–70, 75–6
  exceptions to moral norms,
    77n112
  human nature in, 70–1
  lack of comprehensive theory of,
    71–2, 78
  natural law in, 72–3, 76–8
  sentiment, role of, 72n100
  society, effect on, 251–2
  universalism in, 73–5
  utilitarianism and, 75–6n111
Mornet, Daniel, 5, 211n58
Muller, Jerry Z., 290n82
Multiple "Enlightenments," 6–7, 8n19
Muthu, Sankar, 6–7, 17n41
Myrdal, Gunnar, 224

Nagel, Thomas, 250
National glory, Smith on, 286,
  290–1n83
Native Americans, 54–5, 122–3
The Natural History of Religion
  (Hume), 184
Natural law
 Hume on, 31–2n14, 108–10,
  109n97
 lack of empiricism in, 298

Locke on, 9, 82
Montesquieu on
 morality, 61–5, 62n71, 66–7,
  66n85, 67n89
 political theory, 84–5, 86–7
Smith on, 121–4, 124n139
Voltaire on
 morality, 72–3, 76–8
 political theory, 98–9, 99n58
Natural science. *See* Science
Naves, Raymond, 146
Negative liberty
 commerce and, 261–2
 communitarianism and, 260, 292–3
 Hume on, 278–84
  anarchy and, 278n54
  commerce and, 282–4
  in Holland, 280n57
  political liberty and, 278–81
  republicanism and, 279–81,
    279n56
  rule of law and, 278n52
 Montesquieu on, 264–71
  commerce and, 268–71, 269n23
  in England, 268, 270–1
  in France, 270–1
  in Greece, 266–8
  in Holland, 270–1
  political liberty and, 264–8,
    264n12
  republicanism and, 265–8,
    265n15, 267n20
  in Rome, 266–8
 overview, 22–3, 233, 260–4, 262n6,
  292–3, 301
 republicanism and, 262, 292–3
 Rousseau on, 260
 Smith on, 284–92
  in American colonies, 285–6
  commerce and, 288–92, 292n87
  in England, 285–6
  in Greece, 286–7, 287n75
  political liberty and, 284–8
  republicanism and, 285–7,
    290n81
  in Rome, 286–7, 287n75
 Voltaire on, 272–8

Index

commerce and, 275–8
in England, 272, 276–8
in Geneva, 272–3
in Greece, 273–4
in Holland, 272–3
political liberty and, 272–4
republicanism and, 272–4,
273n36
in Rome, 273–4
Nero (Rome), 128
Neumann, Franz, 89n28, 205n36
Newton, Isaac, 143, 153, 157–8,
160–1, 160n89, 163, 164–5,
165n109, 170
Nietzsche, Friedrich, 11
Nobility
Montesquieu on, 83–4,
84n9, 177–8
Smith on, 128
Voltaire on, 96–7, 103, 211
Normative lessons of pragmatic
Enlightenment, 297–301
Nozick, Robert, 301

Oakeshott, Michael, 191–2, 191n2,
193, 194, 195, 195n12, 200,
204, 205, 208
O'Brien, Karen, 252
Orientalism, Montesquieu on, 17–18,
17n43, 18n45

Paine, Thomas, 230, 299
Pangle, Thomas, 11, 69, 86n18,
87n19, 176, 217n81, 255n56
"Particular usages," 56–8
Pascal, Blaise, 44–5, 45n38, 58
Pascal, Roy, 227n113
Pearson, Roger, 98n54, 144,
170n119, 213
Pellessier, Georges, 207–8
Pensées (Montesquieu)
autonomy of individual in,
254, 255–6
morality in, 61, 63–4, 65
negative liberty in, 264, 265, 266,
267, 268–9
political theory in, 92, 94

progress versus teleology in, 220
reform versus revolution in,
205, 207
religion in, 175, 176, 177–8
science in, 154–5, 155n65
skepticism in, 150–1
Perkins, Merle, 101
The Persian Letters (Montesquieu)
autonomy of individual in, 254
importance of, 60
morality in, 60
negative liberty in, 268
political theory in, 85
progress versus teleology in, 218
reform versus revolution in, 205
religion in, 177
science in, 154n64, 155
*Philosophiae Naturalis
Principia Mathematica*
(Newton), 135–6
Philosophical Dictionary (Voltaire)
autonomy of individual in, 250
morality in, 70, 71, 72, 73–4
negative liberty in, 272, 273, 275
political theory in, 100, 106
reform versus revolution in,
208, 209
religion in, 170–1, 172, 173
science in, 158
skepticism in, 143, 145–6
Physiocrats, 201n26, 202, 202n28
Pitts, Jennifer, 17n41, 57
Pizarro, Francisco, 155
Plato, 57, 181n159
Pocock, J.G.A., 6, 8, 222n97, 262,
262n7
Political rationalism
Hume, opposition to, 195–200
of Locke, 194–5, 206
Montesquieu, opposition to, 204–7
overview, 21, 194–5, 229–30
progress versus teleology
(*see* Progress versus teleology)
reform versus revolution
(*see* Reform versus revolution)
Smith, opposition to, 200–3
Voltaire, opposition to, 207–11

Political theory
  anti-foundationalist approach, 82
  of Hume, 107–19
    abstract principles in, 111–12
    circumstances of justice, 110
    custom and authority, role of,
      117–18
    on England, 115–17, 116n120
    historical analysis in, 112–13,
      118–19
    justice in, 109–11, 109n98
    lack of preference for single sys-
      tem, 114–15
    Locke compared, 111, 117
    monarchy in, 117n121
    natural law in, 108–10, 109n97
    overview, 119
    political liberty in, 113–14,
      113n110
    politics as science, 112n107
    social contract in, 108–9
    universalism in, 108–9, 114–15
    utilitarianism and, 108–9
  of Locke, 19
  of Montesquieu, 83–96
    decentralization of power, 83–4
    despotism in, 87–9, 87n22,
      88n23, 88n25, 90–2, 95n42
    on England, 93–5, 94n39
    flexibility of, 96
    historical and comparative analy-
      sis in, 89–90, 92–3
    humane criminal law, 83–4
    human nature in, 91n34
    Locke compared, 83, 84–5, 86–7,
      86n17
    moderateness of, 96
    natural law in, 84–5, 86–7
    overview, 83–4
    political institutions in, 83–4
    political liberty in, 90n30,
      95n42
    separation of powers, 83–4
    social contract in, 85
    tyranny in, 90n31, 207
  overview, 19–20, 80–3, 130–1
  "politics of decency," 81–2

  of Rawls, 80–1
  of Smith, 120–30
    commerce, role of, 120, 124–6,
      125n140
    on France, 127–8
    historical analysis in,
      121–4, 125–6
    jurisprudence of, 118n125,
      121–2n130
    justice in, 123–4
    lack of preference for single sys-
      tem, 126, 128–9
    Locke compared, 127, 128
    natural law in, 121–4,
      124n139
    non-foundationalist nature
      of, 124–5
    overview, 129–30
    phases of society, 120–1
    social contract in, 120–1
    universalism in, 120, 128–9
  of Voltaire, 96–107
    on China, 105n84
    despotism in, 104–6, 105n82
    empiricism in, 99–100
    on England, 101n68, 102–4,
      102n70, 102n72, 126–8
    "enlightened despotism," 104–6
    flexibility of, 106
    on Geneva, 104
    historical and comparative analy-
      sis in, 100
    on Holland, 104
    lack of preference for single
      system, 100–2
    Locke compared, 97, 99n57
    natural law in, 98–9, 99n58
    overview, 106–7
    political institutions in, 97
    pragmatism of, 99–100
    on Prussia, 104–6
    royalism in, 96–7
    rule of law in, 97–8
    on Russia, 104–6
    social contract in, 98–9
    universalism in, 100–2
  "Politics of decency," 81–2

Index

Popkin, Richard, 141–2n16
Porter, Roy, 5, 28, 193n7, 261
Positivism, 32n15
"Possessive individualism," 261n3
"Pragmatic" Enlightenment. *See also
specific topic*
  "idealistic" Enlightenment versus,
    296–7, 297n10
  outlook of, 8–10
  "radical" Enlightenment
    versus, 7
Pragmatic liberalism. *See* Political
  theory
Price, Richard, 200–1n26
Priestley, Joseph, 229
Progress versus teleology, 211–29
  in Hume, 220–3
  in Montesquieu, 216–20
  overview, 192–3, 194, 211–12,
    229–30
  in Smith, 224–9
  in Voltaire, 212–16
Protestants in France, 168
"Prudent man," 291
Prussia, Voltaire on, 104–7
Ptolemy, 163
Pufendorf, Samuel, 72, 99, 122
Puritanism, 118, 187, 223

Quakers, 172
Quesnay, François, 125, 202n28
Questions on the Encyclopedia
  (Voltaire), 73, 215,
    251, 252

Race
  Hume on, 17–18, 18n44
  Smith on, 17–18, 17n42, 18n45
Radasanu, Andrea, 205n36
Radicalism
  in Enlightenment, 295–6
  Hume on, 195
  pragmatism distinguished, 7
  scholarly views of, 296–7
"Radical" versus "moderate"
  Enlightenment, 296–7,
    297n10

Rahe, Paul, 95n42
Raphael, D.D., 163–4
Rasmussen, Dennis C., 9n24, 12n34,
  120n127, 125n140, 126n142,
  193n8, 228n117, 289n80,
  293n88
Rationalism
  of Bacon, 191–2n2
  of Condorcet, 12n34, 89n27
  Descartes and, 136, 139,
    191–2n2
  empiricism versus, 136n4,
    143, 298
  in Enlightenment, 295–6
  Hobbes and, 16n40, 20, 136, 139,
    139n10, 150
  Hume on, 31, 195, 200, 241
  Kant on, 14, 31
  political rationalism (*see* Political
    rationalism)
  pragmatism versus, 194
  sentiment versus, 299–300
  Smith on, 46
  Voltaire on, 209
Rawls, John
  on autonomy of individual, 258,
    258n64, 300
  circumstances of justice, 110
  criticism of Enlightenment,
    9, 15, 80–1, 81n2, 82,
    130
  Kant and, 14
  on reason, 299–300, 300n12
  veil of ignorance, 234n5
Raynor, David, 48n44
Reason
  blind faith in, 4
  Descartes on, 16n40, 20
  Kant on, 152, 299–300
  limits of (*see* Limits of reason)
  Locke on, 20, 136, 150
  Rawls on, 299–300, 300n12
  religion and, 166–89. (*see also*
    Religion)
  Rousseau on, 135–6
  science and, 165n107. (*see also*
    Science)

344   *Index*

Reason (*cont.*)
  skepticism and, 139–52. (*see also*
    Skepticism)
Reform versus revolution, 194–211
  in Hume, 195–200, 197n17
  in Montesquieu, 204–7
  overview, 191–2, 193–5, 211,
    229–30, 299
  in Smith, 200–3
  in Voltaire, 207–11
Reid, Thomas, 148
Religion, 166–89
  Anglican Church, 103n73
  atheism
    Hume on, 183–4
    Montesquieu on, 174–5,
      174n138
    Voltaire on, 170–2, 171n124
  Catholic Church (*see* Catholic
    Church)
  commerce and, 276–8, 277n51
  deism
    of Hume, 183
    of Montesquieu, 174
    of Smith, 178–9
    of Voltaire, 169–70, 169n117
  in England, 168
  in France, 168
  Hume and, 41–2, 183–9, 183n164,
    184n168, 187n180, 188n182
  Montesquieu and, 173–8, 175n140,
    176n144
  overview, 166–7, 189
  pluralism, 177
  Quakers, 172
  "secular fideism," 189
  separation of church and state,
    182–3, 182n163
  Smith and, 178–83, 179n154,
    180n156
  toleration, 188n182
  Voltaire and, 169–73, 169n116
Republicanism
  Hume on, 279–81, 279n56
  Montesquieu on, 265–8, 265n15,
    267n20
  negative liberty and, 262, 292–3

  Smith on, 285–7, 290n81
  Voltaire on, 104, 272–4, 273n36
Revolution. *See also* Reform versus
  revolution
  French Revolution (*see* French
    Revolution)
  Glorious Revolution of 1688
    (*see* Glorious Revolution
    of 1688)
  Hume on, 196, 197–200
  Locke on, 206, 206n38
  Montesquieu on, 87, 206–7
  Smith on, 202
  Voltaire on, 98–9, 210–11
Richter, Melvin, 66n85, 67, 207
Robertson, John, 8–9, 296
Robertson, William, 12, 54n59
Roche, Daniel, 5
Rome (Ancient)
  Hume on, 280
  Montesquieu on, 217–18, 219, 220,
    266–8, 267n20
  Smith on, 286–7, 287n75
  Voltaire on, 273–4
Rosenberg, Nathan, 290n82
Rothschild, Emma, 45, 164,
    179, 201n26, 203–4n32,
    222, 285
Rousseau, Jean-Jacques, 9n24
  on autonomy of individual, 237n11,
    253n51
  Burke on, 294–5n1
  criticism of Enlightenment, 15
  Montesquieu on, 267n21
  on negative liberty, 260
  radicalism of, 211
  on reason, 135–6
  on state of nature, 236–7, 237n11,
    244, 247–8, 252–4
  Voltaire on, 248n36, 250
Rowe, Constance, 207
Royal Exchange, 276–8
Royalism, Voltaire and, 96–7
Rule of law
  Hume on, 118–19, 278–9, 278n52
  Smith on, 120
  Voltaire on, 97–8, 105–6, 272

Index

Russell, Paul, 142n18, 183
Russia, Voltaire on, 104–7

Sabl, Andrew, 198n20
de Saint-Simon, Comte, 96–7
St. Bartholomew's Day Massacre,
    168n113
Sandel, Michael J., 234–5, 234n5,
    235n8, 239, 258n64, 259
Sayre-McCord, Geoffrey, 34n19
Schaub, Diana, 156n71, 177, 178
Schliesser, Eric, 160n89
Schmidt, James, 6, 8n20, 14, 16n40
Science, 152–66
    Hume and, 112n107, 159–61,
        159n86
    Montesquieu and, 153–6, 153n60,
        154n63, 156n71
    overview, 165–6
    politics as science, 112n107
    Smith and, 161–5, 165n107
    Voltaire and, 156–9
Scottish Enlightenment versus French
    Enlightenment, 294–6, 294n1
de Secondat, Charles-Louis.
    See Montesquieu
The Second Treatise of Government
    (Locke), 150, 235
"Secular fideism," 189
Self-love
    Hume on, 37
    Montesquieu on, 254
    Smith on, 242–3, 243n29
    Voltaire on, 70–1, 250
Sen, Amartya, 49–50, 126n143
Sentiment
    defense of, 29n9
    Hume on, 30–45
    Montesquieu on, 58–9,
        62n73, 63–4
    rationalism versus, 299–300
    Smith on, 46–7, 48–9
    Voltaire on, 72n100
Separation of church and state, 182–3,
    182n163
Separation of powers, 83–4, 83n7
Serfdom, 215n73

Seven Years War, 102
Sextus Empiricus, 148
Shackleton, Robert, 177n146
Shaftesbury, Third Earl of, 39, 53
Shank, J.B., 145n31
Shklar, Judith, 64, 84n10, 151–2,
    153n60, 219n89, 265n13,
    265n15
Sirven, Pierre-Paul, 275
Skepticism, 139–52
    of Hume, 140–3
    of Montesquieu, 149–52
    overview, 152
    of Smith, 146–9
    of Voltaire, 143–6
Skinner, Andrew, 163–4
Slavery, 57n62, 67–9, 67n90, 69n93,
    182n161
Smith, Adam. *See also specific work*
    on autonomy of individual, 242–7
        egoism, rejection of, 243n26
        self-love and, 242–3
        social nature of man, focus
            on, 244–7
        sympathy and, 243, 247
    on Catholic Church, 181
    communitarianism and, 246,
        247n33
    deism of, 178–9
    on education, 289–90, 289n80
    empiricism of, 45–6
    on England, 126–8, 227–8, 285
    epistemology of, 146–9, 146n35
    "four stages" theory (*see* "Four
        stages" theory)
    on France, 129–30
    on Greece, 56–7, 286–7, 287n75
    on human nature, 53–4
    importance of, 10
    invisible hand, 201–2, 224
    on justice, 48n45, 52n55, 123–4,
        287n77
    Kant compared, 287n76
    on mercantilism, 124–5,
        147, 201–2
    on militias, 289n80
    on monarchy, 127, 128, 284–5

Smith, Adam (*cont.*)
  on morality, 45–58 (*see also*
    Morality)
  on national glory, 286, 290–1n83
  on natural law, 121–4, 124n139
  on negative liberty, 284–92
    in American colonies, 285–6
    commerce and, 288–92, 292n87
    in England, 285–6
    in Greece, 286–7, 287n75
    political liberty and, 284–8
    republicanism and, 285–7,
      290n81
    in Rome, 286–7, 287n75
  on nobility, 128
  perceived conservatism of, 13
  on political liberty, 284–8
  political rationalism, opposition
    to, 200–3
  political theory of, 120–30 (*see also*
    Political theory)
  progress versus teleology in, 224–9
  "prudent man," 291n84
  on race, 17–18, 17n42
  on rationalism, 46
  reform versus revolution in, 200–3
  religion and, 178–83, 179n154,
    180n156
  on republicanism, 285–7, 290n81
  on revolution, 202
  on Rome, 286–7, 287n75
  on rule of law, 120
  science and, 161–5, 165n107
  on self-love, 242–3, 243n29
  on sentiment, 46–7, 48–9
  on separation of church and state,
    182–3, 182n163
  skepticism of, 146–9
  on social contract, 120–1
  on state of nature, 120, 244
  on sympathy, 46–7, 243, 247
  system-building and, 147–8,
    147n38
  utilitarianism and, 48
  on women, 17–18, 18n45,
    49n46, 181–2
Smith, Preserved, 135–6

Social contract
  communitarianism and, 236,
    236n10
  Hume on
    political theory, 108–9, 108n95
    rejection by, 238
  lack of empiricism in, 298
  Locke on, 2, 297–8
  Montesquieu on, 85
  Smith on, 120–1
  Voltaire on, 98–9
Social nature of man. *See also*
    Autonomy of individual
  Hume, focus on, 236–8, 239–42
  Montesquieu, focus on, 252–6
  Smith, focus on, 244–7
  Voltaire, focus on, 247–9, 250–1
Socrates, 181n159
Solon, 201, 201n27
Spencer, Herbert, 212
Spencer, Mark G., 279n56
Spinoza, Baruch, 3, 20, 136, 296
The Spirit of the Laws (Montesquieu)
  autonomy of individual in,
    252–4, 255–8
  importance of, 11, 60
  morality in, 59–61, 62, 63, 64,
    65–6, 67–9
  negative liberty in, 264–7, 268–71
  political theory in, 83, 84, 86, 88–9,
    90, 91, 92, 93–5, 101, 103
  progress versus teleology in,
    216–17, 219
  reform versus revolution in, 195,
    204, 205–7
  religion in, 174–8
  science in, 153–4
  scope of, 59–60n66
  skepticism in, 149–50, 151
Stair, Viscount of, 199
Star Chamber, 118n125
Stark, Werner, 67n89
State of nature
  Hobbes on, 236–7, 237n11, 252–4
  Hume on, 108–9, 237
  Montesquieu on, 85, 252–3,
    253n51, 254n53

Index

347

Rousseau on, 236–7, 237n11, 244, 247–8, 252–4
Smith on, 120, 244
Stewart, Dugald, 130, 162, 201n26, 203–4n32
Stewart, Potter, 90
Stigler, George, 242
Stoicism, 176
Strauss, Leo, 135–6
Sullivan, Vickie, 66, 88, 88n24
Sympathy
  Hume on, 239
  Smith on, 46–7, 243, 247
System of Nature (d'Holbach), 171

Talmon, Jacob, 192
Tamerlane, 176
Taylor, Charles, 234, 235, 235n6, 235n8, 239, 259, 260
Taylor, Jacqueline, 39
Teichgraeber, Richard, 53n57
Teleology. *See* Progress versus teleology
The Theory of Moral Sentiments (Smith)
  autonomy of individual in, 242–4, 245–7
  morality in, 45–8, 49, 51–3, 54, 55–7, 58
  negative liberty in, 286, 287–8, 289, 290–1, 292
  political theory in, 121, 122–3, 125
  progress versus teleology in, 224, 226, 228
  reform versus revolution in, 200–1
  religion in, 179–81
  science in, 162
  skepticism in, 146–7
de Tocqueville, Alexis, 15, 192, 268n22
Torrey, Norman, 74–5
Torture, 68n92
Trade. *See* Commerce
A Treatise of Human Nature (Hume)
  autonomy of individual in, 237–40, 241–2
  "Hume's Law," 32–3

morality in, 30, 36, 38, 39, 41, 42, 44, 47
political theory in, 85, 108–10, 111–12, 113, 117–18
reform versus revolution in, 198, 199
science in, 160, 161
skepticism in, 140, 141, 142
A Treatise on Metaphysics (Voltaire)
  autonomy of individual in, 248, 249, 250–1
  morality in, 74, 75–8
  religion in, 170, 171
  skepticism in, 143, 144
Treatise on Tolerance (Voltaire), 173, 208
Tucker, Josiah, 12
Turgot, Anne-Robert-Jacques, 125, 212, 222
Tyranny. *See also* Despotism; Monarchy
  Hume on, 198, 198n20, 199, 278n54
  Montesquieu on, 90n31, 207
  Voltaire on, 104

United Kingdom. *See* England
Universalism
  of Condorcet, 12n34
  criticism of Enlightenment based on, 3–4, 27–8n3, 294, 298–9
  Hume and
    in morality, 35–7, 36n22, 42n34, 45
    in political theory, 108–9, 114–15
  of Kant, 299
  Montesquieu and, 63n76, 66–9
  in morality (*see* Morality)
  in political theory (*see* Political theory)
  Smith and
    in morality, 49–51
    in political theory, 120, 128–9
  Voltaire and
    in morality, 73–5
    in political theory, 100–2

348   Index

Utilitarianism
  Bentham and, 2, 9, 297–8
  Hume and, 33, 33n18, 108–9
  Smith and, 48
  Voltaire and, 75–6n111

Veil of ignorance, 234n5
Verri, Pietro, 12
Virgil, 161
Virtue ethics, 29–30n10
Voegelin, Eric, 137–8n7
Voltaire. *See also specific work*
  on anarchy, 104, 106
  on atheism, 170–2, 171n124
  on autonomy of individual, 247–52
    climate, role of, 251–2
    moral causes, role of, 251–2
    self-love and, 250
    social nature of man, focus on,
      247–9, 250–1
  on Catholic Church, 102, 169, 172,
    210, 215
  on China, 69–70, 105n84
  contes (fictional stories), 144–5,
    213n64, 251
  deism of, 169–70, 169n117
  on Descartes, 143
  empiricism of, 99–100, 143, 159
  on England, 101n68, 102–4,
    102n70, 102n72, 272, 276–8
  epistemology of, 143–6
  French Revolution, influence on,
    207–8, 210–11
  on Greece, 273–4
  on human nature, 70–1
  importance of, 11, 11n32
  on India, 69–70
  on Judaism, 17–18, 17n43
  on justice, 72n101
  on Locke, 143
  Locke compared, 97, 99n57
  on Mandeville, 274–5
  on mercantilism, 283n66
  on monarchy, 101–2, 104–5,
    106–7, 272–3
  on morality, 69–78 (*see also*
    Morality)

  on natural law, 72–3, 76–8, 98–9,
    99n58
  on negative liberty, 272–8
    commerce and, 275–8
    in England, 272, 276–8
    in Geneva, 272–3
    in Greece, 273–4
    in Holland, 272–3
    political liberty and, 272–4
    republicanism and, 272–4,
      273n36
    in Rome, 273–4
  on nobility, 96–7, 103, 211
  on political liberty, 272–4
  political rationalism, opposition to,
    207–11
  political theory of, 96–107 (*see also*
    Political theory)
  progress versus teleology in, 212–16
  on Prussia, 104–7
  on rationalism, 209
  reform versus revolution in, 207–11
  religion and, 169–73, 169n116
  on republicanism, 104, 272–4,
    273n36
  on revolution, 98–9, 210–11
  on Rome, 273–4
  on Rousseau, 248n36, 250
  on rule of law, 97–8, 105–6, 272
  on Russia, 104–7
  science and, 156–9
  on self-love, 70–1, 250
  on sentiment, 72n100
  skepticism of, 143–6
  on social contract, 98–9
  system-building and, 143–5
  on tyranny, 104
  utilitarianism and, 75–6n111
  on women, 17–18, 18n45
Vyverberg, Henry, 69–70n95, 212n60

Waddicor, Mark, 174n138
Wade, Ira, 157, 158–9
Waldinger, Renée, 211n57
Warburton, William, 174, 175n141,
  177n145
Warner, Stuart, 66–7, 112, 114

Index

349

War of the Spanish Succession, 216
Wealth of Nations (Smith). *See
    An Inquiry into the Nature
    and Causes of the Wealth of
    Nations* (Smith)
Weinstein, Jack Russell, 247n33
Whelan, Frederick, 108,
    109n97, 114
Whiggism, 87, 103, 115n117, 127,
    201n26, 206, 221
Whitehead, Alfred North, 143n23
Wieland, Christoph, 12
William III (England), 216, 223
Williams, David, 99, 210
Wilson, James Q., 233
Winch, Donald, 126n144

Without Foundations (Herzog), 120
Wokler, Robert, 5–6, 8, 10, 60
Wollaston, William, 31
Women
    Hume on, 17–18, 18n44
    Montesquieu on, 17–18, 17n43,
        18n45, 176, 270–1
    Smith on, 17–18, 17n42, 18n45,
        48, 181–2
    Voltaire on, 17–18, 17n43, 18n45
Wootton, David, 213–14, 213n65

Yack, Bernard, 166

Zadig (Voltaire), 213n64
Zuckert, Michael, 87n22

Printed in the United States
By Bookmasters